VANITY FAIR'S TALES OF HOLLYWOOD

GRAYDON CARTER has been the editor of *Vanity Fair* since 1992. He is the author of *Vanity Fair's Hollywood* (Viking Studio, 2000), *Oscar Night* (Knopf, 2004), *Vanity Fair: The Portraits* (Abrams, 2008), and *What We've Lost: How the Bush Administration Has Curtailed Our Freedoms, Mortgaged Our Economy, Ravaged Our Environment, and Damaged Our Standing in the World* (Farrar, Straus and Giroux, 2004). Carter served as producer of the films *The Kid Stays in the Picture, Chicago 10, Surfwise,* and *Gonzo,* and has won Emmy and Peabody awards as executive producer of the CBS documentary *9/11,* which aired in 140 countries. Carter, a former writer at *Time* and *Life,* cofounded *Spy* magazine and served as the editor of *The New York Observer.* He is also an owner of the Waverly Inn, a restaurant in New York City's West Village.

VANITY FAIR'S
TALES OF HOLLYWOOD

Rebels, Reds, and Graduates
and the Wild Stories Behind the
Making of 13 Iconic Films

EDITED BY
GRAYDON CARTER

PENGUIN BOOKS

PENGUIN BOOKS
Published by the Penguin Group
Penguin Group (USA) Inc., 375 Hudson Street, New York, New York 10014, U.S.A.
Penguin Group (Canada), 90 Eglinton Avenue East, Suite 700, Toronto, Ontario,
Canada M4P 2Y3 (a division of Pearson Penguin Canada Inc.)
Penguin Books Ltd, 80 Strand, London WC2R 0RL, England
Penguin Ireland, 25 St Stephen's Green, Dublin 2, Ireland (a division of Penguin Books Ltd)
Penguin Group (Australia), 250 Camberwell Road, Camberwell, Victoria 3124, Australia
(a division of Pearson Australia Group Pty Ltd)
Penguin Books India Pvt Ltd, 11 Community Centre, Panchsheel Park,
New Delhi - 110 017, India
Penguin Group (NZ), 67 Apollo Drive, Rosedale, North Shore 0632, New Zealand (a division of
Pearson New Zealand Ltd)
Penguin Books (South Africa) (Pty) Ltd, 24 Sturdee Avenue, Rosebank, Johannesburg 2196,
South Africa

Penguin Books Ltd, Registered Offices:
80 Strand, London WC2R 0RL, England

First published in Penguin Books 2008

10 9 8 7 6 5 4 3 2

Copyright © *Vanity Fair*, a publication of the Condé Nast Publications, 2008
Introduction copyright © Graydon Carter, 2008
All rights reserved

Vanity Fair is a registered trademark of Advance Magazine Publications Inc.

The selections in this book first appeared in issues of *Vanity Fair*.

LIBRARY OF CONGRESS CATALOGING IN PUBLICATION DATA
Vanity fair's tales of Hollywood : Rebels, Reds, and Graduates and the wild stories behind the
making of 13 iconic films / edited by Graydon Carter.
p. cm.
ISBN 978-0-14-311471-0
1. Motion pictures—United States. I. Carter, Graydon. II. Vanity fair (New York, N.Y.)
PN1993.5.U6V36 2009
791.430973—dc22   2008032453

Printed in the United States of America
Set in New Caledonia Medium and AT Sackers Gothic
Designed by Sabrina Bowers

CONTENTS

INTRODUCTION

The Making Of . . .

Put simply, it is the journalist's job to tell the story behind the story. In the case of governments or large corporations, the odds are that whatever line they're peddling, it may look like the truth, smell like the truth, and be labeled as the truth, but it's most certainly anything but the truth. It falls therefore to the journalist to peel away the layers of artifice and avarice, much like one does the leaves of an artichoke, to get to the heart of the matter. It's no accident that both the White House and Wall Street like to release bad news on Fridays— their assumption being that the reading public will skip past the reports of their misdeeds as they skim their Saturday papers before heading off to the mall, a soccer game, or, perhaps, a movie.

Hollywood also likes to release its offerings on Fridays, turds and gems alike. The official story *they* put forward is the one you can see up there on the screen for yourself. It then becomes a meal for pygmies—the sorry lot otherwise known as film critics. The fun part, and here is where the journalist comes in, is telling the story of how that entertainment was conceived, how it was assembled, and generally who did what to whom. "The Making of . . . ," in other words. These are the unreported anecdotes, the filmgoer's equivalent of liner notes, and they're often more interesting than the movies themselves. *Who did the director really want for the lead? Which two (or three) stars were spotted carrying on in the location trailer?* Who doesn't want to know about the knockdowns, the hissy fits, the brawls, and the breakdowns?

In this volume, *Vanity Fair's Tales of Hollywood,* our writers report not only on what almost happened but also on what *really* happened on the locations and back lots of 13 of the most iconic films and classic flops in cinema history. *Vanity Fair* didn't create the "Making of . . . " genre, but our stable of writers is uniquely qualified to tell these stories, having earned their commissions reporting on the old studio system, the Lew Wasserman era, and the brackish tide pool that is today's Hollywood.

A big part of this book's template is the "What if . . . ?" What if *Springtime for Hitler,* a novel that a young television sketch-comedy writer named Mel Brooks planned to write, had ended up as just another paperback sitting on a shelf at the Strand, rather than as the creative nub that spawned *The Producers*? What if Warren Beatty, the director of *Reds,* hadn't been able to wrangle his fellow rake Jack Nicholson into the role of Eugene O'Neill by asking him to suggest which Hollywood leading man could out-Beatty Beatty for Diane Keaton? (Nicholson could think of only one—and he was magnificent in the part.) And what if Warner Bros. had decided to protect its newly minted star, 24-year-old James Dean, and refused to let him appear in Nicholas Ray's electric teen opera, *Rebel Without a Cause*? Finally, what if the late *New York* magazine editor Clay Felker, unimpressed by a piece on outer-borough clubgoers, had killed Nik Cohn's story "Tribal Rites of the New Saturday Night," which eventually became *Saturday Night Fever,* the movie that brought white polyester suits into the 70s mainstream—or, more accurately, got blamed for bringing them into the mainstream? Not incidentally, two other films in this collection were also inspired by magazine articles— a 1946 *Cosmopolitan* piece called "The Wisdom of Eve" provided the basis for *All About Eve,* and a 1948 *Collier's* story, written by Ernest Lehman, called "Hunsecker Fights the World," grew into *Sweet Smell of Success.*

For sheer delight, dip into David Kamp's "When Liz Met Dick," about the making of *Cleopatra,* the four-hour 1963 epic that still takes the honors for being the most expensive movie ever made. It cost a then record $44 million (more than $300 million in current dollars). Joseph Mankiewicz, the director who completed the film, called it "the toughest three pictures I ever made." It took two of everything to get *Cleopatra* in the can: two Twentieth Century Fox studio regimes, two directors (the first was Rouben Mamoulian), and more than two years of shooting. As if that were not enough, *Cleopatra* also had the two biggest stars in the world, Elizabeth Taylor and Richard Burton, engaged in a riotously public adulterous affair that resulted in condemnation not only on the Senate floor but in the fragrant pages of the Vatican newspaper. As Burton said of sleeping with Taylor—and this is one of my favorite lines—"It's like fucking Khrushchev! I've had affairs before—how did I know the woman was so fucking famous!"

Cleopatra was initially considered a flop. As was Alexander MacKendrick's *noir*-ish cocktail, *Sweet Smell of Success*. It was among the first screenplays by Lehman, a former press agent, who went on to become arguably the greatest screenwriter of all time, putting notches in his belt for films as varied as *The Sound of Music, North by Northwest, West Side Story, The King and I, Who's Afraid of Virginia Woolf?, Hello, Dolly!,* and *Sabrina. Sweet Smell of Success*, so dangerous at the time, so written off by critics and audiences alike, so deliciously and unrelentingly dark, is now considered by *The New Yorker*'s David Denby, among others, as being the finest New York film ever made. Indeed, as Sam Kashner writes, *Sweet Smell of Success* did for New York what Billy Wilder's *Sunset Boulevard* had done for Los Angeles. That its central character, an unsavory gossip named J. J. Hunsecker, was based on Walter Winchell—at midcentury, America's most powerful syndicated columnist—made it all the more daring an enterprise. What makes it shine, aside from the brilliant performances of Burt Lancaster, as Hunsecker, and Tony Curtis, as the feral press agent Sidney Falco, is the crispness of the dialogue, a collaboration between Lehman and Clifford Odets, then at his most bitter heights of ennui and disaffection.

And then there's Kashner's "Here's to You, Mr. Nichols," about Mike Nichols's 1967 screen adaptation of Charles Webb's relatively uncelebrated novel *The Graduate*. (Kashner is a protean "The Making of . . ." hand. Five of the pieces presented here are his.) *The Graduate* was set to star Robert Redford and Candice Bergen. The rapacious Mrs. Robinson, who seems to burst from the pages of Flaubert, was initially set aside for Ava Gardner, and Gene Hackman had signed on to play her husband. That Nichols eventually chose a completely different cast, including a young, insecure Off Broadway actor named Dustin Hoffman for the part of Benjamin Braddock—and that Nichols's brother happened to send him a new LP, Simon and Garfunkel's *Parsley, Sage, Rosemary, and Thyme,* during filming—changed the history of the movies, from the way we perceive comedy and drama to the impact of soundtracks on motion pictures.

As perfect as Bette Davis is in the part of Margot Channing, the aging theater warhorse in *All About Eve,* she was not director Joseph Mankiewicz's first choice, according to Sam Stagg's report on the making of the film. Mankiewicz—the brother of screenwriter Herman, who was known as Mank—wanted Claudette Colbert for the part. When she bowed out due to a ruptured disc, he tried to get Gertie Lawrence, a bona fide star of the stage, who was then having Rodgers and Hammerstein adapt *Anna and the King of Siam* into *The King and I* for her. When she turned him down, he approached Davis. That signature deep, raspy, almost guttural voice that Davis employed for the role of Margo was less Method-driven than it was circumstantial. After a torrid fight with her husband, William Sherry, in Los Angeles a few nights earlier, Davis showed up for the first day of filming without her voice. Despite her doctor's advice that she rest, director Mankiewicz patted his actress on the shoulder and asked if she could keep the voice up for a month—it was the pitch-perfect bourbon contralto he had imagined for Margo. Later, Mankiewicz declared Davis, without irony, a director's dream: "the prepared actress."

Elsewhere in this fine volume, Laura Jacobs slips into a black dress to tell the story of *The Best of Everything,* the quintessential young-girls-in-the-big-city tale, in all its 1959 Color by DeLuxe glory. It had a sparkling cast that included Hope Lange, Suzy Parker, Joan Crawford, and Brian Aherne, as smartly British as a racetrack trilby (and, not incidentally, the man Brooke Astor used to tell me was the love of her life). In supporting but no less vital roles were Robert Evans (it was blessedly his last screen appearance before turning to producing) and the Seagram Building.

These tales—all originally written for *Vanity Fair*—are intended not simply for moviegoers but for true film obsessives who mark their memories by the Scorsese movie that was in theaters at a certain time in their lives, or for the old-studio-system-era buffs who know whose arm Elizabeth Taylor hung from way back when. Connoisseurs, who care to know how a movie got made, and why it almost didn't, this is your book. Herewith: the definitive, untold sagas behind the making of 13 unforgettable films.

—GRAYDON CARTER
New York City, 2008

VANITY FAIR'S
TALES OF HOLLYWOOD

THE MAGNIFICENT AMBERSONS

Magnificent Obsession

by David Kamp

There are two great "lost" movies in the annals of Hollywood filmmaking, Erich von Stroheim's *Greed* and Orson Welles's *The Magnificent Ambersons*. Neither film is lost in a literal, vanished-and-gone sense—both are available on video, are occasionally screened in theaters, and are highly regarded by film critics (four stars apiece in Leonard Maltin's *Movie & Video Guide*, for example). Rather, their tragic "lost" status stems from the fact that they exist only in truncated, bowdlerized form, having been wrested from the hands of their visionary directors by studio functionaries who were too craven and bottom-line-obsessed to cut these directors some auteurist slack. Since both films well pre-date the preservationist era of film-as-art-and-heritage—*Greed* was released in 1925, *The Magnificent Ambersons* in 1942—they have suffered the further indignity of being unreconstructible; studios back in those days didn't hang on to excised footage for the sake of future director's cuts on DVD, so the reels upon reels of nitrate film trimmed from the original versions were—depending on which movie you're talking about and which story you believe—burned, thrown in the garbage, dumped into the Pacific, or simply left to decompose in the vaults.

Of the two sagas, *The Magnificent Ambersons'* is the more wrenching case of what might have been. *Greed,* as extraordinary an achievement as it is, comes from the remote era of silent pictures, and von Stroheim's original cut exceeded seven hours—even if it could be reconstructed, it would be a chore to sit through, indigestible to all but the most dogged of cineasts. The fully realized *Magnificent Ambersons,* by contrast, is a more tangible piece of purported great art, a normal-length feature that, some say, would have been as good as or even better than the movie Welles made immediately before it, *Citizen Kane.* Chief among those taking this view was Welles himself, who in the 1970s told the director Peter Bogdanovich, his friend and sometime interlocutor, "It was a much better picture than *Kane*—if they'd just left it as it was." What it *is*—in the Turner Classic Movies version you can rent, the same version RKO Radio Pictures unenthusiastically dumped into a handful of theaters in the summer of '42—is an impressive curio, merely 88 minutes long, a nub of the two-hours-plus version Welles had in mind, with a patched-on, falsely upbeat ending that Welles's assistant director, Freddie Fleck, shot under RKO's orders while Welles was out of the country.

To this day, more than 60 years after it was shot, *The Magnificent Ambersons* remains a rallying cry for film obsessives, the movie equivalent of the Beach Boys' aborted *Smile* album [which was finally completed in 2004] or Truman Capote's phantasmal complete manuscript of *Answered Prayers.* But unlike those tantalizing elusive works, which only ever existed in fragments, the long version of *Ambersons* really was pretty much finished: Welles and his editor, Robert Wise, had assembled a 132-minute cut of the movie before the studio-ordained hacking began. It's this version, which in Welles's view required only some tweaking and burnishing in postproduction, that people are talking about when they talk about the "complete" or "original" *Ambersons,* and it's this version that animates the minds of the many cinephiles who hold out hope that somewhere, somehow, the excised footage still exists, waiting to be discovered and reinstated. "It is clearly the grail now," says the director William Friedkin, a card-carrying *Ambersons* buff. "A lot of directors I know dream of finding it—Bogdanovich, Coppola, we've all talked about it." The film preservationist James Katz, who with his business partner, Robert Harris, has restored Alfred Hitchcock's *Vertigo* and David Lean's *Lawrence of Arabia,* likes to tell the story of how he was milling through a film vault in Van Nuys, California, when the '94 Los Angeles–area earthquake struck, sending a canned print of the forgotten 60s historical epic *The Royal Hunt of the Sun* hurtling toward his head—"and all I could think was, If I'm gonna die, at least let it be from the missing footage from *Ambersons,* not *Royal Hunt of the Sun.*" Harris, who is also a film producer, says that in the early 90s he and Martin Scorsese seriously entertained the notion of remaking *The Magnificent Ambersons* to Welles's exact specifications, proposing to go even so far as to "have actors like De Niro subsume their identities to the old actors in the film, like Joseph Cotten." That scenario never panned out, though in 2002 A&E did broadcast a three-hour telefilm version of *The Magnificent Ambersons,* based on Welles's original shooting script.

———

Orson Welles, who died in 1985, would no doubt have been pleased by this turn of events, for he saw *The Magnificent Ambersons* as his Hollywood waterloo, the dividing line between his early boy-genius years (the "War of the Worlds" broadcast, his Mercury Theatre company, *Citizen Kane*) and the nomadic, semi-tragic life he led thereafter. His oft quoted epigram on the subject—"They destroyed *Ambersons,* and the picture itself destroyed me"—is a bit melodramatic, but it's true that the movie's ultimate failure, at a loss of $625,000, exacerbated the tensions that had already arisen from *Citizen Kane*'s substantial cost overruns, RKO's *Kane*-occasioned battles with William Randolph Hearst (who saw the film as an act of character assassination and tried to suppress it), and the Hollywood establishment's general resentment of Welles. RKO severed its relationship with Welles in the aftermath of *Ambersons,* and, with just a few exceptions, he never worked within the mainstream of the movie industry again. He was not, as he put it, "destroyed"—he would go on to make such accomplished films as *The Lady from Shanghai, Touch of Evil,* and *Chimes at Midnight*—but it's fair to say the *Ambersons* debacle set Welles on the path to becoming the person he's most remembered as today: the rotund raconteur of *Merv Griffin* appearances and Paul Masson wine commercials, an entertaining has-been, forever trying to scrounge up financing from European film companies and individual investors for some pet project that, in the end, wouldn't come off. Furthermore, the circumstances surrounding the butchery of *The Magnificent Ambersons*—he had already moved on to Brazil to begin work on his next film, the ill-fated *It's All True,* while the editing of *Ambersons* was still going on in Los Angeles—launched his reputation as a filmmaker with completion anxiety, a tag that would dog him increasingly as later movies either took years to get done (*Othello, Mr. Arkadin*) or lay on shelves unfinished (*It's All True, Don Quixote, The Other Side of the Wind*). "The myth started that he couldn't finish a movie," says the director Henry Jaglom, Welles's closest confidant in his final years. "He said to me repeatedly that anything bad that happened to him in the next 30, 40 years derived from *Ambersons.*"

And so there's an added poignancy to the hopes and yearnings of those who believe the original version may somewhere still exist: it's about not just restoring a film but also redeeming a man. "If somebody had a sense of what was at stake, they might have secreted away a copy," says Friedkin. "Like Theo van Gogh's wife kept all of Vincent's paintings and got dealers to store them in warehouses when no one, *no one,* wanted to buy a van Gogh. You hope that there's a Mrs. van Gogh out there."

━━━━━━━━

It was through Friedkin, more or less, that I first learned of the breadth and depth of *Ambersons* obsession in cinephile circles. A few years ago, while working on another story, I became acquainted with a film-restoration producer named Michael Arick, who was helping Friedkin restore his 1973 film, *The Exorcist* (a big success in

2001). Arick mentioned to me that Friedkin spoke frequently of his desire to find the missing *Ambersons* footage. The director has an office on the Paramount Studios lot in Hollywood, a chunk of which, bounded by Gower Street and Melrose Avenue on its western and southern sides, is the former Desilu Studios lot, which, before Desi Arnaz and Lucille Ball bought it in 1957, was RKO's main lot. As Arick told it, Friedkin wanted to check the old RKO/Desilu vaults at Paramount to see if there were some canisters of *Ambersons* film sitting around that no one had noticed before. This wasn't as unlikely a notion as it sounds: in the early 1980s, a stack of film cans marked BRAZIL was discovered in these same vaults, and turned out to contain footage Welles had shot in Brazil for the abortive *It's All True* project—footage that had long been presumed to have been destroyed. These materials subsequently became the centerpiece of a documentary feature released in 1993 entitled: *It's All True: Based on an Unfinished Film by Orson Welles.*

If anyone had the pull to gain access to the vaults on the Paramount lot, it was Friedkin; his wife, Sherry Lansing, is C.E.O. of the studio. But when I called him to ask if he wanted to undertake an *Ambersons* search with me tagging along, he demurred. He was happy to talk about the movie, he said, but he didn't want to embark on a publicized search that would likely turn up nothing, "and end up looking like fuckin' Geraldo opening up fuckin' Al Capone's vault."

Anyway, I soon learned that there have been several *Ambersons* searches over the years (more on which later) and that, though nothing's been found and the trail grows ever colder, there are still people out there who *believe.* Among the most ardent is a man named Bill Krohn, the Hollywood correspondent for the venerable French film journal *Cahiers du Cinéma* and a co-writer-director-producer of the '93 version of *It's All True.* "Look, *It's All True* wasn't supposed to be there, and it was," he says. "Film history is smoke and mirrors. You just never know."

―――――

Why anyone thought *The Magnificent Ambersons* would have bright box-office prospects is a mystery. The basis for the movie was Booth Tarkington's 1918 novel of the same name, a nuanced, elegiac story of a genteel Indianapolis family's inability to come to grips with the societal changes wrought by the advent of the automobile; as the times pass them by, their fortune crumbles and their "magnificence" is no more. While it's rich material—indeed, the novel won Tarkington the first of his two Pulitzer Prizes for fiction—it lacked the lightning-rod immediacy of *Citizen Kane*'s media-baron subject matter, and wasn't exactly the kind of lighthearted fare that moviegoers were clamoring for as they sought diversion from the Great Depression and the United States' recent entry into World War II. Welles, in fact, had not originally intended to make *The Magnificent Ambersons* his second film—it was a fallback choice. He'd planned to follow up *Citizen Kane* with a movie based on Arthur Calder-Marshall's 1940 novel, *The Way to Santiago*, an espionage thriller set in Mexico. When the project ran aground for a variety of logistical and political reasons, George Schaefer, the RKO studio chief, suggested a less ambitious espionage thriller that he already had in development, *Journey into Fear*. Welles agreed to this idea, but not for his next film—*Journey into Fear* was a basic genre picture, an insufficiently grand successor to *Kane*, and something more dazzling and far-reaching would have to come between the two films.

———

Welles's Mercury Theatre troupe had done a radio adaptation of *The Magnificent Ambersons* for CBS in 1939, with Welles himself playing George Amberson Minafer, the spoiled third-generation scion whose rash actions hasten the demise of the Amberson dynasty. It was a terrific production (which, if you can somehow get your hands on a laser-disc player, you can hear on the special edition of *The Magnificent Ambersons* released by Voyager), and precisely the kind of low-budget masterstroke that led Schaefer to believe that this East Coast theater and radio prodigy was worth signing to a two-picture deal. Welles had been just 22 when he, with John Houseman, founded the Mercury Theatre in 1937. By the following year, his innovative productions of the classics had landed him on the cover of *Time*, and he'd persuaded CBS to give him a weekly dramatic radio series, *The Mercury Theatre on the Air*. Just four months into that program's run, Welles's fame grew to international proportions on account of his "War of the Worlds" broadcast hoax, which convinced a panicked U.S. citizenry that Martians were invading New Jersey. So by 1939, Schaefer was all too happy to commit to a deal in which Welles would write, direct, produce, and star in two feature films, each to be in the $300,000-to-$500,000 range. If that wasn't enough to stir resentment in Hollywood, given Welles's tender age and lack of track record as a filmmaker, then Schaefer's pledge of near-total artistic control—including the right of final cut—was. "Orson had come out with the damnedest contract that anybody ever had," says Robert Wise, who was RKO's in-house film editor during Welles's time there and went on to become the acclaimed director of *West Side Story* and *The Sound of Music*. [Wise died in 2005, after this article was first published.] "So there was a kind of resentment of him in town, this young genius coming from New York, going to show everyone how to make pictures. When *Kane* was up for all these Academy Awards—in those days they were done on the radio, out of the Biltmore Hotel downtown—every time there was an announcement of the nominees for a category, when it was *Citizen Kane*, there would be boos from the [industry] audience."

Citizen Kane, despite the ecstatic reviews it received, was not a financial success—it was too ahead of its time to connect with a wide commercial audience, and too technically ambitious to come in at the prescribed budget. (Its total cost was $840,000.) Furthermore, Welles had turned out just one picture in his two years under contract, having squandered much of the first year developing an adaptation of Joseph Conrad's *Heart of Darkness* that never got off the ground. So by the time of *The Magnificent Ambersons*, Schaefer was no longer willing to be as indulgent as he'd been. At his urging, Welles signed a new contract specifically for *Ambersons* and *Journey into Fear* in which he yielded his right of final cut to the studio.

———

The *Magnificent Ambersons'* story, as adapted by Welles from Tarkington's novel, works on two levels: first, as a tragic tale of forbidden love, and, second, as a what-price-progress lament on how the buzzy, clamorous 20th century ran roughshod over the bucolic, leisurely 19th. The plot is set in motion when Eugene Morgan (Joseph Cotten), an old flame of Isabel Amberson Minafer's from her youth, returns to town in 1904 as a middle-aged widower and successful automobile manufacturer. Isabel (Dolores Costello), the still-beautiful daughter of the richest man in town, Major Amberson (Richard Bennett), is married to a dull nonentity, Wilbur Minafer (Don Dillaway), with whom she has raised a holy terror of a son, George (Tim Holt). The smug, college-age George, who is inappropriately close to his mother and considers automobiles to be a loathsome fad, takes an instant dislike to Eugene, but falls for his pretty daughter, Lucy (Anne Baxter). When Wilbur Minafer dies, Eugene and Isabel rekindle their old romance. George doesn't immediately catch on, but as soon as he does—thanks to the whispering of his father's spinster sister, Fanny Minafer (Agnes Moorehead)—he flies into a rage and forbids his mother to see Eugene. Reluctantly, she breaks off with him and embarks with George on a long tour of Europe, where she takes ill before returning at death's door. Her death, followed in rapid fashion by her brokenhearted father's, reveals the family's financial affairs to be in disarray. Though the Morgans grow ever more prosperous as Eugene's automobile business thrives, the surviving Ambersons— George and his genial Uncle Jack (Ray Collins), a congressman, plus Aunt Fanny, their dependent—are left virtually penniless, and are forced to give up their home, the grand old Amberson mansion. As George faces a life of reduced circumstances in a city where the Amberson name no longer carries any weight, he finally realizes how wrong he was to keep his mother and Eugene apart. Then, while out walking, he suffers a fateful injury when struck by, of all things, an automobile; Lucy and Eugene go to visit him in the hospital, and at last, George and Eugene, both sadder but wiser, bury the hatchet.

Welles's cast, pictured mucking around convivially in the behind-the-scenes stills that survive, was an appealingly odd mix of ace Mercury Theatre regulars (Cotten, Moorehead, and Collins, all of whom give the performances of their careers) and left-field choices, particularly where the Ambersons themselves were concerned. Though he was still in his 20s, Welles felt he was too mature-looking to play George on film, so he turned the role over, improbably, to Holt, best known for playing cowboys in B-picture Westerns and, later, for playing Humphrey Bogart's sidekick in *The Treasure of the Sierra*

Madre. Bennett was a retired stage actor whom Welles had admired as a youth, and whom he'd tracked down, he later said, "out in Catalina in a little boarding house . . . totally forgotten by the world." Costello was a silent-film star and ex-wife of John Barrymore, whom Welles coaxed out of retirement especially for the film. The presence of Bennett and Costello—he with his white mustache and 19th-century thespian's bearing, she with her Kewpie-doll curls and milky complexion—was a bit of prescient postmodernism on Welles's part. They were living artifacts of a more graceful American past, and with their characters' deaths, two-thirds of the way into the film, so ended both the magnificence of the Ambersons and Indianapolis's age of innocence.

Schaefer's hopes for smooth sailing on the picture were borne out by the advance footage he screened on November 28, 1941, a month into the shooting schedule. Impressed by what he saw, which included the already completed Amberson-ball sequence, now renowned for its virtuosic camerawork and gorgeous mansion interiors, he made encouraging noises to Welles. Principal photography on the movie wound up on January 22, 1942. Wise, who viewed the rushes of each day's shooting as they came in—and who is, in all likelihood, the only person alive today [at the time of this article's publication, in 2002] who has seen the movie in its original form—says, "We all thought we had a smashing picture, a marvelous picture."

Even in its current, mutilated state, *The Magnificent Ambersons* is, in stretches and flashes, the marvelous picture Wise remembers. For starters, its relatively unmolested opening sequence is among the most enchanting ever committed to film, beginning with Welles's dulcet, radio-style narration, condensed from Tarkington's opening pages:

> The magnificence of the Ambersons began in 1873. Their splendor lasted throughout all the years that saw their Midland town spread and darken into a city. . . . In that town in those days, all the women who wore silk or velvet knew all the other women who wore silk or velvet—and everybody knew everybody else's family horse-and-carriage. The only public conveyance was the streetcar. A lady could whistle to it from an upstairs window, and the

car would halt at once, and wait for her, while she shut the window, put on her hat and coat, went downstairs, found an umbrella, told the "girl" what to have for dinner, and came forth from the house. Too slow for us now-a-days, because the faster we're carried, the less time we have to spare . . .

Welles's narration continues over a brisk succession of faintly mocking scenes illustrating the antiquated mores and fads of this vanished society ("Trousers with a crease were considered plebeian; the crease proved that the garment had lain upon a shelf, and hence was 'ready-made'"); inside of three minutes, you're fully briefed on the halcyon world you've entered. Right afterward, the plot is launched no less ingeniously, with a tricked-up interplay of narration and dialogue that's every bit as propulsive as the fake "News on the March" newsreel that opens *Citizen Kane*. When we learn from Welles's narrator that the townspeople hoped to live to see the day when the bratty George "would get his comeuppance," we cut immediately to a woman in the street saying, "His *what?*," and a man responding, "His comeuppance! Something's bound to take him down, someday, I only want to be there." Six or seven minutes in, you feel like you're watching the best, most stylish family-saga movie epic ever made. Which, perhaps, it might once have been.

━━━━━

The trouble with *The Magnificent Ambersons* began, though no one foresaw it as trouble at the time, when the State Department approached Welles in late autumn of '41 about making a film in South America to promote goodwill among the nations of the Western Hemisphere. (With the war on, there was concern that the South American countries might ally themselves with Hitler.) The proposal was the brainchild of Nelson Rockefeller, who was not only a friend of Welles's but a major RKO shareholder and Franklin Roosevelt's coordinator of inter-American affairs. Welles, eager to oblige, had just the right idea: he had for some time been toying with the notion of making an omnibus documentary film called *It's All True*—indeed, it was yet another of his "in development" projects that was causing Schaefer anxiety—and he thought, Why not devote *It's All True* entirely to South American subjects? RKO and the State Department gave this idea their blessing, and it was decided that one segment of the film would be devoted to the annual carnival in Rio de Janeiro. There was only one problem: the carnival would be taking place in February—precisely when Welles would need to be in Los Angeles, readying *The Magnificent Ambersons* for the Easter release date that Schaefer was counting on. So a reshuffling of plans was in order.

The reshuffling went as follows: Welles would turn over the directing chores of *Journey into Fear* to the actor-director Norman Foster, though he would still act in that film in a supporting role; Welles would finish as much editing and postproduction work on *Ambersons* as possible before departing for Brazil in early February, whereupon he would supervise further work from afar through cables and telephone calls to a designated intermediary, Mercury Theatre business manager Jack Moss; and Wise would be sent down to Brazil to screen *Ambersons* footage and discuss possible cuts and changes with Welles, and would implement these changes upon his return to Los Angeles. It was an insanely demanding plan for Welles, who spent much of January directing *Ambersons* by day, acting in *Journey into Fear* by night, and devoting his weekends to the preparation and broadcast of his latest CBS radio program, *The Orson Welles Show*—all the while contemplating the *It's All True* project in the back of his mind. But Welles was known for keeping several irons in the fire, constantly juggling stage productions, radio shows, lecture tours, and writing projects, and the whole scheme proved, for January at least, to be workable.

In early February, Wise hastily assembled a three-hour-long rough cut of *The Magnificent Ambersons* and took it to Miami, where he and Welles—passing through en route to Brazil from a State Department briefing in Washington, D.C.—set up shop in a projection room that RKO had reserved for them at Fleischer Studios, the facility where the *Betty Boop* and *Popeye the Sailor* cartoons were made. For three days and nights, Welles and Wise worked around the clock on fashioning a quasi-final version of *Ambersons,* and Welles, in his bedraggled state, recorded the film's narration. Their work was to continue in Rio, but the U.S. government threw a wrench in their plans: due to wartime restrictions on civilian travel, Wise was denied clearance to go to Brazil. "I was all set, I had my passport and everything," he says, "and then they called and said, 'No way.'" (Welles, as a "cultural ambassador," had special dispensation.) And so, says Wise, "the last I saw of Orson for many, many years is when I saw him off on one of those old flying boats that flew down to South America one morning."

Closely following Welles's instructions from notes he'd taken during their Miami work sessions, Wise beavered away on a master version of *Ambersons,* informing Welles, in a letter dated February 21, of minor revisions he'd made, plans for new line dubbings by the actors, and the imminent completion of the film's music by "Benny," the renowned composer Bernard Herrmann (*Psycho, Taxi Driver*). On March 11, Wise sent a 132-minute composite print (a print with picture and soundtrack synchronized) to Rio for Welles to review. This is the version that scholars and Wellesophiles consider to be the "real" *Magnificent Ambersons.*

Curiously enough, the first blow against this version was dealt not by RKO but by Welles himself. Before he'd even received the composite print, he impulsively ordered Wise to cut 22 minutes from the middle of the film, mostly scenes concerning George Minafer's efforts to keep his mother and Eugene apart. Wise complied, and on March 17, 1942, *The Magnificent Ambersons,* in this form, had its first preview screening, in the Los Angeles suburb of Pomona. Sneak previews are a notoriously unreliable gauge of a film's worth and potential for success, and RKO did *The Magnificent Ambersons* a particular disservice by previewing it before an audience composed mostly of escapism-hungry teenagers, who had come to see the movie at the top of the bill, *The Fleet's In,* a featherlight wartime musical starring William Holden and Dorothy Lamour.

The preview, attended by Wise, Moss, Schaefer, and some other RKO executives, went horribly: "the worst I've ever experienced," says Wise. Seventy-two of the 125 comment cards turned in by the audience were negative, and among the comments were "The worst picture I ever saw," "It stinks," "People like to laff, not be bored to death," and "I could not understand it. Too many plots." Although these critiques were slightly mitigated by the occasional eloquent, favorable assessment—one viewer wrote, "Exceedingly good picture. Photography rivaled that of superb *Citizen Kane*. . . . Too bad audience was so unappreciative"—Wise and his compatriots could not ignore the sense of restlessness in the crowd and the waves of sarcastic laughter that erupted during the film's serious scenes, particularly those involving Agnes Moorehead's flitty, frequently hysterical Aunt Fanny character.

Schaefer was devastated, writing to Welles, "Never in all my experience in the industry have I taken so much punishment or suffered as I did at the Pomona preview. In my 28 years in the business, I have never been present in a theater where the audience acted in such a manner. . . . The picture was too slow, heavy, and topped off with somber music, never did register." But while Welles's 22-minute cut no doubt robbed the movie of some of its dramatic momentum, Schaefer, in entrusting *The Magnificent Ambersons'* fate to a bunch of callow high schoolers, showed some questionable judgment of his own. As Welles later remarked in one of his taped conversations with Peter Bogdanovich, collected in the 1992 book *This Is Orson Welles*, "There'd been no preview of *Kane*. Think what would have happened to *Kane* if there had been one!" And as Henry Jaglom says today, "If I'd gone to the theater to see a Dorothy Lamour movie, I'd have hated *Ambersons*, too!"

The next preview was scheduled for two days later, in the more sophisticated climes of Pasadena. Wise, to his credit, reinstated Welles's cut, trimming other, less crucial scenes instead, and this time the movie received a considerably more favorable response. But Schaefer, still shaken by the Pomona experience and antsy about the $1-million-plus he'd invested in the film—after initially approving an $800,000 budget—already envisioned failure. It was on March 21 that he poured his heart out to Welles in the letter quoted above, adding, "In all our initial discussions, you stressed low costs . . . and on our first two pictures, we have an investment of $2,000,000. We will not make a dollar on *Citizen Kane* . . . [and] the final results on *Ambersons* is [*sic*] still to be told, but it looks 'red.' . . . Orson Welles has got to do something commercial. We have got to get away from 'arty' pictures and get back to earth."

———

Welles was devastated by Schaefer's letter, and pressed for RKO to somehow get Wise down to Brazil. This, however, still proved unfeasible, and RKO, acting within its legal rights, took control of cutting the film, relying on a makeshift committee of Wise, Moss, and Joseph Cotten to fashion yet another, much shorter version of *Ambersons*. (Cotten, as dear a friend to Welles as his *Citizen Kane* character, Jed Leland, was to Charles Foster Kane, was mortified by the compromised position he was in, writing guiltily to Welles, "*Nobody in the Mercury* is trying in any way to take advantage of your absence.") Welles, correctly deducing that the film was slipping away from him, tried to reassert his control by sending painstakingly lengthy cables to Moss detailing every last change and edit he wanted made. (The telephone proved to be unreliable, given the primitiveness of intercontinental connections back then.) But these were effectively stabs in the dark—Welles had no way of knowing how well or how poorly his changes would work if implemented. Not that they would get implemented, anyway. In mid-April, Schaefer gave Wise full authority to whip the film into releasable shape (though his hoped-for Easter release date was no longer a possibility), and on April 20, Freddie Fleck, Welles's assistant director, shot a new, improbably tidy ending to the picture to replace the existing one.

Welles's ending was his most radical departure from the Tarkington novel, a total invention that saw Eugene, after checking in on the injured George in the hospital (a moment seen in neither the release version nor the lost version), visiting Aunt Fanny at the shabby boardinghouse where she'd taken up residence. It was Welles's favorite scene in the entire movie. As he later described it to Bogdanovich, it sounds wonderfully atmospheric and emotionally devastating: "all these awful old people roosting in this sort of half old folk's home, half boarding house," eavesdropping and getting in the way of Eugene and Fanny, two holdovers from a more dignified era. Fanny had always been jealous of Eugene's attentions to her sister-in-law, but now, Welles explained, "there's just nothing left between them at all. Everything is over—her feelings and her world and his world; everything is buried under the parking lots and the cars. That's what it was all about—the deterioration of personality, the way people diminish with age, and particularly with impecunious old age. The end of the communication between people, as well as the end of an era." And an appropriately weighty end to a movie that begins so forcefully.

The ending that Fleck shot—rather artlessly, with lighting and camerawork that bear no resemblance to the rest of the picture—shows Eugene and Fanny meeting in a hospital corridor after the former has just visited George. "How is Georgie?" Fanny asks. "He's going to be *allll* right!" says Eugene, sounding rather like Robert Young at the end of a *Marcus Welby* episode. They talk some more, then drift out of frame, smiling, arm in arm, as saccharine music (not by Herrmann) swells on the soundtrack. It's like having Oskar Schindler wake up at the last moment to realize that all this Holocaust business was just a bad dream.

In May, an 87-minute version of *Ambersons* using this ending was previewed in Long Beach, California, to much better audience response, and in June, after a bit more tinkering, Schaefer cleared a final version for release. Its 88 minutes included not only Fleck's ending but new continuity scenes shot by Wise (his first stab at directing, he says), and even by Moss, the Mercury business manager. Gone were all the scenes that carried heavy inferences of the Oedipal relationship between George and Isabel, and most of the scenes underscoring the town's transformation into a city and the Amberson family's desperate attempts to stave off its decline. (In the script, the Major starts selling lots on the mansion's grounds to developers, who begin excavations for apartment houses.) As such, the movie lost much of its complexity and resonance, becoming more about the basic mechanics of its plot than the greater themes that had drawn Welles to Tarkington's novel in the first place. Another casualty of the severe editing was the film's greatest technical accomplishment, the ball sequence, which included a continuous, carefully choreographed crane shot that wended up the three floors of the Amberson mansion to the ballroom at the top, with various characters moving in and out of the frame as the camera wove around them. To pick up the pace, this shot had a chunk removed from its middle, diluting its rapturous effect. (This would happen to Welles all over again in 1958, when Universal fiddled with *Touch of Evil*'s famous long opening shot; fortunately, a 1998 restoration put that right.) The 132-minute version of *The Magnificent Ambersons* that Welles and Wise had shaped in Miami was never shown publicly.

=====

Wise says he never had any sense that he was desecrating a great work of art by editing down and reshaping the film. "I just knew that we had a sick picture and it needed a doctor," he says. While he grants that "it was a better film in its full length," he maintains that his actions were simply a pragmatic response to the movie's being overlong and ill-suited to its era. "If it had come out a year before or even six months before the war started, it might have had a different reaction," he says. "But by the time the picture came out for previews, you know, guys were going off to training camp and women were working in the aircraft factories. They just didn't have many interests or concerns about the problems of the Amberson family and Indianapolis at the turn of the century." Besides, he adds, "I think the [edited] film is now something of a classic in its own right. It's still considered quite a classic film, isn't it?"

A soft-spoken man of mild temperament, Wise is the last person you'd suspect of pulling Machiavellian power plays, and he seemed genuinely pained in a post-Pomona letter he sent to Welles, writing, "It's so damn hard to put on paper in cold type the many times you die through the showing." But Welles never forgave him—Jaglom remembers Welles referring to "the traitorous cables from Bob Wise"—and it's certainly true that a pragmatic, go-along-to-get-along type like Wise was not the ideal person to defend the interests of an art-or-bust iconoclast like Welles. As for Welles's seemingly loyal Mercury lieutenant, Jack Moss, director Cy Endfield (*Zulu, The Sound of Fury*) had some surprising things to say about him in a 1992 interview with Jonathan Rosenbaum of *Film Comment*. Endfield, as a young man on the make in early 1942, had wangled a low-level job with the Mercury operation because he was good at magic tricks, a passion of Welles's, and Moss wanted a tutor to teach him some tricks that would impress the boss upon his return from Brazil. As such, Endfield was present in Moss's RKO office throughout the *Ambersons–It's All True* period, and even got to see the original version of the former. "I was waiting for another round of the *Citizen Kane* experience," he told Rosenbaum, "and instead I saw a very lyrical, gently persuasive film of a completely different succession of energies." Endfield was less enamored, though, of what he witnessed as things started to go bad:

A telephone with a private line had been installed in Moss's office in the Mercury bungalow that had a number known only to Orson in Brazil. For the first few days, he had a few discussions with Orson and tried to placate him. Then they had started arguing because there were more changes than Orson was prepared to acknowledge. After a few days of this, the phone was just allowed to ring and ring. I conducted many magic lessons with Moss when the phone was ringing uninterruptedly for hours at a time. I saw Jack enter carrying 35- and 40-page cables that had arrived from Brazil; he'd riffle through the cables, say, "This is what Orson wants us to do today," and then, without bothering to read them, toss them into the wastebasket. I was particularly dismayed by the enthusiasm with which the mice played while the cat was away.

The ignominy of the whole situation was compounded by Schaefer's ouster as RKO studio chief at the beginning of the summer of 1942—his undoing attributable, in part, to his financially unsuccessful gamble on Welles. In July, Schaefer's successor, Charles Koerner, ordered the Mercury Theatre staff off the RKO lot and pulled the plug on the floundering *It's All True* project, effectively sacking Welles from RKO in the process. The same month, the Koerner regime, lacking any confidence in *The Magnificent Ambersons*, opened it without fanfare in two theaters in Los Angeles, on a double bill with the Lupe Velez comedy *Mexican Spitfire Sees a Ghost*—an even more incongruous pairing than the Dorothy Lamour one.

After playing at a handful of movie houses around the country, Welles's picture died a quick box-office death. Later that year, on December 10, Koerner authorized James Wilkinson, the head of the editing department, to tell RKO's back-lot managers, who had been complaining of a shortage of storage space, that they could destroy various materials that were no longer of any use to the studio—including all the negatives from *The Magnificent Ambersons*.

Peter Bogdanovich, who was very close to Welles from the late 1960s through the mid-70s, and who for a time even let Welles bunk in his Bel Air home, remembers an incident that took place in the early 70s when he and his then girlfriend, Cybill Shepherd, paid a visit to Welles and his companion, a Croatian actress named Oja Kodar, in Welles's bungalow at the Beverly Hills Hotel. "Orson had this habit—you'd be having a conversation, and food would be there and whatever, and he sat rather near the TV with the clicker," he says. "So he was clicking it and watching it go, with the sound turned down a bit. I had my eye half on the TV, and there was a flash of *Ambersons* that I caught. He was off it almost before I could see it, because he obviously recognized it before I did. But I still saw it, and I said, 'Oh, that was *Ambersons!*' And Oja said, 'Oh, really? I've never seen it.' [*Mimicking Welles's stentorian boom:*] 'Well, you're not going to see it now!' And Cybill said, 'Oh, I want to see it.' We all said, 'Let's see a little bit.' And Orson said no. And then everybody said, 'Oh, *please?*' So Orson flipped to the channel and walked out of the room in a huff.

"So then we all said, 'Orson, come back, we'll turn it off.' [*Wellesian boom again:*] 'No, it's all right, I'll suffer!' So we watched it for a while. And then Oja, who was sitting furthest forward, kind of gestured to me. I looked back, and Orson was leaning in the doorway, watching. And as I remember, he came in and sat down. Nobody said anything. He just came in and sat down rather close to the set and watched for a while, not too long. I couldn't really see him—his back was to me. But I looked over at Oja at one point, who could see him because she was sitting on the other side of the room, and she looked at me and gestured like this. [*Bogdanovich runs a finger down his cheek from his eye, indicating tears.*] And I said, 'Maybe we shouldn't watch this anymore.' And we turned it off, and Orson left the room for a while and then came back."

This incident went undiscussed for a few days, until Bogdanovich summoned the nerve to say, "You were very upset watching *Ambersons* the other day, weren't you?"

"Well, I was upset," Bogdanovich remembers Welles saying, "but not because of the cutting. That just makes me furious. Don't you see? It was because it's the *past*. It's *over*."

—————

Several years later, Henry Jaglom, who had taken over Bogdanovich's role as Welles's protégé and confidant, had a similar experience. "I actually made him watch the movie," Jaglom says. "Around '80, '81, *Ambersons* was going to be on uninterrupted on a thing we had in Los Angeles called the Z Channel, an early form of cable. There were no VCRs and rentals then, so it was an event. It was coming on at 10 at night. I called to tell him to come over, and he kept saying he wouldn't watch it, he wouldn't watch it, until at the last minute he said he'd watch it. So we watched it. He was upset at the very beginning, but once we got into it, he was having a very good time, saying, 'This is pretty good!' He kept a running commentary going the whole time—where they cut this, how he should have done that. But at a certain point, about 20 minutes before it ended, he grabbed the clicker and turned it off. I said, 'What are you doing?' And he said, 'From here on it becomes *their* movie—it becomes bullshit.'"

Welles never stopped thinking about the possibility that he could save *The Magnificent Ambersons*. At one point in the late 60s he seriously considered rounding up the principal actors who were still alive—Cotten, Holt, Baxter, and Moorehead (who was then slumming as Endora on TV's *Bewitched*)—and shooting a new ending to replace the one Freddie Fleck had concocted: an epilogue in which the actors, with no makeup, in their naturally aged states, would depict what had become of their characters 20 years down the line. Cotten was apparently game, and Welles hoped for a new theatrical release and new audience for his movie. "But it never happened—he couldn't get the rights," Bogdanovich says.

Both Bogdanovich and Jaglom pulled whatever strings they

could to get various vaults checked for missing *Ambersons* footage. "Every time I had something to do with Desilu, which was still Desilu then, and then Paramount, I would ask," says Bogdanovich. The closest he ever got was when he found a cutting continuity—a screenplay-style transcription on paper of what appears on the screen—for the 132-minute version that Wise sent to Brazil on March 12, 1942. Bogdanovich also found photographs—"not stills, but actual frame enlargements"—of many of the deleted scenes. These materials form the basis for the most complete scholarly work on the movie, Robert L. Carringer's *The Magnificent Ambersons: A Reconstruction* (University of California Press, 1993), which painstakingly details the movie as Welles envisioned it.

⸻

Another person who looked into the *Ambersons* situation was David Shepard, a pioneer of film preservation and the restorer of *The Cabinet of Dr. Caligari* and various Charlie Chaplin and Buster Keaton shorts. He took his shot in the 1960s, but was dissuaded early in his search by Helen Gregg Seitz, an RKO old-timer, now dead, whose tenure at the company dated all the way back to the days of RKO's corporate predecessor, a silent-picture outfit called FBO. "Helen managed RKO's editorial department for many years, scheduling editors and laboratory work and so on," he says. "And she told me, 'Don't bother.' The standard practice back then was, negatives were disposed of after six months. She said she would have remembered if *The Magnificent Ambersons* had been handled any differently than any other film. And she was the kind of lady who probably remembered what she had for breakfast every day of her life."

⸻

The last, best hope for discovering the missing footage in Welles's lifetime came in the person of Fred Chandler, an employee in Paramount's postproduction department. It had been Chandler who made the much-ballyhooed discovery of the missing *It's All True* footage in the early 80s; a young Welles aficionado, he came upon a bunch of cans in the Paramount vaults labeled BRAZIL, unspooled the film inside one of them, and recognized what he saw—frames depicting fishermen floating on a homemade raft—to be the "Four Men on a Raft" segment (about four poor fishermen who sailed all the way from northern Brazil to Rio to plead for workers' rights) of Welles's long-lost South American movie. A couple of years earlier, Chandler had made Welles's acquaintance when he presented the director with another of his finds, a virgin print (never run on a projector) of Welles's 1962 film, *The Trial,* which he'd salvaged from the garbage. The appreciative Welles enlisted Chandler to do some archival work on his behalf, and, as Chandler puts it, "he put a bug in my ear that if ever a search for *Ambersons* was done, he would have to know about it."

The hoped-for opportunity arose in 1984, when the lab where Paramount got its film developed, Movielab, went out of business. This necessitated the return to Paramount of some 80,000 cans of film negative that Movielab had been storing for years. More important for Welles's purposes, this influx of new material into Paramount's vaults meant that everything already in the vaults had to be examined and catalogued, to see what should be kept, what should be moved elsewhere, and what should be thrown out. "My job was to check all the cans and see what was inside them," says Chandler, who is now a senior vice president of postproduction at Fox. "I had the whole inventory of RKO and Paramount at my fingertips."

Alas, he found nothing. "And I had five or six people checking every can," he says. He even, through discreet inquiries, located a woman, by then retired, who had worked in the stock-film library throughout the RKO and Desilu regimes, and who claimed to have destroyed the negatives of *The Magnificent Ambersons* herself. "Her name was Hazel something—I don't remember what," Chandler says. "She was afraid to talk about it. She was very guarded, an old retired lady. She just said, 'I was given a directive. I took the negative and incinerated it.'" This would make sense: making a few discreet inquiries myself, I learned that the head of RKO's stock-film library in the *Ambersons* era was a woman named Hazel Marshall. David Shepard knew her many years ago, and he says it's entirely plausible that she would have incinerated the negative; studios in those days often burned unneeded nitrate film to salvage the silver in the emulsion. (Although there's also a persistent rumor, which I was unable to verify, that Desilu indiscriminately dumped loads of RKO materials, including *Ambersons* footage, into the Santa Monica Bay upon its acquisition of the studio's lot in the 1950s. Say it ain't so, Lucy!)

Welles got the bad news from Chandler just a year before his 1985 death. "I would never have given Orson that answer—that it was all gone—unless I was pretty sure it was all gone," Chandler says. "I had to look him in the eye and tell him. He broke down and cried in front of me. He said it was the worst thing that had happened to him in his life."

———

In Chandler's view, there's no point in conducting a search like the one I'd wanted to embark on with Friedkin, "because I already did it. And it's all moved now." The only chance for *The Magnificent Ambersons'* survival in its original form, he says, is "some crazy happenstance," such as the footage's languishing somewhere in a mislabeled can, or in the possession of someone who doesn't know what he has.

But there's actually one other chance: that the composite print Wise sent to Welles in Brazil has somehow survived. "Nobody's been able to track it down," says Wise, who has no recollection of the print's ever being returned to RKO. "And as the house editor," he says, "I probably would have received it."

Bill Krohn, as part of the team that put together *It's All True: Based on an Unfinished Film by Orson Welles,* spent a lot of time poring over RKO documents and interviewing Brazilians who remembered Welles, and has his own ideas about what may have happened. Welles, he explains, used a Rio film studio called Cinedia as his base of operations for *It's All True.* Cinedia was owned by a man named Adhemar Gonzaga. Gonzaga was not only a director and producer of repute, but one of the pioneers of Brazilian cinema and a man who held a prescient view of film as art; he collected films before it was common to do so, and even founded a highfalutin Brazilian film journal not unlike France's *Cahiers du Cinéma.* Naturally, he also became friendly with Welles during the latter's time in Brazil.

As Krohn tells it, when RKO pulled the plug on *It's All True* and Welles eventually returned to the United States, he left the composite print of *Ambersons* behind at Cinedia—in other words, in Gonzaga's custody. Gonzaga cabled RKO, inquiring as to what he was supposed to do with the print. RKO, according to Krohn, responded that the print should be destroyed. "So Gonzaga cabled to RKO, PRINT DESTROYED," says Krohn. "But do you believe it? He's a film collector! I would bet dollars to doughnuts that his memo to RKO was not true."

Krohn tells this story from memory, since he doesn't have any copies of the correspondence in question. I tried to track down the cables he describes through Turner Entertainment, which now owns all of RKO's business correspondence from that era, but Turner's attorneys informed me in a letter that I would not be allowed access to the RKO documents "due to legal and practical considerations." However, when I ran Krohn's account past the most thoroughgoing of *Ambersons* experts, Robert Carringer, the author of *The Magnificent Ambersons: A Reconstruction,* he said that it was more or less correct, though he doesn't share Krohn's hope that the Brazilian print might still exist. Carringer provided me with copies of the pertinent RKO documents he came across in his research: an exchange of letters between the studio's New York and Hollywood offices in which the print-service department (in New York) twice asks the editing department (in Hollywood) what the "Brazilian office" is supposed to do with the prints of *The Magnificent Ambersons* and *Journey into Fear* it has in its possession. Intriguingly, this correspondence takes place during the months of December 1944 and January 1945—which means that, at the very least, the Brazilian print of *Ambersons* survived a good two years longer than any American print of the full-length version did. Eventually, the Hollywood office tells the New York office to "instruct the Brazilian office to junk" the Welles material. There's no smoking-gun cable from Gonzaga, Cinedia, or any other Brazilian entity confirming that the deed had been done, but Carringer, for one, accepts RKO-Hollywood's edict as the final word. In his book, he states unequivocally, "The duplicate print sent to Welles in South America was deemed useless and was also destroyed."

Krohn, nevertheless, is confident of the print's existence, if not its condition, saying, "There are eight cans of brown sludge marked

AMBERSONS somewhere in Brazil." Actually, says David Shepard, it's not a foregone conclusion that nitrate film from more than 60 years ago would have decomposed by now. "If it's been kept where other film is stored, in a place that's not too hot or humid, no question it could survive," he says. "I've got an original print of the 1903 *Great Train Robbery*, and it's fine."

=====

So the question is, if the print was indeed saved by Gonzaga, where would it be? Cinedia is still in operation (though it's since moved to a different location in Rio), and it's now run by Gonzaga's daughter, Alice Gonzaga. With the help of Catherine Benamou, a professor of film at the University of Michigan who is fluent in Portuguese and was the chief researcher on the '93 *It's All True* project, I was able to ask Alice Gonzaga, in writing, if she knew anything about such a print's existence. Responding by e-mail, she said that she didn't. Her staff had looked into the matter, and found nothing—"so we should presume that [my father] complied with RKO's request, since this print of *The Magnificent Ambersons* never became part of our film archive." However, Gonzaga noted that Cinedia's recordkeeping was patchy during the *Ambersons–It's All True* period, making it "quite probable that a lot of information" concerning Welles and RKO was lost. She also allowed that "you never know what can happen in this line of work," and mentioned that, a few years ago, a student at Northwestern University named Josh Grossberg had made an inquiry similar to mine.

Krohn had also heard of Grossberg. In the mid-1990s, the student had sought out Krohn's help in producing a documentary, never realized, called *Legend of the Lost Print*. On his own, Grossberg had made two trips to Brazil, in '94 and '96, to investigate the possible whereabouts of the composite print of *The Magnificent Ambersons*. Grossberg is now a New York–based entertainment reporter for the E! Online Web site and an aspiring filmmaker. He says that while in Brazil he was introduced to a man named Michel De Esprito, who had worked in the archives of Cinedia in the 1950s and 60s, and who claimed that Welles's print still existed in that era. "He swears that he saw an original print of *Ambersons* in a can, mislabeled," says Grossberg. "I think he actually projected it. But when he returned a few weeks later to look at the film more intently, it was moved away." De Esprito raised a number of possibilities as to what might have happened to the print—it could have been destroyed, pilfered, or transferred to a private collector. "We pursued some leads, even talking about tracking it through Gypsies," says Grossberg, who has not abandoned hope that the print exists. "But after that, we kind of ran out of leads."

If you've spent any amount of time immersed in the *Ambersons* saga, you begin to imagine, and even dream, that you've screened the movie's missing parts. So it was jarring for me to watch one of the scenes cut from the 132-minute version—of George brooding in a sitting room while Isabel merrily waits for Eugene to collect her, unaware that he has already called and George has rudely sent him away—and not have to shake myself from my reverie. Isabel was being played by Madeleine Stowe. George was being played by Jonathan Rhys-Meyers, best known for his portrayal of a David Bowie–like figure in the glam-rock movie *Velvet Goldmine* and as Henry VIII in TV's *The Tudors*. And the scene was being shot not on RKO's secondary lot in Culver City in autumn 1941 but in a huge mansion called Killruddery in County Wicklow, Ireland, where I was allowed to observe some of the A&E remake-in-progress in autumn 2000.

The new, $16 million production of *The Magnificent Ambersons* had taken over the grounds of the estate, as well as a large lot in industrial northern Dublin where a breathtaking replica of turn-of-the-century downtown Indianapolis had been built, the better to illustrate Welles's lost theme of the town's urbanization. The director, Alfonso Arau, also spoke of reviving Welles's cherished boardinghouse scene, as well as "all the Oedipus, all the Freudian content" that was muted the first time around. His words on the last point were borne out by the lingering hand grasps and longing looks between Stowe and Rhys-Meyers as they went through their paces. (Bruce Greenwood, who played John F. Kennedy in *Thirteen Days*, takes over for Joseph

Cotten as Eugene; James Cromwell, Farmer Hogget in *Babe*, is Major Amberson; Jennifer Tilly is Aunt Fanny; and Gretchen Mol is Lucy Morgan.)

But, for all the reinstatement of flourishes and ideas dear to Welles, the TV film's participants stressed that they were not doing a faithful, frame-by-frame remake of the uncut *Magnificent Ambersons*. "I love *Citizen Kane*, but I'm not crazy about *The Magnificent Ambersons*," Arau told me. "I think in many ways it's old-fashioned. It would be a romantic thought that Orson Welles is sitting on a cloud, applauding me, but I'm not motivated by that at all. The challenge I have is not to follow his act."

Cromwell, his whiskers grown out to Reconstruction length to play the Major, went even further. "I think Welles knew he had a bad film," he said. "It's a horrendous film! It was horrendous before the edit! As a follow-up to a film that essentially rewrote all the rules? C'mon! I just don't believe the performers are compelling. There's no magic between Costello and Cotten. It looks like a second-rate Hollywood period melodrama. I think Welles knew he didn't have anything. Even before he finished the film, he splits? I think he was scared shitless to fight with RKO." (Bear in mind that Cromwell played William Randolph Hearst in *RKO 281*, HBO's 1999 movie about the making of *Citizen Kane*, and could still have been carrying around some osmotic antipathy toward Welles.)

———

Arau and Cromwell had raised the two thoughts most heretical to members of the *Ambersons* cult: (a) that Welles's movie was never that good in the first place, and (b) that Welles himself is ultimately to blame for what happened to it. The first thought is simply a matter of taste; I disagree with it for the most part, and suspect that *The Magnificent Ambersons* was indeed a great film in its 132-minute incarnation. (My only major qualm is with the performance of Holt. His crude, braying line readings are intermittently effective in conveying what a heel George is, but his one-dimensionality ultimately doesn't do justice to what is, on paper, a complex role.)

As for the second thought, it's one of the great debates of film scholarship: was Welles his own worst enemy? In the case of *The*

Magnificent Ambersons, many people think so. It's often alleged that Welles effectively abdicated responsibility for the picture once he got to South America because he was having too good a time drinking rum, taking Brazilian lovelies to bed, and in general gorging on Latin America's rich pageant. "I think, someplace down the line, he got tired of dealing with [*Ambersons*]," says Wise. "He loved the partying, he loved the women, and he kind of forgot about the film, lost interest. It was pretty much 'You take care of this, Bob. I have other things to do.'"

Carringer, too, targets Welles, stating in his book that he "must bear the ultimate responsibility for the film's undoing." But he takes a stranger tack, arguing that Welles was subconsciously uneasy about *The Magnificent Ambersons* from the get-go because its Oedipal themes resonated a little too closely to home, uncomfortably mirroring his own obsession with his mother. This, says Carringer, explains why Welles cast Holt rather than himself in the George role, why he made George more unsympathetic in the screenplay than he is in the novel (a major turnoff for those preview audiences), and why, when the State Department beckoned, Welles jumped at the chance to skedaddle rather than face the task of finishing a troubling and troubled film.

Carringer makes the most of his theory, citing *Citizen Kane*'s theme of "maternal rejection" and Tarkington's deliberate borrowings from *Hamlet,* but it's all too speculative for me to buy, and I don't think Wise is on the mark, either. Welles's long, meticulous, occasionally desperate-sounding cables from Brazil (some of which I was able to see at U.C.L.A.'s Arts Library, which allows limited access to its RKO Radio Pictures Archive) belie the idea that he was disengaged from the editing process, and his desire to do his patriotic duty for the State Department seemed sincere enough. "He felt he was doing a very good thing for the war effort," says Jaglom. "He said, 'Can you imagine me *not* wanting to be present and in control of the editing of my own movie?'"

———

More likely, Welles, who was still just 26 in early 1942, was vainglorious and naïve enough to think he could do it all—*The Magnificent*

Ambersons, Journey into Fear, It's All True, and as many Brazilian girls as possible. He was, lest it be forgotten, a boy wonder, accustomed to getting done what men twice his age couldn't, and to being allowed a degree of control unknown to any other director. Precocious enough to make *Citizen Kane,* he was also callow enough to think he could maintain authorial control over *Ambersons* from a distance, and he paid for this mistake with his job, his film, and his place in Hollywood.

Carringer says that Richard Wilson, Welles's longtime right-hand man in the Mercury Theatre, once told him, "Orson never cared about *Ambersons* until the *auteur* stuff started in the 60s and 70s and people started talking about *Ambersons* as a great film." This statement could well be true. But it still doesn't mean Welles was insincere or fraudulently revisionist in his later bitterness over what had happened to his movie, nor does it mean he was crying crocodile tears in front of Peter Bogdanovich and Fred Chandler. The passing of time often brings with it a sad dawning, a belated understanding of the worth of something that's not there anymore. Was this not, after all, the very message imparted by *The Magnificent Ambersons*?

From *Vanity Fair,* January 2002

ALL ABOUT EVE

Everything About Eve

by Sam Staggs

When I asked Nancy Reagan recently if she had been aware in 1950 that she was under consideration for a part in *All About Eve*, director Joseph L. Mankiewicz's classic film about love and ambition and treachery in the theater, she told me she had had no idea she was in the running. And yet there's the name Nancy Davis on the casting director's sheet, No. 9 in a total of 28 possibilities to play the role of Karen Richards. She's below Ann Sothern and Shirley Booth but above Jessica Tandy and Arlene Dahl. The part went to Celeste Holm.

Nancy Reagan was also unaware that the actor she would marry two years later, in 1952, was on the list. The Twentieth Century Fox casting office had jotted his name under the character of Bill Sampson, along with 24 other contenders. If Ronald Reagan, and not Gary Merrill, had gotten the part in *All About Eve*, it would have been his second movie with Bette Davis, who played the leading role of Margo Channing. It might also have changed the course of history.

For *All About Eve* did change the course of the lives of the actors in it. Critic Ethan Mordden has called it "the film that ruined Davis or the film that made her immortal." Perhaps it did both.

Marilyn Monroe, who played the cameo role of dizzy blonde Miss Casswell, is the only one whose career would ascend. For others in the cast—Anne Baxter, Hugh Marlowe, George Sanders, Thelma Ritter—and for the director, *All About Eve* was the climax. Never again did a single one of them surpass, or even equal, what he or she did so brilliantly, with such verve and wit, in this film.

———

All *About Eve* was based on a real story, which a young actress named Mary Orr fictionalized and sold to *Cosmopolitan* magazine for $800. The story, called "The Wisdom of Eve," was published in the May 1946 issue.

A story editor at Twentieth Century Fox read the short story, and the studio optioned it. Eventually it came to the attention of Joe Mankiewicz, who considered it an excellent starting point for the film he wanted to make about the theater. He persuaded Darryl F. Zanuck, production chief of the studio, to approve the property.

During the summer and early fall of 1949, Mankiewicz completed an 82-page treatment. The first title was *Best Performance*. Reading Mankiewicz's treatment, Zanuck followed his custom of making notes on it in pencil. At one point he underlined a phrase spoken by the Addison DeWitt character: "Eve . . . but more of Eve later. All about Eve, in fact." Sometime during January 1950 the project acquired its new name.

After reading Mankiewicz's lengthy first draft in March 1950, Zanuck praised it highly but suggested changes, most of which involved shortening or condensing. By early April, Mankiewicz had finished revising his screenplay. He kept not a line of dialogue from Mary Orr's story, but he did retain what served him better: the breezy, brittle tone. The story's slick opening sentences—"A young girl is on her way to Hollywood with a contract for one thousand dollars a week from a major film company in her pocketbook. I shall call her Eve Harrington because that is not her name"—match the lacquered narration of Addison DeWitt (played by George Sanders) at the start of the movie.

Mankiewicz and Zanuck were not the final arbiters on all points,

however. The imprimatur of Joseph Ignatius Breen, chief adminis-
trator of the Production Code, was mandatory for this picture, as it
was for virtually every other one. Breen was, in effect, the head cen-
sor of Hollywood at the time, an ardent Catholic who had been director of Code Administration since 1933, first under Will Hays and
after 1945 under Eric Johnston.

Today, *All About Eve* strikes viewers as "adult" in the sense of
sophisticated, but in 1950 certain lines and situations didn't conform
to Code standards of "good taste." Breen asked that on page 15 of the
script "the use of the word 'sex' be changed to something less blunt
in the circumstances." The offending line, spoken by the actress
Margo Channing quoting a lady reporter from the South, was: "That's
why ah don' understand about all these plays about sex-stahved
Suth'n women—sex was one thing we were nevah stahved for in the
South!" In the revised script, "sex" turned into "love."

In the original script, Mankiewicz describes Margo's dressing
room and then adds, "A door leads to an old-fashioned bathroom."
Birdie, the maid (played by Thelma Ritter), makes several trips into
and out of this bathroom. That made Breen nervous. His letter states,
"We presume that there will be no notice of a toilet in the bathroom
in these scenes."

Mankiewicz has Birdie say, "I'll never forget that blizzard the
night we played Cheyenne. A cold night. First time I ever saw a brassiere break like a piece of matzo." Breen noted dryly that "the reference to the brassiere should be changed or eliminated."

It was eliminated, and it's likely Mankiewicz conceded that
Borscht Circuit line as a gambit for retaining another crack of Birdie's:
"Everything but the bloodhounds snappin' at her rear end." Breen
had also found this one "vulgar" and recommended that it be changed
or eliminated.

Colonel Jason S. Joy, Fox's director of public relations, reported
Breen's request to Mankiewicz, adding, "Insomuch as Birdie's line is
at the end of the shot, perhaps you can let it go the way it is and clip
off 'rear end' if we have to, although I don't think we will." Mankiewicz replied, "The word *should* be 'arse.' What do you suggest we
substitute for 'rear end?' 'Backside?' 'Butt?' What would you think of
'snappin' at her transmission?'"

Breen dictated a whole memo about bathrooms: "We suggest that you soften the reference to the 'Ladies' Room' by possibly referring to it as the 'Lounge Room' or the 'Powder Room' or something similar. The line, 'I understand she is now the understudy in there,' seems somewhat vulgar, and we ask that it be changed."

Mankiewicz fired back: "Changing 'Ladies' Room' to 'Powder Room' is not only childish but will most certainly hurt Bill's comment" (the "understudy" line is Bill Sampson's, referring to Eve Harrington). Exhausted from dealing with literal-minded boobs, Mankiewicz concluded rather pedantically, "'Understudy' refers to *ladies* and not to *powder.*"

On this point Mankiewicz got his way, and on Breen's final point he also refused to budge. Referring to the hotel-room scene where Addison slaps Eve and pins her to the bed, Joseph Breen wrote demurely, "We ask that the slap across the face be eliminated."

It wasn't, and when Breen saw this slap on-screen in its context of implied sadomasochism, he must have bemoaned his leniency in letting them get away with it.

———

For Claudette Colbert, April really was the cruelest month—at least in 1950, for that's when she lost the part of Margo Channing. Mankiewicz and Zanuck had agreed on her early on, and she had signed the contract. Then, on the set of *Three Came Home,* directed by Jean Negulesco, she fell and ruptured a disc in her back. Colbert realized that she would never make *All About Eve.* "I cried for days," she said later, adding, "Days? I cried for years."

With Colbert's back in a steel brace, a replacement had to be found. No doubt Mankiewicz was fearful that Zanuck might use Colbert's indisposition as an opportunity for offering Margo to the actress he had favored from the start: Marlene Dietrich. Mankiewicz objected strenuously to Dietrich. He later explained, "I was, and am, a great admirer of Marlene. But from what I knew of her work and equipment as an actress, I simply could not visualize—or 'hear'—her as a possible Margo."

Mankiewicz had a viable second choice. Gertrude Lawrence, at

51, was a decade older than Margo, but with her swooping archness, her great-lady-of-the-stage mannerisms, and a zany sophistication that had served her well in Noël Coward comedies, she deserved the compliment that Lloyd Richards, in the *All About Eve* script, pays his leading lady: "Margo, you haven't got any age." Lawrence, however, declined the role. She had just acquired the rights to *Anna and the King of Siam,* which Rodgers and Hammerstein would soon turn into *The King and I* especially for her.

Mankiewicz and Zanuck turned to Bette Davis as a last resort. Their offer was even more of a last resort for her than for them, because in 1950 Davis was a fading star. *Winter Meeting* (1948) had been the first of her pictures to lose money. Her behavior had become less professional and more unbearable on the set of each new lackluster movie. After *Beyond the Forest,* in 1949, it seemed impossible for her career to get any worse. And since "camp" as an aesthetic concept hadn't yet been invented, no one realized that this movie would fester into immortality once Edward Albee featured a Davis line from it—"What a dump!"—13 years later in his play *Who's Afraid of Virginia Woolf?*

In early April, Davis was filming *Payment on Demand* at RKO. One day, during a lull in shooting, she got word that she was wanted on the phone. She was astonished to hear it was Darryl Zanuck on the other end, for they hadn't spoken in nine years. The last thing he had yelled at her was "You'll never work in Hollywood again!" Now he was saying, "Bette, I've got a script I want you to take a look at. And I hope you'll want to do it."

She thought someone was playing a joke on her, so she assumed an arch, saucy tone. "Anything you say, Darryl dear. If I like it, I shall do it."

"The only thing is, Bette, if you like it you've got to be ready to start shooting in ten days, wardrobe finished and all."

Davis decided to have a little fun herself, string whoever it was along. "Right away, Darryl dear."

"So you're interested in the script?" Zanuck continued.

"Anything you say, Darryl dahling."

"Wouldn't you like to know the name of the picture?"

"Oh, why not surprise me?" Davis said airily.

"Bette, it's the picture Claudette Colbert was going to do before she broke her back."

"Broke her back?" Davis yelped. And then it dawned. "Darryl, is that really you?"

They talked for four or five minutes, during which Zanuck made her one of the best offers any film actress had ever received. Following their conversation, Davis went through a pack of cigarettes in two hours.

A bicycle messenger arrived at RKO in the late afternoon carrying a large envelope with Davis's name on it. She started reading the script as her chauffeur drove off the lot. Her enthusiasm grew with each page she turned, and by the time the driver pulled up to her house at 1991 Ocean Way in Laguna Beach, Davis knew this was the best script she had read in years. She locked herself in her room and, provisioned with plenty of scotch and cigarettes, didn't come out again until she had studied every word of *All About Eve*.

The next morning she phoned Zanuck and said, "Darryl, I'd love to play Margo Channing." Then she called Mankiewicz, who invited her to dinner that night to discuss the project. Decades later, Davis would still recall Mankiewicz's description of Margo Channing: "He said she was the kind of dame who would treat her mink coat like a poncho!"

Bette had five days left on the film at RKO. She had looked forward to a vacation, but now she had to work on two films at once. Edith Head was to design the Margo Channing outfits (but no one else's) for *All About Eve,* and so Davis immediately started going to Head for fittings each night after a long day at RKO.

The reason for this breakneck schedule was that the Curran Theatre in San Francisco had been rented for two weeks of location shooting to begin April 11. With one play closing and another to open soon, the Curran was available only for those two weeks in April. Since a number of scenes in *All About Eve* take place in a cavernous Broadway playhouse, it made sense to shoot them in a real theater.

On April 5, 1950, Davis celebrated her 42nd birthday on the set of *Payment on Demand*. Two days later she signed her contract for *All About Eve*, and four days after that, on the 11th, production began in San Francisco.

———

Darryl Zanuck recoiled when Mankiewicz demanded Gary Merrill for the part of Bill Sampson. He grumbled that Merrill "had only played around airplanes," and he was right, for Merrill's career so far hadn't led him beyond portrayals of lieutenants and commanders in such military aviation films as *Winged Victory* (1944) and *Twelve O'Clock High* (1949). Zanuck's choice for the role was John Garfield. But Mankiewicz stood firm, and Merrill got the part.

"One Sunday in 1950," Merrill later wrote in his memoir, *Bette, Rita, and the Rest of My Life,* "I had been called to the studio for a makeup test with Miss Bette Davis."

"This was the first time I met Gary," Davis wrote in *her* memoir *The Lonely Life*. "They did photographic tests of us together. I was to look older than he as Margo. I did."

Merrill: "I went to the test stage, and there, being turned this way and that on a stool, as though she had just been picked up from a counter at a jewelry store, was the Queen, Bette Davis."

Davis: "I had seen the film *Twelve O'Clock High* and an actor in it named Gary Merrill. I had never seen him before and I was greatly impressed by his performance and looks."

Merrill: "The makeup people . . . were trying to see if our age difference would be too noticeable. . . . Bette had a few character lines around those incredible eyes, but . . . here was a magnetic woman with a compelling aura of femininity who might also be willing to confront dragons. I was irresistibly drawn to her."

Davis told columnist Hedda Hopper, "People get the idea that actresses my age are dying to play younger women. The fact is, we die every time we play one."

Merrill later told author Shaun Considine, "Never in the history of motion pictures has an actress been so perfectly cast."

Sizing each other up, Davis and Merrill liked what they saw. But before any romance could take wing, each one had to shed a marital encumbrance. Davis's third marriage—to William Grant Sherry, variously characterized as "a muscle-bound sailor" who was "an artist of sorts" with a "bohemian attitude and blunt manner"—was already on the rocks. Merrill divorced actress Barbara Leeds four months after he laid eyes on Bette Davis.

———

Zanuck wanted Jeanne Crain to play Eve Harrington. Though the intervening years have reduced her star to the size of an asterisk, in 1950 she was famous. Under contract to Fox, Crain had become a favorite with fans and theater exhibitors. Mankiewicz, however, was unenthusiastic. He had cast her a year earlier in *A Letter to Three Wives* and thought she lacked the "bitch virtuosity" needed to play Eve. Zanuck yielded. Mankiewicz then named the actress he wanted, Anne Baxter, and since she was under contract to Fox, Zanuck O.K.'d her for the role.

Hollywood wasn't sure what to do with Celeste Holm, in part because she preferred acting onstage to appearing in films and made no secret of her preference. Ironically, in *All About Eve* she plays the wife of a playwright; as such, she is referred to as being "of the theater by marriage." She played Margo Channing's best friend, but Holm and Davis disliked each other immediately. "Bette Davis was so rude, so constantly rude," Holm remembered years later. "Why, I walked onto the set about the first or second day and said, 'Good morning,' and do you know her reply? She said, 'Oh shit, good manners.' I never spoke to her again—ever."

Holm felt shy in new situations, and although she had won an Oscar, for *Gentleman's Agreement* (1947), it was for a supporting role. She feared Davis—a two-time winner for best actress, in *Dangerous* (1935) and *Jezebel* (1938)—might hold that against her. It's possible that Davis viewed Holm as something of a goody-goody with a sharp eye for the publicity value of righteousness. Only a year earlier, Holm had starred as a tennis-playing nun in the wholesome Loretta Young vehicle *Come to the Stable*.

Soon this strange group of stars began to descend on San Francisco. Celeste Holm, Gary Merrill, and Hugh Marlowe flew from Los Angeles on Darryl Zanuck's seaplane. But flying, in those days, was not considered the safest way to travel. Bette Davis got the real star treatment: she went by rail. When the train pulled into the station in

San Francisco, reporters and photographers swarmed around her. Davis had her three-year-old daughter, B.D., with her, as well as her secretary, the child's governess, Marion Richards, and a bodyguard, because Davis's estranged husband, William Sherry, had made threats.

Thelma Ritter flew in from her home in Queens, New York; Anne Baxter arrived late that night because she could hardly bear to leave her husband, the actor John Hodiak. George Sanders and his wife, Zsa Zsa Gabor, arrived on the same flight as Marilyn Monroe.

Long after Sanders and Monroe were dead, Zsa Zsa Gabor wrote about the trip: "I met Marilyn for the first time in the commissary and noted that she was extremely adept at wiggling her ass and batting her eyelashes. On the plane to San Francisco, I had the window seat, Marilyn the aisle—with George, appropriately, sandwiched in the middle. Marilyn spent most of the trip batting her eyelashes at George, who turned to me when we were alone and said, with a mixture of sympathy and pride, 'Poor girl, she has it bad.' 'George,' I said, in fury, 'don't flatter yourself, she's having sex with everybody.'"

Monroe later said this about her first encounter with Gabor: "I saw she was one of those blondes who put on ten years if you take a close look at them."

———

On the first day of filming, Bette Davis awoke without a voice. She tried to speak, but no words came. The trouble had started a few nights earlier, in Los Angeles, when she let loose such a lava spill of abuse on William Sherry that she ruptured a small blood vessel in her throat.

A specialist told her to rest her voice for a day or two. He assured her that the problem was neither serious nor permanent. But Joe Mankiewicz turned pale when Davis arrived at the Curran Theatre, pulled him close, and moaned, "Oh, what am I going to do about it?"

He patted her shoulder and with a reassuring smile said, "Honey, we're going to keep it. It's the whiskey-throated voice that Margo should have, a bourbon contralto. Even when your throat improves, I want Margo to sound like this. Can you keep it up for a month?"

Mankiewicz called rehearsal. Although Davis had to guard her voice, she could still say her lines. Later, Mankiewicz said, "Bette was letter-perfect. She was syllable-perfect. The director's dream: the prepared actress."

A clever graffito sums up Hollywood's most famous costume designer: "Edith Head gives good wardrobe." Bette Davis once said, "While other designers were busy starring their clothes in a film, Edith was making clothes to suit a character." That's why Davis chose Head to design Margo Channing's outfits.

At the time, Edith Head was chief designer at Paramount, where she had just dressed Gloria Swanson for *Sunset Boulevard*. Then Davis got the part in *All About Eve* and the race was on to complete Margo's wardrobe in time for filming.

Charles LeMaire, executive director of wardrobe at Fox, happened to be Head's friend. He had already dressed Anne Baxter, Celeste Holm, Thelma Ritter, and Marilyn Monroe for the film.

Reading the script, LeMaire realized that *All About Eve* could end up a very good picture indeed, the kind of picture where the costumes themselves would help characterize the women who wore them. The picture's theatrical setting added to LeMaire's enthusiasm, for he had started out as a costumer on Broadway. "Sure I would have liked to have dressed Bette Davis," he recalled, "but I was already on another film. I had confidence that Edith could do it, so I asked for her on loan."

Tuesday, April 11, was day one of *All About Eve*. By seven A.M., hairdressers and makeup artists were at work on Anne Baxter and Celeste Holm, for that morning they were to film the first meeting of Eve Harrington and Karen Richards. This was an important scene because it gained sympathy for the stagestruck young Eve, whose idolatry of Margo Channing seemed so pure. It set the tempo and timbre of Anne Baxter's entire performance. While Baxter was made to look dowdy in a trench coat and hat, Holm was glamorized in mink. As their makeup was applied, both actresses brushed up their lines with the script clerk.

Mankiewicz had been on the set long before shooting was scheduled to begin. Cinematographer Milton Krasner and his assistants, along with electricians and grips, had also been at work since the crack of dawn to prepare the lighting for the first scene, which was a night shot in the alley beside the Curran Theatre. To film this night scene in daylight, Krasner had the whole area covered with tarpaulins to obscure the sun and its reflections. At nine A.M., the cameras rolled.

The scene begins as Karen Richards gets out of a taxi. She takes a step, hesitates, looks curiously about, then makes her way into the alley, heading for the stage door. As she passes a recess in the theater's exterior wall, Eve steps from the shadows and calls out, "Mrs. Richards."

From nine o'clock until long past lunchtime, they did it over and over again. First the lighting wasn't right, Mankiewicz thought, so they did another take. That time Krasner wasn't satisfied. A streetcar grinding past Geary Street spoiled the third take; then Anne Baxter flubbed a line. Only after the 14th take did the director say, "Print it."

That afternoon, Holm, Baxter, Mankiewicz, and all the others reassembled to shoot the continuation of the sequence, in which Karen leads Eve to Margo's dressing room. By six o'clock the day's shooting was over. Exposed film was packed up and airmailed to Fox's lab in Los Angeles. There the negative would be developed and a positive print of the film and soundtrack would be sent to Barbara McLean, the editor of *All About Eve*.

The next day, Davis made her first appearance before the cameras. Thanks to the throat specialist, her voice had definitely improved. During that first week of shooting, however, another complication arose: Bette Davis and Gary Merrill fell in love. Celeste Holm recalled, "And from then on she didn't care whether the rest of us lived or died."

Gary Merrill said in his memoirs, "There is truth in the idea that an actor's personality is created in the parts he or she plays. My role was that of Bill Sampson, who was in love with Margo Channing, and as the film progressed I became infatuated with Bette. At first, since I love kids, I played games with Bette's three-year-old daughter, B.D., who was often on location. As B.D. (her name is Barbara Davis, but

Bette always called her B.D.) became more comfortable with me, so did her mother. And as I earned more of their trust, Bette opened up and began confiding in me about some of her problems."

Davis revealed in *The Lonely Life,* "The unholy mess of my own life—another divorce, my permanent need for love, my aloneness. Margo Channing was a woman I understood thoroughly. I had hard work to remember I was playing a part."

Merrill: "Before long we were walking about holding hands, going to the movies. From simple compassion, my feelings shifted to an almost uncontrollable lust."

According to Celeste Holm, "It was not a very pretty relationship, as they laughed at other people together. Bette and Gary formed a kind of cabal, like two kids who had learned to spell a dirty word."

Davis: "There was one bitch in the cast—Celeste Holm."

Merrill: "I walked around with an erection for three days."

═══

After interviewing about a dozen young actresses, including Sheree North, for the role of Miss Casswell, Mankiewicz proposed the name of Marilyn Monroe. Zanuck hit the ceiling; he had fired her a couple of years earlier because, Monroe herself later claimed, he considered her unphotogenic. She had played bit parts in several Fox pictures, and Zanuck had excised her from all but one or two.

Why did Mankiewicz want her to play Miss Casswell? "There was a breathlessness and sort of glued-on innocence about her that I found appealing." But Zanuck might have demanded another girl as the "graduate of the Copacabana School of Dramatic Art" if Marilyn's protector, Johnny Hyde, hadn't intervened.

Hyde, 54 years old at the time, was a short, wizened man with severe heart trouble. He was also a top agent at William Morris. Though married, Hyde was in love with Marilyn. He took her to see Joe Mankiewicz. Or, as Mankiewicz said, "He haunted my office."

Once Hyde had convinced the director that Marilyn was the one, he set to work on Zanuck. Hyde, as a top agent, was in a position to overcome Zanuck's resistance, if not his reluctance. "On March 27,

1950, Marilyn Monroe was signed for five hundred dollars a week—on a one-week guarantee," Mankiewicz recalled. This agreement led to a long-term contract with Fox, which remained in effect, with modifications, through June 1962, when the studio fired her a second time. Two months later Marilyn Monroe died.

In the years following *All About Eve,* Marilyn's co-stars seemed dazed that their own careers faltered while hers mushroomed. After her death, when the myth of Marilyn obscured the facts, various members of the cast ransacked their memories for details of the fledgling goddess during that long-ago April.

"And that poor Monroe child—Marilyn—Marilyn was terrified of Bette Davis!" This is George Sanders speaking in 1970, two years before his suicide. "During one scene in a theater lobby involving Monroe, Davis, and me, Davis whispered to me after a shot, within poor Marilyn's hearing: 'That little blonde slut can't act her way out of a paper bag! She thinks if she wiggles her ass and coos away, she can carry her scene. Well, she can't!'"

A few years after *All About Eve* came out, Monroe told Joan Collins (who at that time was filming *The Virgin Queen* with Davis), "That woman hates every female who can walk. She made me feel *so* nervous. She didn't talk to me at all, just sort of swept around the set, nose and cigarette in the air. She's a mean old broad."

Celeste Holm said of Monroe in 1978, "I confess I saw nothing special about her Betty Boop quality. I thought she was quite sweet and terribly dumb, and my natural reaction was, 'Whose girl is that?'"

Anne Baxter wrote in her memoir, *Intermission,* "[Earlier] in 1950 I'd made a movie called *A Ticket to Tomahawk.* Marilyn Monroe played one of a trio of the required dancehall girls. . . . All of us lived in Durango at the Royal Motel, a euphemism, and ate at the local greasy spoon called the Chief Diner. Marilyn Monroe came in with a different crew member every night, wearing the same sweater. She was eminently braless and I particularly remember the pink V-necked angora sweater. It was said she slept in it."

Ten years after Monroe's death, Mankiewicz said, "I thought of her, then, as the loneliest person I had ever known. Throughout our location period in San Francisco, Marilyn would be spotted at one restaurant or another dining alone. Or drinking alone. We'd always ask her to join us, and she would, and seemed pleased, but somehow she never understood or accepted our unspoken assumption that she was one of us. She remained alone. She was not a loner. She was just plain *alone.*"

=====

At the end of the first week's filming, everyone joined Mankiewicz to view the rushes. Even this crude preview bolstered the actors' wavering faith. They were good; they were great. And Monday morning, on the set, they were even better than before. "Every day was like a glorious relay race," Anne Baxter recalled.

Baxter, who made her Broadway debut at 13, later revealed that she had patterned Eve Harrington on her own first understudy. That girl, she said, "was nice to everybody but me and would always be in the wings watching me like a hawk."

Mary Orr's story in *Cosmopolitan,* from which *All About Eve* grew, also had a real understudy as its basis. During the 1943–44 Broadway season, the Austrian actress Elisabeth Bergner (1897–1986) was appearing in a thriller called *The Two Mrs. Carrolls.* Bergner had the role of a devoted and unsuspecting wife who is slowly being poisoned by her husband.

In Europe, Bergner had been called "the Garbo of the stage." She made movies in Germany and also in England, where she immigrated when Hitler came to power. She played Rosalind in the 1936 film version of *As You Like It,* opposite Laurence Olivier. When a German invasion of Great Britain seemed likely, Bergner headed for New York. During her 400-performance run of *The Two Mrs. Carrolls,* she was inadvertently cast, offstage, as a Margo Channing.

Reginald Denham, the director of *The Two Mrs. Carrolls,* was married to the young actress Mary Orr. One weekend they visited Elisabeth Bergner and her husband, Hungarian producer-director Paul Czinner, at their country retreat in Vermont. Here's how Mary Orr [who died in 2006] remembers that evening more than 50 years later: "Elisabeth on the stage was an amazing actress. Offstage, however, she was a little Austrian hausfrau. So that night I watched one of the world's great actresses bread veal and peel potatoes. Before long, she looked at me and said, 'You're a young actress. Let me tell you about the one . . . '

⸻

"Elisabeth always called her 'that terrible girl' or 'that little bitch.' Anyway, the girl—let's call her Miss X—used to stand in the alley beside the theater night after night, wearing a little red coat. I suppose she somehow saw every performance of *The Two Mrs. Carrolls*. Or maybe she only claimed she did.

"Elisabeth told me all this right there in the kitchen. 'So, Mary,' she said, 'wouldn't you be curious? I was too, and so one night I invited her into my dressing room.'

"It seems that from that very night the 'terrible girl' took over Elisabeth's life. Or tried to. The girl lied to her, deceived her, did things behind her back—even went after her husband, Paul Czinner!

"Elisabeth was touched that a very young fan would feel such devotion toward her. And the girl had a faint accent. She was English, she told Elisabeth and Paul, and, like them, she had fled to America for fear the Germans might invade Britain. Elisabeth said the girl's eyes filled with tears. They all became friends that night.

"A few days later Elisabeth arranged for the girl to become a secretary of sorts to Paul. And of course the girl performed to perfection. . . . In the meantime, however, the young secretary-actress had her eye on greater things. It so happened that Irene Worth, who played the ingenue in *The Two Mrs. Carrolls*, was leaving the cast and a replacement had to be found. Miss X volunteered to read Elisabeth's role at the auditions—'so that Miss Bergner won't have to be bothered,' as she put it."

⸻

Bergner was surprised to learn that Miss X had read. It was terribly kind, she thought. And Elisabeth Bergner was generous. She, along with her husband and his co-producer, decided to do something for Miss X.

The three of them approached Actors' Equity to seek permission for the young Englishwoman to make her Broadway debut. Equity investigated. A few days later Paul Czinner got a phone call. "No trouble at all," he was told by the Equity rep. "The girl's not English, she's American."

As deceptive as Tartuffe, the young lady blithely talked her way out of this tight spot by saying she had to find out—in the company of experts—whether her British accent was as convincing as she hoped.

Mary Orr continues: "As for Miss X, Elisabeth thought her talented, and so she helped her get Irene Worth's role. I can't remember whether she also became Elisabeth's understudy, but it stands to reason that she would, even though she was much too young for the part.

"How far did she go in undermining Elisabeth's career, you ask? Not far at all. Maybe she coveted Elisabeth's starring role in *The Two Mrs. Carrolls,* but she never got it, of course. Elisabeth knew how to defend herself."

About the time Mankiewicz was transforming his treatment into the shooting script of *All About Eve,* the real Eve Harrington paid Mary Orr a visit.

"She came to my home one day, very angry," Orr recalls. "Somehow this girl got past the doorman and made her way upstairs. You see, she had read my story in *Cosmopolitan.* I suppose she found my address in the phone book. And she was livid. Now, keep in mind that this was three or four years after the story was published. She was a real Eve, there's no question about it. She rang my bell, and when I answered she pushed in past me, angry and agitated. I had no idea who she was or why she had come, but she threatened to sue me. She had recognized herself in the story, but she never found a lawyer who would take the case."

Others besides Mary Orr have encountered the real Eve. Harry Haun, a Manhattan journalist, looked up from his desk at the New York *Daily News* one day in 1990, and there she stood. She demanded that he write her story. Harry Haun laughed as he told me this in his apartment on Riverside Drive in New York. Haun is a burly native Texan who for many years has been a journalist specializing in celebrity profiles. Among those he has interviewed are Celeste Holm and Joseph L. Mankiewicz.

"Mankiewicz corresponded with her—did you know that?" Haun said. "He showed me the letters. Have you ever heard anything so wild? First Mankiewicz created Eve Harrington, then they become pen pals."

Mankiewicz was in Venice in the mid-1980s to receive the Lion d'Or at the Venice Film Festival. Later he told an interviewer, "I got this telephone call from an absolutely desperate-sounding woman. She said, 'Mr. Mankiewicz, this is Eve.' I said, 'Eve?' She said, 'Yes, the Eve you wrote the movie about. I was the girl who stood outside the theater.' She said, 'I know you don't believe me, so I'm going to send you something.' Sure enough, she sent me a copy of this autobiography of Elisabeth Bergner. She wrote about this girl who was there outside the theater every single night of the run. So that desperate-sounding old woman on the phone in Venice really was Eve."

Harry Haun has revealed the real Eve's name in print: Martina Lawrence. But that seems as false as everything else about Eve. It is, in fact, the name of one of the twin sisters that Elisabeth Bergner played in the 1939 British film *Stolen Life*. (The other twin was called Sylvina Lawrence. By the time Bette Davis starred in the Hollywood remake in 1946, with the title adjusted to *A Stolen Life*, the twins had become Kate and Patricia Bosworth.)

Haun set up a tea party so that Eve could at last tell her side of the affair. Along with Martina Lawrence, he invited Mary Orr. Describing the encounter, Haun says, "The girls eyed each other curiously, suspiciously."

According to Mary Orr, "She and Harry did all the talking. I sat and listened. At first, she wanted Harry to help her write her side of the story. Then she wanted me to rewrite the story from her point of view. I said, 'I have no interest in doing that.' At the end of the tea I excused myself. You see, I had nothing to say to her, really. I had satisfied my curiosity to see her after all those years."

In an article written for *Films in Review* (March–April 1991) to commemorate the 40th anniversary of *All About Eve*, Harry Haun added a postscript about Martina Lawrence. "A former librarian who lives in Venice and works in a bookstore there . . . she insists she was

never the premeditated plotter Mankiewicz made her out to be—that
her skulduggery only existed in the mind of Elisabeth Bergner."

———

Anne Baxter called her director "Joe the Mank." She had a secret
crush on him. "John Hodiak and I were happily married then, but
Joe's wit, his modest perspicacity, and my latent father complex drew
me to him like a magnet," Baxter confessed years later. "In fact, all
the ladies on the set melted and gravitated to him as I did."

Bette Davis suspected there was more than a crush. According
to Davis's longtime secretary, Vik Greenfield, Bette at last came out
with it. "We went to see Anne Baxter in *Applause*," Greenfield said,
"and when we were backstage, Bette asked Anne if she had an affair
with Joe during the making of *All About Eve*. 'No,' said Baxter. 'I always thought you did,' said Bette."

The friendship of Davis and Baxter lasted, and one morning in
1983, while visiting Baxter in Connecticut, Davis stepped out of the
shower and, toweling herself dry, discovered a lump in her breast.
Baxter comforted her 75-year-old houseguest as best she could,
never dreaming that Davis would outlive her by four years.

An interviewer asked Celeste Holm about working with Anne
Baxter. "Oh, she was fine. But of course you know she was what's-his-
name's granddaughter."

"Frank Lloyd Wright," supplied the interviewer.

"Frank Lloyd Wright," repeated Holm. "And so she was very
sophisticated and very 'Have you read the latest Christopher Fry?'"

Perhaps this breezy, left-handed compliment owes something
to an anecdote that Anne Baxter had told earlier about Holm. When
cast and crew left San Francisco to complete filming at the studio in
Los Angeles, they were scheduled to shoot on Stage 9, one of the
smaller soundstages on the Fox lot. As Baxter recalled, "Our assistant, Stan Hough, didn't want to crowd the sets, and after pushing
and fitting five portable dressing rooms here, there and everywhere,
he left Celeste Holm's outside. Out in the cold was more to the point.
Celeste took one look, aimed, fired at everyone in sight, and tearfully
flounced back to her permanent dressing room.

"Everything stopped for two solid hours while Joe, all three assistants, Celeste's agent, and several emissaries from the front office made elaborate apologies. She came back on the set chin high, wet eyes shining resolutely—we couldn't help wondering if she'd toured in *Saint Joan*."

Holm counters that this slight occurred because, sometime earlier, she had quit the studio and Zanuck now wanted to punish her. "Mr. Mankiewicz insisted that I play the part of Karen, and Mr. Zanuck didn't want any part of that. So when I arrived, my dressing room was out in the alley and everybody else's was inside. Mankiewicz said, 'What are you trying to do? Kill an actress?'"

George Sanders believed there was real rivalry on the set. "Davis upstaged Anne Baxter at every turn, and drove Anne to distraction," he later commented. "Playing a woman of 40 who was jealous of a much younger woman, she played it as if it were happening to her personally. Anne caught the underlying tensions and viciousness, and it is to her credit that it spurred her to act even better than she would have with a gracious co-star."

Davis returned his fire. She had heard about Sanders's bisexuality from Henry Fonda, and that led her to characterize Sanders as a "bitch." She claimed he upstaged her at every opportunity. "He won that goddamned award [his Oscar for best supporting actor of 1950] at my expense!" she said.

"Her lack of fundamental graciousness toward her co-players disgusted me," Sanders said. And how gracious was he? "George Sanders never spoke to anyone," Celeste Holm said. "He was a brilliant actor, but he wasn't much fun."

———

One morning, a week into shooting at the Curran Theatre, a stagehand delivered a telegram addressed to Davis just as an assistant called out, "Everybody on the set, please." Davis tore open the envelope, ran her eyes over the message, and grimaced. Moments later she strode onto the set with lips pursed. Her expression indicated grim pleasure.

The telegram was from William Sherry, her estranged husband, who was asking Davis to call off the divorce and try another reconciliation. Davis read the telegram, with sarcastic emphasis and loud laughter, to everyone. Merrill laughed loudly. Hugh Marlowe, the actor playing Lloyd Richards, the playwright, chuckled. Holm lowered her eyes and pretended to pick a speck of lint off her skirt. Since she and Davis weren't speaking, it's doubtful she would have laughed even if she had found Davis's performance hilarious. Baxter concentrated on her lines and pretended not to hear.

In the words of Marion Richards, B.D.'s nanny, the telegram was "beautiful, tender, sweet." Richards claimed that "finally everyone was howling. The only one who didn't go along with ridiculing it was Anne Baxter. She was offended by the whole thing. As was I."

Marion Richards, however, had a vested interest. Before long William Sherry was writing letters to her. Later, Davis would claim that Sherry had fallen in love with the nanny before he and Davis split up. This Richards and Sherry denied. But on August 6, 1950, not long after *All About Eve* was in the can, Marion Richards became Mrs. William Grant Sherry.

———

At the start, Joe Mankiewicz had been more than a little apprehensive about working with Bette Davis. As soon as *Daily Variety* and the other trade papers announced that she was replacing Claudette Colbert, Mankiewicz got several cautionary calls from directors who had worked with her in the past. (Along with one of congratulation: William Wyler, who had directed Davis in *Jezebel*, *The Letter* [1940], and *The Little Foxes* [1941], phoned to tell Mankiewicz that working with her would be a ball.)

The most explicit warning came from Edmund Goulding, a friend of Mankiewicz's who had directed Davis in four films: *That Certain Woman* (1937), *Dark Victory* (1939), *The Old Maid* (1939), and *The Great Lie* (1941). "Dear boy," moaned Goulding, "have you gone mad? This woman will destroy you, she will grind you down to a fine powder and blow you away. You are a writer, dear boy. She will come to the stage with a thick pad of long yellow paper. And pencils. She will write. And then she, not you, will direct. Mark my words."

Mankiewicz, girding his loins, prepared for the worst—"Always a good thing to prepare for, among theatre-folk," he said. But Goulding's forecast proved inaccurate. Long after *All About Eve*, Mankiewicz brimmed with compliments for his leading lady: "Barring grand opera, I can think of nothing beyond her range." And Davis brimmed, too: "Mankiewicz is a genius—the man responsible for the greatest role of my career. He resurrected me from the dead."

Toward the end of their time in San Francisco, Mankiewicz told Davis about Goulding's call. She said, "I suppose my reputation is pretty much as advertised."

"Why haven't I seen any sign of it?" Mankiewicz asked.

"Look, Joe," she said, "you know as well as I that there is nothing more important to an actress than a well-written part—and a director who knows what he wants and knows how to ask for it." She thumped the *All About Eve* script. "*This* is heaven," she said.

At the end of two weeks in San Francisco, *All About Eve* moved to Los Angeles for more than a month of solid work.

"When we left San Francisco," said Gary Merrill, "I got Bette's permission to drive back to her house for the weekend, along with Bette's sister, Bobby, and B.D., with the bodyguard in tow."

After spending the weekend with Davis and members of her family at her house in Laguna Beach, Merrill went home to Malibu. His wife, Barbara Leeds, seems not to have smelled a rat. A few days later the Merrills attended a dinner party where Gary, in an "alcohol haze," as he put it, started talking to some of the other guests about Bette Davis. They asked him if she was really the termagant that some people claimed.

"I'd marry Bette in a heartbeat if she'd have me," Merrill announced. Later, Merrill confessed that his statement was "not exactly the sort of thing to say in front of one's own wife." When the Merrills got home that night, "the dishes began to fly."

A few weeks later Barbara Leeds Merrill, testifying in the divorce proceedings, intimated that "27-year-old Anne Baxter had been Gary's first choice for an affair during *All About Eve*." But, she added, since Baxter was madly in love with her husband, John Hodiak, Gary had settled for Bette Davis, who was 42.

===

On-screen and off, it seemed half of Hollywood was out to get Bette Davis. On top of everything else, her cocktail dress didn't fit.

This dress, which Edith Head had designed for Davis to wear in the party sequence, was everything it should be: snug-bodiced, wasp-waisted, full-skirted, ankle-skimming. Head's original sketch had had a square neckline. The designer said she had high hopes for the dress because the fabric, brown gros de Londres (a heavy silk), photographed magnificently in black and white. To make the dress even more opulent, Head trimmed it in sable.

Because of the tight shooting schedule, the dress wasn't made up until the night before Davis was to wear it in the big scene. Head arrived at the studio early the day of the filming to make sure the dress was pressed and camera-ready. "There was Bette," Head recalled, "already in the dress, looking quizzically at her own reflection in the mirror. I was horrified. The dress didn't fit at all . . . the entire bodice and neckline were too big. There was no time to save anything, and a change would delay the shooting."

Head told Davis not to worry. She would take full responsibility for the mess-up. But she dreaded the hassle. On her way out, Head heard Davis say, "No, wait. Turn around and look, Edith."

Head took one look and her eyes brightened, even behind the tinted glasses she always wore.

"Don't you like it better like this?" Davis asked. She had pulled the neckline off her shoulders, and, as Head approached, she wiggled one bare shoulder seductively.

"I could have hugged her," Head said.

Filming the party scene, that first day on the soundstage in Los Angeles, involved almost everyone in the cast. When Bette Davis arrived, magnificent in her Edith Head gown, not a thing was going on. People were sitting, milling around, talking, yawning. "Why?" Davis asked.

She headed toward Gary Merrill and Hugh Marlowe, who were playing poker. "The new girl," Merrill said. "Marilyn Monroe. She's almost an hour late."

Just then Monroe rushed in, out of breath, as though she had run several blocks. "I'm so sorry," she whispered to everyone and no one.

Mankiewicz talked with her quietly for a few minutes and then asked them all to take their places. Gregory Ratoff, who played producer Max Fabian in the film, gushed to Celeste Holm in his thick Russian accent, "That girl ees going to be a beeg star!"

"Why?" Holm snapped back. "Because she's kept us all waiting an hour?" Holm looked at the irritating starlet. "Besides, she's dressed ridiculously in that *tit*ular number. It's a cocktail party. No one else is in an evening gown."

Charles LeMaire had designed Monroe's "titular" gown precisely as such. The first time he saw the Monroe figure, he knew that Marilyn and décolletage went together like gin and vermouth. Did LeMaire know that the camera would worship Monroe during the brief time she's on-screen? She steals her first scene with Davis without trying.

The actress Constance Bennett, spotting the unknown Monroe at a party during this period, reportedly remarked, "Now there's a broad with her future behind her."

———————

Celeste Holm and Bette Davis had a big scene coming up. The party sequence had taken nearly a week; four days were spent filming the Sarah Siddons Society awards banquet; and finally, with supper in the Cub Room of the Stork Club completed after several full days, all the ensemble scenes were done. Now Mankiewicz concentrated on scenes with two and three people.

And so, on one of the hottest days that spring, while searing lights burned down on them, Davis and Holm bundled up in fur coats and played their car scene. Lloyd and Karen Richards are driving Margo to the station to catch a train back to New York for her evening performance when the car sputters to a halt on a snowy road. Footage of the surrounding wintry landscape, which the film's second unit had shot several months earlier in upstate New York, was projected onto a process screen behind the specially prepared car.

The scene gathers momentum slowly. At first the dialogue is all about what time it is, when the train leaves, and how far it is to the nearest farmhouse. Then, when Lloyd leaves to seek help, the exchange between Margo and Karen becomes a confessional scene of feminine intimacy. The two characters bare their souls to each other and to us. At the climax, Margo has her big speech, which begins: "Funny business, a woman's career. The things you drop on your way up the ladder, so you can move faster. You forget you'll need them again when you get back to being a woman. That's one career all females have in common—whether we like it or not—being a woman."

The two actresses played this scene to the hilt. The soundstage wasn't air-conditioned, and the temperature inside the coupe soon reached 100 degrees. When the scene was over, they, and Mankiewicz, realized what a good job they had done. In spite of the friction between them, Davis even declared that the scene wouldn't have been the same without Holm. "She was perfect," Davis said.

Perfect not once but twice, as it turned out. When Mankiewicz and Zanuck viewed the rushes, they discovered that a glitch with the process film had spoiled several shots. And so once more the following day Lloyd Richards crawled out of the car to go for help while Davis and Holm sweltered in mink as the lights grew hotter and both women, between takes, drank water as though they were field workers.

———

Everyone loved Thelma Ritter. "One of my favorite people in the whole world," Celeste Holm said years later.

Gary Merrill called Ritter "a character actress with great common sense." The common sense shines through in every performance. She couldn't have played a woman who didn't have it. One reason she's perfect in *All About Eve* is that her character, Birdie, who can't stand pretense and deception, is wise to Eve Harrington's machinations from the start.

"I adored her," Mankiewicz said. He, along with Zanuck, started her out in movies. In 1946 the director George Seaton, under contract to Twentieth Century Fox, went to New York in search of character actors for *Miracle on 34th Street*. Seaton's wife, a childhood friend of Thelma Ritter's, introduced them, and Seaton gave Ritter a walk-on part as a harried housewife who berates Santa Claus for promising her son too much during the Christmas rush at Macy's. Darryl Zanuck, after watching the rushes, ordered Ritter's role enlarged. Soon she became a favorite character actress with American audiences.

Ritter had two children, and her maternal quality attracted Marilyn Monroe. The year after *All About Eve,* they worked together again, in *As Young as You Feel.* Ten years later they made their third film together, *The Misfits.* After Marilyn Monroe died, Thelma Ritter said, "I adored that girl from the moment we met."

═══════

On the morning when Bette Davis, Gary Merrill, and Anne Baxter were to film the confrontational scene that lends Bill's coming-home party its "Macbethish" air, Davis was worried. This pivotal scene is Margo's awakening to the threat of Eve Harrington. It functions like a door opening into the rest of the film.

During rehearsal Davis said, "I don't understand how to play this. What can we do so that it's not just a talky scene?"

Mankiewicz puffed his pipe for a few seconds. Then he looked around the set. At last he said, "Do you see that candy jar on the piano?" He took Davis's arm, and they walked over to it. The candy jar was empty. Mankiewicz called over the second prop master, or "best boy," and sent him to get some chocolates.

Later, when it was time to play the scene, Davis recalled what Mankiewicz had told her: "The madder you get, the more you want a piece of candy."

Margo loves candy, according to his reasoning, but she doesn't dare eat it. Actresses are always on a diet, and Margo at 40 is on an even stricter one, because she suspects that her svelte young protégée is after Bill.

The cameras rolled. At Margo's sarcastic line about Eve—"She's a girl of so many interests"—Davis jerked open the candy jar, picked up a chocolate, brought it to her mouth, and almost popped it in, then threw it back into the jar.

Davis made such a peculiar face that Mankiewicz halted the shooting. "What's wrong?" he asked.

"I'm sorry, Joe," Davis said. "I didn't mean to, but I loathe eating chocolates in the morning."

Mankiewicz dispatched a propman to the commissary; he came back with tiny squares of gingerbread to masquerade as chocolates.

Then the scene continued. Margo's anger builds; so does Bill's. Outraged at what he considers her unwarranted jealousy of Eve, Bill lectures: "You have to keep your teeth sharp. All right. But I will not have you sharpen them on me—or on Eve." Margo opens the candy jar again, quickly slams it shut, and snaps back, "What about *her* teeth? What about her fangs?"

Bill persists: "She hasn't cut them yet and you know it! . . . Eve Harrington has never by word, look, thought, or suggestion indicated anything to me but her adoration for you and her happiness at our being in love!" At this, Margo opens the candy jar, grabs a piece of candy, throws it into her mouth, and chews furiously, eyes bulging as she swallows, seething all the while.

And that's how a scene that was already good on the page turned out to be brilliant, thanks to the director's flourishes, and thanks to an actress who knew what to do with "a genius piece of business," in Davis's words.

Perhaps Davis's greatest contribution to her characterization of Margo Channing came the day she spoke what was destined to become an immortal line. It is in the party scene, and Margo's cue comes from Karen, who says, "We know you, we've seen you like this before. Is it over—or is it just beginning?"

Instead of responding immediately as indicated in the script, Margo drains her martini and walks toward the stairs with a shoulder-rolling, hip-swinging swagger. She halts, swerves, regards Karen, Lloyd, and Bill with a scowl, then lets it rip: "Fasten your seatbelts, it's going to be a bumpy night!"

Mankiewicz came up with the line, but the timing was all Davis's. "Those are things that you should be able to do as an actress that a director wouldn't think of telling you to do," she said. "When Margo holds back like that, it lets you know she's collecting more venom."

———

According to Fox records, *All About Eve* was brought in for a modest $1.4 million, the equivalent of $9 million today. The original estimate had been $1,246,500. Just 13 years later, Mankiewicz would direct Elizabeth Taylor and Richard Burton in *Cleopatra*, which would run to an astounding $44 million (about $300 million today).

The cast and crew of *All About Eve* would never again be together. Bette Davis and Gary Merrill, inseparable, lived by the sea in her house in Laguna Beach or at his place in Malibu. Marilyn Monroe retreated to her little apartment at 718 North Palm Drive, and Celeste Holm and Thelma Ritter flew to New York. George Sanders and Zsa Zsa Gabor continued to spar over his flirtations, real and imagined. And Joe Mankiewicz became president of the Screen Directors Guild. He had been nominated by Cecil B. DeMille.

All About Eve went on to receive 14 Academy Award nominations and six subsequent Oscars, including those for best picture and best director. (Bette Davis, Anne Baxter, and Gloria Swanson—for her comeback in *Sunset Boulevard*—all lost out for best actress that year to Judy Holliday for *Born Yesterday*.) Starting out as a fine picture by almost any standard, *All About Eve* soon mutated into something more—a Hollywood classic and, later, a classic of camp.

And whether we watch it for high reasons or low, it seems as fresh today as it did a half-century ago. Sitting there in the audience, we tacitly repeat to everyone in the cast what Eve tells Margo early on: "I could watch you play that scene a thousand times."

From *Vanity Fair*, April 1999

REBEL WITHOUT A CAUSE

Dangerous Talents

by Sam Kashner

James Dean was only 24 years old when he crashed his Porsche Spyder and died on a lonely stretch of highway west of Bakersfield, California. The tragedy occurred on September 30, 1955, scarcely a week before the opening of *Rebel Without a Cause,* the celebrated movie about juvenile delinquents, which would immortalize him as the archetype of the brooding adolescent. "That guy up there's gotta stop; he'll see us" were Dean's last words to his mechanic, Rolf Wutherich, riding next to him, just before he slammed into a Ford sedan making a left turn from the opposite lane.

Dean, however, lives on in our age. The actor continues to exemplify strident youth. And photographs of Dean, to this day, resonate with the young and disaffected across America and around the world.

Rebel, as a result, still seems to be James Dean's show. But, in fact, it was the movie's director, Nicholas Ray, who was the real rebel behind the film. His fourth wife and widow, Susan Schwartz Ray, now in her 50s, wrote in her introduction to his collected lectures, *I Was Interrupted*: "What was all the fuss about Dean when Dean was so clearly—to me anyway—aping Nick?"

Other filmmakers agree, especially the French. Jean-Luc Godard rather famously wrote, "There was theatre (Griffith), poetry (Murnau), painting (Rossellini), dance (Eisenstein), music (Renoir). Henceforth there is cinema. And the cinema is Nicholas Ray." François Truffaut called Ray "the poet of nightfall." American director Jim Jarmusch, a former student of Ray's, called him "my idol—a legend, the outcast Hollywood rebel, white hair, black eye patch, and a head full of subversion and controlled substances."

But, despite such admiration from his peers and three recent retrospectives of Ray's films in London, New York, and Los Angeles, "America still seems unsure whether Ray mattered, whether he even existed," said film historian David Thomson. Forty-three years old when he directed *Rebel Without a Cause,* Ray would live for another 24 years, spending much of that time trying to re-create the dangerous magic he and Dean had conjured together in the movie. Unable to work within the studio system, he wandered through Europe, drinking and gambling recklessly. At the Cannes Film Festival one morning in 1969, film reviewer Vincent Canby noticed a tall, gaunt man, fully dressed in city clothes, haunting the beach. Canby was surprised to see it was Ray. He had come to Cannes, it turned out, not to promote a movie but to make arrangements that would enable him to unload the rights to one he couldn't make himself. He needed the money.

═══

Ray's daughter, Nicca, 43 when interviewed for *Vanity Fair* [in 2005], has made it a quest to learn more about her father. "He was not very present in my life, and yet he was such a huge presence," Nicca explains. "My mom did not talk about him, so I'd go to bookstores to find out about him." Nicca was searching for answers to questions she had had about him since she was a child: "Where is he? Where has he been? Why was he suddenly here when I was 13? Where was he before this? Who were his friends? Why aren't his movies playing in the cinema anymore? Why did his letters stop? Why isn't he coming home?"

Ray was married four times—to writer Jean Abrams (who used the pen name Evans), briefly and notoriously to the actress Gloria Grahame, to dancer and choreographer Betty Utey (Nicca's mother), and finally, toward the end of his life, to Schwartz. His first three marriages ended in divorce.

"I went to college late in life," says Nicca, who lives in New York and is at work on a memoir about her father. "I went to the New School to get my bachelor's degree. I avoided classes that had to do with my father's films, but this teacher started lecturing. . . . 'In *Rebel Without a Cause,* Nick Ray is saying that the family is a ball and chain.' I remember sitting there thinking, Oh my God, my father thought that we were a ball and chain? But when I thought about that film, especially the scene on the staircase where James Dean is saying to his parents, 'Speak to me!,' I think he so desperately wanted there to be a connection. . . . So afterwards I went up to the teacher. I told him I was Nick Ray's daughter." She had wanted to disagree with the teacher, but that was the first time Nicca had spoken to someone outside her family about her relationship with her father. "I felt I didn't have a right to say anything, because people tend to get possessive of my father, or at least their memory of him," she explains. "Their possession made me silent, as if I had nothing to say."

Ray was born Raymond Nicholas Kienzle, in 1911, in Galesville, Wisconsin, the youngest of four children and the only boy. His father, who had two daughters from a previous marriage, was an alcoholic, a lapsed German Catholic who later became a Lutheran; his mother was a smothering woman with artistic leanings. He attended the University of Chicago sporadically for a few years and quit in 1932, moved to New York, and changed his name. Returning to Wisconsin at the invitation of Frank Lloyd Wright, he began to study with the maverick architect at his communal school, Taliesin, but that association didn't end well—Ray later described Wright as "the most outrageous egocentric of our times"—and Ray left Taliesin under a cloud.

With a hundred dollars in his pocket, he took off in a ramshackle

Ford to Mexico, where he lived for a year. When he returned to New York, in 1934, he joined the left-leaning Theatre of Action, a communal, improvisational company, where he met director Elia Kazan. Kazan led his actors to such extremes of improvisation that when they enacted anger, for example, he had to stop them just short of real violence. It was an approach to acting that would leave its mark on Ray. When Kazan went to Hollywood in 1945 to make his first film, *A Tree Grows in Brooklyn,* he took Ray along as his assistant.

Soon Ray was making his own movies, starting with *They Live by Night.* In 1949 he directed *A Woman's Secret,* starring Gloria Grahame, whom he married eight weeks after they finished the movie. That same year he directed Humphrey Bogart in *Knock on Any Door,* which he followed in 1950 with *In a Lonely Place,* a powerful film starring both Bogart and Grahame, about a screenwriter suspected of murder. Then came *Born to Be Bad, Flying Leathernecks* (starring John Wayne), *On Dangerous Ground, The Lusty Men,* and *Johnny Guitar,* which was a hit at the box office.

Fresh off the success of *Johnny Guitar* (which, by the way, Ray loathed, having surrendered control of the picture to its star, Joan Crawford), Ray met with Warner Bros., which asked him to direct *Rebel Without a Cause.* The movie was to be based on Dr. Robert M. Lindner's 1944 clinical study of a disturbed, incarcerated youth, whose violent past was revealed under hypnosis. Warner Bros. had bought the rights to the book in 1946 with two actors in mind for the anguished teenager—Marlon Brando and (surprisingly) Sidney Lumet—but neither worked out. The studio held on to the property for eight years. By then juvenile delinquency had become a staple of the media, endlessly covered in newspapers, magazines, and such films as *Blackboard Jungle.*

At first, Ray wasn't interested. He felt that Lindner's book was too clinical and too focused on abnormal behavior. "It was neither the psychopath nor the son of a poor family that I was interested in," he said. It was only after he began developing his own story, called *The Blind Run*—a violent, 17-page story outline—that the idea for *Rebel* took shape. *The Blind Run* was to begin with a man on fire running toward the camera. It consisted of a series of brutal, shocking scenes of criminal acts, such as a girl stripped to the waist being whipped by three teenagers. Ray could never have made that movie in 1954, but soon he began to work with Warner Bros. producer David Weisbart, who had been a film editor on Tennessee Williams's *A Streetcar Named Desire*, directed by Kazan. At age 39, Weisbart was the youngest contract producer on the lot. Together he and Ray worked to turn *The Blind Run* into an acceptable story. Ray eventually came up with the solution to what he saw as the problem of the book: he made the juvenile delinquents into middle-class malcontents from "nice" homes—they are us. Best-selling novelist Leon Uris and a former schoolteacher, Irving Shulman, wrote early versions of *Rebel* before Ray found his voice in Stewart Stern, a 32-year-old writer from New York, who was brought to Ray's attention by the dynamic young film composer Leonard Rosenman.

Ray had no trouble deciding whom he wanted to play rebellious Jim Stark. James Dean came to Ray's attention through Kazan, who had just finished directing the actor in his first starring role, in *East of Eden*. But Kazan warned Ray against using him. "I became very impatient with the Dean legend. . . . Brando was Dean's hero," recalled Kazan. "Marlon, well trained by Stella Adler, had excellent technique. . . . Dean had no technique." But Kazan perhaps hadn't realized how damaged Ray was, or just how beautifully the two troubled souls would merge.

Both Dean and Ray grew up virtually fatherless. Dean's father, Winton, a dental technician at a veterans' hospital, essentially abandoned his son at age nine to be raised by his aunt and uncle, after the boy's mother died of ovarian cancer. Later, when Dean was a young man trying to break into the movies, he moved back in with his father, who didn't hide his contempt for acting as a profession.

Ray's father, also Raymond Nicholas Kienzle, was a contractor. The director once recalled, "During Prohibition, there were twenty-one saloons and speakeasies on one street. . . . I learned to drive when I was thirteen and I could get my father home safely from his nightly rounds. . . . At the age of fourteen I learned of his mistress. At fifteen I made an unsuccessful pass at her. . . . One night my father could not be found." Ray, then 16, located him, drunk and dying in his mistress's hotel room. He took his father home and nursed him through the night. The next day, Ray came home from school to find his father dead.

As adults, both Dean and Ray were "deeply introverted loners," says writer Gavin Lambert, who was Ray's assistant on 1956's *Bigger than Life*, "distrustful of all authority (but especially studio executives), hungry for love but wary of involvement. . . . Nick liked to confuse and unnerve strangers with long, mysterious silences. Dean preferred to disconcert them by turning a cartwheel when he entered a room." [Lambert died in 2005, after this story was published.]

Kazan invited Ray to see a rough cut of *East of Eden* in the music room of the Warner Bros. studio. Leonard Rosenman, a good friend of Dean's who shared a small apartment with him in New York, was also there. Rosenman had created the searing music for *East of Eden*, and Ray would hire him to score *Rebel Without a Cause*. Jimmy—as everyone called Dean then—was also present, "aloof and solitary," Ray remembered. The two men hardly exchanged a word. Still, Ray was intrigued, and he followed Dean back to New York. There Ray set out to observe, study, court, and finally sign Dean to play the role that would transform a talented kid from Indiana into an icon.

─────

Warner Bros., however, didn't think the choice a good one, either for Dean or for the movie. As late as March 1955—a month before filming—the studio was still considering Robert Wagner, Tab Hunter, or John Kerr, all up-and-coming Hollywood actors, for the lead. At the same time the studio was trying to get Dean to hold out for a bigger picture, preferably one directed by Kazan, George Stevens, or William Wyler. The studio didn't consider *Rebel* to be an important film; it was planned as a black-and-white feature. But Ray was so sure he had his lead rebel that he named the character "Stark"—an anagram of "Trask," Dean's character in *East of Eden*. "But don't tell those bastards," Dean said to Ray (referring to Warner Bros.) after he agreed to play Stark.

Having found his Stark, Ray interviewed a number of actresses to play Stark's girl, the wayward Judy, driven to delinquency by her rejecting father (played by William Hopper), who is disturbed by Judy's budding sexuality. Warner Bros. wanted Debbie Reynolds, Margaret O'Brien, Carroll Baker (recommended by Elia Kazan), or Kathryn Grant (later Mrs. Bing Crosby). Even Jayne Mansfield was briefly in the running. "The original concept of Judy was a much trashier girl," says Faye Mayo, who was the double for Judy in the film. Ray had Mansfield read for a screen test, but he didn't put film in the camera. It was one of several ways in which he tried to thwart the wishes of the Warner Bros. executives.

Natalie Wood desperately wanted the part, but at 16 she had played only juveniles. She knew the role of Judy would help her to break into adult roles, and also to wrest control of her career from her domineering mother, Maria Gurdin. Ray was immediately drawn to Wood, Gavin Lambert recalls. "She was very young, and that was always attractive to Nick," he says. In fact, she was at least five years younger than all the candidates except O'Brien, who was 18. But it was not only her youth that appealed to him, Lambert thought. "How quickly did Natalie realize that he found her extremely desirable, and how soon did Nick make his move? . . . The interview took place in the first week of February, and by the time she made her first screen test, 10 days later, they were lovers," recalls Lambert.

Wood got the part—not just due to her affair with Ray but because he recognized in her a rebellious spirit trying desperately to break out. "There is only one girl who has shown the capacity to play Judy, and she is Natalie Wood," Ray wrote in a Warner Bros. memo. To Wood, Ray seemed "mysterious, laconic and powerful," an "aging Heathcliff."

Sal Mineo was the last of the juveniles to be cast, as Plato, Stark's worshipful friend. He reminded Ray of his son Tony, from his first marriage, "except he was prettier." He had been raised in the Bronx; his father was a coffin-maker. At 16, he had already appeared twice on Broadway, in Tennessee Williams's *The Rose Tattoo* and Rodgers and Hammerstein's musical *The King and I*. Dean and the other cast members were impressed by this Broadway experience. Gore Vidal, then in Hollywood, later speculated in his memoir that Ray had an affair with Mineo as well as Wood, "while the sallow Dean skulked in and out."

Ray was, in fact, bisexual. Lambert recalls that "Nicca called me and said, 'I'm planning to write a book about my father . . . and I'd love to talk to you.' This was two or three years ago. She came over to the apartment. She was very nice—tall—looked quite a bit like Nick. We made some small talk at first, and then I said, 'I think before we get down to business I had better put a card on the table, and that is that Nick and I were on-and-off lovers for a while.' She said, 'Oh, I guessed that,' which I thought was wonderfully cool."

———

After casting the stars, Ray turned his attention to the high-school gang members who surround and threaten Jim Stark. One of the actors he interviewed was Frank Mazzola, the leader of a real gang called the Athenians. Mazzola had been weeded out by the casting director but muscled his way in to see Ray anyway. "They thought that because I was in a gang, I might create problems on the set. I came out of the Depression, really," Mazzola explains in a West Hollywood restaurant, his hair, still jet black, tied back in a ponytail. "We didn't have any pop culture. The guys that we loved flew, like my uncle, a pilot in the Second World War. Everybody I knew wanted to grow up and fly P-38s. . . . And so these clubs started forming—ours was called the Athenians. We defended our turf. You'd probably get in two or three fights a night just defending Hollywood. It was like a sport."

Ray not only cast Mazzola, he gave him an office on the Warner lot, from which he could serve as technical adviser on gang behavior. Ray instructed him to hang out with Dean and take him to meetings of the Athenians. "I want you to get us the cars, tell us what kind of clothes we should be wearing," Ray told him. Mazzola had the wardrobe department buy the gang's clothes at Matson's, on Hollywood Boulevard, where the Athenians bought their club jackets. The wardrobe department then soiled and laundered more than 400 pairs of Levi's for the cast.

"At the time, we were such babies," recalls Beverly Long, a viva-cious brunette, who won out over hundreds of other actresses to play Helen, the tough little girl with the blond ponytail. Today she's a well-respected casting agent; back then she was married to a member of the Athenians. Long recalls her first sight of Nick Ray: "When I walked in the room—I'll never forget it—he was at a desk and he was barefoot and wearing jeans. He was the only director I'd ever worked with who used to be barefoot on the set. He came on very strong, and he wanted to know how I got along with my mother. And I was thinking, Where is that in the script?"

Once the cast was assembled, Ray held script meetings at his Chateau Marmont bungalow. Built in 1929 as an apartment building with turrets and spires, the Chateau was surrounded by bungalows. Ray's own, No. 2, was nestled beside the swimming pool and had three bedrooms, a big kitchen, and a fireplace. He often held Sunday-afternoon parties there, which Dean and much of the cast of *Rebel* attended—it was there that Dean met one of his heroes, the playwright Clifford Odets.

"Nick's whole thing was to make us a family," said Steffi Sidney, who played Mil, one of the girls in the gang. The daughter of Hollywood columnist Sidney Skolsky, she has kept close ties with her fellow actors from the movie, especially Beverly Long and Jack Grinnage, who was cast as Moose (but mistakenly credited as Chick). "Nick was the father that we all needed. I think we would have done anything for him—anything he wanted—at least that's the way I felt," Grinnage says. "He was very open to ideas. One day we just improvised all day, though we never used it."

Natalie Wood's affair with Ray awakened her sexuality—and emboldened her to initiate another love affair, this one with Dennis Hopper, who had been cast as Goon. "I was astonished," Hopper later said. "I came from a very conventional, middle-class family in San Diego . . . and this was the 1950s, when girls who'd turned sixteen only a few months earlier just didn't do things like that." The sexually charged situation created ill will between Ray and Hopper.

Maria Gurdin, having found out about both affairs, complained to Warner Bros. that Hopper was involved with her daughter; ever ambitious for Natalie, she didn't mention that Ray was as well. "I was furious with [Ray]," Hopper said about the incident. "The studio came down on me, and he came out of it as pure as snow."

Grinnage remembers the first time he saw Wood on the set as Judy. "They'd cut her hair, and they'd padded her hips and her butt. I remember Nick said to her, 'What do you have on?' She said, 'Well, they padded me.' He said, 'Take it off.' The wardrobe ladies got very upset because the things didn't fit, so they had to re-do everything."

Beverly Long became friendly with Wood, in spite of Maria Gurdin's scrutinizing every move her daughter made. "I know about how much pain she was in, due to her family. We had a dressing room, a trailer for all of the gang, but Mrs. Gurdin—she took it over. She would go in there and take naps and would not let us in. And what could we do? She wouldn't even speak to us. She got Natalie's tutor to keep Natalie away from us because we swore and we smoked and we were really bad kids. But, of course, Natalie swore, and she smoked more than I did."

———

Shooting began on Wednesday, March 30, at the Griffith Park planetarium. They were to begin by filming the knife fight between Buzz and Stark, as choreographed by Frank Mazzola. Impressed by Mazzola's description of a knife fight he'd had in a Hollywood park, Ray had asked the 19-year-old to describe the fight to Dean and Corey Allen, the young actor and law student who was playing Buzz, Stark's rival for Judy. "'I want you to go to the observatory with Jimmy and Corey, and you just stage the fight, rehearse it the way you just told me, like a boxing match,'" Mazzola recalls Ray's saying to him, adding, "and if you look at that sequence, it is like that—all feints."

But the filming of the actual scene almost didn't happen. A few days before, Dean had disappeared, and no one could find him. The executives at Warner Bros. considered filing a breach-of-contract suit, and talks began about replacing him. "Dean was not certain at first that he trusted Nick," says Lambert, "which I don't think Nick was aware of. . . . Nick always felt that they had an immediate rapport. Well, they did have . . . but then Dean had these second thoughts. He disappeared for a few days, and it unnerved everybody, which I'm sure he enjoyed."

None of the other cast members knew that Dean had taken a powder. An all-points bulletin went out from the studio to locate him. Ray tried calling Dean's apartment, on Sunset Plaza Drive, and messages were left with his service at HO7-5191. He could not be reached in New York either. Finally, Dean called the movie's screenwriter, Stewart Stern, with whom he had developed a friendship, and confided his lack of trust in his director, particularly compared with how he had felt about Kazan—an irony, given Kazan's dislike of Dean. But there may have been other reasons for Dean's flight from the set. Perhaps he sensed that Ray was so obsessed with his character that the line between fact and fiction was disappearing; perhaps he already sensed the degree to which Ray and the movie would devour him. "Remember," Mazzola says, "Jimmy was just starting to come to terms with his fame." In any case, he returned just in time for his first scene.

The film almost derailed again when, after a few days of shooting, Ray was summoned to the office of Steve Trilling, Jack L. Warner's executive assistant, and told to stop production. The executives had seen the rushes and panicked—were Ray's young actors up to the task? Trilling then asked the Warner Bros. projectionist, who had been running the rushes, what he thought of the material. "Mr. Trilling," he said, "frankly, I think it's the only picture worth something on the lot." They gave Ray the go-ahead to finish his movie, and they would reshoot it in color. By now, the studio sensed a hit in the making—*East of Eden* had just been released, and Dean's fan mail had spiked to 400 letters a week.

Beverly Long and the other *Rebel* gang members went to Matson's "to buy something for Jimmy, because the jacket he had didn't work in WarnerColor. So one of the guys tried on that red Windbreaker, and everybody at once said, Yeah, that's it! Just buy it! And that jacket—wow, it became the symbol."

Ray consulted with former Group Theater set designer John

Hamilton, "a great drunk and a great eye," according to the director, and the two men chose colors from *Life* magazine. "The red-on-red for Jimmy evolved as a result of an improvisation in my living room," Ray said. "I had a red couch. . . . Jimmy had been red-on-red on the couch, and it was smoldering danger. All were significant."

One of the early scenes that had to be reshot in color was the opening sequence, in which a drunken Dean rounds the corner and sees a toy monkey on the sidewalk. He lies down next to it and tries to cover it with a scrap of paper. "It was about three in the morning when we shot that scene," recalls Long. "It was freezing, wet, cold outside. I was sitting on a curb and had a blanket wrapped around me. I was so affected by Jimmy—his concentration, his ability to make that work. I was in tears."

=====

Long believes that Stark's shrewish, emasculating mother may have been modeled on Maria Gurdin. "They were both very dark people," she recalls. Without a strong father to anchor the Stark home, it seems in danger of capsizing. In one scene Mrs. Stark comes downstairs into the living room, where Jim is sprawled on the couch; Ray filmed it from Dean's point of view by turning the camera around 180 degrees, a shot that, Ray explained, "came to express my feeling toward the entire scene: here was a house in danger of tipping from side to side."

Ray had spent his entire life in houses in danger of tipping over. He left a trail of broken families, beginning with the one he was born into. "I think he was more comfortable in a student-teacher, director-actor kind of relationship," Nicca explains. "He said that his films were his family. But film sets move and change. You don't have to stay in it and deal with the consequences of your behavior in such an intimate way, as you do with your family. . . . And my father—he had quite a few families."

Ray's first marriage, to Jean Evans, which ended in 1942, produced a son, Anthony "Tony" Ray, an actor and assistant director throughout the 60s and 70s. Ray met Gloria Grahame on the set of his second film, *A Woman's Secret.* In June of 1948 the two married in Las Vegas, at the El Rancho Vegas Hotel. Ray seemed almost instantly to regret the marriage, but Grahame was pregnant at the time, and their son, Timothy, was born five and a half months later. (Timothy has worked as an actor and assistant cameraman.) Ray spent his wedding night at the gaming tables, losing his shirt. He later said about Grahame, "I was infatuated with her, but I didn't like her very much. There was something vindictive about me that made me stay at the crap tables. . . . I wanted to be absolutely broke. . . . I didn't want her to have any money at all. . . . I lost a bundle."

Grahame, who won an Academy Award in 1953 as the ditsy southern belle in *The Bad and the Beautiful* (she also played the bravehearted moll who gets a pot of scalding coffee thrown in her face by Lee Marvin in *The Big Heat,* and the girl who can't say no in *Oklahoma!*), had a rare comic gift and an unusual look, including "an incredible repertoire of mouths" that she outlined in various shades of lipstick. In an era of *noir* blondes, she stood out as unique, touching, and as smart as a whip. Ultimately, none of it mattered to Ray. "You know, Nick didn't like women," Lambert says. "He was often physically attracted to them, but he didn't like them. And I think he resented being attracted."

Cruel as Ray was to Grahame at the beginning of their marriage, Grahame won the final round. Lambert explains, "There was the story that he found her in bed with [his son] Tony. I mean, that's the most Eugene O'Neill moment of Nick Ray's life. Tony was a nice kid; I always liked him very much. I don't know what happened to him, but he adored Nick. And, of course, part of *Rebel* was Nick's own guilt about being a bad and neglectful father."

Nicca thinks the affair between Grahame and Tony came about because "Tony and Gloria shared a mutual hatred toward my father. They had a common enemy, which was him." Nine years after Nick found Grahame in bed with his son, Tony and Grahame married and then had two children. As Nicca observes, "Some families are fucked up differently than others."

———

Filming was completed on May 26, 1955, 11 days behind schedule. On the last night of shooting, Ray and the cast headed for Googie's, a pancake-and-hamburger joint across the street from the Chateau, which had become a second home to the cast. Roger Donoghue, a young boxer who hung around the set, recalled, "Nick had an old '50 or '51 Cadillac that he had bought from Robert Taylor for something like 800 bucks. We all got in the car, Jimmy went ahead on his motorcycle. . . . The kids didn't want it to end, and Nick didn't want it to end, and it was probably the end of Nick that night, too."

Ray knew he had an important piece of work on his hands, but he worried that Jack Warner would try to interfere with the editing, so he tried to postpone screening the movie for him. A few days after the last dubbing session, Ray wrote to Warner, "My name is Nick Ray and I just finished making a picture for you called *Rebel Without a Cause*. I thought maybe you'd forgotten my name. . . . I know you must have been pissed off at me at least once. . . . I know every important frame of [the movie] as if it had been printed on my skin." But when Warner finally saw a rough cut of the film, he wrote a memo to his assistant Steve Trilling: "Do not let them go 'arty' on us." Ray prevailed, however.

———

"I was driving down Sunset Boulevard when I heard the news about Jimmy," recalls Mazzola. "It was weird. It felt like the whole world, like everything, was changed. He wasn't immortal anymore." Beverly Long remembers, "It was dusk when this girl called me, someone I'd gone to high school with. She said, 'Guess what! Guess what! Did you hear? Jimmy Dean died.' I said, 'Oh, sure, right. What are you talking about?' I thought it was so cruel for her to say that. She said, 'I'm not kidding. Turn on the radio.' So I turned on the radio, and they kept breaking in that Jimmy Dean was in a car accident, and they said that he was dead at the scene." *Rebel*'s gang members met that day at a diner to come to terms with Dean's death.

One of the more bizarre aspects of the tragedy was that at the time of the crash Dean, having just completed filming George Stevens's *Giant*, based on the novel by Edna Ferber, was still made up to look like a much older man. The impact broke his neck, nearly decapitating him. Wutherich was thrown from the car and survived. The two men had been on their way to a car race in Salinas. Earlier that day Dean's father, whom he had tried to get close to his entire life, had made a rare appearance; father and son, as well as Jimmy's uncle and Wutherich, had all breakfasted together at the Farmer's Market in Los Angeles.

"Do you think the end of the world will come at nighttime?" Plato asks Stark shortly before the final scene of *Rebel Without a Cause*. "At dawn," Stark says. For Dean, the end came at dusk.

"The night Jimmy died," recalls Judie Gregg Rosenman, Leonard's fourth wife, "Leonard was at a dinner party in upstate New York when he heard the news. And he immediately came back to the city and went to the apartment he'd shared with Jimmy. It was completely ransacked. Leonard was writing the music for an opera with a libretto by Thomas Mann at the time. Everything was cleaned out, including the only copy of Leonard's score, which was never recovered." Fans had broken into the apartment in search of souvenirs. The cult of James Dean had begun.

———

No one felt the shock more than Nick Ray. The two men had been planning to set up a production company that would have allowed Ray the artistic freedom he felt he never had with the studios. "Nick's thing was he always wanted to be independent," remembers Mazzola. "He didn't want to work for the studios. He once turned down a $110,000 check that Howard Hughes gave him to run RKO. And in the 40s, that was an awful lot of money. We were all sitting around talking one night when Nick said, 'You know, if you have the artist in front of the camera, protected by the artist behind the camera, you have your freedom.'"

When Warner Bros. released *Rebel Without a Cause*, barely a week after Dean's death, the publicity focused on him. In spite of mixed reviews for the film, Dean was uniformly praised. "His rare talent and appealing personality even shine through this turgid melodrama," wrote William Zinsser in the *New York Herald Tribune*. Wood, Mineo, and Ray (for motion-picture story) were all nominated for Academy Awards, and the movie was the second-biggest moneymaker for Warner Bros. that year (after *Moby Dick*), grossing $7,197,000 in domestic and foreign screenings. Even after Dean's death, the studio continued to receive 2,000 letters a week addressed to the star. But no man is a hero in his own hometown; back in Indiana, the headline simply read: FAIRMOUNT MAN DIES IN TRAFFIC ACCIDENT IN WEST.

The impact of the movie was immediate, unleashing knife fights and "chickie run" enactments around the world among teenagers, who felt that *Rebel* spoke for them. The film was censored in London. It had to be smuggled into Spain and shown in private screenings, and wasn't formally released in that country until 1964, becoming Spanish exhibitors' favorite film of the year.

Elvis Presley was obsessed with the movie, and he worshipped James Dean. "I was sitting in the cafeteria at MGM one day," Ray recalled, "and Elvis Presley came over. He knew I was a friend of Jimmy's and had directed *Rebel*, so he got down on his knees before me and began to recite whole passages of dialogue from the script. Elvis must have seen *Rebel* a dozen times by then and remembered every one of Jimmy's lines." Martin Sheen—who played the Dean look-alike inspired by spree killer Charlie Starkweather in Terrence Malick's 1973 *Badlands*—once wrote, "There were only two people in the fifties: Elvis Presley who changed the music, and James Dean who changed our lives."

Sal Mineo—so affecting as the essentially fatherless outcast Plato—later commented that he had portrayed the first gay teenager on film. There are little clues: the photograph of Alan Ladd taped to his locker door, his longing looks at Jim Stark, his disguised declaration of love in the abandoned mansion. Ray was aware of Dean's bisexuality and encouraged the actor to use it in certain scenes. Dean instructed Mineo, "Look at me the way I look at Natalie," for their intimate scene in the Getty mansion. It had to be subtle. A Production Code officer had written in a memo to Jack L. Warner on March 22, "It is of course vital that there be no inference of a questionable or homosexual relationship between Plato and Jim."

Filmmakers continue to pay homage to the movie, especially to the "chickie run" scene, in which Dean and Corey Allen (as Buzz, the knife-wielding gang leader) drag-race to the edge of a cliff. Buzz, catching his sleeve on the door handle before he can bail from the car, crashes magnificently into the black Pacific. One film critic described the scene as "an absolute classic of car action that has never,

ever been surpassed. . . . Every action director has been influenced by this scene."

———

Dean's death was the beginning of Ray's downward spiral. "When Jimmy checked out," says Mazzola, "it really took a big chunk away from Nick's dream. It's like De Niro and Scorsese. Can you imagine if De Niro had died really young? No *Raging Bull.* No *GoodFellas.* No nothing. With Jimmy, Ray could've been the biggest thing in the world."

Ray went to Europe to promote the film, and he attempted to set up some independent deals for future projects, but he couldn't bring himself to return to the States to finish editing his next feature, *Hot Blood,* a movie about Gypsy life he had made for Columbia Pictures. Gavin Lambert says, "One of Nick's troubles was that he always wanted to be a sort of avant-garde, independent moviemaker and do daring things on a low budget. At the same time, he wanted the five-star hotel and the limo at his beck and call. And that's not going to work. Another problem was that he was always in debt because of his gambling and was therefore behind in child support and alimony. It was a huge disintegration of a huge personality."

Ray eventually returned to America, to Twentieth Century Fox, where he negotiated a two picture deal. One of them, *Bigger than Life,* starring James Mason, is now regarded as one of Ray's great films; it's based on a *New Yorker* article about a schoolteacher who becomes unhinged as a result of an addiction to cortisone. Ray, Lambert, and Clifford Odets all contributed to the screenplay, which was written by Cyril Hume and Richard Maibaum. Watching *Bigger than Life* on TV one weekend, Ray's fourth wife, Susan, told him, "This is your story before you lived it."

The True Story of Jesse James and *Bitter Victory* were made in 1957, with much difficulty, and *Wind Across the Everglades,* a Budd Schulberg production filmed in Florida, was a disaster. Ray's excessive drinking got him thrown off the project; he had to wait to see the movie, like everybody else, in a theater. On the set of *Party Girl,* an MGM film he directed in 1958, he met the woman who became his third wife, Betty Utey. (They had met once before, on the set of

Androcles and the Lion.) She was 24 years his junior. They had two daughters: Julie, born in 1960, and Nicca, born the following year.

===

Desperate to stay in the game, Ray had agreed to direct two epics, *King of Kings* and *55 Days at Peking.* "What the hell was he doing, directing *55 Days at Peking*?" Nicca asks. "He went from James Dean to Charlton Heston! He had a heart attack on the set of that movie, and they took him to the hospital. He was doing a lot of crystal meth; he had this doctor who was shooting him up. A nurse would come to the house and inject him. He was a London-based doctor, a very frightening person." (The amphetamine was prescribed as a cure for alcoholism!)

Around this time, Ray had planned to make *The Doctor and the Devils,* based on an original screenplay by Dylan Thomas, but the film was never produced—that was the project Ray was looking to sell off at the Cannes Film Festival.

After being fired from *55 Days at Peking,* Ray wandered. He had lost his career, and he was losing his third family. He wound up in Paris during the student upheavals in 1968, which energized him again, igniting his love of rebellion and youth. He began to trade on his relationship with Dean, dead now for 13 years, to win the respect of a younger generation. He once showed a group of Sorbonne radicals a gun he claimed had belonged to Dean. "James Dean gave this to me," he said. "I'm passing it on to you, because you'll know what to do with it."

It's impossible to know if the gun Ray showed to those students at the Sorbonne ever really belonged to James Dean. "My father told a great many lies in his life," says Nicca, "even about James Dean, even about his own outsize life. He felt that's what people wanted to hear."

By this time Ray's troubles went beyond unemployment and alcoholism. His gambling was out of control. "My mom was pretty much paying the bills because he was an incredible gambler," recalls Nicca. "He would drop $30,000 in a night. My mom said he was more excited about losing than he was about winning." Later, while in Europe, Ray was reduced to acting in two fantasy sequences for a 1974 soft-core pornographic film called *Wet Dreams,* assembled by Max Fischer, a Dutch filmmaker in Amsterdam. (He played a preacher and a janitor in the film.)

Ray was first drawn back to the States in 1969 by the Chicago Seven conspiracy trial. For Ray, Abbie Hoffman, Jerry Rubin, and Black Panther Bobby Seale, among others, were the ultimate rebels. "It was like putting James Dean on trial," says Nicca. While shooting some footage about the celebrated case, Ray met the woman who became his fourth wife, a University of Chicago student named Susan Schwartz. They were introduced by William Kunstler, lawyer for the Chicago Seven, while Schwartz was doing research at the trial. Surrounded by young people at the courthouse, Ray was "hard to miss . . . tall and white-maned, the coolest of cats, he came and went as he pleased," Schwartz noted. He looked "like a king who had lost his kingdom." Schwartz was about to turn 18; Ray had just turned 58.

––––––––––

Dennis Hopper helped get Ray a job teaching a film class at Harpur College, in Binghamton, New York, where he worked with his students to make a feature film, *We Can't Go Home Again.* (Ray had been staying with Hopper at his ranch in Taos, New Mexico, running up $30,000-a-month phone bills, and Hopper wanted desperately to get him out of his house.) By then Ray was wearing an eye patch, the result of an embolism that had cost him the use of one eye. "Wearing a black eye patch, black Levi's, black turtleneck, black cowboy boots and a shock of white hair, he was a Hollywood legend who directed James Dean," wrote Tom Farrell, one of his students at Harpur College. Although the student film was never finished to anyone's satisfaction (despite a premiere at Cannes), the experience re-created for Ray some of the joy of directing *Rebel Without a Cause.* "He's always wanted to be cherished by young people. . . . He scorns his own generation, which has rejected him, apparently," said Farrell, who also felt that Ray was "a con artist, and he knows how to manipulate people . . . but that's part of the talent of a director."

Ray made a return visit to Los Angeles, though he was destitute, taking buses everywhere. Frank Mazzola got a frantic call from him one night from Barney's Beanery, just off La Cienega—he didn't have $13 to pay his tab, and the manager was threatening to have him arrested. Ray had taken out a huge, falling-apart address book that he'd carried around with him since the 40s. "It had everyone's phone number in it," says Nicca. "James Dean's old phone numbers, Howard Hughes's private number—everybody's."

On that trip Ray had somehow managed to scrape together enough funds to rent his old bungalow at the Chateau Marmont, and he invited to a lunch as many people as he could from his old Hollywood days to raise money to get *We Can't Go Home Again* ready for Cannes. Only a handful turned up. Two of the guests, however, were Natalie Wood and Robert Wagner. She had remained loyal to the man who had given her her first adult role—in life and in art. Until her own tragic death, in 1981, when she drowned off Catalina Island, Wood always acknowledged *Rebel Without a Cause* as the film that inspired her to become a serious actress.

=====

"I remember when he was living with us for those few weeks in 1974," Nicca recalls. "The father who came home was a mess. He was a coke addict and an alcoholic, and he had the patch on his eye and the crazy hair. I didn't grow up with the father who made *Rebel Without a Cause*. My father was the one who was unemployed." Growing up in Los Angeles, she would be taken to the planetarium at Griffith Park, where she would play, doing cartwheels on the grass. "My mom would say, 'Your father shot a movie here.'"

Before marrying Schwartz and sharing her loft in New York, Ray had become virtually homeless. She described the condition Ray was in: "He drank wine for breakfast. . . . And then there were the medicaments, a briefcase full that went with him everywhere: needles, ampules of methedrine and B-complex, mysterious pills, bags of grass, blocks of hash, and fresh patches for the right eye."

Nicca believes that, near the end of her father's life, "if it hadn't been for these people who loved his work he would have been lost. They took him in. They took care of him. Then [the German director] Wim Wenders came and pretty much brought him back. His passion was making films. It wasn't having dinner with the family. He needed to be out there. He needed to be eating film."

Wenders was one of the generation of filmmakers who had cut their teeth on Ray's films. In 1977 he cast Ray in *The American Friend,* an adaptation of a Patricia Highsmith novel. In a brief but lionhearted performance, Ray played Derwatt, an American painter believed dead who goes underground to increase the value of his artwork. Dennis Hopper played Highsmith's sociopathic hero, Tom Ripley. Wenders and Ray shared the same visionary obsession with the movies, and they embarked on a bold experiment. In 1976, Ray had entered Alcoholics Anonymous, but it was too late: his health was ravaged, and the following year he was diagnosed with cancer. He knew he was dying. "When he found out he was going to die," Nicca explains, "he made the calls, and he said, 'It's time to make a film.'" In what was to be part documentary, part fiction, part home movie, Wenders filmed an emaciated Ray slowly dying on-camera. The movie, titled *Lightning over Water,* offended many of Ray's oldest friends. Gavin Lambert says, "When you think what hit him . . . losing one eye, the cancer, the brain tumor—I mean, it's like a sort of thunderbolt from somewhere. Just extraordinary and terrible. That's why I resented Wenders's film so much. . . . Nick was so wonderful-looking, and to see him reduced in that way was terrible." Lambert viewed the film with producer John Houseman, who had given Ray his first opportunity to direct, with *They Live by Night.* "I remember saying to [Houseman] after the screening, 'Oh my God, this is so awful and so pitiful, and how could Nick do this?' And then I realized, I know why he can do it. He loved the idea of going out in a movie."

───

Nicca was also horrified when she went with her mother, Betty Utey, to see the film at a distributor's screening in 1980, a year after her father's death, on June 16, 1979. "I was 19. I was wearing full-on punk-rock makeup and everything, and I had this jacket with all the spikes in it, thinking, I'm so tough, I'm not going to crack." But after the screening, which was filled with "all these men in suits," Nicca went to a friend's house and shot Demerol. "Why didn't my sister or I get to see him die in real life, and why do these strangers get to see him? Then you think about how he was always more comfortable on a film set."

There's a moment in *Lightning over Water* that follows an improvised scene from *King Lear*—with Ray as the raging king without a kingdom—where he is clearly too weak to continue. He turns to Wenders and speaks the last word he would ever say on film: "Cut."

In the final frame of *Rebel Without a Cause,* after Stark's father has told him that he'll "stand up with" him, a solitary figure appears, his back to the camera, and walks toward the ornate doors of the planetarium. That's Ray, who once remarked, "If they're still showing *Rebel Without a Cause* twenty years from now, then it can stand as my epitaph." Not just his epitaph, but his masterpiece.

From *Vanity Fair,* March 2005

SWEET SMELL
OF SUCCESS

A Movie Marked Danger

by Sam Kashner

Sweet Smell of Success has always
been a dangerous film. It even
had the most powerful gossip
columnist in America pacing
nervously across the street from
Loew's State on Times Square,
where the film was having its pre-
miere in New York on June 27, 1957. Walter Winchell, the fast-
talking, snap-brim-fedora-wearing arbiter of American culture, was
waiting for a handful of his spies to reassure him that the movie was
going to be a flop. And indeed it was. The film that's now regarded as
a delicious morality tale, credited with sullying Winchell's reputation
for all time, failed at the box office.

The public hated it. Earlier, when it was screened for a Northern California audience, one viewer wrote on the preview card,
"Don't touch a foot of this film. Just burn the whole thing."

But a half-century after its release this stylish black-and-white
movie refuses to go away. Its sly influence has cropped up in the
work of directors as diverse as Martin Scorsese, Barry Levinson,
the Coen brothers, and Paul Thomas Anderson. *New Yorker* film

critic David Denby has called it the finest New York film ever—besting even *Annie Hall* and *Taxi Driver* on his personal list. "It was such a tough film," Scorsese has said. "It was vibrant, alive. The images of New York, the location work were all brilliant. . . . It was a world of operators I knew very well."

Why has this film, rejected by its initial audiences in favor of *Peyton Place*, *The Bridge on the River Kwai*, and *Funny Face*, reemerged in all its low-life glory? What is it about *Sweet Smell of Success* that causes the film to live up to its hype: THE MOTION PICTURE THAT WILL NEVER BE FORGIVEN—OR FORGOTTEN!, as its theater posters claimed.

Just about everything.

Sweet Smell of Success—the story of an unethical press agent named Sidney Falco and a power-mad gossip columnist named J. J. Hunsecker—does for New York what *Sunset Boulevard* did for Hollywood. It was conceived as a short story called "Hunsecker Fights the World," published in 1948 in *Collier's* by Ernest Lehman, an unhappy press agent who wanted only to be a novelist and a screenwriter; it was Lehman's attempt to expiate his guilt for being one of the little guys feeding the big columnists the stuff that made Walter Winchell more powerful than presidents.

The writer Michael Herr called Winchell "the wizard of the American vicarious: gossip columnist, failed vaudevillian, power broker, and journalistic demagogue, one of the most powerful and famous men of his time." At the height of his popularity, in the late 1930s, 50 million people—two-thirds of American adults—read Winchell's syndicated column and listened to his Sunday-night radio broadcast. An insecure man, he was quick to perceive slights and avenged them ruthlessly. As he wrote in his autobiography, "I'm not a fighter. I'm a 'waiter.' I wait until I can catch an ingrate with his fly open, and then I take a picture of it." Winchell's special brand of nastiness is the evil heart of *Sweet Smell of Success*.

Among the film's many pleasures is James Wong Howe's chiaroscuro cinematography, which unerringly captures the look and feel of postwar New York City. Howe shot his subjects from low angles so they always seemed to be "knifing up through the air, poised for the kill," as critic and screenwriter Stephen Schiff put it. The city is awash in brilliant shadows—everything shines, seemingly drenched in acid rain: the enormous neon signs above the great buildings, even the newsstand holding down its corner of the sidewalk in front of Nedick's. At one point, after Hunsecker watches a drunk being bounced from a nightclub, he turns away and says, "I love this dirty town." *Sweet Smell of Success* is a corrosive valentine to New York, embracing its energy and its clashing ambitions. But what cineasts really love about this film is its biting dialogue, written by Lehman and that most miserable of urban geniuses, Clifford Odets. Where else would you hear a sinister cop utter the words "Come back, Sidney. I want to chastise you"?

———

The Sturm und Drang of bringing Lehman's morality tale to the screen had a nearly lethal effect on a number of its players: It made Lehman so ill he had to leave the project. It deepened the melancholia of the great Odets. It almost sent Susan Harrison, the fragile actress who played Hunsecker's sister, over the edge. And it helped to derail the career of its talented director, Alexander "Sandy" Mackendrick.

Burt Lancaster plays the villainous J. J. Hunsecker, understood by all audiences—then and now—to be a swipe at Winchell, though Lehman claims he went out of his way to make Hunsecker as different from Winchell as he possibly could. ("Winchell never played golf," Lehman points out. "I put all those golf trophies in Hunsecker's study!") But Hunsecker is Winchell: an unscrupulous, megalomaniac gossipmonger who rules his empire from a table at '21.' (In real life Winchell's was Table 50 at the Stork Club.) Lancaster portrayed Hunsecker as a tight-lipped monster, "the first heartless titan in American film," according to film historian David Thomson. He's obsessed with his own power, destroying careers on a whim, using his column to bludgeon his enemies and friends alike. But then, he has no friends, just lackeys and hangers-on like Sidney Falco who suck up to him, the press agents whose livelihoods depend on getting their clients mentioned in Hunsecker's column. "You're dead, son—get yourself buried!" are nearly the first words that come from his mouth.

What drives the plot is Hunsecker's relationship with his sister, a fragile doll named Susie in an oversize mink, and his resolve to break up Susie's romance with Steve Dallas, a jazz guitarist played by the gleamingly clean-cut Marty Milner. (This was another element that was too close to reality to be a coincidence: Winchell was a smothering father to his beautiful daughter Walda, to the point of ruthlessly hounding her boyfriend, a producer named William Cahn, in an attempt to destroy him.)

Enter Sidney Falco, press agent on the make and uneasy protagonist of this twisted tale, played by Tony Curtis in arguably the greatest role of his long career. Falco is Hunsecker's lapdog—he'll do anything to stay in the columnist's good graces: lie, cheat, pimp his girlfriend. And destroy Steve Dallas by libeling him as a pot-smoking Communist. When Hunsecker says to Falco, "I'd hate to take a bite out of you; you're a cookie full of arsenic," Falco just smiles. It was a hell of a role.

———

In some ways, Ernie Lehman was not a typical press agent. He was probably the only one in history who had been raised by a Czechoslovak nanny. His parents lived in Woodmere, Long Island (one of the affluent Five Towns), but lost their home in 1938, when Lehman was 18. Shy and high-strung, Lehman had the nervous system of a whippet. He went into public relations because it offered financial security. He would soon develop moral qualms about his profession. "I knew Winchell. I was the guy on the other end of the phone. He'd go into a 30-minute tirade about Ed Sullivan, then he'd say, 'Who is this?' The nicest thing you could do was to keep someone out of that world."

"We were a frightened bunch of people," Lehman says about the cadre of press agents and writers who fed the columnists, who made the rounds of all the nightspots in New York in the 40s: '21,' El Morocco, the Stork Club. [Lehman died in 2005, five years after this story was first published.] "We knew [our] lives were in the hands of a small group of columnists. It's hard to believe the columns were that important in those days. There were three in the *Daily News*. There was Nick Kenny and Walter Winchell in the *Mirror,* there was Louis Sobol and Dorothy Kilgallen in the *Journal-American,* there was Lucius Beebe in the *Herald Tribune*. There was George Ross in the *World-Telegram*."

Lehman was still living with his parents on West 75th Street when he was absorbing the world of *Sweet Smell of Success*. Looking back on that whole period, Lehman says that he "was fearful" when he quit his job in 1948, rented a cottage and a writing studio in Provincetown, Massachusetts, with his wife, Jacqueline, and began writing a hundred-page "novelette" extending the short story. "I knew I was playing with fire," he says.

Irving Hoffman was the chief press agent for whom Lehman, as legman and writer of items, had worked. "Irving was a celebrity, really," Lehman recalls, "and he was one of the few men who could stand up to Winchell, tell him where to get off." Hoffman was tall, physically imposing—"a great talker and phone man." He had terrible vision and wore thick glasses. He usually wore a camel-hair coat. He was a star in his own right, a friend of J. Edgar Hoover's, and his clients included a number of the major motion-picture studios. He had his own power, including a column in *The Hollywood Reporter* with the highbrow title "Tales of Hoffman." Lehman contributed to those columns, and to a weekly segment called "Last Week on Broadway."

When Lehman showed his former boss the manuscript of his short novel, which would be published in 1950 in *Cosmopolitan* under the title "Tell Me About It Tomorrow" (Herbert Mayes, *Cosmopolitan*'s editor in chief, didn't want the word "smell" to appear in his magazine), Hoffman was furious.

"Ernie," he asked, "how can you do this to me? Everybody's going to think I'm Sidney! Everybody's going to think Hunsecker is Winchell! You have things in here that only somebody who's close to Winchell would know!"

———

There were similarities. Falco read Hunsecker's column the day before, as Hoffman did Winchell's. Falco had an apartment-cum-office that was very much like Hoffman's. ("I used to visit Irving's office," Lehman recalls. "He would hand the phone over to me so I could hear Truman Capote's voice.") A bedroom lurked behind the front desk, where on at least one occasion Lehman had to knock off a theater review to the sounds of moans and bouncing bedsprings coming from behind the door. Hoffman was a world-class womanizer, a fact confirmed by Lehman's friend the producer David Brown, who has known the writer since they were boys together on Long Island.

Brown was the managing editor of *Cosmopolitan* when Lehman's novelette appeared in the magazine. Brown has said that "Hoffman was afflicted with satyriasis, male nymphomania." But there was one important difference between Sidney Falco and Irving Hoffman: Hoffman didn't have to suck up to Winchell. Lehman tried to explain this crucial difference to his former boss, but it didn't matter. "Irving had a right to feel betrayed," Lehman would later say. In fact, out of respect for Hoffman, he made several small changes in the manuscript: having the secretary address Hunsecker as "boss" instead of "chief," for example, because Winchell's secretary, Rose Bigman, always addressed Winchell as "chief." But Hoffman was not assuaged. "For a year and a half, he didn't talk to me," Lehman admits. "We had a complete break."

Winchell tried to derail the inevitable speculation that came when the novelette was published by calling up rival columnist Louis Sobol and saying, "Hey, did you read that story Ernie wrote about you!" But everyone read it as an attack on Winchell anyway, and that's why, at first, no one in Hollywood would touch it. Lehman's agent in Los Angeles, George Willner, attempted to sell the story to the movie studios even before it appeared in *Cosmopolitan*. He wrote to Lehman in Provincetown in June 1949: "The big problem still remains the resemblance to Winchell. I . . . went to all places where I thought it would do some good, but I still ran up against the same problem. . . . I'll say one thing for your story—it set this town on its ear, and Ernest Lehman's name is probably as well known out here now as any of the top ten or twelve writers."

Ironically, it wasn't the manuscript of "Tell Me About It Tomorrow" that brought Lehman to Hollywood, but his estranged mentor, Irving Hoffman. In 1952, Hoffman finally wanted to make up with Lehman, after they were brought together by a mutual friend, a press agent for Artie Shaw named Sid Garfield. As an olive branch, Hoffman offered Lehman a plug in his column. Better yet, he let Lehman write the whole column himself:

"The world I want to see on film is the world of Toots Shor's at lunch-hour, Sardi's at 11 of an opening night, Lindy's at 2 o'clock of any morning . . . the world of Winchell and Wilson, Sullivan and Sobol . . . of columnists on the prowl for items, press agents on the prowl for columnists . . . " Lehman ended his pitch with "Now I may be wrong (and I don't think I am), but just off his past performances I would say that Ernest Lehman is the guy who can write that kind of picture."

Two weeks later, Paramount called. And none too soon: Lehman, who was writing freelance now, had become a pariah at Lindy's, the Stork Club, '21'—places where he had formerly plied his trade. Press agents got up and left whenever he entered the room.

The film-production company of Hecht-Hill-Lancaster could be a treacherous place to work. Harold Hecht had been a hoofer and a literary agent. Small, clever, and tricky, Hecht laughed a lot and drank a little too much. The skinny on him was that, despite his affability, you shouldn't turn your back: he was given the nickname "the Mule." In *Naming Names,* Victor Navasky's book on Hollywood and the House Committee on Un-American Activities, he is described as "a denigrating informer."

The 32-year-old Burt Lancaster had just made his debut on Broadway in *A Sound of Hunting,* in which he played a tough World War II sergeant, when he met Harold Hecht in 1946. Hecht, 6 years Lancaster's senior, had already spent some 20 years in show business, but with modest success. Hecht recognized Lancaster's immense potential, even though the actor's major credential before the Broadway play was his membership in a two-man trapeze-and-gymnastic act. Lancaster's charisma was instantly apparent, though. His sheer physical presence was overwhelming; his shadow fell over you before he even entered the room.

In order to induce Lancaster to go in with him, Hecht came up with the idea of forming their own film-production company, something unthinkable for a mere actor at the time. "Here we were," Hecht told Lancaster's biographer, "a couple of bums without a quarter between us, discussing producing our own pictures."

James Hill, the third partner in Hecht-Hill-Lancaster, who was brought in seven years after the company's formation, was perennially boyish. He had been a page at NBC before becoming a contract screenwriter at MGM. People wondered why he was made a partner in the company. The truth was Hill "was Burt Lancaster's boy," according to Julius Epstein, who, with his brother Philip, co-wrote the screenplay for *Casablanca*. It had been Lancaster's idea to put Hill's name between Hecht's and his own; Hill would come between the two in other ways as well, most often as a buffer—because Hecht and Lancaster were usually at each other's throats. In return, Lancaster found women for Hill, and not just any women—movie stars. In February 1958, at the age of 41, Hill would marry Rita Hayworth—her fifth marriage, and his first. The marriage would last only three years.

When Hill first came to work at the Hecht-Lancaster building on North Cannon Drive, which had formerly housed the William Morris Agency, he noticed the intense rivalry between his two new partners. "Harold and Burt," Hill recalls, "had as strange a relationship as you could get. People were frightened of Burt, and he never did anything to make people unfrightened of him." [Hill died in 2001.] Another friend described the relationship as "a Freudian can of worms." Not only was Lancaster capable of verbally brutalizing Hecht, he once lifted him into the air and threatened to throw him out the window.

Their contention stemmed from Hecht's desire to "get out from under Burt's shadow," Hill says. Lancaster wasn't just a company figurehead; he was an active and involved partner. Lehman recalled that "Burt had the power. He was the famous movie star. He had the money, which Harold Hecht didn't have. . . . In terms of publicity and power, Burt Lancaster had both. Hecht was the nobody."

Hecht resented Hill's presence in the company, but he wasn't about to go up against Lancaster. "It was old-fashioned jealousy," Lehman says. Once Hill became involved in the making of *Sweet Smell of Success,* Hecht lost all interest in the film, although he was the one who had originally angled for the rights.

From the minute Lehman walked into their plush offices, with an aviary of twittering finches that seemed to fall silent whenever Lancaster passed by, he didn't like his surroundings. "They were profligate," he remembers. "They spent money on everything—$12,000 remodeling the executive washroom." The partners also maintained a luxurious apartment on Wilshire Boulevard for their trysts, replete with gold-plated dinnerware and a Utrillo hanging in the hallway near the bathroom; the antiques and hundred-dollar ashtrays still had their price tags attached.

Lehman's first encounter with Lancaster didn't do much to change his mind: "I was sitting with Harold Hecht. The door opened and in walked a towering, impressive figure. He was zipping up his fly and smiling proudly, saying, 'She swallowed it.' That was my introduction to Burt Lancaster.

"I called my agent and said, 'I'm not going to do this picture. Get me off of it.' Harold Hecht pleaded with me. He got down on his hands and knees and said, 'Please don't leave, or Burt will blame me.'"

Although they were the only producers in town with the courage to show interest in the project, frankly, they scared Lehman—there was a whiff of violence about the place.

———

Lancaster was rumored to have beaten up a girlfriend who was a telephone operator. "He was known to be violent with women," confirms Lehman. *Confidential* magazine published an article in 1955 with the headline THE SECRET'S OUT ABOUT BURT LANCASTER. A woman named Francesca de Scaffa, who at one time had been a mistress of the Shah of Iran and then married the actor Bruce Cabot, who saved Fay Wray from the ape's clutches in *King Kong*, had gone to the scandal sheet and offered her story. She had met with Lancaster to maneuver for a role in the 1954 film *Vera Cruz*, but, she claimed, when she turned down his sexual advances he attacked her, ripping the sleeve from her $400 Jacques Fath dress. "Things went from waltz time into a tempo four times faster than the mambo," the magazine reported in its signature style. "Burt's tendency toward clobbering cuties is rapidly becoming no secret at all among dames in the know in Hollywood."

"The place was rife with womanizing," Lehman remembers. Early on, the screenwriter was invited to a meeting with the three heads of the company, the subject of which was "Who can we find to become our official procurer?"

"I'm ashamed to say," Lehman explains, "that I was a part of this meeting. There we were, scratching around for women. They were the most corrupt group. I really sank into the depths when I decided to work with them."

Lehman remembers being in Palm Springs with his wife when Hecht and Hill tried to persuade him to join them in Acapulco, where they had two women waiting. "I said no, absolutely not. And to this day I can't figure out why they did that. . . . Here I was, married with two young children—my wife was in the next room. . . . What were they trying to do by exporting me to Acapulco? It was very strange."

Paddy Chayefsky was also working for the production company at the time and had just adapted his television play *Marty* for it. He and Lehman would go on long walks together and trade horror stories. "I seemed to have been surrounded by evil," Lehman says today. "But they were the ones who felt a great affinity for *Sweet Smell*. They dug it. Nobody else did, really. The film could only have been made by Hecht-Hill-Lancaster."

It was the unexpected success of *Marty*—in 1956 the film won four Academy Awards, including best picture—that made Lehman change his mind about letting the project go forward. "When *Marty* won the Oscar, I said yes," Lehman recalls. "On the condition that I also direct the picture."

Tony Curtis hounded Burt Lancaster for the part of Sidney Falco, the weaselly press agent who long ago had thrown his moral compass into the East River. Lancaster had been impressed with Curtis the previous year during the making of director Carol Reed's *Trapeze,* the sawdust-and-sweat circus drama in which the two men were teamed as aerialists who fall out over Gina Lollobrigida. The movie was highly successful, but there was more chemistry between the two men in tights than between either man and the girl.

Curtis knew he had been born to play the streetwise Falco. "All they had to tell me was New York. I was raised in that city. I should have done it as the first movie I ever made."

For the role of Hunsecker, Lehman thought of Orson Welles. But while Lehman was working on the first of several drafts of the screenplay, Lancaster would sit in on story conferences. "He was fascinated," Lehman remembers. "It's like he smelled that this could be a different role for him—no hero. One day, Burt just said, 'I'm going to do it.' That's when it became a bigger venture, more important."

With Lancaster now starring in the film, Lehman's sensitive stomach began to give him trouble. "It bothered me a lot," he said. "They used to make jokes about it. I remember at a meeting we had one day when Burt looked at me and he said, 'I can see us all standing around Ernie's grave, and there's a stomach tree growing out of it.' And the three of them laughed. This was the atmosphere I was working in. This was not John Houseman or Billy Wilder." Instead of using the project to atone for "having done some pretty terrible things as a press agent," Lehman felt he'd entered a whole new level of corruption.

———

After United Artists came in with the funds to produce the picture, Hecht fired Lehman as director. The ostensible reason was that Lancaster's first directorial effort, on *The Kentuckian*, a 1955 film with Lancaster and Walter Matthau, had lost money for United Artists, but the truth was, as Hill explains 42 years later, "we were never gonna let Ernie direct!" In fact, Hill believes that "Ernie didn't want to work on the picture at all, or he wouldn't have made a demand like that." Tony Curtis confirms this. "We were talking about getting Orson Welles to play J. J. Hunsecker. They're gonna let Lehman, who's never directed a movie before in his life, direct Orson Welles? They [promised him] that, I feel, because they wanted to get the property. That's the only reason."

Lehman says he was crushed when Hecht called him in to his office to give him the news. He went to his agent, Lew Wasserman, and said, "'Lew, I have terrible news for you.' And Wasserman said, 'I already know.' That was the trouble with MCA in those days, because Wasserman was also their agent! So they made me a producer instead of the director. I kept getting more and more pain in my gut, and more and more stress. And that's when they chose Alexander

Mackendrick. Sandy was already there on another project, so they asked him to direct. It seemed an unlikely choice. What would he know about the world of Broadway and New York nightlife?" He was from Scotland, after all.

In a way, Mackendrick was coming home when he flew to America in 1956. Although he grew up in Glasgow and worked in England, he had actually been born in Boston of Scottish immigrant parents. When his father died in the Spanish-flu epidemic of 1918, it was decided that the experiment of living in America just hadn't worked out. The family returned to Scotland, and Mackendrick was raised by his grandparents. (Mackendrick was fond of telling people that he had been conceived in Hollywood, so his "mistrust of Hollywood was pre-natal.")

Mackendrick had made his reputation directing two of the classic Alec Guinness comedies for Britain's Ealing Studios, *The Man in the White Suit* (1951) and *The Ladykillers* (1955), the latter considered the apotheosis of the Ealing style. His background was in design; he had been a wunderkind at the advertising agency J. Walter Thompson before being hired to create storyboards for Ealing, which he then parlayed into directing. His comedies are known for their dark-edged humor ("Where there is comedy he rims it in black," wrote one critic). Guinness described him as "a man of great charm but of astonished outrage at the wickedness of the world."

Soon after *The Ladykillers* was made, Michael Balcon sold Ealing Studios to the BBC, and Mackendrick sought his fate abroad. "He got a call from his agent one day asking him to come out here and talk to somebody at Paramount," Mackendrick's widow, Hilary, remembers. "It was all rather mysterious, so naturally he was intrigued." Mackendrick, used to the camaraderie of Ealing, turned down offers from big studios such as Paramount and producers such as David O. Selznick, deciding instead to sign with Hecht-Hill-Lancaster, because they promised he could direct an adaptation of George Bernard Shaw's *The Devil's Disciple*.

Mackendrick and his wife settled into a rented house on South Rodeo Drive. Mackendrick's biggest complaint about Hollywood at that time was its lack of pubs. At Ealing Studios each crew member would drink a quart of bonded whiskey a night.

During daily conferences with Mackendrick, Lehman quickly recognized the Scottish director's brilliance. "His words just tumbled over each other; I couldn't quite follow him at times. He was too bright for me, too fast. Working with Sandy was great, but at the same time stressful. You had the feeling he wasn't even listening to you because his mind was going so fast."

———

After one particularly rough story conference, Lancaster walked Lehman out into the hall and put an arm around his shoulder. "We're going to start shooting next week in New York," he said. "You're going to have to do some rewrites behind the camera."

"O.K., Burt, but first I'm going to have to go see my doctor."

Lehman was really suffering. David Brown, then living in Los Angeles and working as an executive at Twentieth Century Fox, drove him in his Mercedes roadster to Cedars of Lebanon Hospital. "When I woke up the next morning," Lehman recalls, "the doctor was seated next to my bed. He said, 'Ernie, we've looked up there with a sigmoidoscope, and you're not going back to work. In fact, you're leaving the country.'"

When the doctor called to say that Lehman was leaving the picture, two of the partners turned to each other and said at the same time: "I hope the son of a bitch dies."

Lehman traveled to Hawaii and then on to Samoa and Tahiti. "I went native," he remembers. "One day I was lying there by myself on a beach, and suddenly I sat up and realized, My God, they're shooting a picture in New York called *Sweet Smell of Success*. I'd forgotten all about it."

———

It was Mackendrick's idea to bring in Clifford Odets, whom he had admired from afar. Odets, who was already adapting A. B. Guthrie's novel *The Way West* for Hecht-Hill-Lancaster, had never gotten over the triumph of having five plays running simultaneously in New York in 1935 when he only 29, including *Waiting for Lefty* and *Awake and Sing!* The "Bernard Shaw of the Bronx" was stocky and handsome, with wild hair like Einstein's that bushed up around his head. "He used to be wonderful to observe at parties," Tony Curtis recalls. "He had an old tuxedo with a vest and he had a very beautiful look about him in those days. No one looked as elegant as he with a martini in his hand. He had a great deal of fire and lust and drive." Odets took many women to bed, including the movie star Luise Rainer, whom he married in 1937.

Odets left New York soon after for California, where he accepted Hollywood's lucre but spent the rest of his life being considered a hypocrite for abandoning the leftist ideals of his great, early plays. It was an opinion that the playwright shared, torturing himself with his sense of self-betrayal.

The playwright Arthur Miller spent some time with Odets in Hollywood in 1958, six years after Odets had been a friendly, though captious, witness for HUAC during the McCarthy bloodletting. Finishing the screenplay for *Sweet Smell of Success*, Odets felt, would give him a way of striking back at that public humiliation. Miller described the embattled playwright as typifying "what it meant to survive as an artist in America. There was something so utterly American in what had betrayed him—he had wanted everything." Miller compared Odets to his wife Marilyn Monroe: "Like her, he was a self-destroying babe in the woods absentmindedly combing back his hair with a loaded pistol."

Harold Clurman, one of the founders of the Group Theatre, which had launched Odets, kept exhorting the playwright to leave Hollywood and return to New York. But Odets knew that the theater world of the 30s, in which he had made his reputation, no longer existed. Even with his tremendous early success, he could not have supported himself there. As Miller observed, there was little to return to: "Only show business and some theatrical real estate."

In 1936, Odets had predicted that "in a few years the movies will have developed into the most important artistic medium the world has ever seen, and it's high time playwrights found out about them." Twenty years later, when he was signed to finish Lehman's script, Odets was living in diminished circumstances—divorced from his second wife, driving a dusty old Lincoln, and caring for his two children, Nora, 11, and Walt, 9. A gifted painter and collector of works by Klee and Matisse, Odets was reduced to selling a number of the paintings from his collection to survive.

———

Tony Curtis remembers his first meeting with Odets. "He used to call me 'boychick,' right from the start." There was a kind of bond between Odets and Curtis—the playwright may have seen in the younger man his own youthful, urban beauty, now rumpled and fading. "The picture is loaded with little references to my looks," Curtis points out, "'the boy with the ice-cream face' . . . and Rita, the cigarette girl, calling me 'Eyelashes.'"

One of the things Odets did was to give Curtis the key to Sidney Falco. He said, "Don't be still with Sidney. Don't ever let Sidney sit down comfortably. I want Sidney constantly moving, like an animal, never quite sure who's behind him or where he is."

Curtis took Odets's suggestions to heart and gave what many consider his breakthrough performance. Up until then he had swashbuckled his way through numerous "tit and sand" movies, such as *Son of Ali Baba*, and made lots of money for Universal, which had transformed a rough-cut Hungarian Jew named Bernard Schwartz from Brooklyn into a brilliantined teen idol who called himself Anthony Curtis. *Sweet Smell of Success* would reverse that transformation.

There's sweet irony in the fact that Curtis went back to his roots—back to being Bernie Schwartz—to unleash the character of Sidney Falco on the world. Falco's little aria on success, delivered to his lugubrious secretary while he's getting dressed in the cramped bedroom behind her desk, could easily have been Curtis's credo as well: "Hunsecker is a golden ladder to the places I wanna get. Way up high, Sam, where it's always balmy and no one snaps his fingers and says, 'Hey, shrimp, rack the balls!' . . . From now on, the best of everything is good enough for me."

"I was really astounded by the twist of it," Curtis says about playing Falco. "I was able to grace the part with little physical innuendos. Not for nothing, I wanted to make him an excellent athlete, growing up in the streets of New York, playing stickball. He punched, he boxed, he did everything, always on his feet, always moving."

Both Mackendrick and Lehman thought Curtis was miraculous as Falco. For Curtis, the role opened doors; other complex and demanding roles would follow—in *The Defiant Ones, Some Like It Hot, The Great Impostor,* and *The Boston Strangler.* And behind all those roles was Sidney Falco: "In all the films I've done, I've never lost Sidney. And I don't want to lose him," Curtis says.

In contrast to Falco, J. J. Hunsecker hardly ever seems to move—he's usually shown sitting, at his table in '21,' at his desk writing his column, in a studio waiting to tape his television show. In one early draft of the script, Lehman put Hunsecker in a wheelchair, tended by a male nurse named Sam. Ambition moves, power stays put.

One of cinematographer James Wong Howe's challenges on the film was to transform the vitally robust Lancaster into a tense, be-spectacled ghoul. How do you shrink this huge man? The solution was to use the glasses to suggest a man who wasn't physically powerful, though with a violent presence. The horn-rimmed glasses are one of the elements that made Lancaster's performance so chilling. He takes them off in only one scene—when Falco is describing Steve Dallas for him and revealing why Susie is so smitten with the musician. As he removes his horn-rims, Hunsecker turns his face into shadow, as if to suggest that this is the instant he realizes he must resort to his darkest side to get rid of Dallas. Lancaster wore glasses in real life, and he fought with Mackendrick about wearing them in the film. But Mackendrick won this battle, and Howe—who had just won an Oscar for his work on *The Rose Tattoo*—used the glasses as a focal point for the light. The shadows cast by the glasses onto Lancaster's face give him the skeletal look of a walking corpse. It's as though Hunsecker were already a dead man, his soul long since squeezed out of him by the machinery of power. "Match me, Sidney," he says, extending his cigarette to Falco from his throne at '21,' in his sadistic little game of dominance and submission.

Howe is rightly credited with the movie's darkly dazzling evocation of Broadway nightlife. It would have been impossible to get the sort of shots he wanted filming inside '21,' so interiors were filmed in Hollywood at Goldwyn Studios' Soundstage 8—they spent $25,000 just re-creating '21,' with movable "wild walls" to make way for Howe's camera. Howe smeared the walls with oil so they would gleam. To capture the smoky atmosphere of New York nightclubs, sets were built two feet off the ground and smoke pots placed underneath, so that Howe could "light the smoke," according to the director Richard Blackburn (*Eating Raoul*).

Production moved to New York City to begin location shooting in the winter of 1956. Odets was brought along to finish the script and furnish script changes as needed. He and Hill traveled east by train because they thought he could get a lot of the writing done that way. By the time they reached Chicago, however, Odets still hadn't written anything. Hill had to resort to devious methods to get Odets to work, such as scribbling an unusable scene himself and saying, "Let's give this to Sandy." Hill knew that Odets "had great pride in his work. He would sometimes write the same scene eight times before he'd let you read it."

But there was another problem. Odets didn't seem to realize until Chicago that they were going on to New York. He complained to Hill, "For Christ's sake, I can't go to New York! I can't face those people!"—meaning the theater people he had left behind, who by now considered him a defector: Harold Clurman, Stella Adler, and other members of the Group Theatre.

Meanwhile, Mackendrick had mixed feelings about Odets's sizzling dialogue, worried that it would sound "stagey." But Odets reassured him: "You're probably worried that the dialogue is exaggerated and may sound implausible. Don't be. Play it real fast—and play the scenes not for the words but for the situations! Play them 'on the run' and they'll work just fine."

═══════

By the time shooting finally began in New York, things had really become chaotic. "One of the most frightening experiences of my life was to start shooting in the middle of Times Square at rush hour with an incomplete script," Mackendrick later said. It was the dead of winter, and it was bitterly cold. "God, you needed all the clothes you could get on, and you were still cold," the production manager, Richard McWhorter, remembered. Adding to this, the mimeographed sheets of Odets's script were often distributed to the cast and crew after the scene had been shot.

Then, one night early in the production, Tony Curtis noticed that Odets was missing from the set. He asked where Odets was, and was told, "We've got him locked up at the Essex House." And sure enough, Curtis remembers, "there was bleary-eyed, stiff-haired Clifford, sitting in his pajamas on a couch, with papers—typewritten, handwritten—all over the joint. I said, 'Let's go out for dinner,' and Hill said, 'What, are you nuts?' They wouldn't let him out until he had completed more work on the script."

Eventually, Hill allowed Odets to leave his hotel room and go down to Times Square. They made room for him and his typewriter in a prop truck.

"I remember," says Curtis, "it was about three or four in the morning, and it was cold, bitter, and miserable. Between shots, I was strolling around, and I heard this *tik-tik-tik* coming from inside the prop truck. So I go and look in, and there's Clifford Odets, sitting in an overcoat, huddled over his typewriter. I said, 'What the hell are you doing here this time of night?'

"He said, 'I've got to finish this sequence. You have two more days shooting here, and I've got to get it done.'"

Curtis joined him in the truck. Odets suddenly looked up and said, "Come here, kid. I want to show you something. Look at what I'm writing."

"I see he's just typed out, 'The cat's in the bag, and the bag's in the river.' It took my breath away, right from his brain to my brain."

———

Mackendrick would note years later, "There never was a final shooting script for the movie. . . . It was all still being revised, even on the last day of principal photography. It was a shambles of a document."

But a bigger problem on the set was the power struggle between Mackendrick and Lancaster. They both wanted to be the man in control. Lancaster would go behind Mackendrick's back, for example, to give Marty Milner direction on how he should play the role of Steve Dallas. Mackendrick would later observe, "The hysteria of that production was the edge of fear. . . . You're working from moment to moment."

Curtis recalls how Mackendrick insisted on absolute silence on the set, or he wouldn't shoot. "Even if everything went perfectly," Curtis says, "he would still want to re-shoot. In the middle of a scene, he'd yell, 'Shut up!' Everyone tiptoed around him on that set. Burt would get mad because they couldn't afford all that reshooting." Mackendrick in fact did an epic number of takes of the scene in which Hunsecker watches a drunk being bounced from a nightclub. They did it over and over and over again, going all night long, and then Mackendrick said, "Print Takes 1 and 2 and let's wrap!"

Lancaster was furious: "Remind me to pay somebody to take the little Limey's legs off," he said.

Elmer Bernstein, who composed the film's powerful, jazzy score, confessed to the director James Mangold (Cop Land), "The combination of people on that movie—Hecht, Lancaster, Odets— was a snake pit. There was a cultural distance between Burt and Sandy. It was like Sandy's heart beat at a different rate.

"Burt was really scary," the composer recalled, "He was a dangerous guy. He had a short fuse. He was very physical. You thought you might get punched out. . . . It was a miracle that [Sandy] finished that film. In fact, I think that film is what finished Sandy." Lancaster would later admit with a grin that Mackendrick considered him "the epitome of evil."

Their biggest fight would be over the ending of the movie. The film critic and screenwriter F. X. Feeney, who would later befriend Mackendrick, knew that "Lancaster was adamant about ending the film in a certain way, which Sandy was opposed to." Mackendrick had been warned by Alan Crosland, the film's editor, that Lancaster intended to take over and re-edit it. "Sandy was at his notepad trying to figure out how he could do it his way, when a big shadow fell over him—it's Lancaster. He had to come clean about what he was doing." He ultimately had to shoot the scene in two different ways, and cut the final ending on his own, behind Lancaster's back.

The choice was, in part, whether to end with Falco's getting beaten up by the sadistic cop Harry Kello—ominously portrayed by character actor Emile Meyer—or to end with Susie Hunsecker's rejecting her brother and walking out into a shaft of sunlight, one of the few to appear in this otherwise dark film. Hill and Lancaster cut the final scenes to end with the pummeling, but when they screened it they could see it wasn't working. "So Sandy tells them," Feeney recalls, "'I've cut the film this way—why don't you look at it?' In a kind of grudging spirit, they all sat down, and Sandy had the rare satisfaction of watching them sink in their chairs and kind of get it—they actually got his ending [with Susie walking out]."

When Lehman returned from Tahiti, Mackendrick called him and said, "Come down, I want to show you the rough cut." Lehman was dazzled by parts of it, but disappointed by the ending and the preceding suicide attempt, in which Susie is prevented by Falco from throwing herself off the balcony of the penthouse apartment she shares with her brother. (Hunsecker keeps her like one of those caged finches, in a little bedroom just off his study.) Lehman had originally written a similar ending, but he changed it to give her character more strength and cunning. Mackendrick, however, felt that the story "needed someone to bring death into the room," so that Falco and Hunsecker can finally be toppled.

Lehman blames himself for planting the idea. "It had to be my stupidity in telling them about the ending I had originally written and thrown out," he says.

The role of Susie Hunsecker went to an 18-year-old actress from the Bronx with no professional experience. Susan Harrison had been a waitress at the Limelight, a Greenwich Village coffeehouse, and a model in the Garment District. She had the delicate, frightened look of a startled deer. At five feet seven she was a willowy, nervous girl with brown eyes and light-brown hair who smoked incessantly. Described by a gossip columnist as "a person with moods," Harrison at the time was thrown into the tough, womanizing partnership of Hecht-Hill-Lancaster, and a number of the cast and crew feared she wasn't going to make it. The fragility she conveyed on-screen was not an act.

———

"I heard the whispers that I was neurotic, difficult—an oddball," she would later say. "I wore long hair, black stockings and oversized sweaters. . . . I didn't know what I was doing when I was in front of the camera, but it looked good."

In preparing for her climactic scene, Mackendrick asked the young actress, "Here, Susan, is where you lock yourself in your room. What would you want to do before you committed suicide?"

Feeney remembers Mackendrick telling him that Harrison had "admitted to a fascination with high buildings—she had an impulse to throw herself off. Sandy said, 'Just give us that,' but he saw something in her that was a little frightening. He was genuinely prescient about people."

What Mackendrick didn't know was that shortly before beginning work on the film Harrison *had* fallen 10 feet during a photographic shoot with the German-born photographer Peter Basch. It had happened in a private house behind the Chateau Marmont in West Hollywood; she fell through a second-story awning onto a patio. Harrison later admitted that her fall might have been a veiled suicide attempt. "I had a thought, deep down, of killing myself because I was very depressed."

Peter Basch remembers the accident, and he vividly recalls Harrison's unusual beauty. Basch has photographed many ingenues, including Tuesday Weld, Jane Fonda, and Natalie Wood, when they were barely in their teens. "What I found fascinating about her was that she was not the girl next door," Basch recalls. [Basch died in 2004.] "She was a young woman with a strong erotic component; she could have worked all over Europe. The Italians would have loved her." Harrison was so luckless that not only did she fall 10 feet to a concrete floor, the ambulance called to rescue her crashed on its way to the house. Her injuries were slight, though, and she ended up suing Basch and the owner of the house. "Her choice of men—I think that's what tripped her up, finally," says Basch.

When Falco tells Susie Hunsecker toward the end of the film, "Look at yourself, you're nineteen years old, just a kid, and you're falling apart at the seams . . . with a fatality for doing wrong, picking wrong, and giving up even before you start a fight," he could have been speaking about Harrison herself. It was one of those many moments when the line was blurred between life and art.

Curtis says that "working with those guys was tough. We all came in with barrels loaded, we all came in to fight. Susan had no experience at all, so we drove her down into nowhere." She seems lost in the film.

———

There were a number of reasons why *Sweet Smell of Success* failed at the box office. The movie was just too cynical for the times—in 1957, America was in no mood to see a film about its dark side. And the public wasn't ready to see two popular stars, Curtis and Lancaster, cast as villains. They had been so winning in *Trapeze*. One film executive marveled that the film seemed to have been made "almost in defiance of the box office."

The Hollywood reporter Ezra Goodman accompanied Hill, Hecht, and Lancaster to San Francisco for a preview. After the screening, Hecht approached Goodman and asked him what he thought of the picture.

"I told him that I thought it was poor. Hecht was overjoyed. His face broke out into a wide CinemaScope-type smile and I became his buddy. [The movie] was a flop and lost a great deal of money, but Hecht was happy." Once Hill had ended up getting the producer's credit on the film, Hecht was glad to see it fail.

At a party at Hill's Los Angeles apartment after the preview, Lehman sat at a table with Lancaster, who turned to him suddenly and said, "You weren't that sick, Ernie. You didn't have to leave the picture. I ought to punch you in the jaw right here and now."

Lehman said, "Go ahead, Burt. I need the money."

"They resented me," Lehman says now. "They considered me an enemy in their midst. I never saw Clifford again. He was off on another picture. They got rid of everyone."

One of the people they got rid of was Mackendrick, two weeks into the filming of *The Devil's Disciple,* the film he had initially been hired to direct. Lancaster claimed that the director was simply taking too long, driving up the budget. "Sandy was a very brilliant man," Lancaster explained, "but we hadn't the time or the money for him. That's the truth."

Hilary Mackendrick recalls that her husband "was let go from *Devil's Disciple* after he had already shot sequences with Laurence Olivier. . . . He had no idea why it happened. He was particularly annoyed that Harold Hecht did not speak to him personally but sent in the production manager. It was very crushing for him. He became depressed." It's possible that Mackendrick was being made a scapegoat for the box-office failure of *Sweet Smell of Success,* despite the critics' appreciation of the film and the fact that it made *Time*'s and the *New York Herald Tribune*'s 10-best lists for 1957.

Mackendrick returned to England, where he made a few more films before he came back to Hollywood in 1969. He spent 10 years developing a film based on the life of Mary, Queen of Scots, which he felt would have been his masterwork, only to have Universal cancel the project. His last film would turn out to be a silly 60s comedy with Tony Curtis and Sharon Tate called *Don't Make Waves,* which was plagued by problems—including the death of a stuntman. Mackendrick came to the conclusion that in Hollywood "the deal is the real product, the movie is the by-product of the deal." When the California Institute of the Arts began looking for someone to head up its new film program, it asked Mackendrick. He accepted, was its dean for 9 years and a much-beloved teacher until his death at the age of 81 in 1993. He never made another film. "Without him," Anthony Lane wrote in *The New Yorker,* "the landscape of cinema has grown dimmer."

"He was cynical, cynical about everything," Hilary Mackendrick says. "He took to calling *Sweet Smell of Success* a piece of hokum, but that was his nature. He just couldn't bring himself to acknowledge that he had made a masterpiece."

In 1960, three years after the movie was released, Hecht, Hill, and Lancaster dissolved their partnership. In 1965, Susan Harrison sued Hecht for $25,000, claiming that he had "fraudulently induced" her into abandoning a contract she had with Hecht-Hill-Lancaster. After that, she seemed just to disappear. Except for a 1960 teen-exploitation movie, *Key Witness,* she did not work again in Hollywood. In October 1965, Harrison was given a suspended 90-day jail sentence by a superior-court judge in Los Angeles for child neglect, after she failed to give her two-year-old son urgently needed medical attention. The boy, Daniel, had sustained a brain injury after having fallen. (As this story was being reported, in 2000, repeated attempts to locate Harrison, even by a private detective, were unsuccessful.)

Walter Winchell refused even to see *Sweet Smell of Success.* "I don't fool with the Lehmans of the world," he allegedly said when asked why he didn't retaliate in his column. It wasn't until the end of the year, nearly six months after its run, that Winchell acknowledged the film at all, reporting matter-of-factly that Hecht-Hill-Lancaster would stand to lose $500,000 on it. But, as Winchell's latest biographer, Neal Gabler, wrote, Lehman's novelette and Mackendrick's movie "helped sully Walter Winchell's name forever." He lived another 14 years, long enough to see his power and influence evaporate. The power of the tabloid gossip column had ebbed with the coming of television—and Winchell, though he briefly tried television, was really a radio man. David Brown describes his last encounter with Winchell, not long before his death: "It was at Danny's Hideaway. He was all alone in the booth, surrounded by his clippings. He had totally abandoned his column, he had been fired, but he still had that incredible ego. At his funeral, you know, nobody was there who wasn't paid to be there." According to Gabler, Winchell's daughter Walda discouraged people from attending the funeral.

As for Odets, he continued to work on films, often uncredited. He had always been a cynic about *Sweet Smell of Success.* "Hell," Odets once said to Burt Lancaster, "you can get killed just yearning for Hollywood."

Odets was hired to write *Wild in the Country* (1961) for Elvis

Presley, but when he had Presley commit suicide at the end of the picture, he was told to rewrite the ending. He did so because he needed the money. "Everything he was against at the beginning of his career," observed his friend the pianist Oscar Levant, "he wound up doing himself."

Odets lived for six more years after the release of *Sweet Smell of Success*. Just as he had accepted the inevitability of movies, he accepted the inevitability of television, and agreed to be a writer for *The Richard Boone Show*. But when a stomach complaint turned out to be cancer, Odets was hospitalized. All his old friends from Broadway, the ones he had avoided during location shooting in New York—Harold Clurman, Elia Kazan, Lee Strasberg—showed up at his bedside to pay homage to their former golden boy. His death received modest notice in the press: *Time* magazine dismissed his long career in a flippant epitaph: "Odets, where is thy sting?"

But Odets, near the end of his life, had written his own epitaph: "That miserable patch of events, that mélange of nothing, while you were looking ahead for something to happen, that was it! That was life! You lived it!"

———

Lehman, on the other hand, has had a spectacular career as a screenwriter in Hollywood. His credits include *Sabrina*, *The King and I*, *Somebody Up There Likes Me*, *North by Northwest*, *West Side Story*, *The Sound of Music*, *Who's Afraid of Virginia Woolf?*, *Hello, Dolly!*, and Hitchcock's last film, *Family Plot*. In 2002, he co-produced with David Brown a musical adaptation of *Sweet Smell of Success* for Broadway.

Sweet Smell of Success has come full circle, to, perhaps, where it belongs. It had always been David Brown's dream to make it into a Broadway musical: "After all," Brown suggests, "it's a fable. And a musical lends itself to a fable. We are now living in a tabloid era— not the era of wonderful nonsense, but an era of character assassination, of instant celebrity. In my view, it was all invented by J. J. Hunsecker."

As for Lehman, he remained on the West Coast, content not to involve himself creatively in this new incarnation of the novelette he wrote 50 years ago in a Provincetown studio. "I wrote the novel, the screenplay—it's theirs now," he says. "I'm staying away from it. I just hope they have a good press agent. Maybe Sidney Falco will get the job."

From *Vanity Fair*, April 2000

THE BEST OF EVERYTHING

The Lipstick Jungle

by Laura Jacobs

The genre was a winner for the movies, right from the start. Requirements were minimal: a big city, three pretty faces, some wolves. *Sally, Irene and Mary* was the first—silent but scrappy in 1925—a tale of three chorus girls looking for love and limelight in New York, New York (one of them was a hungry young actress named Joan Crawford). In *Our Blushing Brides,* 1930, it was three shopgirls—one of them, again, Joan Crawford. In 1932's *Three on a Match,* the girls were childhood friends, all grown up and sharing bites of the Big Apple—shiny, wormy—only this time the Joan was blonde, as in Blondell. Throughout the 30s and into the 40s, three-girls-in-the-city had to make room for three-boys-back-from-war. (In those days returning soldiers were as hopeful, as vulnerable, as young women.) Two is just two: left and right, yes and no, Goofus and Gallant. Four is fine for TV—see HBO's *Sex and the City*—but one too many for film (*A Letter to Four Wives* was fixed by subtraction: *A Letter to Three Wives* won the Oscars). Three is destiny. When blushing brides play with matches, one girl wins, one draws, one dies.

Who would have thought the ultimate three-girls-in-the-city flick would premiere not in the flapper-fast 20s, the satin-slouch 30s, or the shoulder-pad 40s, but in the white-glove, bullet-bra 50s? In 1959, with considerable fanfare, Twentieth Century Fox premiered *The Best of Everything*, a title it took seriously. The movie was in CinemaScope, of course, as were all major Fox films after 1953, and the color was by DeLuxe. Indeed, "deluxe" was the operative word, from the orchestral score, as plush as expensive perfume (Shalimar is the boss's last name), to the running time of 121 minutes (twice that of *Three on a Match*), to the skyline-and-sidewalk location work that opens the movie up while holding it down to earth (un-deluxing it a little, letting it breathe). The credit sequence alone is a perk, a thrill, a tone poem to arrival, home movies meet Hart Crane. The camera flies in over a hazy Manhattan at dawn, eyes the city from the far side of the East River (a barge floats by), then glides along Park Avenue like a limo with the windows down. The streets are empty, a strange and lovely sight to any New Yorker, then slowly the rush begins, cars in tunnels and curving off ramps, girls coming up subway stairs at Rockefeller Center, girls swinging hatboxes from Bonwit's as they step out of bomb-shaped buses (Fox in the 50s loved buses).

"All that sublime photography of New York that is also so incredibly dull," says fashion designer Isaac Mizrahi, host of the 1996 New York screening of *The Best of Everything*, a revival-reunion sponsored by American Movie Classics. "They just had a really good day and they shot it, at a slightly good angle. And they're all going to work. You see hundreds of people going to work. It's *so inspiring.*"

Not least because it's carried on the voice of young Johnny Mathis—Cognac and cream—who sings the Alfred Newman–Sammy Cahn title song as if he were hovering between the last longing of the night and the first reverie of the day (sample lyric: "That one little sigh—is treasure / you cannot buy—or measure").

"I loved it," Mathis says of the Oscar-nominated song. "It was absolutely at the beginning. I was living in a broom closet at the Wellington Hotel"—seriously, the manager had put a bed in there—"and

I walked to the studio, which was a long way away, but I composed myself as I was walking."

A slim melody, long-line like the girdles everyone was wearing, it has a rising inflection, lonely, yearning. This was the last song Newman wrote as Fox music director—a legendary run of 20 years—and he marked the score "Moderately (*with much feeling*)," not only setting the tone of the movie, the smooth, poised pace, but also capturing something of the era, the steady surface, the heart's bottled-up position within parentheses. Few movies are such pleasurably perfect time capsules, but then, perfection was a 50s ideal. There would be nothing moderate about the next big three-girl movie: in 1967, *Valley of the Dolls* popped open the bottle and gulped down the time capsule, along with anything else in reach.

No, *The Best of Everything* was a class act. "It was not just another movie," says Julian Myers, a publicist at Fox from 1948 to 1961 "The making of it was relatively high-charged. It had more energy and it had more meaning." It also had a pride of Fox's most promising young stars—Hope (*Peyton Place*) Lange, Stephen (*Ben-Hur*) Boyd, Suzy (top model in the world) Parker, Diane (*Diary of Anne Frank*) Baker, Martha (future wife of producer Hal B. Wallis) Hyer, Robert (future head of production at Paramount Pictures) Evans—and two excellent older men: Brian (English stage actor) Aherne and Louis (*Gigi*) Jourdan. And by God if the queen of the genre doesn't come up at the end of the acting credits, but there it is, "Joan Crawford as Amanda Farrow," a name to make film buffs weep at the rightness (and also the wrong: her first supporting role). The most important credit, though, the muscle behind the movie—the might, really, behind Fox in the late 50s—is the one that comes up first, before the title: "Jerry Wald's Production of."

That apostrophe *s* says it all. No producer in Hollywood history had a bigger embrace than Jerry Wald, or possessed the stuff of movies—genres, plots, scenes, routines, even lines of dialogue—with such brio. His mind, as director Philip Dunne writes in *Take Two*, "was a magpie's nest crammed with situations, characters, and plot devices he had gleaned from his omnivorous reading of every writer from

Euripides to Proust." And his file cabinets were famous in the business, filled with newspaper and magazine stories—"no matter how weird, outlandish, or esoteric," remembers director Richard Fleischer—that might someday point to a film project, a movie the public was growing ready for. For instance, Wald developed the W.W. II movie *Destination Tokyo* from an article in *Time*.

"Wald was bigger than life," says Julian Myers, "not really that tall but big around, and a very colorful guy. Quick to laugh, smile, be jolly, and didn't worry too much about who owned what. His legs moved too fast and richly to be concerned with little things like that."

"He didn't trample on anybody," says actor and director Mel Ferrer, a good friend of Wald's. [Ferrer died in 2008.] Yet Wald never stopped sifting the air for ideas. "He was the only person I ever knew who could write in his pocket," Ferrer continues. "He had a little pad and pencil, and if he had an idea when he was talking to somebody, or when he was looking at a picture, his hand would go into his pocket and he would be writing down his ideas for the plot."

"The important thing about Jerry was his passion for movies," says writer Gavin Lambert, who worked with Wald at Fox and wrote the screenplay for *Sons and Lovers*, a literary property close to Wald's heart. "It was a medium that was his life. No producers are like him today. You see, today, most producers have very little training in movies." [Lambert died in 2005.]

In 1956, still only 44, Wald arrived at the Fox lot with a lifetime of training in movies—not to mention an Irving G. Thalberg Award bestowed in 1948, when he was only 36. A New York City kid born in 1911, the son of a dry-goods salesman, Wald was light on his feet. In college he fast-talked his way into a radio column at the *New York Evening Graphic*, jumped from there to film with a series of two-reelers featuring radio stars, and then landed at Warner Bros. in Hollywood, where he took up screenwriting (*The Roaring Twenties, Torrid Zone, They Drive by Night*). By 1942 he had his first producing credit—a film adaptation of the play *The Man Who Came to Dinner*. Some of the biggest Warner movies of the 40s were Wald's: *Objective Burma!, Mildred Pierce, Humoresque, Johnny Belinda.*

"Just go, go, go all the time," recalls Mel Ferrer, who in 1950 advised Howard Hughes to hire Wald and Norman Krasna to run RKO, which Hughes did (Wald-Krasna Productions, 1950–52, the "Whiz Kids," because of their initials W-K). Hughes got reports from "people" at Warner who said, " 'Jerry Wald will envision a picture and he'll be shooting in seven days,' and it was not entirely untrue," says Ferrer.

Not only that, adds Julian Myers, "he would promote a film before he started it."

"There was a ceaseless flow of fanciful press releases from his office," writes Richard Fleischer in *Just Tell Me When to Cry*. "He made up titles of pictures, attached the biggest star names in town to them, and gave them to a gullible, eager press who unhesitatingly printed everything. If a star bothered to deny it publicly, which rarely happened, Wald would get his name mentioned all over again. Two for one."

———

Despite the fact that Wald was a mensch, beloved by those he worked with, the speed of his rise, his frightening energy, plus his panache with publicity led some to compare him to that infamous Hollywood operator Sammy Glick, the main character of Budd Schulberg's 1941 best-seller, *What Makes Sammy Run?* It wasn't a compliment. Wald laughed it off, but friends are still quick to his defense, chalking the charge up to jealousy.

Julian Myers: "Jerry was not like that. Jerry Wald was a hail-fellow-well-met."

Gavin Lambert: "Oh God, there were so many candidates for [Glick]. Jerry had a lot of energy, that's true. But he did not have Sammy Glick's attitude to movies, which was a purely cynical one. And Sammy Glick was a sort of semi-illiterate. Well, that's not Jerry at all."

Says the book's author, Budd Schulberg, himself an admiring friend: "It was ironic we should end up working together on two projects [*The Harder They Fall, The Enemy Within*], insofar as many people did point to Jerry Wald as being the model for Sammy Glick." And was he? "One. But not the only one. He had an enormous enthusiasm for movies, and he also wanted to do some more honest kinds of films. So in that way I'd say he was quite different from Sammy."

Wald went to Fox as an independent producer who would release through the studio. And Fox needed him. The studio chief and founder, Darryl Zanuck, was off in France making flops with French girlfriends, and the studio was in the hands of suits who could see nothing higher than the bottom line. Wald had his own lot, separate from the rest, tantamount to a little empire within a larger one ("Quite unique," says Myers). In no time he was producing more movies—often three or four simultaneously—than all of Fox's other producers combined. In 1957 this "one-man studio," as *The New York Times* would call him, sent out his first mega-hit for Fox, *Peyton Place*. It was just the kind of "front page" producing he liked: social issues, sensation, location shooting, and a title with potential as a catchphrase. That same year one of Wald's files was whispering. He could see the movie; he needed the book.

If there was one thing Wald loved as much as movies, it was writers. Perhaps because he'd been one, he knew, as Schulberg puts it, "he didn't have the qualities of a serious writer, and I think he both envied and very much respected those qualities in writers. He catered to writers in a way that a Zanuck never would." And it didn't matter if they were famous (Wald knew William Faulkner and was close with Clifford Odets) or just starting out.

"He treated you as an equal, never pulled rank," says Gavin Lambert. "Working on the script was, I think, the part of moviemaking he liked most."

———

Making the rounds of New York publishing houses, talking to top editors about upcoming books with movie potential, and looking for new writers who might have what he needed, Wald was waiting to see Jack Goodman, editor in chief of Simon & Schuster, when a 25-year-old Radcliffe grad came in to meet her college friend Phyllis Levy, who was Goodman's secretary. Phyllis introduced Rona Jaffe to Jerry Wald. Goodman entered the room and said, "Rona's going to write a hell of a novel someday."

"And we're going to publish it," Phyllis added.

To which Wald said, "I'm looking for a modern *Kitty Foyle*. A book about working girls in New York."

It was a reference to the 1940 film that won Ginger Rogers an Oscar for best actress. *Kitty Foyle* wasn't a three-girl movie (though Kitty does have two roommates), but it was a successful woman's pic, the story, according to the movie's prologue, "of a white-collar girl" who braves "that 5:30 feeling" while waiting for Mr. Right. And it had a hospital scene actresses kill for, super sudsy, a soliloquy of sorrow for Rogers—face framed in white sheets—who has just lost her out-of-wedlock baby.

Jaffe read the book by Christopher Morley and thought it was dumb. "He kept making an issue about Kitty getting her period," says Jaffe. [She died in 2005, a year after she spoke with *Vanity Fair*.] "I thought, He doesn't know anything about women. I know about women. I'm in an office." Still, she let it drop. But when Jaffe and Levy went to Hollywood on vacation, they called up Wald for lunch, and Jaffe, casting about for conversation, said, "'I'm going to write that working-girl book.'

"So he said he was going to produce it, and he sent me over this ton of scrapbooks that he'd collected on girls, with all this stuff like Tampax ads—it was really crazy. And then coming back on the train from California, coming into New York I got this vision of the beginning of the book, which is all the girls walking to work." The train ride produced a title too, a phrase remembered from *The New York Times*, a help-wanted ad that began: You Deserve the Best of Everything.

Jaffe wrote under the daily supervision of S&S's rising star and eventual editor in chief, Robert Gottlieb (Goodman had died suddenly of a heart attack). Charging her to "look back in horror and write," he called Jaffe every morning to hear what she'd be working on, then called back at five to hear what she'd written. Meanwhile, Wald was churning out press releases, announcing stars who were signed to *The Best of Everything*, even though none were, names like Paul Newman, Lee Remick, Orson Welles (basically, the cast of Wald's terrific *The Long Hot Summer*). When Jaffe wrote to say she was pleased they'd cast Newman, Wald answered, "Paul Newman will never be in *The Best of Everything*. He's under contract to Warner's. And Jack Warner wouldn't even give you his earwax."

"Jerry was encouraging in a kind of scary way," says Jaffe, "because there was stuff in the paper every day about how he was doing this movie of a book I hadn't written, which he hadn't seen."

The 437-page novel was finished in five months and five days, and Fox bought it for $100,000 before it was even edited. As Michael Korda, another Young Turk S&S editor at that time, has written, *The Best of Everything* was "the very prototype of the hot 'women's novel.'" Wald's synergistic purchase gave the book landmark status in publishing: it meant the studio would help with the marketing. And it put a big spotlight on a young writer. The first-edition book jacket wears an expensive photograph by Philippe Halsman—a chill gray Rockefeller Center on a chill gray day—and half shadowed in the foreground (not stuck in black and white on the back) is the author herself in red kid gloves, a pulp accent on the hands that typed this "unabashed, fact-facing" novel. Despite condescending reviews from sniffy—dare one say sexist?—male critics (*Time:* "It would have been too much to ask that Author Jaffe produce a second *Sister Carrie . . .*"), *The Best of Everything* made the *New York Times* bestseller list by September 21, 1958, two weeks after publication.

"People were just waiting," says Jaffe. "They ran ads for a long time before it came out, things like 'The girl who's in love with the married man is in *The Best of Everything*.' And the second it came out, everybody was reading it."

Though the book is full of white collars and 5:30 feelings, Fox didn't acquire Kitty Foyle exactly—or, rather, it got five Kitty Foyles. The flap copy says, "These are the girls who didn't become wives at twenty. . . . They are today's girls who gravitate to New York to play at careers while they wait for what they really want: a husband and a home." And Jaffe would know. She interviewed 50 women about their lives to make sure her own experiences weren't an anomaly. "This is a sociological novel," she says. Sequences like April Morrison's abortion, when she's driven in a black Cadillac to a doctor in New Jersey—more shocking, sad, and true than Mary McCarthy's famous "pessary" scene in 1963's *The Group*—are based on the confessions of friends. "These things happened to people," says Jaffe. "They didn't even give you anesthetic, because they thought they might be raided and they wanted you to be up, to run away." Sensation, social issues, and a winning title. While the book was enjoying its five months on the best-seller list, the movie was well under way.

Jaffe decided not to do the screenplay, because she didn't know how. She wasn't thrilled, though, when the writer they hired, first-timer Mann Rubin (his background was in television), said, according to Jaffe, "'Oh, I know these girls. They're the ones that wouldn't go out with me when I lived in New York. I'm going to show them.' I thought, Oh my God, he hates my girls."

"I never said that," insists Rubin, who went on to an award-winning career and is proud of his contribution to the script. "I got the assignment from Jerry Wald, who asked me if I'd ever dated young career women in New York. And I said, 'Every chance I got.'"

Dates or no dates, it wasn't a match. Having written three drafts, Rubin—young, feisty, and not the least bit interested in teaming on the screenplay—was replaced by Edith Sommer, a reliable hand.

"Edith was a very good solid writer," says Gavin Lambert. "And *The Best of Everything* was the kind of thing she was best at, what *Variety* used to call 'a good programmer,' which meant a superior commercial movie."

And who better to direct a superior commercial movie than Hollywood pro, Zanuck favorite, and crown prince of the three-girl movie Jean Negulesco?

———

He was a Wald favorite, too. Negulesco had come up through Warner Bros. in the 40s, directing movies in which his *noir* flair in black and white—developed as a painter in Paris in the 20s and as a Hollywood sketch artist for title designs in the 30s—blossomed darkly, orchids in the dusk. In fact, some cite Negulesco's first success, *The Mask of Dimitrios* (1944), as the first *film noir*. It was at Warner that Negulesco forged a friendship with Wald, doing superb work directing two Wald greats, *Humoresque* and *Johnny Belinda*. Jack Warner fired Negulesco for the latter, mid-picture, hating the pictorial approach: too much silence, too many mood shots. Wald told Warner, "If Negulesco leaves the picture I leave the studio." In 1948, *Johnny Belinda* was nominated for 12 Academy Awards. Negulesco, however, was done with Jack Warner. He'd been summoned by Zanuck, and that same year he made an odd, compelling, *noir*-ish hit for Fox, *Road House*, starring Ida Lupino. Still, his *noir* days were numbered.

———

Of Romanian birth, Negulesco was charming, worldly, a womanizer supreme—his bungalow on the Fox lot, where he invited ladies for lunch, was known as his "bangalow," where he sometimes had *them* for lunch. "Poor Dusty," Wald's widow, Connie, says of Negulesco's beautiful wife, "[she] had to put up with a lot." The couple quickly became members of Zanuck's croquet-playing inner circle (Zanuck on Negulesco: "Jesus, he was cunning. . . . He was always complaining that someone had committed a foul on his ball"), and Fox was good to Negulesco materially. But, artistically, he would soon be up against huge odds—how to be stylish within the vast, static, cruise-ship bloat of CinemaScope in DeLuxe color, Hollywood's panoramic answer to the audience-stealing TV screen. Negulesco's last regular-format, black-and-white film at Fox—*Titanic*—feels like an omen. Film critic Andrew Sarris, in his book *The American Cinema*, puts it bluntly: "Jean Negulesco's career can be divided into two periods labeled B.C. and A.C., or Before CinemaScope and After CinemaScope."

Sarris sees it as a qualitative difference, but the divide is also gender-oriented—a creative, masculine dynamic in black and white versus the slower, chattier, color-me-spring woman's picture. Negulesco happened to be very good with women.

"He adored women, was terrific with them," says Leslie Astaire, whose father, Monty Berman, of the famous costume company Berman's, was a good friend of Negulesco's. "He made you feel that he was concentrating on you."

And there were a lot of women at Fox on whom to concentrate (Zanuck concentrated on a new one daily, from 4 to 4:30). When CinemaScope came in and the three-girl movie seemed a good way to fill out that wide screen, Negulesco was Zanuck's pick to direct. And the movies made money. Where *Johnny Belinda* was Negulesco's greatest critical success, it was 1953's *How to Marry a Millionaire*, his first movie in CinemaScope and his first try at three-girls-in-the-city, that drew the biggest box office of his career. In 1954 he directed two more three-girl hits: *Three Coins in the Fountain*, much of it shot in Rome,

and *Woman's World,* back in New York. All three films had long location openings under the credits, like travelogues or tourist snapshots—
the most interesting camerawork on each reel (yet none comparable to
The Best of Everything's opening). In scenes done on Fox sets, it's
pretty much actresses trying to look natural in football-field living
rooms with prop-shop furniture oddly scaled. There were some delicious performances—Monroe in *Millionaire,* hilarious in Coke-bottle
lenses; Arlene Dahl in *Woman's World,* a whipped-cream diva—but
Negulesco doesn't have much to do in these mindless rooms. As for
the three-girl genre, where once it had been a classic cautionary tale,
in these films it was a bit sitcom, the girls all good, if silly to various
degrees, and the ending happy, if padded out like the decade's worst
Dior cocktail dresses. The tale had lost its teeth.

———

The Best of Everything was different. To begin with, the book had
five girls, and bad things happened to them. There's virginal Caroline
Bender, who throws herself into work after her fiancé marries another; Gregg Adams, the aspiring actress who loves, then stalks, a
controlling theater director; April Morrison, a daisy plucked and
tossed; Barbara Lemont, a divorcée in love with a married man; and
plain Mary Agnes, busy planning her wedding. Furthermore, the
movie had a conscience—Rona Jaffe—who was involved every step
of the way. The most important thing, she told Negulesco again and
again, "is that it is real, real, real." She was "a true believer in details,"
Negulesco wrote in his autobiography, *Things I Did . . . and Things I
Think I Did*—"sets, clothes for the girls, their way of living."

Negulesco heeded Jaffe, as did cinematographer William C.
Mellor and the team of three art and two set directors. *The Best of
Everything* rewards the eye at every turn, beginning with the very
first scene, when Hope Lange (Caroline) is about to enter Fabian
Publishing—i.e., the Seagram Building in all its spanking, gleaming,
one-year-old grandeur. As she pauses in front of the building, Lange's
little crop jacket flies open to reveal a polka-dot lining—so right, so
Traina-Norell. In an interview before her death last December,
Lange said it wasn't planned, no wind machine—it just happened.
And that's how the camera works, never pointing anything out, just

gliding like that limousine and taking in details. The Fabian offices—
a set modeled on Pocket Books Inc., the paperback publishers of *The
Best of Everything*—are a Mondrian you could live in, "Broadway
Boogie Woogie" in coral, mustard, French blue. The Fabian desk
lamps, they're like Balenciaga hats. The cramped apartments of editor Amanda Farrow (her chandelier hangs at a mesmerizing shoulder
height) and theater director David Wilder Savage (books, books, and
African art) are two versions of Michael Greer midcentury chic. Look
at the way Lange leans against a wall—that *Vogue* slouch taken straight
from 30s movies—and the way Suzy Parker sleeps on the bus ride to
the company picnic (Fox in the 50s loved company picnics), as if Avedon were only rows away, focusing his Rollei. Notice the pearls, one
strand, two, three, as if the number designated rank within the company. And that subtle code—who wears a hat and who doesn't.

Other details, however, did change. Jaffe remembers what she
calls the Great Virgin Conference, something between *Playboy* and
playing house, where the top men, in all sincerity, "sat around deciding which girl should be a virgin and which shouldn't. They didn't
care what was in the book. They decided this one is and this one isn't.
They decided that Caroline had to have had an affair in college.
And who should be pretty, who should be blonde, who should be
brunette."

There was, as well, a sixth character to consider, Amanda Farrow, the girls' superior at Fabian, an icy older woman mostly absent,
off to matinees (and we don't mean The Theatah) with a married
company V.P. Wald had an idea that the role should go to Joan Crawford. In the 40s he had rescued her career by championing her for
the part of Mildred Pierce (if Crawford owed that Oscar to anyone,
she owed it to Jerry Wald). He'd let her do *Humoresque,* even though
he thought the part too small for her. And when her fourth husband,
Alfred Steele, chairman of Pepsi-Cola, died suddenly of a heart attack, Wald called Crawford a week later. "I thought that coming out
to Hollywood and working would take her mind off her troubles and
be good therapy for her," he told *Life* magazine.

"But it's a nothing part," Negulesco had argued. "She'll never
do it."

Wald: "Not after I put in the scene that every actress will sell her soul to play." He then described the exact same getting-drunk-in-a-smoky-bar scene that Crawford had done in *Humoresque*. Negulesco pointed out the similarity, adding, "It doesn't belong here."

Wald: "It's a good scene, Johnny. And it may get us Crawford." Which it did. (When *The Best of Everything* came out, the scene was gone.)

And then there was the Hays Office. Just as 1957's *Peyton Place* never quite uses the word "rape" (*Anatomy of a Murder,* two years later, was thought daring for tossing the word around), *The Best of Everything* could not use the word "abortion"—in the movie it's "an operation"—and heaven knows the censors couldn't let April-the-innocent (adorable Diane Baker, straight from filming *Journey to the Center of the Earth,* with Pat Boone) actually have one. Instead, in a scene that required stopping all traffic in Central Park for a day, cad boyfriend Dexter Key tells April he's driving her to a doctor—forget marriage—and she jumps out of the moving car, conveniently losing the baby. When she wakes up between white sheets, Caroline bending over her, it's none other than that *Kitty Foyle* hospital scene, but with a 50s twist: the definitive, and probably the most dated, line of the movie (which Jaffe didn't write and thinks "stupid"). Diane Baker delivers the line *with much feeling:* "I'm so ashamed"—face turns away—"now I'm just somebody who's had *an affair."*

"I'm so ashamed," quotes Isaac Mizrahi. "Exactly. I think that's why the movie resonates with homosexual men. The whole plight of women in that time period, it's like homosexuals are living that today. We're like 50 years behind the times. It's true, I tell you, it's true."

April is rewarded for her suffering with a handsome young doctor—played by Ted Otis, a clever extra who was Johnny-on-the-spot when it came time to fill this bit part. Hmm—Kitty Foyle ended up with a doctor, too.

"The handsome doctor," Rona Jaffe harrumphs. "I thought that was more immoral than in the book. Because that's not the way life works."

———————

Casting was done with the usual Wald esprit—contract players, plus catch-as-catch-can. Hope Lange, of the deep-blue angel eyes, and

Diane Baker, both Fox ingenues, were coming off critical successes: Lange in *Peyton Place*, where she played incest victim Selena Cross, and Baker in *Diary of Anne Frank*, where she played Anne's older sister. And for the glam-tragic role of Gregg Adams, why not the most glamorous face in America?

"I wanted Suzy Parker," Jaffe recalls. "I met her on the beach in St. Thomas, when I took myself on vacation. I went up to her and said that I had written a book and I wanted her to be in it. And then I guess she read it and sent Jerry Wald a little note saying she wanted to be Gregg."

Parker, 26, was under contract at Fox, having been recommended for her first real film role (in *Kiss Them for Me*) by Audrey Hepburn. Wald thought she could be a big star, a new Grace Kelly, and in 1959, Parker certainly had presence. Her breeziness, knowingness—those pussycat cheekbones, that tumbling red hair—the way she tips up her chin, lowers her sunglasses, all lend the movie a kind of haunting sophistication, a sensation of the real thing. Nevertheless, Gregg Adams wasn't an easy role. Dumped by theater director David Wilder Savage, Gregg becomes obsessed, unhinged, picks through his garbage, spies from his fire escape. As Parker's Gregg grows needier, the camera tilts and the movie darkens. "It sort of set a tone for my life," confesses Isaac Mizrahi. "The whole loneliness of all the different romances gone wrong. Suzy Parker and Louis Jourdan—oh, that's such a sad, horrible plot." (During filming, Parker was early in her first pregnancy—a happy thing, daughter Georgia—which may have added to her bloom.)

Though Hope Lange was the unspoken star of the movie, it became quite clear that Joan Crawford, then 55, was the star of the set. She arrived at the studio in a limousine. She swept in, dressed to the nines, with an entourage that included a hairdresser, makeup artist, wardrobe mistress, secretary, chauffeur, and stand-in (all the other girls shared Fox staffers), and nobody would say good morning until she said it first. Crawford played the ice-queen editor in the movie, and, fittingly, when she was on the set it was kept cold, very cold, six degrees below normal temperature, and not just because she had coolers full of Pepsi for the cast and crew, and a special cooler of 140-proof vodka for herself.

"That was my first awareness," remembers Diane Baker, "that an artist had that kind of [power]. She had to have the set freezing. People caught cold. We all tried to figure it out. Someone came up with the solution; it had to be because of her makeup."

———

And yet, despite the cold, Crawford was in meltdown. She was mourning the loss of Steele, the end of her happiest marriage, and was desperate about money. She told gossip columnist Louella Parsons that she accepted the small role (for which Wald reportedly paid her $65,000) because Steele's death had left her "flat broke." This in turn infuriated the executives at Pepsi-Cola, who felt smeared, so Crawford had to recant the comment, saying there was a "misinterpretation" (which teed off Parsons, who never forgave her). Crawford's drinking was an open secret on the set, and though she was never visibly drunk, Jaffe once saw Madame Perfectionist in mismatched sandals, one turquoise, one beige. Crawford would later say to writer Roy Newquist, "After Alfred died and I was really alone, the vodka controlled me. It dulled the morning, the afternoon, and the night." Did it? On-camera, Crawford was a consummate professional. But off-camera, to the young women around her, she seemed out of control.

"She was pretty much a vulnerable, tear-ridden person, trying to hold it together," says Diane Baker. "She was crying one day, before a take. She was scared to death. I just gave her a positive sign, like 'Yes, you're going to be fine.' It sort of solidified a . . . kindness." In turn, Crawford adopted Baker as a protégée, which was fine until they met again on the set of *Strait-Jacket*, and a recovered Crawford—"She was the boss again"—cut Baker and her scenes down to size.

Suzy Parker, disturbed that some of the younger actresses were treating Crawford like an old has-been, was quick to help her. Parker befriended the aging star, acting, her husband Bradford Dillman says, "as kind of a shield to Joan." What she couldn't know was that she herself, her status as the top model in America, intimidated Crawford. Eve Arnold, who photographed Crawford on the set for *Life* magazine, says, "Joan was in competition with Suzy—she was very much in the news. [But] Joan was smart enough to leave that alone."

The only outright tension was between Hope Lange and Craw-ford, between the star with first billing and the name that came last. Amanda Farrow, after all, was Crawford's first supporting role—a comedown.

"I was fortunate because there was tension," said Lange. "Our scenes were built-in with tension. It had to have been tough to have all of these young upstarts, and there she was in a non-starring role."

Asked just how in or out of control Crawford was on *The Best of Everything*, Eve Arnold says, "Joan Crawford was an actress. It was hard to tell what state of mind she was in. Indeed, she played the part of the widowed wife—little black hat, dressed all in black, sitting at the Pepsi-Cola boardroom table for *Life* magazine."

No doubt Crawford was feeling vulnerable, but clearly she knew how to use that vulnerability. And when it came to delivering her lines, baiting repartee punched up by Gavin Lambert, her darts over the desk take the skin off your nose. Years later, in conversation with Newquist, more baiting: "The youngsters did all right," Crawford said, "but for some reason or other I'm proud to say I sort of walked off with the film. Perhaps it was the part—I had all the balls—but I think it was a matter of experience, knowing how to make the most of every scene I had."

Still later, with biographer Lawrence J. Quirk, the truth: "All those young bitches," she called them.

⸻

The men were easier. Both Louis Jourdan and Brian Aherne did the movie as a favor to their good friend Negulesco. (Jourdan was also in Zanuck's croquet circle, and the best player of all.) Aherne, who'd cut his teeth touring with the playwright Dion Boucicault, Jr., and who'd conquered Broadway with actress Katharine Cornell, plays the lascivi-ous Mr. Shalimar with a twinkle and a sigh, twirling his lines like the ends of a mustache. (Note to film queens: Marlene Dietrich report-edly rated Aherne the best lover she'd ever had.) As David Wilder Savage, Jourdan plays with a light touch and a cold eye. Both men brought their skills to bear on the script (Wald was known for endless tinkering), with Aherne writing a scene of cozy camaraderie between

Shalimar and Farrow, and Louis Jourdan adding the Ping-Pong ball speech—"You're reaching for your hat with every word."

Dashing Stephen Boyd was a coup for the movie, considered a hot property because of his big role in the upcoming spectacle *Ben-Hur*. There, he was the sadistic Messala, stealing scenes from Charlton Heston; here, he's editor Mike Rice, a lush and a gent, the man who waits for Caroline, who in turn rescues him. Boyd was well liked, a nice guy with a quiet side, an actor's actor, as respected by his colleagues as the other young male lead, gleaming Robert Evans, a part-time actor, part-time businessman (Evan Picone, women's sportswear), was not.

"I suppose the title of my current picture, *The Best of Everything*, sounds like the story of my life," Evans told *The Saturday Evening Post*. "The truth is that I've been bedeviled by frustrations since I started balancing two careers. . . . In Hollywood most actors give me the big-freeze treatment when I walk onto a set. To them I'm a pants manufacturer out for kicks."

Norma Shearer groomed Evans to play her husband Irving Thalberg in *Man of a Thousand Faces*. Zanuck groomed Evans to play a Valentino of a matador in *The Sun Also Rises*. Now Wald was grooming Evans as the new Tyrone Power. "Groomed" was the word. Lange, Baker, and Jaffe all describe young Evans the same way— "slick"—beginning with the Brylcreem. Negulesco, who took an instant dislike to Evans, got furious every time Evans went into the bathroom: "He's in there combing his hair," Negulesco would fume. In fact, he didn't even want to audition Evans. "Over my dead body," he roared when Jaffe suggested it. She, however, saw the likeness between Robert Evans and Dexter Key—"I thought it was a compliment," Evans says, "until I read the book"—and as Evans was dying for the part, she got him a reading. He wasn't bad, and watching the movie you can't say he's not convincing as a cad. But if he was hoping for more respect as an actor, *The Best of Everything* didn't bring it. Evans's fourth film was his last.

———

There tended to be a merry atmosphere on Wald sets. He was a great family man, that rare Hollywood mover who was true to his wife. His ebullience, his kindness (he was ruthless where he needed to be, when it came to the finances of moviemaking), made people want to be around him. Diane Baker: "I used to go back to his office whenever I wasn't on the set or working. I'd pop over and, usually, guess who was there. Bob Evans. He spent a lot of time trying to learn producing from Jerry Wald."

"That's very true," says Evans. "I knew one thing. I wanted to move on. I wanted to be him and not me." Evans did move on, producing such critical and popular successes as *Rosemary's Baby, Love Story, The Godfather,* Parts One and Two, and *Chinatown*—a hit parade described in his memoir (and the award-winning film), *The Kid Stays in the Picture.*

Negulesco was as easygoing as Wald. "He was a kick to work with," said Hope Lange. "He was a big flirt. He used to call me Miss Slivovitz. At the same time, he was disciplined. He knew what he wanted."

"He exactly knew what he wanted us to do," seconds Baker. "And we just did it. And for that reason I think it was great fun to be on that picture. And you can tell it."

The scenes with Lange, Parker, and Baker—the three roommates—"those scenes with the three of us were fun scenes to play," says Baker. Suzy Parker, "she was very funny and we all laughed. Hope was great. Working with all of the girls, and in that atmosphere, it took a lot of the strain off of you."

Negulesco even softened on Robert Evans, ending up good friends with him. "He gave me a great line," Evans recalls. Quote: "When I was your age, Bob, I used to love to make love. As I got older I used to like to watch people make love. Today I like to watch the people who watch the people make love."

Again, the only pea under the pillow was Crawford. And as far as Negulesco was concerned, it was been-there-done-that. Back in 1946, on the set of *Humoresque,* Crawford had cried when she felt she wasn't getting enough input from Negulesco into her character, Helen Wright. Negulesco solved the problem by drawing a flattering portrait of Crawford as Wright (plus another form of input: they reputedly had an affair). In 1959, Negulesco was no longer swayed by those tears. In fact, he caused a flood of them when, in front of the entire cast, he criticized Crawford's "lousy taste" in art, those kitschy big-eyed Margaret Keanes she collected (of course, he collected Bernard Buffet, iffy in another way). And when Wald asked Crawford to introduce a young actress in a test scene, another contretemps. Crawford insisted on playing the scene holding a bottle of Pepsi (her condition for doing the scene for free). Negulesco objected, to which she said, "No Pepsi-Cola bottle, and Joan Crawford goes home." He replied, "No, Joan. Pepsi-Cola stays, but Negulesco goes home." Again, waterworks. "Crash, tragedy, hysteria," Negulesco reports in his autobiography. "Joan put on menthol tears."

Filming took two months, and when it was done, Wald had a movie considerably longer than the optimal two hours. Test audiences weren't responding to the Martha Hyer–Donald Harron pairing— the most heartrending romance in Jaffe's book, and the most popular. Both were strong actors. For her performance in *Some Came Running*, Hyer had been nominated for an Oscar, and Harron had done serious work on Broadway. The problem was his age; he just didn't meet audience expectations of the older and wiser Sidney Carter. Bit by bit Hyer and Harron were cut from the movie until theirs was merely a mirage of a romance, a glance here, a meeting there, then gone. Gossipy Mary Agnes, played by nightclub comedienne Sue Carson, was never more than a secondary character, salt of the Bronx. No, as *The Best of Everything* moved through final edit, that inviolate law of filmdom imposed itself: No More Than Three. Lange, Baker, Parker. By the time it was finished, *The Best of Everything* was a throwback: *Our Blushing Brides* in Mollie Parnis and pearls.

Press for the movie was very Jerry, an aggressive, creative campaign—the bullet-bra approach. While *The Best of Everything* was much more sophisticated than *Peyton Place*, it was aimed at the same audience (and with the same cinematographer, the movies had a similar look). "There weren't many openly sexy movies at that time, and *Peyton Place* was supposed to be one," says Julian Myers. "It was sort of a naughty picture, so we tried to ride on that notoriety."

Ride they did. In some ads, the *o* in the title's "of" was a wedding band, and the text read, "The story of the girls who claw and scratch their way to the top . . . only to realize too late—there's no wedding ring on their finger!" Snapshots of each couple, each containing a line of dialogue (example: "I had the finest husband . . . too bad he wasn't mine"), would wheel in a circle, or run vertically, like those photo-booth strips. The Halsman cover of Jaffe's book was often reproduced within the ad—a seal of approval—even as Jaffe's sympathetic portrait of single women was being hyped as "The Female Jungle Exposed." A steady drumbeat of coverage led up to the film's release, splashy photo spreads in *Life* magazine on Suzy Parker ("A Gay Soaking for Suzy"), Martha Hyer ("Nothing but the Best"), and Joan Crawford ("The Durable Charms of Joan the Queen"). And in big cities around the country secretaries vied for the title Miss Best of Everything Secretary. The winner got a line in the movie, playing an assistant who chases after Caroline. (She calls, "Oh, Caroline," and Hope Lange answers, "Not now, later, Dinah.")

This promotional strategy—potboiler in pearls!—belies the gentle, contemplative quality that paces the movie, and those Negulesco grace notes, none lovelier than the movie's ending, when Hope Lange leaves the office at five on a Friday, coming out to a blue sky and cool sun, and finds Stephen Boyd waiting. Looking up at him, never speaking, she removes her hat and smooths her hair—a two-part gesture that would be lost to the culture by the mid-60s. Then they turn, never touching, and walk south on Park together. It's all, it's nothing, it's perfect.

———

The Best of Everything had a lavish premiere at New York's Paramount Theatre, a grand old movie house on Broadway. When the reviews began appearing on October 9, 1959, they were mostly positive, though male critics continued to condescend. *Time:* "The Hollywood version of the big city is a sort of cautiously diluted Scotch-and-Sodom."

"Women's picture!" says Jaffe. "They said to me, 'Do you mind that you're known for writing women's books?' I said, 'Why? Because women write about stupid things like relationships, and men write about really important things like killing?' You know, that was their attitude."

"Bound to, I think," says Gavin Lambert. "Because it was that kind of movie. It was deliberately aimed to be a popular hit. It was very successful."

"It was one of the big pictures of the year," says Robert Evans. "And I was the heel of the year."

"A huge hit," says Jaffe. "It was a date movie. I have friends who were married, and their first date was *The Best of Everything*."

As for romance on the set, if the bangalow was busy, it wasn't with any of the stars. Hope Lange and Stephen Boyd lunched daily together in the commissary, and because of these lunches several columnists began to imply that the two were in love. Lange, then married to actor Don Murray, "became so upset over these rumors," wrote *Photoplay*, "that she nearly suffered a nervous breakdown." But of Boyd, who died in 1977, Lange had only fond memories (and she still wondered what aftershave lotion he wore)· "During the film we had a great cama raderie. He had that wonderful Irish charm, and wonderful humor. And anyone who has humor I'm a sucker for."

And the "heel of the year," when it comes to all those pretty Fabian secretaries, he's a gentleman. "I wanted every one of them," says Robert Evans. "And I'm not going to tell you who I got."

But Jaffe's talking. "The only affair on the set I knew of was mine." Who?

"Donald Harron. Just the week he was in New York. He and Martha Hyer were doing a scene in the sculpture garden at MoMA"— it didn't make it into the movie—"and when I saw him I just thought he was so cute. He said, 'You must hate me because I'm so wrong for the part.' And he was—he was much too young. I said I didn't hate him, and then we talked, and then he said, 'Do you want to fall in love with me?' And I said, 'Yes.'

"Isn't that heaven? So 1959. It was so out of *The Best of Everything*."

From *Vanity Fair*, March 2004

CLEOPATRA

When Liz Met Dick

by David Kamp

RIVOLI THEATER, NEW YORK CITY, JUNE 12, 1963

Back in the studio, Johnny Carson was in stitches. *The Tonight Show* had taken the unusual step of hooking up by live remote to the world premiere of *Cleopatra*, and the man he'd deputized to stand outside the Rivoli Theater in Times Square, Bert Parks, couldn't elicit a single upbeat comment from the film's director, Joseph L. Mankiewicz. "Congratulations, Mr. Mankiewicz!" said Parks, agleam with Brylcreem and headwaiter unction. "A wonderful, wonderful achievement!"

Mankiewicz, a stocky, impassive-looking man, had the mien of a Wall Street executive strong-armed into addressing his wife's garden club. "Well," he said warily, "you must know something I don't."

The studio audience roared with laughter. Carson's chuckling bled over the audio track. Parks persevered. "I want to ask you," he said conspiratorially, "whether you are *personally* going to control the sound on the showing of *Cleopatra* tonight. That's the rumor!"

"No," said Mankiewicz, "I think everything connected with *Cleopatra* is beyond my control at the moment."

The studio audience roared again. "Is some of the tension gone?" said Parks, changing tack. "Do you feel a little more at ease now?"

"No, I, uh . . . " Mankiewicz smiled thinly. "I feel as though the guillotine were about to drop."

With that ringing directorial endorsement, the four-hour epic *Cleopatra* unspooled before the public for the first time. It was a crack-up to Carson and company because poor Parks was evidently the only man in town willing to keep up appearances, to pretend that the world had trained its cameras on the *Cleopatra* premiere because it heralded the arrival of a spectacular new filmed entertainment in Todd-AO with color by DeLuxe. The truth was that everyone had come to see the train wreck. Everyone knew that *Cleopatra* was an extraordinarily botched production that had cost $44 million—an unheard-of sum for 1963 which was all the more astounding considering that Hollywood's previous all-time budget record setter, *Ben-Hur*, had only four years earlier cost a mere $15 million, chariot race and all. Everyone knew that *Cleopatra* had nearly gutted the studio that made it, Twentieth Century Fox. Everyone knew that it had taken two directors, two separate casts, two Fox regimes, and two and a half years of stop-start filmmaking in England, Italy, Egypt, and Spain to get the damned thing done.

Above all, everyone knew that *Cleopatra* had given the world "Liz and Dick," the adulterous pairing of Elizabeth Taylor and Richard Burton, irresistibly cast as Cleopatra and Mark Antony. Never before had celebrity scandal pushed so far into global consciousness, with Taylor-Burton pre-empting John Glenn's orbiting of the Earth on tabloid front pages, denunciations being sounded on the Senate floor, and even the Vatican newspaper publishing an "open letter" that excoriated Taylor for "erotic vagrancy." When she signed on for the role, Taylor had already been four times a bride, once a widow, and once a purported home wrecker, but it was during the making of *Cleopatra* that she truly transcended the label of mere "movie star" and became, once and for all, *Elizabeth Taylor*, the protagonist in a still-running extra-vocational melodrama of star-crossed romance, exquisite jewelry, and periodic emergency hospitalizations.

"It was probably the most chaotic time of my life. That hasn't changed," says Taylor, who has seldom discussed the *Cleopatra* experience publicly. "What with *le scandale,* the Vatican banning me, people making threats on my life, falling madly in love . . . It was fun and it was dark—oceans of tears, but some good times too."

For old Hollywood, *Cleopatra* represented the moment when the jig was up. No longer would anyone buy the studio system's sanitized, pre-packaged lives of the stars, nor would the stars and their agents bow in obeisance to the aging moguls who'd founded the place. It was the moment when every schnook on the street became an industry insider, fluent in *Variety*ese, up to speed on Liz's "deal" ($1 million against 10 percent of the gross), aware that a given film was *x* million dollars overbudget and needed to earn back *y* million dollars just to break even. *Heaven's Gate, Ishtar, Waterworld*—the modern narrative of the "troubled production" began here, though none of these films would come close to matching *Cleopatra* for sheer anarchy, overreach, and bad Karma. Here, too, originated the mixed-blessing concept of "the most expensive movie ever made": in strict economic terms, *Cleopatra* still holds the title. *Variety* estimated *Cleopatra*'s cost in current-day dollars to be $300 million, a full $100 million more than *Titanic*'s. Even if you perform a straightforward consumer-price-index conversion of the $44 million figure, *Cleopatra*'s adjusted-for-inflation budget comes out at $231 million.

———

Mankiewicz called *Cleopatra* "the toughest three pictures I ever made," and his epitaph for the film—that it was "conceived in a state of emergency, shot in confusion, and wound up in a blind panic"—is one of filmdom's most famous quotes. Even now the movie's survivors talk of its making almost as if they're discussing a paranormal experience. "There was a certain . . . madness to it all," says Hume Cronyn, who played Sosigenes, Cleopatra's scholarly adviser. [Cronyn died in 2003.] "It wasn't anything as clear as 'Richard Burton is moving out on his wife, Elizabeth is leaving Eddie Fisher.' It was much more complicated, more levels than that. . . . Paparazzi in the trees. . . . We were weeks behind. . . . Hanky-panky going on in this corner and that. . . . There were wheels within wheels within wheels. *God,* it was a messy situation."

Although it ended up turning a small profit and winning modest critical acclaim, *Cleopatra* had grim aftereffects on many of its principals. Mankiewicz would never again attain the brilliance and prolificacy of his late-40s-to-late-50s peak, during which he pulled off the still-unmatched feat of winning four Oscars in two years: for writing and directing *A Letter to Three Wives* (1949) and *All About Eve* (1950). "*Cleopatra* affected him the rest of his life," says his widow, Rosemary, who worked as his assistant on the film. "It made him more sensitive to the other blows that would come along." Mankiewicz would make only three more features, concluding with the minor gem *Sleuth* in 1972, and then spend his final 21 years disillusioned and idle, "finding reasons not to work," in the words of his son Tom.

Taylor and Burton, in *Cleopatra*'s aftermath, would marry each other twice, make one good movie together, Mike Nichols's *Who's Afraid of Virginia Woolf?*, and otherwise fritter away their acting careers on a series of blowsy, drink-sodden exhibitions of international jet-set filmmaking: *The V.I.P.s, The Sandpiper, The Taming of the Shrew, Dr. Faustus, The Comedians, Boom!, Divorce His, Divorce Hers*.

As for the film's producer, the 68-year-old legend Walter Wanger, he would never make another movie. He had meant for *Cleopatra* to be a happy culmination of a distinguished career that had begun in 1921, when he persuaded Paramount to put Rudolph Valentino in *The Sheik*. Instead, he was forced on premiere night to sit queasily through a movie he hadn't seen, having been aced out of *Cleopatra*'s postproduction phase by Twentieth Century Fox president Darryl F. Zanuck, who targeted him as a prime suspect in the whole mess. And though the concept had been his in the first place, Wanger stood outside the ropes with the hoi polloi, watching as Mankiewicz, Zanuck, Rex Harrison (who played Julius Caesar), and Roddy McDowall (who played Octavian) made their entrances.

And where on this magical night at the Rivoli were the two people everyone wanted to see, Taylor and Burton? In England, where Burton was filming *Becket*. "We'd just had it with *Cleopatra* by then," says Taylor. "The whole thing. It was years of my life." A few weeks later, however, Taylor reluctantly hosted a London screening of the film. She dutifully sat through the picture, mortified by the memories it evoked and the butchery, as she perceived it, of Mankiewicz's vision. Immediately afterward, she hurried back to the Dorchester Hotel, where she was staying—and threw up.

AN INAUSPICIOUS BEGINNING:
NEW YORK, LOS ANGELES, 1958–59

> *"He would never have pulled the plug on* Cleopatra. *That would have been like giving up a child."*
> —STEPHANIE GUEST, DAUGHTER OF WALTER WANGER

Everyone in the movie business loved Walter Wanger—he spoke well, was Dartmouth-educated, wore Savile Row suits, and was reliably couth and hail-fellow-well-met, the antithesis of the shouters who ran things.

Wanger had wanted to do a Cleopatra picture for years. There had been others—a 1917 silent version with Theda Bara; the opulent Cecil B. DeMille version of 1934, featuring Claudette Colbert; and, in 1946, a soporific British adaptation of George Bernard Shaw's play *Caesar and Cleopatra,* starring Claude Rains and Vivien Leigh. But Wanger hoped to surpass them all with an intelligent treatment and a star in the lead who was, in his words, "the quintessence of youthful femininity, of womanliness and strength." He found his ideal Queen of the Nile in 1951, when he saw Elizabeth Taylor in George Stevens's *A Place in the Sun.*

But that year Wanger was not in the best position to do a deal. After a couple of decades as one of Hollywood's more successful independent producers, responsible for such films as *Queen Christina,* with Greta Garbo, and John Ford's *Stagecoach,* he'd fallen upon a hitless period, the ignominy of which was compounded by the discovery that his wife, the actress Joan Bennett, was having an affair with her agent, Jennings Lang of MCA. On December 13, 1951, in an act that froze Hollywood in disbelief, Wanger staked out Bennett and Lang in the MCA parking lot, pulled out a pistol, and shot Lang in the groin. That Wanger got off as lightly as he did—serving only a four-month sentence at a Southern California "honor farm" in mid-1952—was in large part a testament to how well liked he was: Samuel Goldwyn, Harry and Jack Warner, Walt Disney, and Darryl Zanuck contributed to his legal fund.

By 1958, Wanger's comeback was in full swing (he had recently produced Don Siegel's thriller *Invasion of the Body Snatchers* and Robert Wise's *I Want to Live!*, for which Susan Hayward would win the 1959 Academy Award for best actress), and his thoughts returned to his dream project. On September 30 he took his first meeting about *Cleopatra* with Spyros Skouras, then the president of Twentieth Century Fox. Skouras, a snow-haired contemporary of Wanger's, was amenable, but he envisioned something more modest than what Wanger had in mind. During their meeting, Skouras had a secretary excavate the ancient script for the soundless 1917 *Cleopatra*—produced by the Fox Film Corporation, Twentieth Century Fox's progenitor—and said, "All this needs is a little rewriting. Just give me this over again and we'll make a lot of money."

Fox was not a well-run operation in the late 50s. All the studios were suffering from the rise of television and the court-ordered dissolution of the studio system, but Skouras and company were having a particularly rough time of it—an internal report published in 1962 reported a four-year loss of about $61 million. "We were the only people who could put John Wayne, Elvis Presley, and Marilyn Monroe in movies and *not* have them do any business," says Jack Brodsky, a Fox publicist during the *Cleopatra* years. [Brodsky died in 2003.]

One reason for Fox's weak programming was the departure in 1956 of its founder and resident genius-dynamo, chief of production Darryl Zanuck, who, burned out after 23 years on the job, quit to become an independent producer. Zanuck's replacement was Buddy Adler, who had produced *From Here to Eternity* and *Love Is a Many Splendored Thing* but proved to be an ineffectual executive. As long as Zanuck had been in place, the New York–based Skouras, a Greek immigrant who'd worked his way up from owning a single movie theater in St. Louis, had kept his distance from Los Angeles and the filmmaking process. With Adler, however, Skouras felt no such inhibitions, and began to meddle heavily.

———————

Skouras was no creative genius, but he had made one important strategic move that temporarily "saved" the industry from television— namely, he kicked off the wide-screen era by making *The Robe,* a 1953 biblical epic starring Richard Burton, with the studio's new CinemaScope technology. That film's success ($17 million gross on a budget of $5 million) made Skouras a hero in Hollywood, and soon every studio was rushing out mastodonic sandswept period epics in rival wide-screen processes such as WarnerScope, TechniScope, and VistaVision.

But by the time Wanger was trying to get *Cleopatra* off the ground, the bloom of CinemaScope had withered. The budget-minded Adler envisioned a modest backlot picture, costing perhaps a million dollars or two, starring a Fox contract player such as Joan Collins, Joanne Woodward, or Suzy Parker. Wanger continued to argue his case for Taylor, whom Skouras didn't want, because "she'll be too much trouble."

On June 19, 1959, Wanger received his first preliminary operating budget for *Cleopatra:* 64 days' shooting at a cost of $2,955,700, exclusive of cast and director salaries— expensive by melodrama standards, but a piddling amount for an epic. The decade had seen one record-setting megaproduction after another, starting with Mervyn LeRoy's *Quo Vadis* (1951, $7 million) and continuing on with Richard Fleischer's Jules Verne fantasy, *20,000 Leagues Under the Sea* (1954, $9 million), Cecil B. DeMille's *The Ten Commandments* (1956, $13 million), and William Wyler's *Ben-Hur* (1959, $15 million).

By late summer, a reputable British writer named Nigel Balchin had been hired to put together a script, a $5 million budget was deemed acceptable, and the names of Taylor, Audrey Hepburn, Sophia Loren, Gina Lollobrigida, and Susan Hayward were being discussed for the title role. On September 1, Wanger made his first formal overture to Taylor, who was in London filming *Suddenly Last Summer* with Joseph Mankiewicz. Over the telephone, she demanded—

half-jokingly, she would later say—a million dollars, something no actress had ever been paid for one movie.

Finally, on October 15 Fox staged a photo opportunity at which Taylor pretended to sign her million-dollar contract. The wire services sent out the photo to newspapers across the country, and now Wanger's idea was the world's: Elizabeth Taylor as Cleopatra.

GETTING NOWHERE:
NEW YORK, LOS ANGELES, LONDON, 1959-60

> *"Gentlemen: You are wasting money on Liz Taylor.*
> *Nobody wants to see her after the way she treated that*
> *sweet little Debbie Reynolds. Everyone loves Debbie. She*
> *is what the teenagers call a doll. Ginger Rogers is still*
> *popular, but Liz is not liked anymore. I heard a group of*
> *teenagers talking about Liz. They said, 'She is a stinker.'*
> *They're right."* —LETTER SENT TO BUDDY ADLER AND
> WALTER WANGER BY A WOMAN IN BEAUMONT, CALIFORNIA,
> OCTOBER 1959

It is the wisdom of those who consider themselves experts on the subject that Mike Todd, the producer-showman behind *Around the World in 80 Days,* was "the love of Elizabeth Taylor's life." But less than six months after Todd died in a plane crash outside Albuquerque in March 1958—leaving the 26-year-old Taylor alone with an infant daughter, Liza, and the two sons she'd had with her second husband, Michael Wilding—she was seen stepping out with her late husband's friend and protégé, Eddie Fisher. Fisher, a pompadoured, haimish 30-year-old pop idol, was famous for his shrewdly publicized union with Debbie Reynolds; together they had two children and were known as "America's sweethearts." But by the time Taylor and Fisher married in Las Vegas in May of 1959, the public goodwill both had built up had evaporated, and they were the target of constant moral dudgeon and tabloid surveillance.

Skouras's intuition that Taylor would be "trouble" wasn't entirely unfounded, in that she had a predisposition toward illness, and alarmed moralists. Then again, she had soldiered on through *Cat on a Hot Tin Roof,* the film she was in the midst of making when Todd died, fulfilled her obligation to *Butterfield 8,* the last film she owed to MGM under her contract there, and delivered a first-rate performance in *Suddenly Last Summer.*

Reaching over Wanger's head, Skouras tapped an old friend, Rouben Mamoulian, to be *Cleopatra's* director. The 61-year-old Mamoulian was a gifted visualist, was accustomed to policing large groups of people, and had directed the original Broadway productions of *Porgy and Bess, Oklahoma!,* and *Carousel,* as well as the films *Dr. Jekyll and Mr. Hyde, Becky Sharp,* and *Silk Stockings.* But he had a reputation for being temperamental, and his filmmaking skills were rusty—apart from *Silk Stockings,* from 1957, he had made only one movie in the last 17 years. The screenwriter Nunnally Johnson (*The Grapes of Wrath*), whom Fox had hired to write additional dialogue for Balchin's screenplay, was skeptical. "I bet Walter Wanger that [Mamoulian] would never go to bat," Johnson wrote to his friend Groucho Marx. "All he wants to do is 'prepare.' A hell of a preparer. Tests, wardrobe, hair, toenails. . . . [But] if you make him start this picture, he will never forgive you to his dying day. This chap is a natural born martyr."

———

Late in 1959, the Fox hierarchy committed its first howler of a mistake: deciding, despite obvious meteorological evidence to the contrary, that England was an ideal place to shoot a sunbaked Egyptian-Roman epic. The decision was money-driven—the British government offered generous subsidies to foreign productions that employed a certain percentage of British crew.

Adler died of cancer the following July. His death created even more of a power vacuum at the studio, but the movie's chief detractor at Fox was out of the way. On July 28, 1960, Taylor finally signed a real contract. The film was to be shot not in CinemaScope but in Todd-AO, a rival wide-screen process developed by Mike Todd, which meant that Taylor, as Todd's beneficiary, would receive additional royalties. It was announced that Peter Finch would play Caesar and that Stephen Boyd, Charlton Heston's co-star in *Ben-Hur,* would play Antony. At the Pinewood Studios, located just outside

London, John DeCuir, one of the best art directors in the business, began construction on a gorgeous, $600,000 Alexandria set covering 20 acres, featuring palm trees flown in from Los Angeles and four 52-foot-high sphinxes.

Right from the start, Mamoulian's *Cleopatra* was a farce. The first day of shooting, September 28, saw two work stoppages by the movie's British hairdressers, who took issue with the presence of Taylor's specially imported American stylist, Sidney Guilaroff. Only after several weeks of negotiation by Wanger was a fragile truce arranged—Guilaroff would style Taylor at her double penthouse suite in the Dorchester, but would not set foot in Pinewood.

Not that Taylor's presence at Pinewood ever became much of an issue. She called in sick on the third day of shooting, saying she had a cold. The cold grew into a lingering fever, and for the next few weeks she remained ensconced in her suite—attended by her husband and several doctors, including Lord Evans, Queen Elizabeth's physician.

Physically and spiritually, the Eddie Fishers were not a healthy couple at the time. Fisher missed the singing career he'd largely forsaken for Taylor, and knew the $150,000 he was being paid by Fox for vague junior-producer duties was really for being Taylor's professional minder. Furthermore, he was strung out on methamphetamine, having gotten hooked in his grueling touring days on "pep" shots administered by Max Jacobson, the notorious "Dr. Feelgood" who provided similar services to John F. Kennedy.

Taylor was in a continual funk because of her ill health, residual grief over the death of Mike Todd, the grim English weather, and the correct intuition that she'd lent her star power to a doomed, disorganized production. In response, she took to drinking and taking painkillers and sedatives. "She could take an enormous amount of drugs," Fisher told Brad Geagley, a senior producer at Walt Disney, in an unpublished 1991 interview for a never completed book concerning *Cleopatra*. "She's written up in medical journals somewhere—that's what she's always told me, and I believe her." (Fisher declined to be interviewed for this story, on the grounds that he wants to save his "explosive, blockbuster stuff" for a memoir he's working on.) [Fisher's *Been There, Done That* came out in 1999.]

While Taylor spent the autumn shuttling between the Dorchester and the London Clinic, where she was variously diagnosed with a virus, an abscessed tooth, and a bacterial infection known as Malta fever, Mamoulian was having his own troubles. Balchin's script remained unsatisfactory to him, and in the rare moments when the sky was clear, the illusion of Egypt was nevertheless shattered by the steam visibly emanating from the actors' and horses' mouths.

Production ground to a halt on November 18, when there was simply no more Mamoulian could do without Taylor and an improved script. The plan was for shooting to resume in January, by which time Taylor would presumably be well and Nunnally Johnson would have finished another script polish.

Back in New York, Skouras sent a copy of the current shooting script to Joseph Mankiewicz, who had made his two Oscar-winning pictures for Fox, and asked the director for a frank critique. Mankiewicz was merciless: "Cleopatra, as written, is a strange, frustrating mixture of an American soap-opera virgin and an hysterical Slavic vamp of the type Nazimova used to play . . ."

On January 18, 1961, with production resumed but still moving at a glacial pace, Mamoulian, bitter and frustrated, cabled his resignation to Skouras. He left behind about 10 minutes of footage, none of it featuring Taylor, and a loss of $7 million.

A NEAR-DEATH EXPERIENCE: LONDON, 1960–61

"I began to look at my life, and I saw a tough situation. In the hospital all the time—I mean, I became a nurse. I was giving her injections of Demerol. I didn't want the doctors to come. I felt sorry for the doctors. I did it for two nights, and whooo-ee. . . . After two nights I said, 'This is crazy.' I actually faked appendicitis to get away." —EDDIE FISHER, RECALLING THE WINTER OF 1960–61

A couple days after Skouras accepted Mamoulian's resignation, a desperate voice broke through the static on Hume Cronyn's telephone in the Bahamas, where he owned a remote island with his wife, Jessica Tandy. "Hume?" said the voice. "Where the hell is Joe?"

It was Charles Feldman, Joe Mankiewicz's Hollywood agent. Mankiewicz was staying with the Cronyns, preparing the screenplay for *Justine,* his planned follow-up to *Suddenly Last Summer.* Feldman told Mankiewicz that Skouras was offering the moon for him to rescue *Cleopatra.* The director was skeptical, but that didn't stop him from flying immediately to New York to meet Skouras for lunch at the Colony.

"Spyros," he said, "why would I want to make *Cleopatra?* I wouldn't even go see *Cleopatra.*"

Indeed, gifted as he was, Mankiewicz seemed the last person qualified (or inclined) to helm a big-budget spectacle. "His movies were dialogue-based and staged like plays, like *All About Eve,* where most of the action, where there *is* action, is people coming down stairs or going in and out of doors," says Chris Mankiewicz, the director's older son, who took time off from college to work on *Cleopatra.* Skouras recognized, however, that the elder Mankiewicz was a great writer and skilled diva-wrangler, having finessed the egos of Taylor and Katharine Hepburn on *Suddenly Last Summer,* and Bette Davis on *All About Eve.*

Mankiewicz consented to take over the project when Skouras made an offer he couldn't refuse: Fox would not only place him on salary, but also pay $3 million for Figaro, the production company he co-owned with NBC. For a 51-year-old man whose glorious career had never quite made him rich, the prospect of overnight million-airedom was irresistible. "He was seduced by the opportunity," says Chris Mankiewicz. "He never saw a penny from *All About Eve.* Now, for once in his life, they were all coming to him. All of a sudden you've got the 'Fuck you' money."

Cleopatra seemed, for a flicker of a moment, to be in good, sane hands. Mankiewicz, citing as his inspirations Shaw, Shakespeare, and Plutarch, set about creating a totally new script for the movie. He enlisted two writers to help him, the novelist Lawrence Durrell (whose *Alexandria Quartet* was the basis for Mankiewicz's *Justine* script) and the screenwriter Sidney Buchman (*Mr. Smith Goes to Washington*). Wanger, elated by Mankiewicz's "modern, psychiatrically rooted concept of the film," thought he was at last getting the upscale *Cleopatra* he'd dreamed of.

Alas, this period of promise was when Taylor suffered what probably still qualifies as her nearest near-death experience. Late in February she returned to London from a vacation on the Continent with what her doctors described as "Asian flu," caught while rushing back to attend to her suddenly "appendicitis"-stricken husband. By March, the Asian flu, or whatever it was, had complicated itself into double pneumonia, and Taylor was sedated and prone in an oxygen tent in the Dorchester. On the night of March 4, 1961, she fell comatose. She was rushed once again to the London Clinic, Fisher at her side screaming, "Let her alone! Let her alone!," as paparazzi leaned in to get photographs of her unconscious. The diligence of the Fleet Street press ensured that within hours an international deathwatch was in place, some papers already reporting that Taylor was dead.

"I was pronounced dead four times," says Taylor. "Once, I didn't breathe for five minutes, which must be a record." Doctors performed an emergency tracheotomy to alleviate congestion in her bronchial passages. The operation saved her life, and by the end of the month she was back home with Fisher in Los Angeles, convalescing. Several months later she underwent plastic surgery to conceal the incision mark at the base of her throat, but it wasn't successful; the scar is visible in the finished film.

Calamitous as the whole episode was, it produced two seemingly serendipitous effects. First, it bought Mankiewicz six months to get his *Cleopatra* together while Taylor recovered. Second, Taylor's public image was overnight transformed from home-wrecking pariah to heartstring-pulling survivor; the London Clinic received truckloads of flowers and sympathetic fan mail, even a get-well telegram from Debbie Reynolds. "I had the chance to read my own obituaries," says Taylor. "They were the best reviews I'd ever gotten." During her convalescence, she collected a sympathy best-actress Oscar for *Butterfield 8*, a movie she hated.

Mankiewicz decided to junk Mamoulian's footage and reconstruct the movie from scratch—only Taylor, Wanger, and John De-Cuir, the art director, would carry over to the new incarnation of

Cleopatra. To replace Finch and Boyd, Mankiewicz pursued Trevor Howard and Marlon Brando, the latter of whom had played Mark Antony in the director's 1953 adaptation of Shakespeare's *Julius Caesar.* But neither actor was available, so Mankiewicz set his sights on Rex Harrison, whom he had directed in *The Ghost and Mrs. Muir,* and Richard Burton, then starring on Broadway in *Camelot.*

Skouras hated both choices. Harrison, he said, had never made a profitable movie for Fox, and Burton "doesn't mean a thing at the box office." Indeed, Burton, the 36-year-old product of a dirt-poor Welsh mining family, was perceived in Hollywood to be a great stage actor whose film career had never really taken off. But grudgingly, after strenuous lobbying from Mankiewicz, Skouras gave in. Fox bought out the remainder of Burton's *Camelot* contract for $50,000, signed the actor for $250,000, and got Harrison for $200,000.

———

If you had to peg one of *Cleopatra*'s two male stars as a potential troublemaker on the set, it would be Harrison; Wanger later expressed surprise that he had turned out to be "the good boy." Described by several of his surviving castmates as "the Cunt," Harrison was known for being tetchy, difficult, and condescending. Burton, by contrast, was a charmer, adored by his peers for his erudition, basso speaking voice, Welsh-barroom raconteurship, and sexual magnetism. Though notorious for his philandering—he had romanced such co-stars as Claire Bloom, Jean Simmons, and Susan Strasberg, and had shown up at his first meeting with Wanger, at New York's '21' Club, with a Copacabana dancer on his arm—he invariably returned to his wife, the dignified, mumsie-looking Sybil Burton.

One of the few people who remained oblivious to Burton's charms, in fact, was Elizabeth Taylor. She had met him years before *Cleopatra* at a party at Stewart Granger's house, back when she was a contract player at MGM. "He flirted like mad with me, with everyone, with any girl who was even remotely pretty," she says. "I just thought, 'Ohhh, boy—I'm not gonna become a notch on *his* belt.'"

"ENGLAND ALL OVER AGAIN": ROME, 1961

"It appears that the responsibility for increased costs in connection with the production falls into four categories, namely
   (1) Elizabeth Taylor
   (2) Lack of Planning
   (3) Corruption on part of employees
   (4) Friction between American and Italian Heads
No effort was made at this time to review the first category, due to the danger involved." —Excerpt from a report prepared by Nathan Frankel, C.P.A., who was retained by Twentieth Century Fox in 1962 to determine how the studio's money was being spent on *Cleopatra*

The second go-round of *Cleopatra*, in Italy, was a folly of proportions nearly as epic as the finished film. Once again, the production rushed ahead without a completed script or adequate preparation, an indication of how desperately Skouras wanted to present Twentieth Century Fox's board of directors with a ready-to-release film that would bring in cash and save his regime. Wanger later estimated that if he and Mankiewicz had been given more time to regroup and plan, *Cleopatra* would have cost about $15 million. But Skouras was not exactly at his managerial best in 1961. Taylor, Fisher, and Mankiewicz got a sense of his addled state of mind one night when he joined them for drinks in New York. The others in the group couldn't help but notice that Skouras was addressing Taylor only as "Cleopatra."

"You don't know my name, do you?" Taylor said suspiciously. "You can't remember my name!"

"You are Cleopatra!" Skouras responded.

"You're paying me a million dollars," Taylor said, "and you can't remember my name. Spyros, tell me my name! I'll give you half the money back!"

"Ehh . . . ehh . . . ," Skouras sputtered, "you are Cleopatra!"

By the summer of 1961, *Cleopatra* was practically all Fox had left; short of funds, the studio had canceled most of its other features and had pinned much of its hope on television. The latest in Fox's series of regent studio chiefs was Peter Levathes, a Skouras protégé who had won good notices as the head of the company's television division.

"We decided to move the production to Rome because we thought Elizabeth Taylor would show up more," says Levathes. "The climate would be more to her liking, and she wouldn't call in sick all the time." At Levathes's urging, Skouras granted Fisher's request to fly in Taylor's personal physician, Rex Kennamer of Beverly Hills, for a fee of $25,000.

Interiors and Roman exteriors were now to be shot at Cinecittà, the massive studio complex six miles outside of central Rome. Ancient Alexandria was being reconstructed at Torre Astura, a hunting estate on the Tyrrhenian Sea owned by Prince Stefano Borghese. Some additional work, mostly battle sequences, would be filmed in the Egyptian desert.

Trawling through the voluminous files and correspondence left in *Cleopatra*'s wake, what one takes away is the abject terror Taylor inspired in powerful men. (As Fisher would later say, "One thing I learned from Elizabeth—if you ever need anything, yell and scream for it.") Privately, Wanger, Mankiewicz, Skouras, and Levathes complained about her fragility and erratic work habits, and talked about how she deserved a good telling-off. But in her presence they lost their resolve and genuflected. Skouras and Levathes tried (unsuccessfully) in 1961 to sign her to a four-picture deal with Fox. Wanger set her up in a 14-room mansion in Rome called the Villa Papa, and flew in chili from Chasen's for her. Mankiewicz reportedly shuffled shooting schedules to accommodate her menstrual cycle. "We could only shoot Roman scenes in the Senate [which did not involve Taylor] when Elizabeth was having her period," says Kenneth Haigh, who played Brutus. "She said, 'Look, if I'm playing the most beautiful woman in the world, I want to look my best.'"

But by the time the production had moved to Rome, these men had an even better reason to coddle Taylor than the usual keep-the-talent-happy ethos. Taylor, in the wake of her near-death episode, was now uninsurable. If she walked off or fell ill, the movie—which *was* Elizabeth Taylor—would represent nothing but red ink.

Mankiewicz, between scouting locations, assembling a cast, and consulting with department heads, wasn't close to having a finished screenplay when shooting began on September 25: a mere 132 pages out of an eventual 327, or most of the film's first half ("Caesar and Cleopatra") and none of its second half ("Antony and Cleopatra"). This meant that the film would be shot in continuity, a costly process that would eventually result in 96 hours of raw Todd-AO negative.

Skouras insisted on moving ahead anyway, arguing that "the girl is on salary"—an allusion to Taylor's renegotiated contract, which called for her to work for 16 weeks beginning August 1, with a guarantee of $50,000 for every week *Cleopatra* ran over. Consequently, Mankiewicz would spend the remainder of the production directing by day and writing by night, an impossibly taxing task that, says his widow, "damn near killed him." (Yet another screenwriter, Ranald MacDougall [*Mildred Pierce*], was drafted in, but Mankiewicz still insisted on writing the actual shooting script.)

Casting was done on the fly: a mid-September flurry of telephone calls brought aboard such actors as Hume Cronyn, Martin Landau, and Carroll O'Connor from America and Kenneth Haigh, Robert Stephens, and Michael Hordern from England. But when the actors arrived in Rome, they discovered half-finished sets, incomplete wardrobes, and an exhausted writer-director who hadn't yet written their parts. Says Cronyn, "I arrived the same day as Burton, September 19, 1961. Neither one of us worked until after Christmas."

"I had a 15-week contract, which was long for those days, but it wound up being almost 10 months," says O'Connor, who played Casca, a Roman senator who puts the first knife into Caesar's back. "In all that time, I worked 17 days." [O'Connor died in 2001.]

The chop-chop pace demanded by Skouras resulted in all manner of jaw-dropping blunders that might have been circumvented had there been adequate time to prepare. The beach at Torre Astura, where DeCuir's massive replica of Alexandria was under construction, turned out to be laced with live mines left over from World War II; a $22,000 "mine-dredging" expenditure was added to *Cleopatra*'s ledger. On top of that, the set was adjacent to a NATO firing range. Wrote

Wanger in his diary, "We will have to arrange our schedule so we are not working when the big guns are blasting." And because Italy had no facilities for processing Todd-AO film, the day's rushes had to be sent all the way to Hollywood and then back to Rome before the director could view them.

DeCuir's sets were grandiose and beautiful, but because no one had kept close tabs on his work, Mankiewicz and his crew discovered too late that they were almost unmanageably big. The fake Roman Forum (which cost $1.5 million to build) dwarfed the real one up the road; so much steel tubing was required to hold it up that *Cleopatra* exacerbated a country-wide shortage, palpably affecting the Italian construction business.

As DeCuir's Rome grew, Twentieth Century Fox began to shrink. Earlier in the year, Skouras, desperate to stanch the hemorrhaging of the company's resources, had engineered the sale of the studio's 260-acre Los Angeles lot to the Aluminum Company of America for $43 million, a transaction that would come to resemble Peter Minuit's $24 deal for Manhattan. Though the studio continued to lease 75 acres for its own use (eventually reacquired), the remaining acreage was now being developed into Century City, the gigantic office-building-and-shopping-center complex that stands south of Beverly Hills today. "You could see the village from *The Song of Bernadette,* New York, castles, a real railroad station," recalled Cesare Danova, a Fox contract player who portrayed Apollodorus, Cleopatra's majordomo. "And the first thing that I saw [upon returning to the lot in 1962] was a truck from the Acme Wrecking Company. Everything was coming down. This was a potent sign for me—that the end had come to an entire world."

The sheer size and obvious disorganization of *Cleopatra* made it an easy mark for anyone practiced in the art of graft—a circumstance not lost on many of the Italians hired to work on the picture. "The Italians are wonderful at designing things, but they have this natural proclivity for larceny," says Tom Mankiewicz, the director's younger son, who, like his brother, Chris, took time off from college to work on the film. "Once you start saying, 'All right, I need 500 Praetorianguard outfits, I need 600 Nubian-slave outfits, I need 10,000 soldier outfits'—this is like an *invitation*. And there was no one to stay on top of it all. If you wanted to buy some new dinnerware or a set of glasses for your house, it was the easiest thing to put it on the budget of *Cleopatra*."

"Later I got to see the studio's breakdown on the money waste," says Taylor. "They had $3 million for 'miscellaneous,' and $100,000 for paper cups. They said I ate 12 chickens and 40 pounds of bacon every day for breakfast. *What?*"

Skouras, though the man with ultimate authority, placed a lot of the blame for the film's rampant disorganization on Wanger. "You have to know Walter Wanger well," Skouras later told an interviewer. "He is a fine man, but he likes to have lots of people to help him. Off the record, he does not want to work so hard." Levathes felt that Mankiewicz was a prima donna whose extravagant requests were being indulged by Skouras regardless of financial consequence. Wanger complained with some justification that Skouras and Levathes were undermining his authority by circumventing him in favor of Mankiewicz and the department heads, but too often he merely complained. The surviving actors and crew remember the producer eventually devolving into a sweet but powerless "greeter" whose most visible duty was to escort visiting European royals to the set.

As a bout of torrential, London-like weather precluded outdoor shooting for much of the fall of '61 (at a cost of $40,000 to $75,000 for every day rained out), many of the film's principal actors realized that they were going to be in Rome at least through the spring of '62. So they moved out of the luxurious Grand Hotel and into their own apartments, becoming idle, semi-permanent residents of the city. Given that Fox had to keep the actors on salary the whole time—Hume Cronyn at $5,000 a week, Roddy McDowall at $2,500 a week, Martin Landau at $850 a week, etc.—the cost pileups were tremendous.

At one point in autumn, Skouras and Levathes approached Burton to see if he'd mind terribly if the movie ended with Caesar's assassination, thereby cutting out half of the plot and roughly 95 percent of Antony's part. Burton was succinct. "I'll sue you until you're puce," he told them.

Given the messy state of affairs, morale remained remarkably high on the set. "Everyone was in a very gay way," says O'Connor. "We knew the picture was going to be O.K., even if it wasn't going to be one of the greats." The rushes were impressive enough to prompt hope in some quarters that the film *was* en route to greatness. On Christmas Eve, Fox publicist Jack Brodsky wrote the following to Nathan Weiss, his colleague in New York: "The first 50 pages of the second act have just come from Mank's pen and they're fabulous. Burton and Taylor will set off sparks, and already Fisher is jealous of the lines Burton has."

HELL BREAKS LOOSE: ROME, WINTER 1962

> *"For the past several days uncontrolled rumors have been growing about Elizabeth and myself. Statements attributed to me have been distorted out of proportion, and a series of coincidences has lent plausibility to a situation which has become damaging to Elizabeth . . . "* —STATEMENT ISSUED BY RICHARD BURTON, THEN DISAVOWED BY HIM, ON FEBRUARY 19, 1962

L*e scandale,* as Taylor and Burton later termed their affair, didn't begin until their work together did, in December or January, after Mankiewicz had written enough material for them to start rehearsing the film's second half. "For the first scene, there was no dialogue—we had to just look at each other," says Taylor. "And that was it—I was another notch." Burton further endeared himself to Taylor by showing up hung over. She had feared that he would lord his talent over her and make fun of her lack of theatrical training; instead, she found herself steadying his trembling hands as he lifted a coffee cup to his lips. "He was probably putting it on," Taylor says. "He knew it would get me."

As for Eddie Fisher, he had not been having the best of times in Rome. Though he was on the *Cleopatra* payroll and was trying to learn how to become a movie producer, his presence wasn't expected or needed at Cinecittà. "I remember Eddie one day walking onto the set, trying to be funny, and shouting to Mankiewicz, 'O.K., Joe, let's make this one!'" says Brodsky. "No one reacted. It cast a pall."

"Eddie and I had drifted *way* apart," says Taylor. "It was only a matter of time for us. The clock was ticking."

But right through the end of January, the only suspicion that Fisher held was that Burton was encouraging his wife to drink too much. In his self-described capacity as a nurse, Fisher took exception to the influence the Welshman's prodigious boozing and peaty *joie de vivre* were having on Taylor, who had grown tired of her husband's predilection for dining in. "Remember," says someone who worked on the production, "Elizabeth was a very self-indulgent person at that time, a sensualist who'd just been confronted with possible death, and was probably rebounding from it by tasting as much life as possible."

Several people associated with *Cleopatra* point out that sensualism and high living were the order of the day in Rome, particularly with so little work for the actors to do. "There was a tremendous sense of being in the right place at the right time," says Jean Marsh, who played Antony's Roman wife, Octavia, well before her PBS fame as the creator and star of *Upstairs, Downstairs*. "Fellini was there, and Italy was the capital of film. And the film was so extravagant, so louche, it affected everyone's lives. It was a hotbed of romance— Richard and Elizabeth weren't the only people who had an affair."

Taylor and Burton filmed their first scene together on January 22. Wanger happily noted in his diary, "There comes a time during the making of a movie when the actors become the characters they play. . . . That happened today. . . . It was quiet, and you could almost feel the electricity between Liz and Burton."

Some people on the set, including Mankiewicz, knew already that there was more going on than just electricity. At one point Burton had stridden triumphantly into the men's makeup trailer and announced to those present, "Gentlemen, I've just fucked Elizabeth Taylor in the back of my Cadillac!" Whether or not this boast was for real, it *was* true that he and Taylor were using the apartment of her secretary, Dick Hanley, for trysts.

On January 26, Mankiewicz summoned Wanger to his room at the Grand Hotel. "I have been sitting on a volcano all alone for too long, and I want to give you some facts you ought to know," he said. "Liz and Burton are not just *playing* Antony and Cleopatra."

"Confidentially," Wanger later told Joe Hyams, his collaborator on *My Life with Cleopatra*, a rush-job account of the film's travails published in 1963, "we all figured it might just be a once-over-lightly. That is what Mr. Burton figured, too. I know it. He told me."

Several firsthand accounts support the idea that Burton began his dalliance with Taylor with only short-term pleasure in mind. Brodsky recalls the actor's genuine surprise, as the weeks advanced, to find himself in the midst of both an intense affair and an international incident: "He said to me, 'It's like fucking Khrushchev! I've had affairs before—how did I know the woman was so fucking famous!'"

Mankiewicz and Wanger harbored hopes in the early going that the situation would simply blow over. But Taylor's notoriety since her grieving-widow days had made her the most hunted tabloid prey in the world. Well before the affair had begun, the Roman gutter press had planted informants in Cinecittà and arranged paparazzi stakeouts of the Villa Papa. Word got out fast, even before Fisher knew anything was going on.

As February dawned, rumors were swirling so madly around Rome—"the whispering gallery of Europe," as Wanger called it— that Fisher could no longer ignore or brush off the gossip. One night early that month, as he lay in bed beside Taylor, he received a heads-up telephone call from Bob Abrams, his old army buddy and Jilly Rizzo–like amanuensis.

Fisher hung up the phone and turned to his wife. "Is it true that something is going on between you and Burton?" he asked her.

"Yes," she said softly.

Quietly, defeatedly, Fisher packed and spent the night at Abrams's place. The following day, he returned to the Villa Papa, and for about two weeks slept by Taylor's side, hoping that the situation would somehow resolve itself. There was never any kind of knock-down-drag-out confrontation. "She just wasn't 'there' anymore," Fisher said in 1991. "She was with *him*. And I wasn't 'there.' She talked to him once at the studio, in my office, with all kinds of people around. And she was talking love to him on the telephone. 'Oh, dahling, are you all right?' With this new British accent."

By mid-February the rumors had gone worldwide, and Taylor-Burton innuendo was everywhere. *The Perry Como Show* ran a comic "Cleopatra" sketch in which a slave named Eddie kept getting in Mark Antony's way. Taylor was visibly upset, and the entire production was in a bad way. Mankiewicz, run-down from his Sisyphean work schedule, had become feverishly ill. So had Martin Landau, who had a large part (as Rufio), and whose illness necessitated the cancellation of a day's worth of shooting. Leon Shamroy, the cinematographer, a cigar-chomping sexagenarian known for his seen-it-all stoicism (he had shot the Fox epics *The Robe, The Egyptian,* and *The King and I,* as well as the Gene Tierney classic *Leave Her to Heaven*), collapsed from exhaustion. Forrest "Johnny" Johnston, the film's production manager, fell gravely ill and died in Los Angeles in May.

Morale back home was also low. Pro- and anti-Skouras factions were taking shape on the Fox board, and rumors swirled of a coming putsch. "This was where my hair went gray," says Levathes, 86 [at the time this article first appeared, in 1998]. "I used to look younger." [Levathes died in 2002.]

Burton, contrite, met with Wanger and volunteered to quit the production if that was what was best. Wanger counseled against this option, arguing that "what would solve the problem [is] putting an end to any basis for the rumors."

In the meantime, Burton's older brother Ifor, a powerfully built man who functioned as the actor's bodyguard factotum, used his fists to get the message across. "Ifor beat the living shit out of Burton," says a *Cleopatra* crew member. "For what he was doing to Sybil. Beat him up so that Richard couldn't work the next day. He had a black eye and a cut cheek."

———

Both Fisher and Sybil Burton decided it best to flee the situation. He headed by car for Gstaad, where he and Taylor owned a chalet; she left for New York. But before either had gone, Fisher paid a visit to the Burtons' villa for a heart-to-heart talk with Sybil. "I said, 'You know, they're continuing their affair,'" Fisher recalled. "And she said, 'He's had these affairs, and he always comes home to me.' And I said, 'But they're still having their affair.' And she went to the studio, and they closed [production] down. And that cost them $100,000. And the day I left Rome, it cost them another $100,000. Elizabeth screamed and carried on. Work stopped that day. They had that in honor of me."

When Fisher, having driven as far as Florence, called Rome to determine his wife's whereabouts, he discovered that Taylor was in Hanley's apartment, accompanied by Burton, who was enraged that the singer had meddled in his marriage to Sybil. Burton took the telephone. "You nothing, you spleen," he said to Fisher. "I'm going to come up there and kill you."

Instead, Burton summoned the courage to tell Taylor their affair was over, and left for a short trip to Paris, where he was playing a small part in Darryl Zanuck's Normandy epic, *The Longest Day*. That night, Hanley called Wanger to say that Taylor would be unable to work the next day. "She's hysterical," Wanger wrote in his diary. "Total rejection came sooner than expected."

The following day, February 17, Taylor was rushed to the Salvator Mundi Hospital. The official explanation was food poisoning. Wanger, who cooked up a story about some bad beef she had eaten, had, in fact, discovered Taylor splayed on her bed in the Villa Papa, groggy from an overdose of Seconal, a prescription sedative. "It wasn't a suicide attempt," says Taylor. "I'm not that kind of person, and Richard despised weakness. It was more hysteria. I needed the rest, I was hysterical, and I needed to get away."

Taylor recovered quickly, but news of her hospitalization compelled both Fisher and Burton to fly back to Rome, which only fanned the flames of rumor. On February 19, Burton, eager to extinguish these flames, issued a statement addressing the "uncontrolled rumors . . . about Elizabeth and myself." The statement took pains to provide reasons why Sybil and Eddie had left town (she was visiting Burton's sick foster father; he had business matters to attend to), but never outright denied that an affair was going on. It was a crucially unsavvy nondenial denial, and the Fox publicity team was apoplectic. The studio got Burton to disavow the statement and pin the blame for its release on his press agent, but it was too late: now the papers had a peg upon which they could hang their "affair" stories. Taylor-Burton was an out-in-the-open phenomenon.

"It was not a help to the production," says a crew member. "You know how she got time off for her period? Now she was having three or four periods a month."

THE WHIRLWIND: ROME, SPRING 1962

> *"It's true—Elizabeth Taylor has fallen madly in love with Richard Burton. It's the end of the road for Liz and Eddie Fisher."* —LOUELLA PARSONS'S SYNDICATED COLUMN, MARCH 10, 1962

> *"The report is ridiculous."* —EDDIE FISHER'S RESPONSE, MARCH 10

In the aftermath of Taylor's hospitalization, all the aggrieved parties tried to re-arrange themselves as they had been before. Fisher threw his wife a 30th-birthday party on February 27 and presented her with a $10,000 diamond ring and an emerald-studded Bulgari mirror. Burton told the press he had no intention of divorcing Sybil. But it was to no avail—the Taylor-Burton affair continued, as did the reporters' pursuit.

Privately, there were cruel scenes between Burton and Fisher, with the former visiting Villa Papa and boasting to the latter, "You don't know how to use her!," or turning to Taylor and saying, with Fisher present, "Who do you love? Who do you love?" Fisher never fought back. Where others saw wimpiness and retreat, Wanger, in recorded conversations with Joe Hyams, his book collaborator, ascribed a kind of nobility to the singer's pacifism. "Eddie always took the position that this is an evil man, and he had to stand and protect her when she was misled by this terrible guy," he said. "He wanted to hold his family together." Fisher left Rome for good on March 21, 1962.

Cleopatra was now about halfway finished, but it still lacked its biggest, most challenging scenes: Cleopatra's procession into Rome, the arrival of her barge at Tarsus, the battles of Pharsalia, Philippi, Moongate, and Actium. Moreover, there remained several weeks' worth of "Antony and Cleopatra" scenes to be filmed. The fictive and the personal dovetailed to the point where even the actors got confused. "I feel as if I'm intruding," Mankiewicz said one day as his shouts of "Cut!" went unabided by Taylor and Burton during a love scene. In a less pleasant coincidence, the very day that Burton announced to the press he would never leave Sybil was the day Taylor had to film the scene in which Cleopatra discovers that Antony has returned to Rome and taken another wife, Octavia. The screenplay called for Cleopatra to enter Antony's deserted chambers in Alexandria, pick up his dagger, and stab his bed and belongings in a rage. Taylor went at it with such gusto that she banged her hand and needed to go to the hospital for X-rays. She was unable to work the next day.

The day-to-day developments of Taylor-Burton were now a full-time news beat. Martin Landau remembers a night shoot on the island of Ischia involving Taylor and Burton where the crew's spotlights, once turned on, revealed paparazzi bunched up like moths. "Behind us was this cliff, with shrubbery and growth coming out of it," he says, "and there were 20 photographers hanging off these things, with long lenses. A couple of them fell—30 feet!"

In actuality, the affair was, as Taylor would note a few years after the fact, "more off than on." "We did try and resist," she says today. "My marriage with Eddie was over, but we didn't want to do anything to hurt Sybil. She was—is—such a lovely lady." Taylor still won't discuss the scenes and machinations that went on between the Fishers and the Burtons, calling the subject matter "too personal," but other observers on the set remember moments when the lovers' similarly combustible personalities caused near explosions. In the midst of le scandale, Burton was also carrying on with the Copacabana dancer he'd been seeing in his Camelot days; one day Taylor took exception to her presence on the set, prompting Burton to shove Taylor slightly and snarl, "Don't get my Welsh temper up." In another instance, Burton showed up for work wrecked, again with the "Copa cutie," as she was known on the set, in tow. When he finally rallied himself into performing condition, Taylor admonished him, "You kept us all waiting." To which Burton responded, "It's about time somebody kept you waiting. It's a real switch."

Far more so than Taylor, Burton was flummoxed, unable to choose between his wife and lover, desperate to have it both ways. Speaking to Kenneth Tynan in *Playboy* after *Cleopatra* had wrapped, he futilely tried to defend the Liz-Sybil arrangement with a choice bit of baroque doggerel. "What I have done," he said, "is to move outside the accepted idea of monogamy without investing the other person with anything that makes me feel guilty. So that I remain inviolate, untouched."

For all its unpleasant side effects, Burton was elated by his new worldwide fame. Kenneth Haigh remembers him "calling me into his room and saying, 'Look at this! There are about 300 scripts! The offers are piling up everywhere!'" Hugh French, Burton's Hollywood agent, began boasting that his client now commanded $500,000 per picture. "Maybe I should give Elizabeth Taylor 10 percent," said Burton.

=====

Alas, the seesaw nature of the affair was not conducive to the efficient completion of what was now routinely described in the papers as a "$20 million picture." Between his euphoric highs, Burton was drinking heavily on the set. Taylor, too, became erratic, alternately showing up unprecedentedly early to work on scenes with Burton and failing to show up at all. A production document titled "Elizabeth Taylor Diary" indicates that on March 21, the day Fisher departed, Taylor was dismissed from Cinecittà at 12:25 P.M. after "having great difficulty delivering dialogue."

The unexpected work stoppages didn't always bother Mankiewicz, who welcomed the opportunity to catch up on his writing and his sleep. He was by now a physical ruin, sometimes writing scenes the night before they were to be shot. A stress-related dermatological disorder caused the skin on his hands to crack open, forcing him to wear thin white film cutter's gloves as he wrote the script longhand. Somehow, he retained his equanimity and sense of humor. When an Italian newspaper alleged that Burton was a "shuffle-footed idiot" deployed by the director to cover up the real scandal—that it was Mankiewicz who was having an affair with Taylor—Mankiewicz released a statement declaring, "The real story is that I'm in love with Richard Burton, and Elizabeth Taylor is the cover-up for us." (The same day, Burton shuffled up to Mankiewicz on the set and said, "Duh, Mister Mankeawitz, sir, do I have to sleep with her again tonight?")

Astonishingly, there had been a time, early on in Rome, when the Fox brass had chastised their publicity department for not getting *Cleopatra* enough attention. By April and May of 1962, as *le scandale* superseded news coverage of the Mercury-Atlas space missions and the U.S.-Soviet tensions that were leading up to the Cuban missile crisis, it was almost impossible to keep up with the whirlwind. Fisher was briefly hospitalized in New York with exhaustion, and after his release took to opening his nightclub act with the song "Arrivederci, Roma." A congresswoman from Georgia named Iris Blitch called on the attorney general to block Taylor and Burton from re-entering the country, "on grounds of undesirability." And in April, the Vatican City weekly, *L'Osservatore della Domenica,* printed a 500-word "open letter," signed only "X.Y.," that began "Dear Madam" and went on to say, "Even considering the [husband] that was finished by a natural solution, there remain three husbands buried with no other motive than a greater love that killed the one before. But if we start using these standards and this sort of competition between the first, second, third, and the hundredth love, where are we all going to end up? Right where you will finish—in an erotic vagrancy . . . without end or without a safe port."

The complicity of the Catholic Church in the sport of Liz-bashing undid Taylor's nerves at the worst possible moment for the production. She was due at last to film Cleopatra's entrance into Rome, the centerpiece of the entire picture. The premise of the sequence, commonly known as the procession, is that Cleopatra, having borne a son to Caesar in Egypt, must now go to her lover's home turf to present herself to the Roman public. If they accept her, then her dream of a globe-straddling Egyptian-Roman empire is realized; if they boo and hiss, she is finished. Mankiewicz, hewing to Plutarch, addressed the situation precisely as Cleopatra did: by devising the most lavish, eyeball-popping spectacle he could think of, a NASA-budgeted half-time show.

As Caesar and the senators watched, agog, from the Forum's reviewing stand, a seemingly endless parade of exotica would stream through the Arch of Titus: fanfaring trumpeters, charioteers, scantily clad dancing girls with streamers, an old hag who changes magically into a young girl, dwarfs tossing sweets from atop painted donkeys, comely young women tossing gold coins from atop painted elephants, painted Watusi warriors, dancers shooting plumes of colored smoke into the air, a pyramid that bursts open to release thousands of doves, Arabian horses, and, for the finale, a two-ton, three-story-high, black sphinx drawn by 300 Nubian slaves, upon which would sit Cleopatra and her boy, Caesarion, both resplendent in gold raiment.

Originally the procession was to have been one of the first things shot, in October, but bad weather and inadequate preparation made a hash of that plan, forcing Fox to pay out money to various dancers, acrobats, and circus-animal trainers to ensure their availability through the spring. (Furthermore, the original elephants that had been hired proved to be unruly and destructive, one of them running amok on the Cinecittà soundstages and pulling up stakes; the elephants' owner, Ennio Togni, later attempted to sue Fox for slander when word got out that his pachyderms had been "fired." Said a disbelieving Skouras, "How do you slander an elephant?")

Six thousand extras had been hired to cheer the queen's entrance and ad-lib reactions of "Cleopatra! Cleopatra!," but Taylor, mindful of their Roman Catholicism and the Vatican's recent condemnation, feared an impromptu stoning. Comforted by Burton and Mankiewicz, she summoned the courage to be hoisted atop the sphinx. When the cameras started rolling, she assumed a facial expression of blank hauteur and felt the sphinx rolling through the arch. "Oh my God," she thought, "here it comes."

But the Roman extras neither booed nor (for the most part) shouted "Cleopatra! Cleopatra!" Instead, they cheered and yelled, "Leez! Leez! *Baci! Baci!*," while blowing kisses her way.

OPERATION HOMESTRETCH:
ROME, ISCHIA, EGYPT, SPRING-SUMMER 1962

> *"Mr. Skouras faces the future with courage,*
> *determination . . . and terror."* —GROUCHO MARX,
> SPEAKING AT A TESTIMONIAL DINNER HELD IN HONOR OF
> SPYROS SKOURAS AT THE WALDORF-ASTORIA IN
> NEW YORK, APRIL 12, 1962

In the spring of '62, Skouras saw the writing on the wall. He knew that his reign as Fox president wasn't going to last much longer. By May he was stricken with prostate trouble, and when he arrived in Rome on May 8 to screen a five-hour rough cut of *Cleopatra*-to-date, he had been fitted with a temporary catheter and was heavily sedated—and fell asleep several times during the screening. Satisfied nevertheless with what he saw, he began a push to finish the film as quickly as possible.

The month had begun with Taylor indisposed on account of what Wanger described as "the most serious situation to date." On April 21, Taylor and Burton, without forewarning any members of the production, left Rome to spend the Easter weekend at Porto Santo Stefano, a coastal resort town a hundred miles to the north. Unprotected by handlers and publicists, they were surveilled the entire time by a swarm of reporters and paparazzi, and the following day newspapers around the world ran pictorial stories of their "tryst at seaside."

"It was like hell," says Taylor. "There was no place to hide, not in this tiny cottage we had rented. When we were driving somewhere, they ran us into a ditch by jumping in front of the car. It was either Richard hits them or he swerves over, so we swerved over."

One of the Porto Santo Stefano "tryst" stories appeared in the London *Times,* which infuriated Sybil Burton, who was at home in England with the Burtons' two small daughters, Kate and Jessica. Sybil had studiously ignored the London tabloids, but to have the Taylor-Burton affair splashed across the *Times* was the last straw. She went to Rome on April 23 to await her husband's return. Wanger, fearing a public scene, detained her at the Grand Hotel for as long as he could.

In the meantime, Taylor returned abruptly and solo from Porto Santo Stefano, and was rushed, for the second time in four months, to the Salvator Mundi Hospital. The following day's papers carried news of a "violent quarrel" that had prompted Taylor to walk out on Burton as he stood, smoldering, on the porch of the stucco bungalow they were staying in. "Burton told her to go and get rid of herself, and she tried to," Wanger later said confidentially. "This was the one time that she really took an overdose and she was really in danger." Taylor again denies that suicide was her intent, saying that, as had been the case in February, she needed some respite.

The hospitalization could be explained away with the old stand-bys "exhaustion" and "food poisoning," but the reason she didn't work again until May 7—that she had a black eye and facial bruises—could not be so tidily addressed. Skouras, in a letter to Darryl Zanuck several months later, matter-of-factly referred to "the beating Burton gave her in Santo Stefano. She got two black eyes, her nose was out of shape, and it took 22 days for her to recover enough in order to resume filming." But Taylor maintains that the truth was what the press was told—that her bruises were incurred during the ride back from Porto Santo Stefano. "I was sleeping in the backseat of the car," she says, "and the driver went around a curve, and I bumped my nose on an ashtray."

Once Taylor's bruises healed, she went back to work. But more bad luck followed. The winds came up on some of the days the extras and dancers had been convened to continue work on the procession, canceling shooting at a cost of $250,000. A successfully completed scene that required Antony to slap Cleopatra to the ground—a loaded proposition made more so by the fact that Taylor had a bad back—was erased when the film was damaged in transit back to the United States; June retakes would be necessary. Then, on May 28, word slipped out to Levathes that Taylor had filmed Cleopatra's death scene, in which she commits suicide by letting an asp bite her hand.

The death scene was, in the eyes of Fox's impatient executives, the one sequence the film could absolutely not do without. Knowing it existed, Levathes headed for Rome to shut down the picture.

On June 1, Wanger met with Levathes and learned that, effective the following day, he was being taken off salary and expenses. This was in every sense a quasi-firing, in that no one discouraged him from continuing to work on the film. So continue he did, contesting, with Mankiewicz, the New York office's demands that Taylor's last day be June 9, that the battle of Pharsalia sequence be canceled, and that all photography be completed by June 30. (A week later, back in the States, Levathes fired Marilyn Monroe from her abortive final film, *Something's Got to Give*. A Fox spokesman said, "No company can afford Monroe and Taylor.")

———

In haste, the *Cleopatra* production moved to the Italian island of Ischia, which was standing in for both Actium, the ancient Greek town near whose shores Octavian defeated Antony, and Tarsus, the Turkish port of the Roman Empire where Cleopatra made her second great entrance, aboard a barge. (The barge, complete with gilded stern and Dacron purple sails flown in from California, cost $277,000.)

It was off Ischia that a paparazzo named Marcello Geppetti took the photograph that most enduringly represents the Taylor-Burton affair: a shot of Burton planting a kiss on a smiling Taylor as both sun themselves in bathing suits on the deck of an anchored boat.

Taylor completed a successful take of Cleopatra's arrival aboard her barge on June 23. By studio decree, it was her last day on the picture—272 days after Mankiewicz had begun at Cinecittà, 632 days after Mamoulian had commenced shooting at Pinewood.

Battle-sequence work in Egypt would keep Mankiewicz busy through July, and battles with Fox occupied him in the weeks prior. While still on Ischia, the director learned that Fox was killing yet another crucial sequence, the battle of Philippi. Mankiewicz was enraged, having planned for the Philippi conflict to open the film's second half. On June 29, he sent a strongly worded telegram to Skouras and the Fox brass:

WITHOUT PHARSALIA IN MY OPINION OPENING OF FILM AND FOL-
LOWING SEQUENCES SEVERELY DAMAGED STOP BUT WITHOUT PHILIPPI
THERE IS LITERALLY NO OPENING FOR SECOND HALF SINCE INTERIOR
TENT SCENES ALREADY SHOT SIMPLY CANNOT BE INTELLIGIBLY PUT TO-
GETHER STOP . . . WITH MUTUAL APPRECIATION OF RESPONSIBILITIES
AND SUGGESTING THAT MINE TOWARD THE STOCKHOLDERS IS NO LESS
THAN YOURS I SUGGEST THAT YOU REPLACE ME SOONEST POSSIBLE BY
SOMEONE LESS CRITICAL OF YOUR DIRECTIVES AND LESS DEDICATED TO
THE EVENTUAL SUCCESS OF CLEOPATRA.

Fox placated Mankiewicz by allowing Pharsalia to be partially
reconstituted via two days' worth of hasty shooting in some craggy
Italian hills—and then *Cleopatra* moved on to Egypt for additional
battle work.

The Egypt trip, from July 15 to July 24, was the by-now-
customary fiasco, marred by delays, poor sanitary conditions, a
threatened strike by the locally hired extras, and government wire-
taps on the telephones of Jewish cast and crew members; adding injury to insult, there was the further deterioration of Mankiewicz's
physical condition—he required daily B_{12} shots to keep going, and
one shot hit his sciatic nerve, rendering him barely able to walk.

Principal photography was now complete. But Mankiewicz
would have more to contend with in the film's lengthy postproduction phase: a new Fox regime. Back on June 26, under pressure,
Skouras had announced his resignation as president, effective September 20.

ENTER THE MUSTACHE:
NEW YORK, LOS ANGELES, PARIS, LONDON, SPAIN, 1962-63

> *IT LOOKS LIKE MUSTACHE WITH ZEUS AS PLANKHEAD.*
> —CABLE SENT FROM JACK BRODSKY (IN FOX'S NEW YORK OFFICE)
> TO NATHAN WEISS (IN FOX'S TEMPORARY ROME OFFICE),
> JULY 6, 1962

"Mustache" was Darryl Zanuck. "Zeus" was Skouras. Upon Skouras's resignation, Zanuck, whose family was still the single largest
shareholder of Fox stock, made a play to take control of the faltering

company he had co-founded in 1933. By outmaneuvering the various board factions and their designees for president, he engineered a coup that by summertime had installed him as president and relegated Skouras to a largely ceremonial chairman-of-the-board position (ergo, "Zeus as plankhead").

Zanuck surveyed the state of affairs at Fox like a police chief arriving at a morbid crime scene—*move away, pal, show's over.* He shut down virtually all Fox productions save *Cleopatra,* dismissed most of the studio's employees and executives, lowered the thermostats, shuttered most of the buildings on the shrunken back lot, and replaced Levathes with his own son, producer Richard Zanuck.

Mankiewicz and Darryl Zanuck had a complex love-hate relationship that more often tipped toward the latter. But the director was relieved to know there was now a decisive man at the top, and someone who knew the ins and outs of picture-making to boot. "When I finished a screenplay, the first person I wanted to read it was Darryl," Mankiewicz said in 1982, recalling the days when Zanuck was Fox's chief of production. It was Zanuck who resolved one of Mankiewicz's biggest writerly dilemmas—how to pare down an overlong screenplay entitled *A Letter to Four Wives*—by suggesting that Mankiewicz eliminate one of the wives.

Back in Los Angeles, Mankiewicz and his editor, Dorothy Spencer, prepared a rough cut of *Cleopatra* that ran five hours and twenty minutes and reflected his desire to present *Cleopatra* in two concurrently released parts, with separate tickets required for each: *Caesar and Cleopatra,* followed by *Antony and Cleopatra.* Fox had long been against the idea, because of the exhibition logistics involved and because no one was interested in seeing Taylor make love to Rex Harrison.

Mankiewicz made a date with Zanuck to screen the film on October 13 in Paris, where the new Fox president lived (and continued to work, even though he was running an American studio). As this date approached, Wanger sent Zanuck a series of obsequious letters and telegrams, begging to be fully reinstated as producer: I BESEECH YOU, DARRYL . . . NOT TO AGGRAVATE THIS SITUATION AND FURTHER DAMAGE MY STATUS AS PRODUCER OF CLEOPATRA BY NOT

BRINGING ME TO PARIS . . . I APPEAL TO YOU AS A MAN NOT TO DO THIS TO ME. Zanuck's cold-shoulder reply was that Wanger was welcome to come along provided he paid his own way.

The October 13 screening did not go particularly well. Zanuck said little to Mankiewicz as the lights went up except "If any woman behaved toward me the way Cleopatra treated Antony, I would cut her balls off."

Mankiewicz grew nervous when a week passed without him hearing anything further. On October 20, he sent a letter to Zanuck requesting an "honest and unequivocal statement of where I stand in relation to *Cleopatra*."

On October 21, he got his statement. "On completion of the dubbing, your official services will be terminated," Zanuck wrote. "If you are available and willing, I will call upon you to screen the re-edited version of the film." Elsewhere in the letter, which ran to nine single-spaced pages, Zanuck described the existing battle sequences as "awkward, amateurish . . . second-rate film making" with a "B-picture" look; said that the film "over-emphasized in some places the *Esquire*-type of sex"; described Wanger as "impotent"; contrasted Mankiewicz's handling of *Cleopatra* unfavorably with his own handling of *The Longest Day;* and alleged, "You were not the official producer, yet in the history of motion pictures no one man has ever been given such authority. The records show that you made every single decision and that your word was law."

A few days later, Zanuck released the following statement to the press: "In exchange for top compensation and a considerable expense account, Mr. Joseph Mankiewicz has for two years spent his time, talent, and $35,000,000 of 20th Century-Fox's shareholders' money to direct and complete the first cut of the film *Cleopatra*. He has earned a well-deserved rest."

In response, the director told the press, "I made the first cut, but after that, it's the studio's property. They could cut it up into banjo picks if they want."

Privately, Mankiewicz sent Zanuck yet another letter that painstakingly refuted every charge made against him in the October 21 correspondence: "I am, I suppose, an old whore on this beat, Darryl, and it takes quite a bit to shock me . . . but never could I imagine the phantasmagoria of frantic lies and frenzied phony buck-passing that you report [in] your letter!"

By December, however, the two men's temperatures had cooled, and they recognized that their cooperation was necessary to get *Cleopatra* into releasable form. Zanuck conceded to Mankiewicz that the previous regime's cutbacks on Pharsalia and Philippi had been a mistake, and so, in February 1963—at a cost of $2 million— *Cleopatra*'s company of soldiers was reconvened in Almería, Spain, to do battle. Further bits and pieces were shot in—irony of ironies— Pinewood Studios in England, where the whole mess had begun with Mamoulian 29 months earlier.

When the reshoots were done, Mankiewicz, with Zanuck looking over his shoulder, edited *Cleopatra* down to its 243-minute premiere length. Though they were publicly allies again, the director was unhappy with this version and still thought Zanuck had done him a disservice by not allowing *Cleopatra* to be shown in two parts. When Mankiewicz was asked to participate in a fluffy NBC tribute program called *The World of Darryl Zanuck*, he said he'd do it only if they retitled it *Stop the World of Darryl Zanuck*.

Nevertheless, *Cleopatra,* at last, was done.

CODA: NEW YORK, ETC., 1963–

> *"She is an entirely physical creature, no depth of emotion apparent in her kohl-laden eyes, no modulation in her voice that too often rises to fishwife levels. Out of royal regalia, en negligee or au naturel, she gives the impression that she is really carrying on in one of Miami Beach's more exotic resorts than inhabiting a palace in ancient Alexandria."* —JUDITH CRIST, EVALUATING TAYLOR'S PERFORMANCE IN HER REVIEW OF *CLEOPATRA* FOR THE *NEW YORK HERALD TRIBUNE*, JUNE 13, 1963

Cleopatra opened at the Rivoli Theater to mixed reviews, Crist's being the most damning, Bosley Crowther's, in *The New York Times,* being the most enthusiastic ("a surpassing entertainment, one of the great epic films of our day"). A viewing unprejudiced by temporal context reveals the movie to be mediocre-to-good, a tribute to Mankiewicz's salvaging abilities and the fact that, for all the waste, you do see a lot of the money up on the screen—the movie looks handsome and expensive in an old-fashioned, 2,000-artisans-at-work way, as opposed to the contemporary, postproduced-in-the-computer-lab way. The procession sequence is as mind-boggling as it's supposed to be.

Taylor's Cleopatra comes off as an imperious harridan, a seething Imelda, but she's actually effective—you believe her dream of empire. Still, you can't help but notice the inconsistency of her physical appearance throughout the film, a consequence of the events and upheavals she was enduring. At times, she's skinny and youthful; other times, she's fleshy but ravishing; still other times, damned if she isn't Mrs. John Warner foretold. The male leads' fortunes are more contingent upon the circumstances under which Mankiewicz wrote their parts. Whereas Harrison gets all the good lines, Burton looks ludicrous and spends most of his screen time shouting, flaring his nostrils, and huffing around Alexandria in a strangely tiny mini-toga (he shows more leg than Cyd Charisse). Not that poor writing was entirely to blame—Mankiewicz's completed screenplay contains nuanced, character building Antony scenes that never should have ended up on the cutting-room floor.

Business at the Rivoli was good, and the movie sold out for the next four months; Skouras, his exhibitor's skills coming to the fore, had shrewdly arranged a deal whereby Fox collected $1.25 million in advance guarantees from the theater before a single ticket had been sold. Applying this strategy worldwide, he collected $20 million in pre-release grosses.

The movie was never the runaway hit Wanger had dreamed of, but a year after its release it was one of the top-10 grossers of all time, and in 1966, when Fox sold the television broadcast rights to ABC for $5 million, Cleopatra passed the break-even mark. The studio had by then rehabilitated itself—The Sound of Music, which had come out a year earlier and cost $8 million to make, was an unexpected megahit, grossing more than $100 million.

But the travails of *Cleopatra* did not end at the Rivoli. Subsequent to the New York premiere, Fox chopped the film down further. For the Washington, D.C., and London premieres, a three-hour forty-seven-minute version was shown. When the film went into wide release, it was even shorter, running at three hours and twelve minutes. If big-city moviegoers were gypped out of seeing Mankiewicz's vision realized, most Americans were gypped out of seeing a comprehensible film.

Recently, with the support of the Mankiewicz family and Fox's current studio chief, Bill Mechanic, archivists have been laboring to reconstruct a six-hour "director's cut" of the film that would do better justice to Burton's part, and the film as a whole, than the 243-minute "opening night" version currently available on video. Their efforts have revealed that Mankiewicz's cynical divination of *Cleopatra*'s ultimate fate—that it would end up as the world's most expensive banjo picks—wasn't that far off. The *Cleopatra* he envisioned has scattered to the winds. Some missing footage has turned up in the hands of private collectors. Other bits and pieces have been discovered, uncatalogued and a mile deep in the earth, in an underground storage facility in Kansas. Further bits have turned up in even stranger places: Richard Green and Geoffrey Sharpe, two eagle-eyed *Cleopatra* enthusiasts in London who are assisting Fox in the restoration efforts, noticed that Charlton Heston used chunks of excised Mankiewicz footage to flesh out his 1972 low-budget vanity production of Shakespeare's *Antony and Cleopatra*.

Appropriately, the saga of *Cleopatra* dragged unhappily on for several more years after its release, a dénouement of bad blood, threats, and lawsuits. Taylor, Burton, and Fisher sued Fox for their proper shares of the grosses. Fox sued Taylor and Burton for breach of contract, specifically citing the former for, among other things, "suffering herself to be held up to scorn, ridicule, and unfavorable publicity as a result of her conduct and deportment." Wanger sued Skouras, Zanuck, and Fox for breach of contract. Fox sued Wanger right back on the same grounds. Skouras contemplated a libel suit against Wanger for the way he was portrayed in the 1963 book *My*

Life with Cleopatra, and another suit against the publicists Brodsky and Weiss for the way he came across in *their* book from 1963, *The Cleopatra Papers.* By the late 60s, after several GATT-like rounds of depositions and negotiations, all of these various actions were eventually resolved.

The matter of the Fishers and the Burtons also stretched well beyond *Cleopatra's* production life span. When principal filming was completed, Burton returned once more to his wife, and Taylor, for the first time in years, had no man in her life. By early 1963, however, the two had reunited to do another movie, *The V.I.P.s,* a London-based production that gave them an excuse to take adjacent suites in the Dorchester. Sybil Burton filed for divorce that December; Fisher, after months of ugly public exchanges with Taylor over the division of their property, finally gave up the ghost on March 5, 1964, when he failed to contest her petition for a Mexican divorce.

Burton was playing Hamlet in Toronto when Taylor's divorce was finalized; she was with him. They married in Montreal on March 15. The following night, Burton was back in Toronto playing the Dane. After taking his curtain call, he presented his wife to the audience and declaimed, to the audience's delight, "I would just like to quote from the play—Act III, Scene I: 'We will have no more marriages.'"

From *Vanity Fair,* April 1998

THE GRADUATE

Here's to You, Mr. Nichols

by Sam Kashner

Imagine a movie called *The Gradu-ate*. It stars Robert Redford as Ben-jamin Braddock, the blond and bronzed, newly minted college graduate adrift in his parents' opulent home in Beverly Hills. And Candice Bergen as his girlfriend, the overprotected Elaine Robin-son. Ava Gardner plays the preda-tory Mrs. Robinson, the desperate housewife and mother who ensnares Benjamin. Gene Hackman is her cuckolded husband. It nearly happened that way. That it didn't made all the difference.

It all began with a book review. On October 30, 1963, a 36-year-old movie producer named Lawrence Turman read Orville Prescott's review of Charles Webb's first novel, *The Graduate,* in *The New York Times.* Though Prescott described the satirical novel as "a fictional failure," he compared Webb's misfit, malaise-ridden hero, Benjamin Braddock, to Holden Caulfield, the hero of J. D. Salinger's classic *The Catcher in the Rye.* Turman was intrigued. "The book haunted me—I identified with it," he says. Now 81, Turman is lean, with white hair and bright eyes. Over lunch in West Hollywood, he recalls how he fell in love particularly with two of the novel's images: "a boy in a scuba suit in his own swimming pool, and then that same boy on a bus, his shirttail out, with a girl in a wedding dress. I liked it so much, I took out an option with my own money—something I counsel my students not to do. Because no one else bid on the novel, I optioned the rights for $1,000." Turman, who now chairs the Peter Stark Producing Program at the University of Southern California School of Cinematic Arts, considered himself something of an industry outsider, though by 1963 he had already produced several films (including *The Young Doctors,* with Fredric March and Ben Gazzara; *I Could Go On Singing,* with Judy Garland; and Gore Vidal's *The Best Man*).

Perhaps he still feels like an outsider because he started life in the garment industry, following in his father's footsteps, although he had majored in English literature at U.C.L.A. "Everyone always says how tough show biz is," Turman says, "and, of course, they're right, but it's kid stuff compared to the garment business, where someone will cut your heart out for a quarter-cent a yard. I'd carry bolts of cloth five blocks after making a sale, only to learn that the customer bought it cheaper, and I had to schlep the bolts of cloth back to my dad's office." He can still vividly recall working his way down 14 flights of a manufacturing building, "getting rejected at every floor." After five years of working with his father, he pounced on a blind ad in *Variety:* "Experienced Agent Wanted." He got the job at the Kurt Frings Agency, a four-person operation specializing in European actors, including Audrey Hepburn, by candidly confessing that he "had zero experience, but was full of energy and would work very cheaply"—$50 a week.

After optioning *The Graduate,* Turman needed a director. He immediately thought of another industry outsider, the comedian turned Broadway director Mike Nichols, then 33 years old. At the time, Nichols had just had a great success directing Robert Redford and Elizabeth Ashley on Broadway in Neil Simon's *Barefoot in the Park,* but before that he had been half of the legendary satirical comedy team Mike Nichols and Elaine May. Their sharp, skewed portrayals of "Age of Anxiety" couples struck a deep chord in American life, and their comedy sketches were hilarious, such as the one about a pushy mother and her put-upon rocket-scientist son: "I feel awful," the son says after his mother berates him for not calling. "If I could believe that," she says, "I'd be the happiest mother in the world." They were improvisation geniuses and could perform sketches in the style of everyone from Faulkner to Kierkegaard.

Elaine May was the daughter of a Yiddish actor named Jack Berlin. Nichols met his dark-haired muse at the University of Chicago, where he was a pre-med student, but like Benjamin Braddock, wanted his future "to be different." Both he and May were members of the off-campus Playwright's Theatre, which later became the improvisational group the Compass Players (a precursor to Chicago's Second City). By 1958 they were performing in New York's Greenwich Village, at the Blue Angel and the Village Vanguard, and then began appearing on television shows such as *The Steve Allen Show* and *Omnibus*. The height of their success was *An Evening with Mike Nichols and Elaine May*, a 1960 Broadway hit at New York's Golden Theatre, directed by Arthur Penn.

Then they walked away from it all. It was Elaine May's idea. She wanted to devote more time to writing and she also felt, with Kennedy just installed in the White House, there had been a seismic shift in the country's mood, and the duo's uptight, Eisenhower-era targets were no longer relevant. On July 1, 1961, they gave their last performance. "I stopped being a comedian," Nichols now says, not the least bit wistfully. "Stand-up comedy is a very hard thing on the spirit. There are people who transcend it, like Jack Benny and Steve Martin, but in its essence, it's soul destroying. It tends to turn people into control freaks." Though he never did stand-up (or sit-down) comedy again, his canny, satirical edge would inform everything else Nichols later undertook as a theater and movie director.

"Mike Nichols was an intuitive hunch," Turman reflects. "Webb's book is funny, but mordant. Nichols and May's humor seemed like a hand-in-glove fit to me." When they finally got together in New York to discuss the project, Turman, ever known for his candor, told Nichols, "I have the book, but I don't have any money. I don't have any

studio. I have nothing, so let's do this. We'll make this movie together, and whatever money comes in, we'll split 50-50." Nichols
agreed on the spot.

"So I got *The Graduate* and Mike Nichols," Turman recounts,
"and I beat my brains out." They sent the book to Brian Keith to read
for the part of Mr. Robinson. "He came into our office," Nichols recalls. "We sat down, and I asked if he had read the book. He said he
had. 'What do you think?' I asked. He said, 'I think it's the biggest
piece of shit I've ever read.' I said, 'Well, then we won't do it. You
agree, Larry?' Turman said, 'Absolutely.' I said, 'Thank you, Mr.
Keith. You've saved us a lot of trouble.' Turman and I both stood up,
and Keith had to get up and leave. It was fun."

For nearly two years, Turman was turned down by every major
studio: "No one thought the book was funny, and no one in Hollywood had even heard of Mike Nichols," but that didn't matter by the
time he approached producer Joseph E. Levine. By then, Nichols
had followed *Barefoot in the Park* with three more Broadway hits,
The Knack, Murray Schisgal's *Luv,* and Neil Simon's *The Odd Couple,* which made a Broadway star out of Walter Matthau. And Nichols had been chosen by Elizabeth Taylor to direct her and Richard
Burton in the movie of Edward Albee's scandalous Broadway hit,
Who's Afraid of Virginia Woolf? It became the most controversial
film of 1966, winning Taylor her second Academy Award.

———————

Joseph E. Levine was known as "an enormously successful schlock-
meister," says Turman. "He would buy junky films, like *Hercules,*
have an aggressive ad campaign, plaster his own name all over them,
and make a lot of money for himself in the bargain. He was a great,
flamboyant, throwback salesman." His company, called Embassy
Pictures, had graduated to classier fare—*Marriage Italian Style,* 8½,
Two Women, Darling—by the time Turman approached him. "I
don't know if Joe Levine even 'got' the book, but Mike had cachet,
which Joe didn't have," recalls Turman. "I think Levine got on board
to be in business with Mike Nichols." Turman gave his word that he
could make the movie for a million dollars. Levine said yes. For the

first time, Turman no longer felt like a fish out of water. "It's always better to be inside than looking at it from outside," he says.

With his money and his director in place, Turman needed a screenwriter. In February of 1965—one year after optioning the rights—he signed Calder Willingham to write the screenplay. Willingham was a novelist and screenwriter known for his strong, often daring sexual content (*End as a Man*). Problem was, he really didn't like the novel. In a note to Turman he wrote, "The whole thing of a young man marrying a girl after screwing her mother's ears off is a mess . . . and it must be handled with art and care or we are dead. This goddamned schizophrenic and amateurish book . . . If my script is unacceptable . . . then hire another writer, but don't go to Charles Webb!"

"Calder turned in a script," Turman recalls, "but it was vulgar. He even added some gratuitous homosexual and man-woman sex." He handed it over to Mike Nichols, warning him, "I don't like it." Neither did Nichols. (There had been an earlier false start with playwright William Hanley.) So Nichols suggested a bright, young comedic actor and story editor, Buck Henry.

"He wasn't a screenwriter when I asked him to write the screenplay. He improvised comedy," Nichols recalls. "He had not, to my knowledge, written anything. And I said, 'I think you could do it; I think you should do it.' And he could, and he did."

Like Nichols, Buck Henry had acted in improvisational theater and had worked as a writer-performer for a few television shows, including *The New Steve Allen Show* and *That Was the Week That Was*, but his big break came as co-creator with Mel Brooks of the television series *Get Smart*, starring Don Adams as the incompetent CONTROL agent 86, Maxwell Smart. The boyish-looking, bespectacled writer was in his second year as story editor for the spy spoof, but he had written only one, unproduced screenplay.

"Turman, Nichols, and I related to *The Graduate* in exactly the same way," Henry recalls. "We all thought we were Benjamin Braddock. Plus, it's an absolutely first-class novel, with great characters, great dialogue, a terrific theme. Who could resist it? I read it and I said, 'Yes, let's go.'"

Born Buck Henry Zuckerman, the writer and actor was living in Hollywood's Chateau Marmont at the time, working on *Get Smart* by day and writing the screenplay for *The Graduate* at night, collaborating closely with Nichols. His mother was Ruth Zuckerman, known as Ruth Taylor, a smoky-eyed silent-screen film actress, so he had, in a sense, been born into show business. He claims that as a little boy he watched the filming of a scene from *The Maltese Falcon,* and that Humphrey Bogart gave him a wad of movie money. And, having been impressed by his mother's glamorous actress friends, he completely got the allure of women of a certain age—his mother's—as embodied by Mrs. Robinson.

"I always thought *The Graduate* was the best pitch I ever heard: this kid graduates college, has an affair with his parents' best friend, and then falls in love with the friend's daughter," says Henry. "Give that to 20 writers and you've got 20 scripts. It's just odd to me it hasn't been done a hundred times." (In 1992, Henry would get the chance to pitch *The Graduate,* albeit as an actor in Robert Altman's *The Player.* Only, this time it's a sequel, and Mrs. Robinson has just had a stroke.)

A great deal of dialogue came directly from the book, but one memorable scene was entirely Henry's, and it would elicit some of the biggest laughs in the movie. At Benjamin Braddock's homecoming party, Mr. McGuire, one of his father's friends, takes Ben and steers him out by the pool:

"Ben, come with me for a minute. . . . I just want to say one word to you—just one word."
"Yes, sir."
"Are you listening?"
"Yes I am."
"Plastics."

Mr. McGuire goes back into the house and we never hear from him again. But the scene has been with us for 40 years—it was even reprised in an ad for VISTA, the domestic Peace Corps, and the word "plastics" was given new life in the vernacular as a symbol for phony commercialism. Henry recalls that audiences who had seen the movie several times would yell out the line "Plastics," as if it were the lyrics to a song.

———

Nichols couldn't have been more pleased with the final screenplay, which he credits entirely to Henry, though Calder Willingham ended up with first billing. "I didn't even know there were other scripts until I was finished," recalls Henry, "but Willingham sued for credit, and won. I was stunned at first, but it's interesting, because from that moment on, I never gave a shit about credit. Give me the money, credit whom you want. And in some cases, I don't really want my name on the movie!"

When it came to casting, the problems really began. It should have been easy. Charles Webb himself was a fair-haired, lanky, fresh-faced graduate of Williams College, in Williamstown, Massachusetts, and had grown up in a decidedly Wasp enclave in Pasadena. "I interviewed hundreds, maybe thousands, of men," Nichols told an enthusiastic crowd at the Directors Guild of America Theatre in New York, in 2003, at a screening of *The Graduate*. He even discussed the role with his friend Robert Redford, who was eager for the part. "I said, 'You can't play it. You can never play a loser.' And Redford said, 'What do you mean? Of course I can play a loser.' And I said, 'O.K., have you ever struck out with a girl?' and he said, 'What do you mean?' *And he wasn't joking.*"

Shortly after hiring Nichols, Larry Turman started a wish list for the roles of Benjamin Braddock and Elaine Robinson. For "Elaine," he wrote, "Natalie Wood, Ann-Margret, Jane Fonda, Tuesday Weld, Carroll Baker, Sue Lyon, Lee Remick, Suzanne Pleshette, Carol Lynley, Elizabeth Ashley, Yvette Mimieux, Pamela Tiffin, Patty Duke, Hayley Mills." Under the "Ben" column, he listed "Warren Beatty, Steve McQueen, Bob Redford, [George] Peppard, George Hamilton, Tony Perkins, Keir Dullea, Brandon De Wilde, Michael Parks."

"When we started talking about actors," Buck Henry noticed, "they were tall and blond. We were talking Southern California." Robert Redford, fresh from *Barefoot in the Park*, auditioned with Candice Bergen, and Charles Grodin, who had made his Broadway debut in 1962 opposite Anthony Quinn in *Tchin-Tchin,* also read for the part. Turman thought that Grodin "gave a wonderful reading," and the actor was strongly considered. Nichols and Turman knew the casting of Benjamin was crucial: "Everything is story, everything is script," Turman says, "but if you don't have an appealing actor, you're dead in the water." He remembers Nichols finally turning to him and saying, "Turman, you S.O.B., you got me into a movie that can't be cast!"

Then two things happened to change Nichols's mind. He was reading Henry James's novella "The Beast in the Jungle," about a young man who lets life and love pass him by while he waits for a cataclysmic event to transform him. And he auditioned a young New York actor, Dustin Hoffman.

"When I was auditioning for this part," Dustin Hoffman recalls for *Vanity Fair,* "I had finally made some inroads in my career." After 10 years as a struggling actor in New York, Hoffman had won an Obie Award in 1966 for best Off Broadway actor, in Ronald Ribman's *The Journey of the Fifth Horse.* He'd been supporting himself with a series of odd jobs—selling toys at Macy's, working as an attendant at the New York Psychiatric Institute, on West 168th Street, waiting tables at the Village Gate—and sharing an apartment with Gene Hackman and his wife. After he won the Obie, his performance as Valentine Brose, a schizophrenic night watchman in an Off Broadway British farce called *Eh?,* landed him on the cover of the Arts & Leisure section of *The New York Times.* And in a daily review, the *Times* described his performance as "a sort of cross between Ringo Starr and Buster Keaton."

"I was riding high, so I felt that I was going to have a career in the theater, which is what I wanted. So when the part came along, I read the book, I talked to Mike Nichols on the phone, and I said, 'I'm not right for this part, sir. This is a Gentile. This is a Wasp. This is Robert Redford.' In fact, I remember there was a *Time* magazine on the coffee table in my apartment, and it had the 'Man of the Year' on the cover, which was 'Youth Under 25,' with a kind of sketch of a young guy who looked like Matt Damon. So I said, 'Did you see this week's *Time* magazine? *That's* Benjamin Braddock!' Nichols replied, *'You mean he's not Jewish?'* 'Yes, this guy is a super-Wasp. Boston

Brahmin.' And Mike said, 'Maybe he's Jewish *inside*. Why don't you come out and audition for us?'"

He took three days off from *Eh?* and flew to L.A. for the screen test, which took place at rented offices in the Paramount Studio lot on Melrose Avenue. "I couldn't sleep, I was so nervous," Hoffman said in an interview accompanying the 40th-anniversary DVD edition of *The Graduate*. He had stayed up all night on the airplane, trying to memorize his lines. The next day, he walked into the high-ceilinged, interconnected offices and met Nichols, who was waiting for him, seated at a fully appointed bar. Nichols casually offered him a drink.

"I'm immediately feeling miserable," Hoffman remembered. "I just have bad feelings about the whole thing. This is not the part for me. I'm not supposed to be in movies. I'm supposed to be where I belong—an ethnic actor is supposed to be in ethnic New York, in an ethnic, Off Broadway show! I know my place." (Harry Hoffman, Dustin's father, of Russian-Jewish ancestry, worked as a set dresser for Columbia Studios before launching his own short-lived furniture company.)

For the audition, Nichols had also brought in Katharine Ross, a 24-year-old actress and California native who had made her film debut in 1965 as Jimmy Stewart's daughter-in-law in *Shenandoah*. The French actress Simone Signoret, with whom Ross had worked in the 1967 film *Games*, had recommended Ross to Nichols. "I remember meeting Dustin in Mike's office," says Ross, seated at an outdoor café in Malibu, not far from the home she shares with her husband, the actor Sam Elliott. "Dustin was from New York. He was all dressed in black, and you know, we're all tan out here," she says, laughing. "He looked like he had crawled out from under a rock. He wasn't at all interested in being in a movie or anything—or at least that's what he said. He was very funny, very fresh. He just kind of said whatever was on his mind. Now nothing shocks anybody, but back then . . . !"

Hoffman was bowled over by the chestnut-haired ingénue. "The idea that the director was connecting me with someone as beautiful as her," Hoffman explained, "became an even uglier joke. It was like a Jewish nightmare." Preparing him for the screen test was another humiliation. Makeup worked on him for two hours, plucking his eyebrows, shading his nose, and hiding his muscular neck in a turtleneck sweater.

It went downhill from there, as far as Dustin was concerned. To relax them both, he gave Katharine a little pinch on her backside, and she whirled around and said, "Don't you ever do that to me again. How dare you!" The audition seemed to go on for hours, and he felt that the takes they printed just weren't any good. He knew he'd blown it. "I couldn't wait to go back to New York," he recalled. The final humiliation occurred when, saying good-bye to the crew, he pulled his hand out of his pocket and a fistful of subway tokens spilled to the floor. The propman picked them up and handed them back, saying, "Here, kid. You're going to need these."

Back in New York, Hoffman got word from his agent to call Mike Nichols. He reached Nichols on the phone, afraid he had woken him up. After a long pause, the director uttered the most beautiful words an actor can hear: "Well, you got it." Those four words changed Dustin Hoffman's life.

"We looked and looked and looked," recalls Nichols, "and when we saw Dustin Hoffman on film, we said, 'That's it.' And I had come all the way from seeing the character as a super-goy to being John Marcher in 'The Beast in the Jungle.' He had to be the dark, ungainly artist. He couldn't be a blond, blue-eyed person, because then why is he having trouble in the country of the blond, blue-eyed people? It took me a long time to figure that out—it's not in the material at all. And once I figured that out, and found Dustin, it began to form itself around that idea."

It was a revolutionary about-face. For generations, Jewish moguls had created fantasies for and about Wasps. Jewish actors and directors routinely Anglicized their names—such as Julius Garfinkle and Bernie Schwartz becoming John Garfield and Tony Curtis—as a kind of camouflage that was especially useful during the McCarthy-era witch hunts, which targeted not just the motion-picture industry but Jewish writers, actors, and producers. Nichols himself was born Michael Igor Peschkowsky, in Berlin, to Russian-Jewish émigrés, in 1931. "When I was seven and my brother four," recalls Nichols, "we came to the U.S. in '39 without either parent, because our father, a doctor, had come [alone] the previous year to take his medical exams, as he had after going from Russia to study in Germany. Our mother at the time was still in Berlin, as she was sick and in the hospital. She came on an even later ship. Bob and I came on the *Bremen* from Hamburg, taken care of by a stewardess. As the *Bremen* landed in New York and we were re-united with our father on the dock, I noticed across the street a delicatessen with Hebrew letters in its neon sign. I said to my father, 'Is that allowed?' He said, 'It is here.' This was only the beginning of our excitement in the U.S. Next were Rice Krispies and Coca-Cola: we had never had food that made noise. It was great."

Buck Henry—who had seen Hoffman in *Eh?* and had been duly impressed—embraced the idea of casting him. "You know my theory about California genetics?" he asks wryly. "Jews from New York came to the Land of Plenty, and within one generation the Malibu sand had gotten into their genes and turned them into tall, Nordic powerhouses. Walking surfboards. We were thinking about how these Nordic people have Dustin as a son, and it's got to be a genetic throwback to some previous generation."

What Nichols didn't realize at the time were the parallels between Dustin Hoffman's and Benjamin Braddock's lives. Hoffman had grown up in Los Angeles, "always despising it," he says. "And that's not an overstatement. I lived in anti-Semitic neighborhoods, and I never felt a part of it, and I used to go to the Saturday-matinee movies to see the Dead End Kids jumping into the East River, and I wanted to be one of them." When he turned 20 and left college, he moved to New York, a place imbued with the spirit of the Beat generation and coffeehouse intellectuals. "We thought of ourselves as artists, and that's what we wanted. It was 180 degrees from today. I felt I was home. New York is Jewish, L.A. is not Jewish. L.A. called you a 'kike' in the 1940s and 50s."

So, much like Benjamin Braddock, when Hoffman went back to

Los Angeles to make the film, he moved in with his parents in their home off Mulholland Drive. But it lasted only about a week, and then he checked into the Chateau Marmont, at his own expense, where he would hang out at the pool after a day of filming. "I was so aware of people sitting around the pool and of how different I looked from them. I remembered this was how I felt when I'd moved out of this town 10 years [earlier]. So, yes, I was right back where I didn't want to be."

Larry Turman had a slew of actresses under consideration for the now iconic role of Mrs. Robinson: Patricia Neal, Geraldine Page, Deborah Kerr, Lana Turner, Susan Hayward, Rita Hayworth, Shelley Winters, Eva Marie Saint, Ingrid Bergman, and Ava Gardner. He also gave a copy of Webb's novel to Doris Day's husband and manager, Martin Melcher. "I sent him the book, but he hated it—he thought it was dirty—and wouldn't even pass it along to her," he recalls.

Mike Nichols went to see Ava Gardner at her suite in the Regency Hotel, in New York, a memory he now treasures, though "it was scary at the time." When he arrived at two P.M., he was a bit taken aback to find hanging around the suite "a group of men who could only be called lounge lizards: pin-striped suits, smoking in the European way—underhand—with greased-back hair. To my complete horror, Ava Gardner said, 'Everybody out! I want to talk to my director. Out, out, out!'" She then asked for the phone, saying, "I've been trying to call Papa all day!"

Nichols thought to himself, I can't do this. I don't think I can do this whole thing, especially since Ernest "Papa" Hemingway, with whom Gardner had worked and been friendly, had died in 1961.

The 44-year-old actress then told Nichols, "The first thing you must know is I don't take my clothes off for anybody."

"Well, I don't think that would be required," replied Nichols.

She then confided, "The truth is, you know, I can't act. I just can't act! The best have tried."

Nichols answered, "Oh, Miss Gardner, that's simply not true! I think you're a great movie actress."

"The main thing is—she's Ava Gardner!" he recalls now. "Not the youngest, but incredibly sexy and gorgeous—almost superhuman in that way. My heart was pounding."

Nonetheless, Nichols quickly recognized the impossibility of working with her and an offer was never made.

Nichols and Turman also discussed the sultry French actress Jeanne Moreau for the role, but "it became apparent that Mrs. Robinson had to be American or it was all over." In truth, there really was only one actor in Nichols's mind to play the well-heeled seductress: Anne Bancroft.

Born Anna Maria Louisa Italiano, in the Bronx, the 35-year-old Bancroft had won a Tony Award in 1958 for her first Broadway role, Gittel Mosca, the bohemian girl who falls in love with a midwestern lawyer in *Two for the Seesaw*. She won another Tony in 1960 as Annie Sullivan, Helen Keller's devoted teacher in *The Miracle Worker*, a role that landed her on the cover of *Time* magazine. She reprised that role on-screen in 1962, winning an Academy Award for best actress. Two years later, she married comedic actor and writer Mel Brooks.

"We didn't offer the role to anyone else except Annie," Nichols says. "Everyone cautioned her to turn it down. How can you go from the saintly Annie Sullivan to the Medusa-like Mrs. Robinson? Too risky." But Mel Brooks—who was then working on his comic masterpiece, *The Producers*—persuaded her to do it because he liked the script, written by his co-creator of *Get Smart*. Once signed, she was the biggest name attached to the film.

And perhaps for Nichols there was another element at play. Is it possible that Anne Bancroft reminded him—both in her intonations and in her appearance—of Elaine May? Just close your eyes and you'll hear a Mike Nichols–Elaine May routine in any number of scenes, such as the exchange between Benjamin and Mrs. Robinson in the Taft Hotel—filmed at the Ambassador, in Los Angeles—where Benjamin has just nervously rented a room for their first assignation. He calls her from the hotel-lobby pay phone and she asks:

"Isn't there something you want to tell me?"
"To tell you?"

"Yes."

"Well, I want you to know how much I appreciate this—really—"

"The number."

"What?"

"The room number, Benjamin. I think you ought to tell me that."

"Oh, you're absolutely right. It's 568."

"Thank you."

"You're welcome. Well, I'll see you later, Mrs. Robinson."

The intonation is dead-on, not just Bancroft's line readings, but Hoffman's as well. Buck Henry noticed it: "Dustin picked up all these Nichols habits, which he used in the character. Those little noises he makes are straight from Mike."

Though he wasn't aware of it at the time, Hoffman now thinks that Nichols, on some level, saw Benjamin as "his alter ego, meaning that he always felt that he was the outsider, born in Germany, coming to this country at an early age, perhaps feeling that he was odd-looking, like me, at least in terms of what we call the leading man. He guided me in such a way that I was an alter ego of a younger version of himself. He saw himself in the character."

Forty years after *The Graduate* first appeared, Mrs. Robinson now seems the most complex and compelling character in the film, in part due to Anne Bancroft's stunning performance. That she's an alcoholic, that she's trapped in a sexless marriage, that she's predatory, cool, and ironic—those are the traits that make her dangerous. That she was once an art major, a fact she reluctantly reveals to Benjamin in his one attempt at pillow talk, makes her vulnerable. We suddenly understand her—her bitterness, her deep pool of sadness. It's the key to her character, Buck Henry believes: "That's when I realized that I knew Mrs. Robinson. That she had *been* Benjamin. She is a very intelligent and cynical woman. She knows what's happening to her."

"I think Anne and Mike Nichols made a very critical decision," Hoffman muses, "which was not to judge the character. It's Nichols's style—he walks that edge of really going as far as he can without falling over the cliff, into disbelief. It's not caricature. That's the highest compliment for satire."

To underscore her predatory nature, Nichols and Richard Sylbert, the Brooklyn-born production designer, created a jungle effect in Mrs. Robinson's well-appointed den, where she begins her seduction of Benjamin. Throughout the film, she's dressed in animal prints such as tiger stripes and $25,000 worth of furs, including a Somalian leopardskin wrap.

"I kept thinking about 'The Beast in the Jungle,'" Nichols recalls. "Let's have animal skins." Sylbert made a tremendous contribution to how Bancroft appeared on film, even down to the tan lines on her shoulders when she removes her brassiere. "We wanted beautiful actresses," Nichols says, "but we wanted them to look like real people."

Sylbert had begun his film career as an art director for Elia Kazan on the set of Tennessee Williams's *Baby Doll* in 1956. After that he worked on *Splendor in the Grass*, *Long Day's Journey into Night*, *The Manchurian Candidate*, and, for Nichols, *Who's Afraid of Virginia Woolf?*, for which he won an Academy Award for art direction. (His identical twin brother, Paul Sylbert, also has had a long and stellar career as a production designer, having won an Academy Award in 1979 for his work on *Heaven Can Wait* and a nomination in 1992 for *The Prince of Tides*.)

"They spoke the same language, they consulted the same dictionary, they read all the same books," Richard Sylbert's widow, Sharmagne, recalls from her home in Laurel Canyon. The production designer and Nichols held lengthy conversations about how to capture on film what they considered the essence of Beverly Hills— its flora and fauna trapped, as it were, behind all that expensive glass. Beginning with the shot of Benjamin viewed through his boyhood aquarium, we have the feeling of someone cut off, suffocating. The aquarium motif itself underlines both the feeling of being separated from the world and the sense, in Nichols's words, of people "drowning in their wealth." Benjamin sees the world through glass: his aquarium tank, his scuba mask, even at the film's climax, when he bangs on the plate-glass window in the church where Elaine is marrying his rival, and the voices of the enraged wedding party are silenced, except for Elaine's glass-shattering cry to her last-minute rescuer—"Be-n-n-n!"

Before filming began, Nichols rehearsed his cast for three weeks, a luxury by today's standards. "We could have taken *The Graduate* on the road, we knew it so well," Katharine Ross recalls. "We rehearsed on a soundstage complete with tape marks and rehearsal furniture. Mike had just come off directing all those Neil Simon hits."

Hoffman didn't know at the time that it "was unusual to rehearse as if we were doing a play, finding the character, which is what you do in theater. This was my first film, so I thought that was it! It was the best rehearsal I'd ever had, and the most creative time. But once we started shooting, I felt more frightened and insecure, brought on by my fear that Mike thought he had made a mistake in casting me. At a certain point, I was terrified that I was going to get fired."

In fact, Gene Hackman—who was playing Mr. Robinson—was fired, three weeks into rehearsal. "Gene said to me while he was taking a leak in the men's room," Hoffman remembers, " 'I think I'm getting fired.' And he was, and I thought I was next. So by the time we started shooting I was on pins and needles, terrified that Mike didn't like what I was doing. He was never satisfied; he was always looking for the exquisite take. I was dubbed a perfectionist for years, and all I could think was 'I learned from Mike Nichols.' "

It had become clear during rehearsals that Hackman was simply too young to play Mr. Robinson. "Unlike Anne and Dustin, in the parts of Benjamin and Mrs. Robinson, the actors needed to be a whole generation apart," says Nichols. The mere six-year age difference between Bancroft and Hoffman didn't really matter, though. "Both actors seemed to be the ages their characters were. That's *acting*."

"Mike is ruthless when it comes to artistic decisions," Buck Henry says. "The play's the thing. He will shut a film down, he'll throw a film away, he'll fire someone, he'll do some really mean stuff in the editing." But it was a good move for everyone, Buck Henry felt, "because Gene went immediately on to *Bonnie and Clyde* and worked for Mike in other films," during a 40-year friendship with the director. Mr. Robinson's shoes were admirably filled by Murray Hamilton.

In retrospect, Dustin Hoffman felt that there was a special relationship between Nichols and Anne Bancroft. Hoffman, then 29, says he was "a neophyte, and [Bancroft] was an accomplished actress who knew what film was. We were friends afterwards. I loved her and I still love her. You're either working with people who are going for the same truth as you are or you're not. She was. She had a character." Anne Bancroft, at 35, but playing 45, doesn't have the dewiness of Katharine Ross—and she smokes, drinks, and has the regrets of an adult—but she's sexy and beautiful.

"We were all in love with Katharine Ross, of course," confesses Buck Henry. "She had a boyfriend at the time who used to hide behind trees and bushes when we were on location—to watch, just to make sure. It was some nice, school-type kid, long before Sam Elliott. I don't think Sam Elliott would hide like that."

Though playing mother and daughter, Bancroft and Ross never actually have a scene together. The closest they come is when Benjamin bursts into Elaine's bedroom to confess his affair with her mother, and Mrs. Robinson, rain-drenched and desperate, stands outside the door, too late to stop him. Her elegant face is framed just above Elaine's own. "You see Mrs. Robinson, disillusioned and bitter. It's one of those very subtle moments that only a great actress can pull off. In that moment you see the story of her life," says Ross.

Robert Surtees, the film's cinematographer, who died in 1985, had been in Hollywood since the advent of the talking picture. He'd earned a dozen Academy Award nominations and won three Oscars, for *The Bad and the Beautiful, King Solomon's Mines,* and *Ben-Hur.* "It took everything I had learned over 30 years to be able to do the job," Surtees said about shooting *The Graduate.* "I knew before we even started shooting that this wasn't going to be an ordinary picture. I had seen *Who's Afraid of Virginia Woolf?,* and I knew that Mike Nichols was a young director who went in for a lot of camera. In fact,

I told my operator and my assistants, 'You fellows be prepared because you're going to do some way-out shots.'"

"We did more things in this picture than I ever did in one film," Surtees wrote in a piece titled "Using the Camera Emotionally" for *Action* magazine in 1967. "We used the gamut of lenses . . . hidden cameras, pre-fogged film," as well as handheld cameras. In one particularly difficult shot that a special camera operator had to rehearse for two days, Surtees's camera acts as Benjamin, as he walks out of the house in wetsuit, diving mask, and flippers, dives into his parents' pool, swims underwater, resurfaces, only to be pushed back into the pool by his father. "We would do whatever we could think of to express the mood, the emotion of the scene," Surtees remembered. Turman was impressed when Surtees gave Nichols a real compliment by saying, " 'You're not asking for any over-the-shoulder shots [a clichéd shot of two people talking, with one person's back to the camera]. Neither did John Ford.' That's quite something coming from a crusty guy like Surtees."

The camerawork wasn't the only innovative element of *The Graduate*. About halfway through shooting, Nichols's brother, a physician, sent him the 1966 Columbia LP *Parsley, Sage, Rosemary, and Thyme*. Nichols listened to it continually for four weeks, then played a track for his actors. The New York actor William Daniels, who perfectly embodied Ben's uptight father in the movie, recalls, "Mike Nichols said to us, 'I have these two kids. One's very tall and one's sort of small. And I'm thinking of them to do the music for the picture.' And so he played 'The Sound of Silence.' And I thought, Oh, wait a minute. That changed the whole idea of the picture for me." For Daniels, who had originated the role of Peter in Edward Albee's *The Zoo Story*, it was no longer just a comedy.

═══════

Paul Simon and Art Garfunkel had been together since 1957, when they called themselves Tom and Jerry, and had even appeared on ABC's *American Bandstand*, fashioning themselves after the Everly Brothers. But when Nichols approached the musicians with his idea, they seemed uninterested, even blasé. This was the 60s, after all, and troubadours had better things to do than write for movies. Turman, however, made a deal with them to write three new songs, but they became so busy touring that Simon—a slow and careful composer—didn't have the time to do it.

When Nichols began editing the film, he and Sam O'Steen, his film editor, began laying in songs that Nichols had already fallen in love with: "The Sound of Silence," "Scarborough Fair," "April Come She Will." The one song Paul Simon did get around to writing, called "Punky's Dilemma," Nichols didn't like. It was written for the scene, Turman explains, "in which Dustin alternates swimming and fucking and fucking and swimming, from the hotel to his parents' pool." They ended up not using it, but Nichols was intrigued when he heard a few chords of a new song Paul Simon was working on, a kind of nostalgia lyric called "Mrs. Roosevelt." Nichols wanted it, so he suggested that he change the name to "Mrs. Robinson." The rest is pop-music history.

Art Garfunkel, who would be directed by Nichols as an actor in his next two films, *Catch-22* and *Carnal Knowledge,* was impressed with the director. "He always makes you feel like the smartest guy in the room," Garfunkel told *Vanity Fair* recently on the phone, before embarking on a brief solo tour. "You know how smart you have to be to do that?" Nichols had them record half-written songs on a Hollywood soundstage. The missing verses for "Mrs. Robinson" would appear in April 1968 on Simon and Garfunkel's *Bookends,* the LP with a striking Richard Avedon cover portrait of the two musicians.

Simon and Garfunkel's lucid, poetic lyrics serve as Ben's interior monologue as he makes his way through the empty opulence of his parents' suburban paradise. The juxtaposition of "The Sound of Silence," a deeply personal *cri de coeur,* against the Los Angeles airport terminal—as Ben is carried robotically along a moving walkway—is both touching and funny. Right away we know we're in a fish-out-of-water story, and Ben's inarticulate, deeply felt musings will suffocate in this environment.

In some ways, the ironic use of Simon and Garfunkel's music—"April Come She Will" while Ben sits in bed in the Taft Hotel, drinking a can of soda, catatonically watching television while Mrs. Robinson flits back and forth in various stages of undress, or Paul Simon's acoustic guitar slowing down and sputtering as Ben's Alfa

Romeo runs out of gas during his desperate race to the church—prefigured the music video. You might say MTV was born out of *The Graduate*.

═══

After the film was completed, Larry Turman began screening it in "the show-business halls of Hollywood," in Hoffman's phrase. The results were not good. Turman feared the film was going to be unsuccessful, because at all those Hollywood homes, industry insiders would come up to him afterward and say, "This could have been a great film if Nichols hadn't badly miscast the lead."

Joe Levine was so worried that he decided to release *The Graduate* as an art-house film, Hoffman recalls, "which, in those days, meant 'soft porn.' And so I got a phone call that he wanted me to come in and pose with Anne Bancroft. She would be sitting on a bed, and I would be facing her, standing up—naked—and she would have her hands around me, holding my buttocks! The only reason that didn't happen was that Nichols found out and put an end to it."

Hoffman saw the film for the first time at a sneak preview on East 84th Street, in New York. "I was sitting in the balcony," he recalls, "and suddenly it was like a train gaining momentum, and by the time we were halfway through, the film was having a wild response. By the time I'm running to the church [at the film's climax], the audience was just standing up, screaming and yelling. It was a profound experience—I was literally shaking through the whole film."

When the movie ended, Hoffman and Anne Byrne, his girlfriend, whom he would soon marry (and divorce from in 1980), waited until everybody had left. "The thought of being recognized? I was traumatized. Everyone left, and we went downstairs, and a woman walking with a cane, slower than everyone else, saw me. She pointed her cane at me and said, 'You're Dustin Hoffman, aren't you? You're the Graduate.' I'd never been recognized in public before. She said, 'Life is never going to be the same for you from this moment on.'"

Hoffman came out of the theater, and "I remember it was snowing, and [I was] trying to get a cab, which was a luxury for us then, and I remember looking up at the snow and saying, 'Annie, now, *that's* real. What we just went through *ain't.*'"

The woman with the cane was Radie Harris, a prominent gossip columnist, but it would take some time before her prophecy came true. Next, Hoffman was summoned to the opening at the Coronet Theater in New York. "All the suits were there, friends of Joe Levine," Hoffman remembers. "There wasn't a laugh during the entire film. That picture bombed! I walked out saying to Anne, 'It's a flop.'"

That's when Levine asked Hoffman and Nichols to tour college campuses, to help build "a word-of-mouth audience." ("They don't even use that phrase anymore—the movies don't stay long enough in the theaters," says Hoffman.) Levine paid Hoffman $500 a week, "more than I got for shooting it," and threw in some perks to get the actor on board.

Nichols wasn't crazy about the idea. He accompanied Hoffman on the tour, and "in college after college, there was one question: Why isn't the movie about Vietnam? You had to be outraged about Vietnam or it was shit. No matter what you were doing—if you ran a laundry, your shirts had to be outraged about Vietnam."

And yet, despite the initial resistance, despite the doomsaying of the suits in Hollywood, the groundswell began. After the movie opened, on December 21, 1967, at the Coronet, on 59th Street and Third Avenue, and the Lincoln Art Theater, on 57th and Broadway, huge lines began to form. Film critic Hollis Alpert, writing in *The Saturday Review*, noticed that from his window he could see "lines extended around the corner, all the way down the block. . . . *The Graduate* is not merely a success; it has become a phenomenon of multiple attendances by young people. One boy . . . bragg[ed] that he had seen *The Graduate* more than any of his friends, no less than 15 times. . . . Marlon Brando, the revered James Dean, and [Elvis] Presley never came near doing that [kind of business]."

Turman, who had prevailed after countless turndowns from the studios, got the last laugh. At one preview, at Loew's on 72nd Street, "there were like 2,000 people and they tore the roof off the theater—

it's like we orchestrated it! It was just fantastic. In the lobby I ran into [producer] David Picker, who had turned it down, and very ungraciously I walked up to him and said, 'Not funny, huh?'" At another theater, Turman ran into a studio head standing in line to see the movie, who said to him, "Larry, why didn't you *make* me make *The Graduate!*"

The film, which cost $3 million to make, became the highest-grossing motion picture of 1968. It earned $35 million in its first six months, after playing in only 350 theaters around the country. *The New Yorker* devoted 26 pages of its July 27, 1968, issue to Jacob Brackman's critical dissection of the film, in which he called it "the biggest success in the history of movies." Despite such high praise, though, Nichols felt that a lot of the reviews missed the mark, describing it as a film about the generation gap. "At that particular moment, 'the generation gap' was everything. It never even entered our minds! The generation gap? Was it worse than Romeo and Juliet? What're they talking about?"

Though the movie may not have been about the generation gap, it was inextricably linked with its time, an era of incredible social and political upheaval. During the spring 1968 student takeover of Columbia University, members of the radical Students for a Democratic Society took turns sneaking out of the occupied president's office to go see *The Graduate.* On June 5, 1968, Robert Kennedy was assassinated in the pantry of the Ambassador Hotel, where parts of *The Graduate* had been filmed. That very week, "Mrs. Robinson" was the No. 1 pop song in America.

=====

"**M**rs. Robinson" earned Simon and Garfunkel the Grammy Award for record of the year in 1969. And despite the dearth of new material by the pair (though it included six original compositions by film composer Dave Grusin that had been used in the movie), the *Graduate* soundtrack album won another Grammy for Paul Simon. *The Graduate* received seven Academy Award nominations (which must have baffled Bob Hope, that year's master of ceremonies): best picture, best actor (Hoffman), best actress (Bancroft), best supporting actress (Ross), best director (Nichols), best screenplay based on another medium (Willingham and Henry), and best cinematography (Surtees). Only Nichols won, however. His decision to cast Hoffman to represent the perpetual outsider, the artist-refugee adrift in a world of plastics, had paid off handsomely, earning him a Golden Globe and best-director awards from the New York Film Critics Circle and the Directors Guild as well.

"I don't know of another instance of a director at the height of his powers who would take a chance and cast someone like me in that part," Hoffman says. "It took enormous artistic courage." Hoffman's affecting, understated performance sanctified Nichols's big gamble. And Hoffman's emergence as a leading man, you might say, made cinema safe for ethnic actors soon to follow, such as Al Pacino and John Travolta and even Woody Allen, who could go from playing comic stooges in *Casino Royale* and *Take the Money and Run* to credibly romancing *shiksa* dream-dates Diane Keaton and Mariel Hemingway in *Annie Hall* and *Manhattan*. After Hoffman, conventional good looks didn't matter as much as wit, or toughness, or sexiness. "It was like rock 'n' roll," Buck Henry observes. "A whole generation changed its idea of what guys should look like, because the girls went for the musicians. I think Dustin's physical being brought a sort of social and visual change, in the same way you talk about Bogart. They called *him* ugly—this, the most handsome man in films. But his generation thought he was awful-looking, until one day he wasn't."

Anne Bancroft, who died in 2005, is unforgettable as Mrs. Robinson, and she was forever after identified with the role, to the point where, later in life, she had to remind people, "I've made other films, you know!" Hoffman escaped that fate. His post-*Graduate* career has been nothing short of miraculous. He has a protean quality that has allowed him to morph into beings as varied as Ratso Rizzo, the tubercular lowlife in *Midnight Cowboy*, the *Washington Post* reporter Carl Bernstein in *All the President's Men*, the much-harassed comic Lenny Bruce, the idiot-savant hero of *Rain Man*, even a lovable man in drag in *Tootsie*. He's garnered seven Academy Award nominations for best actor, and he's won twice, for *Kramer vs. Kramer* and *Rain Man*.

In the past 40 years, *The Graduate* has served as a kind of film-school course for new generations of filmmakers, including Steven Soderbergh, Harold Ramis, Todd Haynes, Mark Foster, the Coen brothers, and Paul Thomas Anderson. When asked why she believes *The Graduate*'s impact has lasted so long, Katharine Ross just laughs and, channeling Sam Elliott in *The Big Lebowski,* says, "The Dude abides."

"It really belongs to nobody now," Mike Nichols reflects, sitting back in his chair at the Polo Lounge, sipping an Arnold Palmer. "It certainly doesn't belong to Charles Webb. I don't think it served to unbalance him, but it served to age and confound him. It was whipped away from him. We didn't do it. We just made the movie! But then again, I think everybody feels it was whipped away from them."

Charles Webb, 68, and his wife, Fred (she had her name changed from Eve in solidarity with a now defunct support group for men with low self-esteem), currently live in East Sussex, England. Renouncing material success, Webb turned down an inheritance from his father, sold his film rights to *The Graduate* for $20,000, then gave the copyright to the Anti-Defamation League. He and his wife home-schooled their two sons and worked as dishwashers, housecleaners, and clerks at Kmart, living in campgrounds and trailer parks. They even lived in a Motel 6 for a while, in the small California coastal town of Carpinteria, before moving to England, where two years ago they were threatened with eviction from their apartment above a pet shop.

Considering himself a literary and not a commercial writer, Webb both distanced and disinherited himself from the success of the movie. (Two other movies based on his books were made: *The Marriage of a Young Stockbroker,* in 1971, and *Hope Springs,* in 2003.) One of his sons, who became a performance artist, even cooked and ate a copy of *The Graduate* with cranberry sauce, a stunt that was mentioned in the English press. "Millions and millions were made from *The Graduate,* and here I am," Webb told the BBC, "searching around for a couple of quid to buy my sandwich—people love that." He did publish seven more novels, including *Home School,* a sequel to *The Graduate,* which picks up in the mid-70s, with Benjamin and Elaine living in Westchester County, with their two boys, and crossing paths again with Mrs. Robinson. When Thomas Dunne/ St. Martin's released the American edition, in January 2008, Webb told the *New York Post* that he "thought it would be my final bow to fiction, to go back to the beginning to find the ending. And then on to something else."

After claiming not to have seen the movie of *The Graduate* for many years, he now calls it "excellent," giving it "four and a half out of four stars."

Throughout his long career, Mike Nichols has won at least one of every major entertainment award: the Oscar, the Emmy, the Tony (seven of them), and the Grammy (for best comedy album, with Elaine May). He's done such fine work for so long that he is in danger of being taken for granted. When he's asked what was different about making movies back in the 1960s, now that his career has entered its sixth decade and he has amassed a formidable body of work (including *Who's Afraid of Virginia Woolf?*, *Silkwood*, *Working Girl*, *Postcards from the Edge*, *Primary Colors*, *Wit*, *Angels in America*, and *Closer*), the ghost of a smile crosses Nichols's face. "I was just thinking," he says, "about how happy we were making *The Graduate*. What was different? Of course, *we* were different then. There's nothing better than discovering, to your own astonishment, what you're meant to do. It's like falling in love."

From *Vanity Fair*, March 2008

THE PRODUCERS

Producing The Producers

by Sam Kashner

They call me the producer.
Pray for me. —SIDNEY GLAZIER

The Producers, one of the most lauded and successful Broadway musicals in recent memory, began life some 40 years ago as a movie that got queasy reviews and quickly sank at the box office. It was the brainchild of the comic genius Mel Brooks, but it couldn't have been made without the efforts of larger-than-life producers Sidney Glazier and Joseph E. Levine, and a collection of singularly talented New Yorkers who were, for the most part, flying by the seat of their pants. Alfa-Betty Olsen, a writer and performer who worked closely with Brooks and cast the movie, knew that from the beginning. "I used to say to Mel, 'You know, we're doing this for the Thalia [an art and revival movie house on Manhattan's Upper West Side].' It was really a home movie," she explains at a corner table at Café Loup in Manhattan. "A very, very small movie with a small budget, done in New York City with all New York people." What they ended up with was a film, in Olsen's words, "so unique it exists out of time."

When it opened, in 1968, the movie got mixed notices, with such words as "vile" and "tasteless" cropping up in the prominent reviews. For one thing, it was considered unthinkable to satirize Hitler only 23 years after the end of World War II. For another, what chance did a send-up of show business—New York, vaudeville, showgirls-with-pretzels-on-their-tits kind of show business—have in the era of Vietnam and student rebellions and acid rock? Not much.

"It started out in life as just a title," Brooks likes to say: *Springtime for Hitler.* The phrase leapt to Brooks's lips during a press conference for a 1962 musical called *All American,* starring comedian Ray Bolger, for which Brooks had written the book. A reporter yelled, "What are you going to do next?" and Brooks answered, "*Springtime for Hitler.*" He was just being outrageous, riffing, perhaps, on the title of a forgotten 1931 comedy called *Springtime for Henry,* but the phrase stuck.

Next came the hero's name: Leo Bloom. Brooks borrowed it from James Joyce's epic novel *Ulysses.* "I don't know what it meant to James Joyce," Brooks told the theater critic Kenneth Tynan in a 1978 interview for *The New Yorker,* "but to me Leo Bloom always meant a vulnerable Jew with curly hair."

Before *The Producers* was a movie, it was supposed to have been a novel. Thing was, Brooks never thought of himself as a writer until he saw his name in the credits for Sid Caesar's television comedy series *Your Show of Shows.* Brooks was one of several sketch writers it employed from 1950 to 1954 (others included Woody Allen, Larry Gelbart, and Neil Simon). "I figured I'd better find out what these bastards do," he said. So he went to the library and took home all the books he could carry: "Conrad, Fielding, Dostoyevsky, Tolstoy." Eventually he realized he wasn't really a writer, he was a talker. "I wished they'd changed my billing on the show," he told Tynan, "so that it said 'Funny Talking by Mel Brooks.'" It was, in fact, that gift for funny talking—improvisation—that made Brooks's reputation.

Brooks first got into movies with a short called "The Critic," which took advantage of his genius for comic patter: it consisted of geometric patterns with the running commentary—in voice-over—of a cranky, clueless Jewish guy who wanders into the movie house and doesn't get it. ("Vat da hell is it? . . . I don't know much about psych-analysis, but I'd say this was a doity picture.") It was essentially a filmed comedy routine—and it won Brooks an Oscar for best short film.

Still, Brooks felt that impromptu dialogue and stand-up comedy didn't have class—*writing* had class. But when he tried to turn *Springtime for Hitler* into a novel, it didn't work. He then tried it as a play, but soon realized that as a movie "it could go places, it wouldn't have to stay in the office"—the action could spread all over New York. Brooks had found his métier. He was going to make a movie, a real movie, like, well, the way Ed Wood did! Looking back, Brooks says, "I loved that movie *Ed Wood*," referring to the 1994 Tim Burton film about the world's most amateurish *auteur*. "I bought it and run it all the time. Marty [Martin Landau] is great in it as Bela Lugosi. When he calls Boris Karloff a 'cocksucker'—I love it! It's so real. I identify with Ed Wood—that's me."

Now he had to write the screenplay.

"One day," Alfa-Betty Olsen remembers, "Mel called up and he had the story. He had the dopey, repressed accountant, and he had [the crooked producer] Max Bialystock." Olsen, who was raised in a Norwegian neighborhood in Brooklyn, lived on 15th Street in Manhattan then, with a roommate named Candace. Brooks would visit during the long doldrums after *Your Show of Shows* went off the air, and his salary had plummeted from $5,000 to $85 a week for free-lance writing jobs.

———

It was a bleak period in Brooks's life. For five years he couldn't get work. *All American* had ended its brief run. Jerry Lewis hired him as a screenwriter for *The Ladies Man* and then fired him. An original screenplay called *Marriage Is a Dirty, Rotten Fraud* (written as Brooks's first marriage, to dancer Florence Baum, unraveled) went begging. Brooks was reduced to living in a fourth-floor walk-up on Perry Street in Greenwich Village.

Then, in 1965, his luck changed. With comedy writer Buck Henry, he created *Get Smart,* the popular secret-agent spoof, for television. That success didn't fill him with joy, however, because now he feared he would spend his entire career in television. He felt boxed in; he had wanted a life larger than that. Even during the glory years of *Your Show of Shows*, he had told Sid Caesar, "Enough—let's do movies!"

The success of *Get Smart* relieved Brooks of financial worries, but it also highlighted a problem that would become something of a pattern in his career. Buck Henry resented the billing "by Mel Brooks with Buck Henry," and the two men fell out over it. Henry later said that he had once bet that Mel Brooks's name would appear five times on the credits of *High Anxiety*, Brooks's 1978 parody of Hitchcock's thrillers.

"Tell him from me he's wrong," Brooks said. "The correct number is six" (for writer, director, actor, producer, composer, and lyricist).

Once Brooks had the characters and the basic plot, he wrote the treatment and screenplay, with Olsen's help, in theatrical producer Lore Noto's West 46th Street office. Noto, who produced the longest-running musical in American history, *The Fantasticks*, had recently produced one of the shortest-running, a musical version of Marjorie Kinnan Rawlings's novel *The Yearling*, about a boy and his pet fawn; it closed on Broadway after three performances.

"In return for looking after Noto's mail and things, we had an office, and that's where we wrote it," Olsen says. "Lore would come in after lunch, and then, around two o'clock, the phone would ring, and it would be Anne Bancroft," the elegant, Academy Award–winning actress whom Brooks had married in August 1964. "Anne would get Lore on the phone and ask him, 'Is my husband there?' That's how it went. We also cast the movie out of that office. Everything was kind of makeshift. . . . And it was just so evident that Mel wanted it very much. You could feel him reaching for the brass ring. Writing *The Producers* was Mel creating himself; he wanted to declare himself on the world."

When they weren't in Noto's office, they continued to write the screenplay out on Fire Island, at Brooks and Bancroft's house on the beach. They worked in their bathing suits on the deck, with a portable electric typewriter set up on a small table among the folding chairs. Olsen was a good secretary, but more than that, she was a singularly funny woman with a strong background in theater. She had been in on the creation of *Get Smart*. "I was thrilled, I was in seventh heaven to be working with Mel," Olsen says. "After all, he had written for Sid Caesar."

The plot was simple: A seedy, has-been producer (Max Bialystock) finances his shows by romancing and fleecing elderly women. When a timid accountant (Leo Bloom) shows up to do Bialystock's books, he discovers that a producer can make more money on a flop than on a success, by raising more than the show actually costs to produce and pocketing the leftover lucre. The conniving Bialystock sees the beauty of a simple idea: the I.R.S. never audits a flop, especially if it closes after just one performance. He persuades the neurotic Bloom to go along with his scheme, and they set out to find the worst play ever. They do. It's *Springtime for Hitler*, written by a crazed, unreconstructed Nazi (Franz Liebkind) who keeps pigeons and lives in a shabby walk-up in Greenwich Village. To make sure that Liebkind's play will flop, they hire the most incompetent director they can find, a cross-dressing Busby Berkeley reject (Roger De Bris; *bris* is the Yiddish word for the circumcision ceremony), and cast a zonked-out hippie on parole to play Hitler (Dick Shawn as Lorenzo St. DuBois, better known as "L.S.D."). They oversell the show by 25,000 percent, and, in a *coup de grâce*, Bialystock tries to bribe the *New York Times* theater critic and succeeds in earning his ire. The show, as expected, is a horror, but the two producers hadn't counted on the pleasures of satire. The audience, convulsed with laughter, decides that *Springtime for Hitler* is a comedy and that it will run for years! Bialystock and Bloom are ruined. They have to pay profits to the mass of investors they'd hoped to bilk—an impossibility.

Brooks didn't have to look far for models for Max Bialystock. He had once worked for "a guy well into his 60s who made love to a different little old lady every afternoon on a leather couch in his office," and he knew another producer who made his living by producing flops. (Brooks won't supply their names.) And the Great White Way was full of producers who kept two sets of books. *Time* magazine suggested that Bialystock was in fact a parody of David Merrick, the cranky, mustachioed producer of *Hello, Dolly!* and many other hits.

But Brooks says he also looked to himself: "Max and Leo are me, the ego and id of my personality. Bialystock—tough, scheming, full of ideas, bluster, ambition, wounded pride. And Leo, this magical child."

———

It took six years to bring the concept to the screen. Once Brooks had started to make the rounds with his 30-page treatment, he quickly found that all the major studio heads recoiled at the idea of Hitler as a comic figure. It was just too tasteless, too outrageous. So Brooks tried independent producers and found much the same reaction, until a friend set up a meeting at a coffee shop in Manhattan with an independent producer named Sidney Glazier.

"Sidney Glazier was larger than life," recalls Michael Hertzberg, sitting in his spacious home office, in the Hollywood Hills, surrounded by framed movie stills from films he's worked on as a director, writer, and producer (including several of Brooks's movies, as well as *Johnny Dangerously* and *Entrapment*). As a young man, Hertzberg was an assistant director on *The Producers*.

"Sidney was just loud and big," Hertzberg recalls. "He was more like Bialystock, [but] you'd look into his past and discover he'd already won the Oscar for [the 1965 documentary] *The Eleanor Roosevelt Story*. He had a huge, huge heart—gigantic. So who took a risk on this crazy man with this crazy thing—*Springtime for Hitler*? If it wasn't for Sidney, there would be no *Producers*, there would be no Broadway show, there would be no nothing."

Glazier, a handsome, dark-haired man then in his 50s who, like Brooks, had served in the Second World War, was having lunch at the Hello Coffee Shop when Brooks arrived for their first meeting. Glazier recalled that Brooks began by telling jokes, "some of which weren't too funny, and I was a little uncomfortable." But then he asked Brooks to read him the treatment, so Mel acted out all the parts with such slapstick bravura that Glazier nearly choked on his lunch. "He's sitting there, eating his tuna sandwich and drinking black coffee, and I'm reading it to him," Brooks recalls, "and the tuna fish is flying out of his mouth, and the coffee cup gets knocked off the table. And he's on the floor, and he's yelling, 'We're gonna make it! I don't know how, but we're gonna make this movie!'"

Glazier's own story was a harrowing one. "Basically, I grew up in an orphanage," Glazier told journalist Timothy White in a 1997 interview for *Billboard*, "the Hebrew Orphan Home on Green Lane in Philadelphia, but I didn't start out in that terrible place. I was put there." Born in 1916, he was the second of three sons of a Russian-Polish couple from Minsk. When his father, Jake Glazier, died suddenly in the influenza epidemic of 1918, his widow, Sophie, took up with another man, who already had three children. "Basically, this man didn't care to raise me or my two brothers," Sidney recalled, "and my mother, in her awful irrationality, decided my brothers and I would be better off in this Orthodox institution. . . . Back then, you were supposed to have no living parents in order to be admitted to an orphan home; years later, we learned that she actually paid to bend the rules. I can still see the glow of the globe-shaped desk lamps on either side of the police chamber where these matters were decided." He tried to run away from the orphanage and its "constant chill, lousy food, and bare beds," but had nowhere else to live; he left for good when he was 15.

"My mother let me stay with her second family for just a month, but then I had to go." Sidney found a job as an usher at the Bijou, a burlesque theater in Philadelphia, "for $9.00 a week"—just enough to rent a room. That's when he realized that movies were "the loveliest and best escape from the troubled life I inherited."

Karen Glazier, Sidney's daughter and a novelist who teaches at Williams College, recently described her father as one who was "proud of overcoming obstacles. His was a Horatio Alger story, a Jewish Dickens story." She never really thought of him as "a film person," however. "I always thought of him as being in the fund-raising business," she explains. "He was a genius at raising money, at charming people. . . . He was a very good-looking guy with a big voice who looked good in a suit. Nice shoulders. But he was impossible to live with. My father was married four times, and he demanded huge amounts of attention."

Perhaps not surprisingly, given his upbringing, "Sidney battled depression," says Karen. "He was incredibly manic, he could be incredibly depressed. He might have been bipolar. He moved between self-destructive tendencies and the will to survive."

Glazier took the screenplay of *The Producers* to Florida and gave it to his trusted cousin Len Glazer and his wife, Zelda, to read. Len and Zelda's son, the screenwriter Mitch Glazer (*Great Expectations, The Recruit*), remembers his father reading the screenplay, which was in a red folder, on their porch in Florida. "He was in hysterics," Mitch recalls. "But then my mother said, 'You can't make this, Sid. It's completely offensive! You've got an Academy Award, you're on the road to stardom, your career would be ruined!' But he didn't listen," according to Mitch. "He had made up his mind."

———

Karen recalls that her father "admired on-your-feet, spontaneous talk. I'm sure that's what he saw in Mel at first." But there were other things that attracted him, such as the similarities in their Russian-Jewish backgrounds. For another, Brooks's father had died suddenly of kidney disease when Mel was two years old. But, unlike Glazier, Brooks had experienced the adoration of his mother and her extended family, even as she worked 10 hours a day during the Depression to support her children. Kenneth Mars, hilarious as the German playwright, Franz Liebkind, in *The Producers,* said recently that he had once asked Brooks about the key to his success, and Brooks answered, "'You know, my feet never touched the floor until I was two because they were always passing me around and kissing and hugging me.' I think that's a key: the kind of image he has of himself of the evergreen child, the child who brings you fun," Mars commented.

Glazier had a little company, U-M Productions, Inc., located in both New York and Florida. His partner was Louis Wolfson, who, Brooks recalls, was "a big guy in the stock market. They took me to a horse-racing stable whose big horse was Affirmed [which would later win the Triple Crown, the last to do so], and I acted out all the parts for Louie and the horse." (Like Bialystock and Bloom, Wolfson would end up going to prison, but his crime was violating securities laws.)

Then, Brooks recalls, "we went to one studio after another. We went to Lew Wasserman at Universal. Wasserman said, 'I like it, ex-

cept for one change.' 'What's that, Lew?' 'Instead of Hitler, make it
Mussolini. *Springtime for Mussolini.* Mussolini's nicer.' 'Lew,' I said,
'I'm afraid you just don't get it.' So, finally, Joe Levine [head of Em-
bassy Pictures] agreed to put up the other half of the money." They
had 40 days, a budget of $941,000, "and we couldn't go a penny over,"
Brooks recalls.

If Glazier was a producer, Joseph E. Levine was a mogul. Among
other jobs, he'd been a scrap-iron dealer before turning himself into
one of the most successful film producers and distributors of his day.
At five feet four and more than 200 pounds, he described himself in
one of his own press releases as "a colossus towering above the lesser
moguls of filmdom." Levine had made his fortune distributing *Hercules* and *Hercules Unchained,* beefcake pictures starring the muscle-
bound Steve Reeves. "He bought Hercules for $120,000, swathed
it in $1,156,000 worth of publicity . . . and grossed, so far, $20 million," gushed the L.A. *Times* in 1966. But if his career began with
Hercules, Godzilla, and Attila, by the mid-60s he had left most of the
schlock behind and began backing art films. Joseph E. Levine Pre-
sents bought the North American distribution rights to Vittorio De
Sica's *Two Women,* starring Sophia Loren, after seeing only three
minutes of the rushes. Through shrewd advertising and campaigning, he helped the sultry Italian star win an Academy Award for best
actress—the first time anyone had won for a performance in a foreign language. Levine went on to produce or distribute Fellini's *8½,
The Lion in Winter, Darling, A Bridge Too Far, The Graduate,* and
Carnal Knowledge.

Like Bialystock, Levine had learned to "flaunt it." The rich and
powerful mogul maintained legions of assistants ("He practically invented the personal assistant," says Olsen), a 96-foot yacht, an estate
in Greenwich, Connecticut, and a fabulous art collection.

Like Brooks and Glazier, the short, portly Levine had grown up
poor and fatherless, the youngest of six children born to a Russian-
immigrant tailor. "He had a funny office," Olsen recalls. "There was
a hallway that was paved to look like the street in Boston where he
began [Billerica Street]. It was designed to make you—and him—
never forget where he came from." Levine once said that he couldn't
recall "one happy day growing up." He had spent his childhood "hus-

tling pennies as a shoeshine boy." He also sold newspapers, lugged suitcases, drove an ambulance, and "manufactured little statues of Daddy Grace, a black evangelist." Olsen saw in Levine the boy who never had a childhood: "He did magic tricks in his office. When you came in, he made a silver dollar stick to his forehead. It was kind of appealing, actually."

Hertzberg recalls the first meeting between Levine and Brooks: "Levine was a child of the Depression, and in his office he kept a bowl of apples. So when Mel goes up to see him, Joe says, 'Mel, my job is to get the money for you to make the movie. Your job is to make the movie. My job is to steal the money from you. And your job is to find out how I do it. Here, have an apple.'"

Once the deal was made, Levine asked, "Who do we get to direct?"

Without missing a beat, Brooks said, "Me. I know everything about this picture. I know where every character has to stand." But Levine needed proof that he was up to it, so Brooks agreed to direct a commercial for Frito-Lay, with Olsen as casting director and Gene Wilder appearing as a daredevil aviator, complete with white silk scarf.

It was a success, and Levine agreed to let Brooks direct, but under one new condition: he had to change the name of the movie. *Springtime for Hitler* had to go. "No Jewish exhibitor will put *Springtime for Hitler* on his marquee," Levine told him. Brooks reluctantly changed the title to something Levine could live with: *The Producers*. It wasn't as striking as the original, but it was more appropriate than most people would ever know—no more colorful team of producers could be found to mount a movie than Glazier and Levine.

Brooks never had anyone else in mind to play Max Bialystock but Zero Mostel.

Mostel, the rotund, rubber-faced comic actor—an inspired clown of Falstaffian proportions—had won three Tony Awards practically back-to-back for his performances in Eugene Ionesco's *Rhinoceros* in 1961, in Stephen Sondheim's *A Funny Thing Happened on the Way to the Forum* in 1963, and—most famously—as Tevye in

Fiddler on the Roof in 1965, which had made him a Jewish icon. His friend the writer A. Alvarez once described him as "a galleon in full sail, laden with pleasure." He was perfect for the part of the loud, grasping, overwhelming Bialystock, except for one little problem: he didn't want to do it.

Glazier sent Mostel the script, but he heard nothing back. Karen Glazier recalls, "It bugged my father that Zero hadn't bothered to answer him. Later, he ran into Zero and his wife, Kate." "Schmuck!" Sidney said. "You don't return letters with scripts attached to them?"

"What's he talking about?" Mostel asked his wife. Mostel had never even seen the script. "His agent read it first and thought it was offensive, and he had kept it from him," Karen explains. So Sidney gave the script to Kate, the former Kathryn Harkin from Philadelphia, a dancer and ex-Rockette.

Kate liked it, but still Mostel didn't want to do it. He didn't want to follow up his role as the beloved Tevye by playing "a Jewish producer going to bed with old women on the brink of the grave." But finally Kate persuaded him to take the role. "You son of a bitch," Mostel told Brooks, "I'm gonna do it. My wife talked me into it."

If Glazier and Brooks "were like cat and dog," as Karen Glazier says, then with Mostel thrown into the mix, "there was a lot of yelling."

"Zero Mostel was heaven and hell" to work with, Brooks recalls. "When in a good mood, he was cooperative. He would do seven takes and give me something ecstatic, something of joy . . . or lunacy. A year before, he was hit by a bus, so he would say, 'My leg is killing me, I'm going home.' I'd beg him to stay. . . . He'd say, 'That's it. Shut up. I'm going home. Fuck you.' On one of the good days, Zero would get up on a chair and announce, 'Coffee nearly ready,' and he'd imitate a percolator. I mean, you would never get anything as glorious as Zero Mostel doing coffee! Or he would say, 'No, fuck you, I'm going to do it as written.' He was ebullient, sweet, creative, and impossible. It was like working in the middle of a thunderstorm. Bolts of Zero—blinding flashes of Zero!—were all around you."

Indeed, Mostel's injury was serious enough to threaten to derail shooting on a number of occasions. In January of 1960 he had stepped out of a New York City cab and was struck by a bus, shattering his left leg. Despite numerous operations, the injury would plague him for the rest of his life.

Mostel was often difficult on the set, but the day they shot the trial scene at 60 Centre Street he seemed especially agitated and unwilling to work. No one knew why. It dawned on Hertzberg some 30 years later that the courthouse was the problem. "It was the blacklist. It colored everything for him," he says.

Mostel had been listed in *Red Channels,* a compilation of 151 alleged subversives, which began circulating among studios in Hollywood in the early 1950s. One of his cabaret creations, a blustery, know-nothing southern senator called Polltax T. Pellagra ("What the hell was Hawaii doing in the Pacific Ocean, anyway?"), had attracted the attention of southern conservatives. On October 14, 1955, Mostel was called before the House Committee on Un-American Activities. He had refused to name names by invoking the Fifth Amendment, which meant he remained blacklisted, and the unproven taint of subversiveness clung to him. As a result, he did not work in films for more than 10 years. Showing up at the Federal Courthouse on Centre Street must have stirred up bitter memories of his testimony before HUAC.

———

Gene Wilder had never set out to become a comic actor. He had trained in the Method. It was Anne Bancroft who brought him to her husband's attention. "He was in [Bertolt Brecht's] *Mother Courage and Her Children* with Anne," Brooks recalls, "and I met him backstage, and he was complaining that they were laughing at his serious performance. He couldn't understand it. 'Because you're funny!' I told him. 'Gene, you're funny. Get used to it. Go with what works!' Then, three years later, he was in *Luv,* the Murray Schisgal play, and he was great in it. And I went to his dressing room and threw the script of *The Producers* on the desk and said, 'There it is. You are Leo Bloom. You didn't think I forgot, did you?' And he burst into tears."

The comedic actress Renée Taylor, who played Fran Drescher's wisecracking mother on television's *The Nanny,* was appearing with Wilder in *Luv* when Brooks went to see the show. "He saw me, and that's how I got to be in the movie" (in an all-too-brief comic turn as Eva Braun), Taylor recalls over lunch at Kate Mantilini in Los Angeles. "I knew Gene Wilder. I was in Lee Strasberg's class with him. His name [then] was Jerome Silberman, and he was very shy. He was such a stickler for the Method—but talk about not being funny!" When Brooks approached him for *The Producers,* Wilder had just made his film debut as a hysterical undertaker in *Bonnie and Clyde.* "Gene was amazing in it," says Hertzberg. "He kind of invented that role of the hysteric."

Perhaps hysteria—and its opposite, repression—came easily to Wilder. When he was a six-year-old in Milwaukee, his mother, a pianist, had a heart attack. From then on, he lived in fear that if he got her excited she might die of another one. "I had to hold back everything all the time," he remembered, "but you can't hold back without paying a big price."

———

There was one enormous obstacle to casting Wilder in the part of Leo Bloom: Brooks had promised Mostel that Wilder would read for the part. But Wilder hated to audition—he was practically psychotic on the subject. Wilder confessed to his psychiatrist that he really wanted the part, and that he believed if he were turned down he would spend the rest of his life as a character actor. "You see," he said, "I knew Leo Bloom could make me a star." After reading Brooks's script, he recognized that he was "exactly at the same stage of life as Leo. . . . Bloom was a man ready to bloom, a man who changes dramatically when he meets his catalyst, Max Bialystock." Reluctantly, he agreed to audition for Mostel.

"I went up the elevator and my heart was pounding," Wilder recalled to Jared Brown, Mostel's biographer. "I knock at the door. There's Mel and Sidney and Zero. Zero gets up and walks toward me, and I'm thinking, Oh God, why do I have to go through this again? I hate auditions, I *hate* them. Zero reached out his hand as if to shake hands, and then put it around my waist and pulled me up to him . . . and gave me a big kiss on the lips, and all my fear dissolved."

Wilder may have been Brooks's first choice, but another Off Broadway actor, who was getting good reviews in Ronald Ribman's *Journey of the Fifth Horse,* was also a possibility: Dustin Hoffman.

After they all caught his performance, "Dustin came back with us to Mel's apartment," Olsen recalls. "Mel and Anne lived on 11th Street, in a town house. Sidney liked Dustin really a lot." But after reading the script, Dustin wanted to play Liebkind, the addled Nazi playwright. "But of course that was impossible; nobody wanted him to be the German," remembers Olsen.

And then, one night, Brooks recalls, "someone woke me up, throwing pebbles at the window. 'It's me, it's Dusty.' 'What do you want?' I said. 'I can't read Franz Liebkind,' he said. 'I'm going to L.A. to audition for Mike Nichols to be in a movie with your wife.' 'Don't worry,' I told him, 'you're a mutt. They're going to get a better-looking guy for the part—you'll be back, and the part will be waiting for you.'"

But Hoffman got the role he auditioned for—that of a disaffected college student who's seduced to the sounds of Simon & Garfunkel by an older woman, played, ironically, by Anne Bancroft, then just 37. The movie was *The Graduate* and it made Hoffman a star. "It's a good thing he went," says Brooks, "for him, and for *The Producers,* because we got that genius Kenneth Mars."

At the time, Mars was probably the most sought-after actor in television commercials. "I was doing a lot of commercials, and I'd always wind up going down Broadway. I would see Mel on my rounds, and he would stop me and say, 'I'm writing this great picture and you're in it, and you're going to be fantastic,' and so on. Finally, he sent me a script," Mars recalls. "The part he wanted me to play was the gay director, Roger De Bris. . . . I was playing a sort of gay psychiatrist [in a show called *Best Laid Plans*], and Mel loved that character."

Mars came in to audition, but he announced, "'Well, De Bris is a good part, but I'm not playing it. I'm playing the German.' 'No you're not,' Mel said. 'Yes I am.' 'No you're not.' 'Yes I am.'" Mars was called in three times to read; at last, Olsen said, "Hire him, he's terrific."

It was Mars's first film role, and he was thrilled. But he quickly came up against Brooks's stubborn control of every aspect of the movie. When Mars suggested putting pigeon droppings on Liebkind's Nazi helmet (after all, he keeps birds—"doity, disgusting . . . boids"), Brooks resisted. He finally gave in, but then the two men haggled over how many droppings. They settled on four.

Brooks did not want his actors to improvise lines—or add pigeon droppings—but Mars is proud of some beauties he contributed that made it all the way to the Broadway incarnation: "Churchill . . . and his rotten paintings. The Fuhrer. Here was a painter! He could paint an entire apartment in von afternoon—two coats!"

For the eight weeks of shooting, Mars lived in his costume—stained suspenders; ratty, military-issue woolen underwear; a Nazi helmet. "That may have set Zero off, I think," Mars says. "In the beginning it was O.K., because I told him how much I admired him—I had seen him in *Ulysses in Nighttown,* in which he was brilliant—and he said, 'Oh, thank you, my boy, thank you, dear boy . . .'

"Then I got my first laugh from the crew," Mars remembers, "and I was in trouble from Zero. Anyway, my smelling to high heaven may have [reminded] Zero of some less-than-fun days." Mars's ability to stay in character throughout the entire shoot also made a deep impression on Wilder, who later admitted, "I didn't know if the character Kenneth Mars was playing was crazy or if Kenneth Mars was crazy."

———

"It wasn't a studio film," remembers Hertzberg. "There was no one to call if you needed more money, so the guys who were trained in New York had a certain way of getting things done. We made *The Producers* for $941,000, not $942,000. There wasn't the extra thousand. Forty days in New York, and that was it." That was a challenge Hertzberg could live with. In 1967 he was a good-looking, dark-haired kid who smoked a pipe to make himself look older.

Shooting for *The Producers* began on May 22, 1967, at the Production Center at 221 West 26th Street, "somewhere between Cuba and the Dominican Republic," Hertzberg recalls, "also known as the Hy Brown Studios," owned by two brothers. "These were the two cheapest guys who ever lived. In the wintertime, you couldn't knock on the pipes [to get heat]. But every day there would be fresh flowers. I went over to Mendy [Brown] and said, 'Mendy, you're the cheapest guy I ever met in my life. How do you have fresh flowers in the studio every day?' He said that when Hy, his brother, comes in from Long Island, he stops at the cemetery, picks up the flowers, and brings them into the studio. From graves."

At first there was camaraderie on the set. Olsen recalls that "after the day's shoot, we would see the dailies, and then we went to [hipster hangout] Max's Kansas City for dinner every night." Even Mostel, with his bad leg, would make it to Max's, where he would greet the drag queens with a sloppy kiss on the lips.

It wasn't long, however, before Brooks's lack of experience, the pressure of directing his first movie, and his need for utter control of all aspects of filmmaking took its toll on cast and crew. "The first thing Brooks said when he got on the set was 'Cut!'" Hertzberg recalls. "No," he explained to Brooks, "wait a minute—first you say 'Action,' and when you're done you say 'Cut.' It was that rudimentary. We all just stood around waiting for him to say something."

"By the end of the first morning on the set, Mel was already becoming jittery," according to Ralph Rosenblum, the film's editor (who died in 1995), in his 1979 book, *When the Shooting Stops . . . the Cutting Begins.* Rosenblum was beginning to wonder if Brooks was prepared for the differences between television and film. "Did he know that in the movies you could shoot only about five minutes of usable film in a day? . . . Brooks couldn't stand the waiting, and his impatience quickly extended to the cast. He soon found himself in a head-on conflict with the mountainous Mostel. The first time the star couldn't perform with just the inflection Brooks wanted, the entire project seemed to be slipping from the director's grasp. After several faulty takes, he started to shout, 'Goddamn it, why can't you . . . ' But Mostel turned his head like a roving artillery gun and barked, 'One more tone like that and I'm leaving.'"

Soon, the two men headed enemy camps. "'Is that fat pig ready yet?' Mel would sputter, and Mostel would say, 'The director? What director? There's a director here?'" recalled Rosenblum.

"There were no camps," Hertzberg says in response to Rosenblum's characterization. "Zero didn't have a camp. Zero *was* the camp. [Mel and Zero] didn't get along that well. For one thing, Zero had it in his contract that he didn't have to work past 5:30 if he didn't want to, because of his bad leg. And he used that a lot. Zero had a huge problem with authority."

———

Hertzberg realized Brooks's lack of experience when he saw that he had no idea where to put the camera. But Hertzberg did. "So when the cameraman Joe Coffey gave Mel a lot of crap, because Coffey didn't understand the comedy, I was able to interpret. After the first few days, when we saw the rushes, the actors looked like they were standing on stumps . . . cut off at the ankles." Coffey finally blew his cool. "You can't do that! It's not cinematic!" he shouted. They had to reshoot, and that was the end of the camaraderie between Brooks and Coffey.

Brooks continued to goad Mostel on the set, trying to get the "blinding flashes of Zero" that he needed to illuminate his movie. Olsen saw that "the really terrible part was that Mel had insomnia. Mike Hertzberg was just carrying him around." Glazier noticed that Brooks was "gray with fatigue" by the end of the day.

The film took eight weeks to shoot and months to edit, with Brooks fighting Rosenblum on every cut. When, halfway through shooting, Rosenblum ran the first 20 minutes of edited film at the MovieLab screening room, Brooks bulldozed his way to the front of the room, planted himself in front of the screen, and faced Rosenblum and Glazier. As Rosenblum recalled, "Brooks growled . . . 'I don't want you to touch this fuckin' film again! You understand? . . . I'll do it all myself. Don't *touch* it until I finish shooting!'"

Rosenblum was deeply shaken by the tirade. Driving back home to New Rochelle, he gave Glazier a lift, and the two men sat in the car in stunned disbelief. Glazier finally blurted out, "I don't know why Mel has to do this. Why does he have to make it so difficult?"

One day a young writer for *The New York Times* named Joan Barthel arrived on the set to write a feature on the making of *The Producers*. Glazier was delighted; what they needed was good publicity, but, to Glazier's horror, Brooks went out of his way to be offensive. "What the fuck do you want?" he barked at Barthel. "What do you want to know, honey? Want me to tell you the truth? Want me to give you the real dirt? Want me to tell you what's in my heart?" At first Barthel thought this was a put-on, part of Mel Brooks's shtick; then it dawned on her that she was being attacked. "Throughout much of the morning, on the set," she later wrote, "as he hurled vivid invective at one of his staff people, and sarcasm at a visiting photographer . . . he had seemed—well, cranky."

Glazier picked his way through some cables to rescue the hapless writer, and introduced himself, adding, "They call me the producer. Pray for me." What should have been found gold—free publicity—turned into a nightmare for Glazier. The article ran with an unflattering photograph of Brooks in mid-tirade, the portrait of a man losing his grip.

Then, several weeks into the shooting, Brooks banned Glazier from the set. Glazier obliged; his nerves were frazzled, and he was smoking three packs of cigarettes a day. But eventually he returned, anyway.

And yet. Despite all the murderous complaints, despite the temper tantrums, despite the insomnia and the insecurity (or perhaps because of them), Brooks got inspired performances from all his actors, including Mostel, whose best work up to that point was generally considered to have happened onstage, in live theater. "Zero was a very old-fashioned kind of performer," Olsen says. "Film was not his medium. He didn't have a clue. But what he did on *The Producers* was quite nice; it was always the lowest take, the take with the least volume, the most human take, that was chosen." Film is a medium which rewards subtlety; critics tend to prefer Wilder's hysterical sweetness to Zero's histrionics. Yet *The Producers* is probably Mostel's best captured performance, the one that will be remembered by posterity.

The Playhouse Theatre on West 48th Street in Manhattan was the actual set for *Springtime for Hitler,* the musical-within-the-movie. (It was demolished in 1969.) On Monday, June 25, 1967, the entire company moved into the theater.

Word had spread among actors that they were casting Hitlers. Olsen recalls, "The tenor from [the Frank Loesser musical] *The Most Happy Fella* came in with a guy from *Fiddler on the Roof.* They were Broadway guys. They didn't want to tell me, because they thought it would turn me off. But, no, I hired them. Agents called for people who had leads in Broadway shows. John Cullum's agent called, but we couldn't use him."

Charles Rosen, *The Producers'* set designer, recalls, "We chose the theater because we needed the alley [for scenes that were eventually cut]. It was four blocks down from Rockefeller Center. There used to be a drugstore there, in the lobby, with a counter. The actors dressed as SS officers would walk down Sixth Avenue in their uniforms," complete with Nazi armbands and polished boots. The sight of dozens of actors dressed as Hitler, taking their lunch break in a coffee shop in Rockefeller Center, caused a near riot, according to Rosen.

All the other scenes were filmed on location whenever possible. It was Olsen's idea to use the Revson Fountain at Lincoln Center. They were looking for a place to film the moment when Bloom agrees to become Bialystock's partner in crime. Olsen was at the Library for the Performing Arts at Lincoln Center, researching possible songs to use during the audition scene, when she walked past the Revson Fountain. "I thought, This is kind of good. We could use the fountain."

It was the last scene they shot, but they almost didn't finish it, because Mostel and Brooks were so furious with each other that Mostel was threatening to walk off the picture for good. Glazier was at the dentist when he heard, and, with his mouth bloody, he rushed over to Lincoln Center. He succeeded in getting Brooks and Mostel to tolerate each other long enough to finish the movie. "Something about the water made Zero angry," Glazier later said.

Around 5:30 in the morning on July 15, 1967, the fountain came to life in the pre-dawn light. Hertzberg recalls, "If you look at that wonderful scene where the fountain comes up, look above and see what color the sky is. It was dawn. We shot all night. We just had enough darkness left to do it, but it was a blue sky, not black. Then we went down to Chinatown for breakfast, like we used to do. It's a memorable scene."

"It was a long night," Olsen remembers. "It was wet and slippery, but Gene Wilder ran around the whole fountain," celebrating his decision to seize the day. It's the "I want everything I've ever seen in the movies!" scene, the *cri de coeur* straight from Mel Brooks through his alter ego Leo Bloom.

━━━━

Too bad the movie bombed. The earliest screenings were held in late November in a small theater in suburban Philadelphia. "There was no promotion, minimal advertising," recalls Olsen. "It would follow *Helga, An Outstanding Film of Childbirth*—no one under 13 admitted." At one screening, there were only about 38 people in the theater, including a bag lady and Joe Levine and some of his people from Embassy Pictures, who had taken limos down from New York. But it soon became apparent there was something wrong. Nobody was laughing. Levine turned to Glazier and said, "You and Brooks are full of shit. You lied to me. Stick this picture up your ass." He pointed to the bag lady in the audience and said, "Look, even she fell asleep."

It's possible that Levine really didn't like the picture, but in truth he had something else up his sleeve. He had already decided to put his resources behind another movie that was already being talked about—*The Graduate*. To add insult to rivalry, it had been written by Brooks's co-creator on *Get Smart*—Buck Henry. Like many of the old-time moguls, Levine could smell a hit, and that hit was going to be *The Graduate*, not *The Producers*. *The Producers* finished its three weeks in Philadelphia and limped into New York.

But just as it seemed the movie would be buried and forgotten, Peter Sellers saw it, almost by accident. While in Los Angeles making Paul Mazursky's *I Love You, Alice B. Toklas*, Sellers had organized a movie club—with dinner—and the night they were supposed to see

Fellini's *I Vitelloni*, it couldn't be found to accompany the spaghetti Bolognese that had been prepared by Mazursky's wife. So the projectionist ran *The Producers* instead. Sellers loved it. That same night, he called Levine back East, waking him up at two A.M. to say *The Producers* is "a masterpiece, Joe!" Three days later, Sellers paid for a full-page ad in *Variety:* "Last night I saw the ultimate film," it began. When the movie opened in New York, Sellers took out another full-page ad, in *The New York Times*. The movie broke box-office records at the Fine Arts Theatre that first week.

But it didn't go over well in the provinces. "It didn't make a lot of money, ever," Brooks says. "I mean, it played in the big cities, but would people in Kansas understand about raising 1,000 percent to put on a Broadway show?" Hertzberg agrees. "It was only accepted among Jews! If you went to Des Moines, forget it."

And then there were the reviews. Some critics found the movie hilarious, but most objected to what they saw as tasteless. Pauline Kael wrote in *The New Yorker*, "That's not screenwriting; it's gag-writing."

"Renata Adler [of *The New York Times*]—she was the *worst*," Brooks remembers, still wincing. "I never thought black comedy of this dilute order could be made with the word or idea of Hitler in it anywhere. . . . I suppose we will have cancer, Hiroshima, and malformity musicals next," she wrote.

Brooks was very depressed. "I remember telling Annie, my wife, 'They thought it was in bad taste. It's back to television. It's back to *Your Show of Shows.*'" Sellers's rave—though it didn't make *The Producers* a hit—may have influenced the Academy of Motion Picture Arts and Sciences to award Brooks an Oscar for best original screenplay (after all, it was always about the words), but the award didn't bring him many offers, because the film didn't make any money. His second movie, *The Twelve Chairs*, came out two years later and crashed. So he went back to wandering the streets of New York, nearly broke, when one day he ran into David Begelman, then an agent at Creative Management Associates. Begelman "brought him out of the desert. He even had a new father figure to replace

Sidney," Hertzberg says. "*Blazing Saddles* [in 1974] came out of that meeting—another script, another idea that can't miss. Lucky for Mel, it didn't. He made a fortune. The checks are still coming in for that one."

———

Although *The Producers* was not commercially successful, over the years it began to acquire cult status. Lines of dialogue and phrases from the movie started cropping up in the language, such as "creative accounting" and "When you've got it, flaunt it" (which appeared in a Braniff Airways advertisement as the caption to a photograph of Andy Warhol seated next to boxer Sonny Liston).

With the musical Brooks has come full circle, back to Broadway. "Thirty-five years later, it's a hit on Broadway—it has a new life now," Brooks says in his office in Beverly Hills, where the desk, the pens, the canisters of film, and the ashtrays are most definitely all his. "*The Producers* is like Halley's comet," he says. "It'll have a metamorphosis, like Ovid. I'm proud of it. After all, it started out as a title."

Hertzberg says, "Brooks owns 25,000 percent of the musical. Well, not really, but he's pretty heavily invested in it; he owns a very large piece. After all, he did write the book, the songs, and he'd play all the parts if he could."

This may be just the beginning of Brooks's third act in show business; *Young Frankenstein* has had a nice run on Broadway [and TV's *Get Smart* recently hit the big screen]. As Hertzberg says, "Brooks is hoping to live forever."

———

Before his death, in December of 2002, Sidney Glazier watched as Brooks, on television, accepted a record-breaking number of Tony Awards—12—for the Broadway incarnation of *The Producers*. Like Kenneth Mars, Glazier stayed away from the Broadway musical of *The Producers*, and the movie's set designer, Charles Rosen, has yet to see it. But Gene Wilder did go and, according to a friend, "is all right with it."

After Brooks swept the Tonys and thanked Glazier in his acceptance speech, the producer got a congratulatory call from his nephew Mitch, who regarded Sidney as a father figure. "All of a sudden," Mitch recalls, "the big voice was back. He'd had time to think things over."

"The son of a bitch owes me money," Glazier yelled into the phone, a producer to the end.

From *Vanity Fair*, January 2004

MIDNIGHT COWBOY

Midnight Revolution

by Peter Biskind

From where we stand now, four decades after the 42nd Academy Awards, it is impossible to imagine an X-rated film winning best picture. But that is exactly what *Midnight Cowboy* did on a spring night in 1970, earning as well Oscars for its director, John Schlesinger, and its writer, Waldo Salt. This was a dramatic moment, pregnant with historic significance, marking as it did the symbolic transfer of power from Old Hollywood to New. *Bonnie and Clyde* had paved the way two years earlier, but despite 10 nominations that film was passed over in all the major categories on Oscar night. Audiences may have been flocking to New Hollywood pictures, but the Academy's Old Guard, the Bob Hopes, Frank Sinatras, and John Waynes, the guys with the stars on Hollywood Boulevard, were not eager to give their blessing to a bunch of longhairs. Yet despite a nod to Wayne that year (he won best actor for *True Grit*), the tide was too strong. After April 7, 1970, Hollywood would never be the same.

For a variety of reasons—partly having to do with *auteur*-driven film history that discounts Schlesinger, owing to his indifferent subsequent output (with the signal exception of *Sunday Bloody Sunday*), and partly due to *Midnight Cowboy*'s undeniable flaws—the picture has often been slighted. Neither Pauline Kael nor Andrew Sarris, the Scylla and Charybdis of film reviewing in those days, gave it unqualified support, even though when the film works, which is most of the time, it spectacularly fulfills ambitions rarely imagined, much less realized, in commercial American movies of any era. Today, *Midnight Cowboy* provides a spellbinding glimpse—etched in acid—of how we lived then that bears comparison to the work of great documentary still photographers, such as Weegee, or to the lurid excesses of tabloid filmmakers, such as Sam Fuller, or to the hallucinatory sensibilities of a Fellini. At the same time, *Midnight Cowboy* makes us a gift of one of the landmark performances of movie history: Dustin Hoffman's Ratso Rizzo, with Jon Voight's Joe Buck a close second. From a cesspool of dark, foul, even taboo material—drugs, illness, passionless sex, both straight and gay—it rescues a true humanism that need not hide its name.

"You couldn't make *Midnight Cowboy* now," Schlesinger, who died in 2003, said in 1994. "I was recently at dinner with a top studio executive, and I said, 'If I brought you a story about this dishwasher from Texas who goes to New York dressed as a cowboy to fulfill his fantasy of living off rich women, doesn't, is desperate, meets a crippled consumptive who later pisses his pants and dies on a bus, would you—' and he said, 'I'd show you the door.'"

———

By the mid-1960s, John Schlesinger had suddenly become a very hot director. Born in London in 1926, the son of a pediatrician, he was an Oxford-educated, cultured man with a dry, cutting sense of humor. He had directed two British hits in a row: *Billy Liar* (1963) and *Darling* (1965), the second of which won three Oscars, among them best actress for Julie Christie. He was hot enough to attract the attention of producer Jerome Hellman, who, after seeing *Billy Liar* and its predecessor, *A Kind of Loving*, had flown to London to persuade the director to sign on to a project he was developing for United Artists.

Hellman, a former agent, had produced one hit, *The World of Henry Orient* (1964), with Peter Sellers, and one flop, *A Fine Madness* (1966), with Sean Connery. A former Marine, Hellman was the physical opposite of Schlesinger, small where Schlesinger was large, sharp where Schlesinger was round, brash where Schlesinger was courtly. And direct. As he says, "I was very serious about what little work I did. And I tried to work with guys who were equally serious." Schlesinger was serious, too, and though he dropped out of Hellman's project, the relationship they had established would eventually flower.

In 1965, a friend had given the director an unsettling new novel that contained several scenes of homosexual sex. It was called *Midnight Cowboy* and had been written by James Leo Herlihy. It told the story of Joe Buck, a sexually ambiguous, Texas-born stud-slash-dishwasher who travels east in hopes of preying on sex-starved New York matrons as a gigolo, but ends up in an ostensibly platonic but freighted relationship with a consumptive street hustler—Ratso Rizzo. Schlesinger liked the book enough to pass it along to his longtime producer, Joe Janni, as a possible film property. But Janni, a volatile Italian, hated it, saying something like "John, oh my God, are you crazy? This is faggot stuff. This will destroy your career." Disappointed, Schlesinger moved on. But *Midnight Cowboy* stayed with him. He read it again, called Hellman, and said, "Look, I've read a book that's very strange. It's nothing like the film you brought me. But I would like you to read it and tell me what you think." Hellman did, told him that it was fascinating material, but that it would be very difficult to execute. "I thought that the relationship between the two guys was something that would work," the producer recalls. "But that if there was any hint of homosexuality it would be a catastrophe. I was a little embarrassed to say that, because when I met John he was still carrying on this charade of being a straight man. In the little house on Peel Street, he had a guy living in the attic, but he never let me meet him. He told me I was not supposed to know that there was a guy scurrying in and out. So I knew he was gay, but he absolutely agreed with me [about *Midnight Cowboy*]. I said, 'O.K., look, it'll be very hard to get money for it—we'll have to work for nothing—but I'd love to try to do it with you.'"

———

Hellman had made *The World of Henry Orient* for United Artists, the filmmaker-friendly company that was then run by the triumvirate of Arthur Krim, Bob Benjamin, and Arnold Picker. It was the company of choice for many world-class filmmakers. The head of production was Arnold's nephew, a prescient young man named David Picker, who had snagged the rights to Richard Lester's Beatles film *A Hard Day's Night* as well as *The Pink Panther* and a series of pictures based on Ian Fleming's spy novels, featuring James Bond.

Picker was also a fan of Schlesinger's work, and so the director and Hellman met with him to discuss *Midnight Cowboy*. The executive said he liked Herlihy's novel and wanted to make it, but added, according to Hellman, "My partners here, the older men in the company, aren't going to understand it. So it's got to be [no more than] $1 million, all-in!" Hellman swallowed. Even in those days that was very little money for a film budget. On the other hand, it appeared that they had a go picture, and both men felt U.A. was the best place for a movie as raw and potentially controversial as this.

They hired a playwright named Jack Gelber to adapt the novel. He seemed a good fit: Gelber's hip junkie drama, *The Connection*, had won three Obies in 1959. One day Gelber told Hellman, "Look, there's a play Off Broadway, and it's called *Eh?* I think that we should go to see it, because there's a young actor in it—he might be a terrific Ratso." As Hellman recalls, "It was a one-character drama, a caretaker in the basement of a factory. And the caretaker was Dustin Hoffman. I was bowled over. I went, 'Oh, shit, this guy was born to play Ratso Rizzo.'" The producer also loved the idea of hiring an Off Broadway actor because he'd come cheap. Hellman sent the book to Hoffman, who read it, liked it, and told the producer he'd do the part.

Meanwhile, Gelber wrote two drafts that neither Schlesinger nor Hellman felt worked. They were back to square one. Then, one day, George Litto walked into Hellman's office. Litto, a bluff, stocky man, was an agent with an eccentric client list, including a number of blacklisted screenwriters, among them Ring Lardner Jr. and Waldo Salt. Litto was pushing Salt for *Midnight Cowboy*.

Like many in the Hollywood of the 1930s, Salt had joined the Communist Party—in his case, on his 24th birthday. Twelve years later, in 1950, with his writing career flourishing, Salt was called in front of the House Un-American Activities Committee. Taking the Fifth Amendment, he refused to name names, and in an instant his brilliant career was over. He scraped by writing for television under his wife's name. But as the 1950s wore on, the blacklist began to crumble, and in 1962 Salt succeeded in getting his first script credit in 12 years, for *Taras Bulba*. He quickly wrote two more movies, *Flight from Ashiya* and *Wild and Wonderful*. But he knew that all three of them were junk. Ironically, now that he had finally regained his right to write, he couldn't do it. He left his wife and two daughters and holed up in the seedy Paris Hotel, on New York's Upper West Side, washed up at 50. Hopeless and depressed, he binged on vodka. Recalls his daughter Jennifer, then an actress who would get a small part in *Midnight Cowboy* (she would become a writer on TV's *Nip/Tuck*), "He was a very unpleasant drunk, and nobody wanted to be around him. I didn't. I was terrified of him when he was drunk. But those three pictures kind of turned it around for him, and he just made the decision that he was going to take his work as seriously as he possibly could. It just carried him." He began writing a script about a Vietnam War draft resister.

"I checked Waldo out as much as I could, and he had these terrible credits," recalls Hellman. "George explained about his blacklisting, having to write shit just to survive. But I declined to see him. George said, 'Look, I've got 36, 38 pages of original script that Waldo is writing. It's called *The Artful Dodger*. If you promise to read it, I promise you that if you don't want to meet this guy I will never set foot in your office again.' Who could turn down something like that? So I read it.

"What John had tried to communicate to Gelber," Hellman continues, "was the idea that there should be a certain energy about

Midnight Cowboy—a New York energy. And that it would involve the present, the past, reality and fantasy, almost a mosaic. Well, that's exactly what Waldo was doing with *The Artful Dodger*. It had that totally fragmented feeling that we'd been searching for. I hadn't read five pages when I got really excited. I called George, and I asked to see Waldo, right away. Of course, then it was all over, because Waldo, who I think was the most brilliant guy I've ever met, came in so prepared. He had analyzed the book and he'd analyzed the characters and he had a memo for me, outlining his approach to the film. I sent it off to John, who was shooting *Far from the Madding Crowd* [his follow-up to *Darling*], and with it a note of my own, saying that I thought this guy might be the answer to our prayers. I got a wire back saying, 'Just hire him immediately, and start work.' So I did."

When Schlesinger finished *Far from the Madding Crowd*, a sprawling adaptation of the Thomas Hardy novel, with Christie, Terence Stamp, and Alan Bates, MGM's suits professed a lively passion for it: "This is a blockbuster. This is going to be a gigantic smash," etc., etc. The studio flew him over to Los Angeles in mid-October 1967 for a screening and after-party, and then the premiere. But the screening was a disaster, the party a wake, and the movie subsequently tanked. "I thought I was going to get him on a real high," Hellman recalls. "But John was very susceptible to his moods, and instead he was absolutely devastated."

Hellman, whose wife had walked out on him, taking their two children, was himself not in much better shape than Schlesinger. *Midnight Cowboy* proved to be one of those happy accidents: a perfect storm created by a handful of lavishly talented people who had all bottomed out. Reflects Hellman, "John was deeply depressed. So, in a way, we were kind of ideally suited to one another. [Along with Waldo], we were three depressed people really looking for a break."

———

Salt was famous for his snail-like pace, but when his draft finally came in, Schlesinger liked it. Still, it needed work. Schlesinger, Hellman, and Salt started meeting every morning at the beach house the director had rented in Malibu, and batted around ideas. In the afternoons, Salt went home and incorporated the morning's work into the script. "It was like extracting teeth to get pages out of Waldo," says Hellman. "But when the pages came, they were tremendously exciting. This process lasted a long time, months and months and months of work." There was one key structural problem to solve: the filmmakers wanted to focus on the novel's second half, after Joe Buck gets to New York, but what to do with the first half, which takes place in Texas? "None of them liked the standard flashback," recalls Jennifer Salt. "My dad sort of developed this notion of a 'flash-present,' where Joe Buck's past is seen through his eyes in the present as memories."

Hellman submitted Salt's pages to U.A., and the three men waited anxiously for a response. When it finally came, the news was good. "This is fucking great," said Picker. "Brilliant. We love it. Let's get going." The only thing that was not discussed was that it was clear that the script, with its hundreds, if not thousands, of fragments and images, which would make up the "flash-present"s—every one of which had to be orchestrated—could not be shot for $1 million. And there was another problem: while waiting for *Midnight Cowboy* to get off the ground, Dustin Hoffman had made *The Graduate* for director Mike Nichols, and on December 21, 1967, the film opened to ecstatic reviews and phenomenal box office. Suddenly, Hellman recalls, "this Hoffman guy, who was an Off Broadway actor, starving to death, was a huge star."

After *The Graduate* Hoffman was turning down everything he was sent. "I was a theater person," he says. "That's how my friends were, too, Gene Hackman and Bobby Duvall. I wasn't going to be a movie star. I wasn't going to sell out. We wanted to be really good actors. After Brando did *A Streetcar Named Desire,* he was getting on an airplane to L.A., and he said, 'I'm going out to make this movie. Don't worry, I'm coming right back.' There was a dignity to being against success."

But *Midnight Cowboy* wasn't the usual dreck, and Hoffman still wanted to do it. Mike Nichols, who was looking out for him, called him up. Hoffman remembers, "He said to me, 'So I hear you're going to do this thing, you're going to play the male prostitute.' 'No, no, I'm going to play the other role.' He knew the material, and he was stunned. What troubled him was that it was a supporting character.

With a certain amount of Nichols-esque wryness, he said, 'I made you a star, and you're going to throw it all away? You're a leading man and now you're going to play this? *The Graduate* was so clean, and this is so dirty.'"

But it was the very contrast between Benjamin Braddock, his preppy character in *The Graduate,* and Ratso Rizzo that appealed to Hoffman. "I had become troubled, to say the least, by the reviews that I had read of *The Graduate* in that I kept seeing over and over again that I was not a character actor, which I liked to think of myself as, but that Mike had found this guy, this nebbish, and gotten a performance out of him. It hurt me. Some of the stuff in the press was brutal. I felt there was a kind of disguised anti-Semitism. They would describe me in the way that the cartoons in Nazi Germany in the 30s pictured Jews—beak-nosed, squinty eyes. And nasal. I was determined to show them, in big letters, THEM, that I was an actor. Revenge is always a good motive in creativity."

But Schlesinger wasn't sold on Hoffman. The actor's performance as Benjamin, with his button-down shirts and crewneck sweaters, was so convincing, and so far from Ratso, that Schlesinger seemed unable to comprehend the fact that he was acting. Continues Hoffman, "I was told that he didn't want to meet me, because, artist that he was, he was not going to cast somebody who's hot, when I wasn't right." Hoffman invited Schlesinger to meet him at an Automat in the heart of the old, ungentrified, un-Disneyized Times Square. "I asked to meet there so I could dress as the character, in a dirty raincoat," he says. "Maybe I slicked back my hair or something. Maybe a couple days of growth. Late, because I had been there late and it got very seedy. And John, whom I loved from the very beginning, looked at me, and he looked around, and he said, 'I've only seen you in the context of *The Graduate,* but you'll do quite well.'" Hoffman promised the director that he would lose weight and stay out of the sun.

"We had had the same image of the character," Hoffman says. "More important, I connected with the role. I felt very unattractive growing up. The acne, the blah-blah. I was always on the periphery. I was never in the club. The whole center of Ratso was something that was not acting. An actor loves being able to play the essence of a character that he feels is him, that he doesn't have to act. That's when you do your best work. Directors, the few really great ones, cast the essence, rather than an actor acting the essence. It was almost criminal in some circles that Nichols had cast me in *The Graduate,* because the role was written as Robert Redford in the book—blond hair, debating squad, champion runner. I didn't even want to test for it. But somehow Nichols cast an essence that he felt was the character and was also me. Kind of alien, not connected to family, outsiders. Benjamin has no friends, and neither does Ratso. Ratso needs somebody, and he becomes the catalyst to changing that person's life."

At the Automat, Hoffman and Schlesinger lingered over their food and talked. "John was very self-conscious, because he was from London. He kept saying, 'I don't know if I understand the American experience.' I thought, Why did they get a British director?"

Hoffman had no idea that Schlesinger was gay: "I said, 'You're not married?' He said, 'No.'

"'You think you'll ever get married?'

"'No, no, I don't think so.'

"'Why not?'

"'Why not? I just don't, I just don't like the idea of waking up with a woman lying next to me.'

"'Why?'

"'I just would guess, I don't know, it'd be horrifying.' I just looked at him. I had this stupid grin on my face. I was so naïve, it didn't occur to me. Finally I said, 'Well, how come?'

"'Oh, because I'm a homosexual.' Oh, O.K."

———

Schlesinger had given up trying to conceal his sexual orientation ever since he had fallen in love with a young, dazzlingly handsome photographer named Michael Childers, whom he had met on a blind date when he was in L.A. for the premiere of *Far from the Madding Crowd.* "We were one of Hollywood's first out couples," says Childers. "He took me everywhere. I felt a little bit uncomfortable at times, but John never did. He said, 'Fuck 'em.' George Cukor was a friend of ours. He said, 'I was never able to do that. I admire you and John.'" Schlesinger hired Childers as his assistant on *Cowboy*.

The director was now sold on Hoffman, but there was still the matter of salary. The actor's agent, Jane Oliver, told Hoffman there was an offer of $75,000 on the table. "Whoa! That was a lot of money in those days," Hoffman says. "And I, who have never been a businessman and certainly wasn't one then, it just came into my head out of nowhere: I said, 'See if you can get double.' It was the first time I'd ever uttered a sentence like that in my life. She called me back the next day, said, 'I got great news: I got it.' My stomach sank, because I knew I had made a huge mistake. I knew if they said 'Yes' that fast something was very wrong. Then I met some guy who later became my manager, who said, 'What points did they give you?' And I swear to God, I thought of the tips of a fork. 'Points? What do you mean, "points"?' I didn't, you know, *know*."

———

To Hellman, the good news was that they had their Ratso. The bad news was that the producer had to go to Picker and ask for more money, say, "Hey, look, this guy is our Ratso Rizzo, we've been on him for years, and now we've gotta sign him. But he's a hot commodity." U.A. allowed Hellman to offer Hoffman his $150,000, which was more than producer, director, and screenwriter combined were getting paid. But the money was worth it. For the first time, Schlesinger and Hellman looked at each other and thought, in Hellman's words, "Hey, we're going to get to make this fucking movie, because U.A.'s not going to want to blow their $150,000."

Once Hellman and Schlesinger had their Ratso, it was time to cast their Joe Buck, their midnight cowboy. Word was out that they had a hot script, and all sorts of actors wanted the part. According to Childers, "Elvis Presley's person from MGM said, 'If you'd clean up this script, get rid of some of the smut, it could be a vee-hicle for Elvis!'" But the casting director, Marion Dougherty, had other ideas. Dougherty, who was casting all the New Hollywood films—she had worked on *Bonnie and Clyde* and *The Graduate*—was turning the business upside down. When she started working, in the early 1960s, casting was still in the Dark Ages. "They had all these people under contract, so you selected one from Line A and one from Line B," she says. "It was like ordering Chinese dinner." Dougherty, on the other hand, shunned the Tabs and the Troys, the look-alikes who flocked to L.A. Instead, she haunted the New York theater—Broadway, Off Broadway, Off Off Broadway, the clubs, the downtown lofts and church basements, Long Island and New Jersey even, searching for interesting faces and new talent. She was pushing a young actor named Jon Voight, who had made a mark in Ulu Grosbard's 1965 production of *A View from the Bridge,* with an up-and-coming Robert Duvall in the lead and Voight as the antagonist. Hoffman knew Grosbard and had worked on the play as an assistant stage manager and assistant director. "I didn't know who Dustin was, but people were saying, 'Oh, he's a genius,'" Voight recalls. "Like it was like a job description. What he did was he spent a lot of time with the female understudies. He *was* a genius. He found his way to the best job in New York City." According to Hoffman, Voight had analogous skills: "My God, the girls loved him. He was tall, blond, and handsome— everything I wasn't. They'd come backstage. They wanted to marry him and mother him. He was a matinee idol Off Broadway."

Hoffman and Voight were competitive from the get-go. "Actors are like women," Hoffman continues. "Women check each other out in a way that men don't. They look at the breasts, they look at the legs, they look at the ass, they look at what she chooses to wear. Because they're in competition with each other. Actors check each other out in a not dissimilar way. So it was charged."

Voight was young, idealistic, and passionate. Recalls Jennifer Salt, "Jon always had that kind of I'd-like-to-save-the-world-with-my-work attitude." (The two would become an item during the production.) Voight knew Schlesinger's films and was desperate for the role. He says, "The way I saw my industry in the 60s was that the movies we were making weren't about anything. In the English-speaking world, we didn't have the equivalent of a Kurosawa or a Bergman or a Fellini. I thought, If I can only get one of those guys, if I can only be the actor, the Max von Sydow for an American Bergman, you know? Schlesinger was the answer for me."

Hellman liked Voight, but Schlesinger had a different idea for

Joe Buck, someone darker, sexier. Voight had vertical creases on either side of his mouth, which the director thought made him look like a little Dutch boy. Schlesinger also doubted that Voight could do the Texas accent. "I thought he was . . . too butch looking, baby-faced, or whatever," the director explained in 1970. But Dougherty, the casting agent, persisted. "You guys are crazy," she said. "Test Jon Voight. If you don't, you're going to really regret it." Hellman and Schlesinger finally agreed, and added him to the list of candidates for screen tests.

Voight was confident he could do the part. "I had figured out what it needed, and that if it went in the wrong direction it could easily be disastrous," he says. "You have to care for this guy, and the way you would care for him is not through his arrogance and swagger, but the fact that it's all an act, an empty pose. Who knows why a kid growing up in Yonkers, New York, like I did, would feel that stuff in his character. But I did."

Schlesinger, however, settled on the actor Michael Sarrazin instead. Sarrazin, who hadn't done much besides Westerns and a surfing movie, was still considered an up-and-comer. He was under contract to Universal, and when Hellman called the studio, it tripled the price Hellman had previously agreed on. The producer remembers, "I said to John, 'I want to hang up on the prick.' He said, 'Go ahead.' I slammed the fucking phone down."

=====

Hoffman, meanwhile, was spending a year at David Wheeler's well-regarded Theatre Company of Boston, where he ran into Voight again. "It was backstage, in the dark," Hoffman recalls. "There was Jon, looking down at me, because I come up to his breastbone. He had heard that the guy they wanted [for Joe Buck] wasn't going to play the part and could I, uh—is it too late to get him seen again by John Schlesinger? It was uncomfortable for him, because the last time he saw me he was the star, and two years had passed, and I'd become the star, and he was still kicking around trying to get that part or whatever, that break. He was fumbling out these words. He said, 'Tell them I'm an actor and I'll go down to Denton or whatever,

Texas. I'll take a tape recorder. I'll work on the accent.' I said, 'Sure, of course, yeah.' And I did."

Schlesinger and Hellman went back to the screen tests they had done of Sarrazin and Voight. Schlesinger said, "The more I look at these tests, the more I like Jon Voight and the less interested I'm becoming with Michael Sarrazin. Let's get Dustin up here." Hoffman had performed with the aspiring Joe Bucks in every test, and after watching them he hemmed and hawed, saying, "Look, they're both good actors. I will be happy to make the picture with either of them. But I will tell you one thing. When I was watching these tests with Michael, I was looking at myself. When I was watching the test with Jon Voight, I was looking at Jon Voight." That tipped the balance in Voight's favor. (Sarrazin went on to do Sydney Pollack's *They Shoot Horses, Don't They?*, which got nine Oscar nominations in 1969.)

Hellman had already called Voight to tell him that he was not going to get the role. The actor recalls, "I felt just like there was a death in my family, I felt so strongly that I was supposed to do that part, because I felt I knew how to do it. That was the thing that made me heartsick." Now Hellman was calling to say that he was going to get the part after all. Voight was incredulous. "Now, wait a minute," he said. "Yesterday you said it was Michael Sarrazin. Today it's—is this for real? Can I count on it?" Hellman replied, "Yeah, you sure can. We're committed, we're going forward." Adds Voight, "It was a big, big deal for me, because it was something I dreamed of—getting a part that I really loved where I knew I was going to work with people that I respected. It doesn't get any better than that. And then the other thing: I was going to be a movie actor. I saw what happened to Dusty. I mean, all of a sudden, Dustin Hoffman was a household word."

Meanwhile, Roman Polanski put in a call to Schlesinger. Word was out that Schlesinger was shopping for a cinematographer. Polanski told him there was a childhood friend of his living in New York, Adam Holender, a wonderful cameraman who had studied, as Polanski had, at the state-run film school in Lodz. He brought a hard-edged, documentary style to his work that Schlesinger liked, and he got the job. One night, Holender recalls, Schlesinger happened to see *The Thomas Crown Affair,* the hit caper movie with Steve McQueen. Schlesinger thought it was slick and soul-less. "It infuriated him," Holender says. "Schlesinger sat us down, Voight, Hoffman, myself, gave us a 15-minute lecture about what the responsibility of an artist is, what kind of films one should do, what kind of films one shouldn't do, and what one should not be tempted by in this business."

Hellman had long known there was no way he could do the film for the original $1 million. But by the time he finished casting and hired the crew, the budget had tripled, to about $3.1 million. He presented the new figures, which included small raises for Schlesinger and himself, to Picker at U.A. "John and I, we'd been working for two and a half or three years, we'd brought them a star, everyone loved the script—and we hadn't gotten a dime," recalls Hellman. "And now we were looking at another year. David was outraged. From their point of view, 'We allowed them to hire Dustin Hoffman, gave them total creative control, and now these fuckers want more money.' There was a firestorm at U.A. And it was only David's total commitment to this that kept them from letting us walk. So they came back with a final offer. It was $800,000 shy of what we needed—$2.3 million, instead of the $3.1 million." Hellman slashed the budget by $800,000. Picker came back a day later, and he said, "O.K., you've got a green light. Go."

———————

It was one thing to out yourself in L.A., making the Bel Air scene, where nobody cared. It was another to out yourself in New York to a crew of tough Irish and Italians from the Bronx and Queens. "John was totally torn up, because part of him wanted to just embrace this, and another part of him was in terror," recalls Hellman. "He had these fantasies that if he were openly gay on a film set, that if he tried to give the crew an order, they would turn on him. I don't know whether he thought they would beat him up, but he certainly thought they'd say, 'You fucking faggot, you're not telling me what to do—go fuck yourself.' I said to him, 'John, look, you're the director. It's your movie. I'm the producer, but I'm your partner. There's nobody who can challenge your authority. If someone speaks out of line to you, they'll be fired the same minute.'"

Schlesinger was reassured. By this time, too, he had recovered from *Far from the Madding Crowd,* buoyed by the enthusiasm of Hellman and Salt as well as by his relationship with Childers. "One of the reasons the film is great was that John was working on a high that he'd never experienced before in his life," says Hellman. "He was so in love, and so excited, and so passionate—we couldn't go anywhere without him saying, 'That's gotta be in the picture, that's gotta be in the picture.' The first thing I heard from certain friends, when I announced that I was doing *Midnight Cowboy* with John Schlesinger, was 'Oh, you're bringing a Brit to make a film in New York? Why are you doing that? You need Sidney Lumet.' We, as New Yorkers, take certain things for granted, but John was seeing this for the very first time." As Schlesinger said in 1970, "Somehow one was always confronted by something worse on the street than one was putting into the film. . . . People said, 'Isn't it a bit much having a man lying on the sidewalk outside Tiffany?' I said, 'Why?' I suppose I may have seen it at Bonwit Teller's."

Midnight Cowboy is packed with iconic, impossible-to-forget images—Joe Buck strutting down the mean streets of Times Square in his fringed jacket, black cowboy hat, and boots, with his transistor radio glued to his ear—and startling vignettes, some observed by Schlesinger during his perambulations about New York, others invented by him and Salt. Like the stoned woman in the Automat running a toy mouse over her son's face (observed), or the sequence in which Joe Buck naïvely picks up a woman, played by Sylvia Miles, who turns the financial tables on him. The scene came from the novel, but the filmmakers added their own twist: as the couple service each other in her apartment, an errant remote, crushed beneath them (Schlesinger had never seen one until he came to America), changes the channels on the TV, an electronic Greek chorus bespeaking the banality of mass culture—a trite conceit, maybe, but with a singular effect. Everything was fodder for Schlesinger's eye: not only inane talk shows featuring poodles in wigs, but also garish neon street signage, billboards, movie one-sheets, acid-inflected light shows, and store windows, while the Vietnam War lurks at the edges of the frame, all the more insistent for being virtually absent.

Another reason the film works as well as it does was the explosive chemistry between Hoffman and Voight, who were still competitive. Says Voight about Hoffman, "He tests things, he goes that extra step to see what will happen. He's an adventurer, an emotional adventurer." For his part, Hoffman recalls, "There was a lot of electricity in the air between us because we were young actors, vying actors. It's not that you don't want the other one to be good, you just don't want to look bad. On the other hand, we were kind of rooting for each other because we're all kind of the underdog. We were so *for* each other doing our best work. We loved working together, Voight and Schlesinger and myself." Adds Jennifer Salt, who played Voight's Texas sweetheart, "They did these amazing improvisations which they would put on tape and give to my dad, and he would construct scenes out of their insane conversations."

Even before production proper started, the actors were sparring with each other. Schlesinger wanted to do a long shot with a telephoto lens of the two of them walking away from the camera over a bridge, without sound. "I panicked, as Jon did, because I thought, Oh God, I don't know the character yet," Hoffman recalls. "I don't know how I'm going to walk. I don't know how I'm going to cough. We were doing take after take. We were trying to act up a storm, not knowing what the fuck we were doing. And because I was so nervous that I was going to come across fraudulent and not have the right cough, I tried to do the cough as realistically as I could. Each time, I tried to do it more realistically until, finally, I did it so realistically I threw up all over Jon. My lunch came up. All over his cowboy boots. Jon looked down. He said, 'Man, why'd you do that?' He thought I did it on purpose. Later, Schlesinger told me that Jon had gone up to him afterwards and said—he was so happy to have gotten the part, and he knew that I gave him a good word—'You know, Dustin's a great actor and everything, and I'm just asking you because I don't want to tell him how to play his character, but is he going to do that in a lot of scenes?' He thought I'd steal every scene if I threw up on him. He thought that was a choice I made, like the gloves were off."

Both Voight and Hoffman had done their homework. Voight went to Texas to work on his accent, while Hoffman hung around the Bowery and studied street people. He looked for his limp. One day he was standing on a corner waiting for the light, and he saw a man with a gimpy leg and thought, There's my guy. Hoffman put a stone in his shoe to facilitate the limp. "Why pebbles? It's not like you're playing a role on Broadway for six months where you're so used to it, limping becomes second nature. The stone makes you limp, and you don't have to think about it. No one can tell you that's not acting. Acting is whatever you want it to be. You get the help you need."

Hoffman also got help from costume designer Ann Roth, who had done both of Hellman's pictures and would become a Schlesinger fixture, as well as a regular for Mike Nichols and many of the great directors of the subsequent decades. "I imagined that Ratso Rizzo was a guy who slept on pool tables on 42nd Street, but he fantasized himself as a sort of Marcello Mastroianni character," she says. Which is why, in a couple of scenes, he is wearing an incongruously natty white suit. "The white jacket came from a garbage can near the Port Authority Bus Terminal that was left over from a guy's prom," Roth continues. "I think he threw up on it. What you want to do is put something on the actor that he never thought of. For Dustin, it turned out to be the shoes. They were these cockroach-in-the-corner shoes, *cucaracha* shoes, very pointed toes. He hadn't seen that end of his body in the mirror in his mind. So when they got on him, they threw him into a different posture, and suddenly there was somebody in front of me who was not Dustin Hoffman."

———

Once principal photography began, the felicitous interplay between competition and compassion that characterized the relationship between both the actors and their characters became extremely fruitful. There's a pivotal scene toward the end of the movie where Ratso, whose cough is getting worse and worse, finally acknowledges he's seriously ill. Hoffman recalls, "It got to be eight o'clock [in the evening], and suddenly they called for one of the most important pieces of coverage. Ratso is dying. [In the scene] I get emotional, because I say, 'I can't walk anymore,' and I've got a fever and I'm spitting up blood. But I just didn't have the energy to do it. I asked, 'You want to come back and do it in the morning?' No, they can't. Jon says, 'You know, we have to do it now.' 'I don't have it.'" They shot a couple of takes. Voight said, "You'd better do better than that or they're going to cut the scene on you," meaning that the scene would be edited to favor Voight. Hoffman continues, "He was just so lovely, and he told me that he loved me, that I was a good actor. He petted me. He petted me! He went, 'C'mon, c'mon.' And he got me to where I had to be. I'll never forget it."

The sexual component of the characters' relationship was always the 800-pound gorilla in the room—or on the set, as it were. "Both Voight and I are actors, and it hit us. 'Hey, these guys are queer,'" observes Hoffman. "I think it came out of the fact that we were in the abandoned tenement [where the characters share a flat]. We were looking around the set, and I said, 'So? Where do I sleep? Why do I sleep here and he sleeps there? Why does he have the really nice bed? Why aren't I—yeah, why aren't we sleeping together? C'mon.' Schlesinger, who was wonderful because he was so courageous in his outing himself at a time when that wasn't common, got very troubled. He said, 'Oh God! Please! It was hard enough to get the financing. Now all we have to do is tell them that we're making a homosexual film. I was hoping we would get the college crowd. We'll get no one.' He absolutely—and I'm sure he was right—did not want to make it explicit."

Bob Balaban (whose uncle Barney Balaban was president of Paramount for three decades) was cast as a student who says he'll pay to go down on Joe Buck in the balcony of a Times Square grind house and then, after the deed is done, reveals he's broke. It was Balaban's first picture, and he was very excited. He called his parents to tell them about it. He said, "I have a scene with Jon Voight." His parents asked, "What's the scene?" "Well, it's in a movie theater. We kind of meet in the bathroom." "Do you have any lines?" "No, not many lines." "So it's a walk-on . . . ?" "Well, at least it's with the star—I give him a blow job."

———

The movie's most iconic scene, the one where Ratso slaps the hood of a taxi and roars, in his hoarse, consumptive voice, "I'm walkin' heah!," was improvised. "They didn't have the money to close down a New York street," Hoffman says, "so they were going to steal it," meaning the plan was to shoot the scene on the fly without getting the necessary permits. "The camera was in the van across the street," Hoffman continues. "It was a difficult scene logistically because those were real pedestrians and there was real traffic, and Schlesinger wanted to do it in one shot—he didn't want to cut. He wanted us to walk, like, a half a block, and the first times we did it the signal turned red. We had to stand there talking, and it was killing us, because Schlesinger was getting very upset. He came rushing out of the van, saying, 'Oh, oh, you've got to keep walking.' 'We can't, man. There's fucking traffic.' 'Well, you've got to time it.' 'Well, we're *trying* to time it.' It's the actors that always get the heat. It was many takes, and then the timing was right. Suddenly we were doing this take and we knew it was going to work. We got to the signal just as it went green, so we could keep walking. But it just happened—there was a real cab trying to beat the signal. Almost hit us. John, who couldn't see anything in the van, came running out, saying, 'What was that all about? Why did you ruin it by hitting the cab? Why were you yelling?' I said, 'You know, he almost hit us.' I guess the brain works so quickly, it said, in a split of a second, Don't go out of character. So I said, 'I'm walking here,' meaning, 'We're shooting a scene here, and this is the first time we ever got it right, and you have fucked us up.' Schlesinger started laughing. He clapped his hands and said, 'We must have that, we must have that,' and re-did it two or three times, because he loved it."

Drugged-out party scenes were *de rigueur* for any movie that even touched on the counterculture, but they invariably rang false—except for the one in *Midnight Cowboy*, owing perhaps to the vibes provided by Andy Warhol and company. Shot at Filmways Studio, in Harlem, the scene featured real-life Factory "superstars" such as Viva, Ultra Violet, International Velvet, and Taylor Mead drifting through like exotic tropical fish in an aquarium. (Warhol himself would have joined in the fun had he not been inconveniently shot in the stomach by Valerie Solanas around the time principal photography began.) "Schlesinger thought they were great," says the actress Brenda Vaccaro, who played a socialite who picks up Joe Buck at the party. "He'd say, 'Dahling, they're so wonderfully eccentric.' He got every wacko in town." Adds Hellman, "It was like a six-day bacchanal. Pot in vast quantities. And these kids, floating around, fucking in the toilets, fucking in the dressing rooms, fucking in the wardrobe rooms. We had to establish certain characters, so we were worried about people not coming back [and thus not appearing in subsequent scenes]—boy, they were back. They couldn't wait to get back."

===

There was little that was routine about *Midnight Cowboy,* and in Schlesinger's hands the sex scene between Vaccaro and Voight is far from business as usual. Joe Buck can't get it up, so the couple divert themselves by playing Scribbage. At one point, as the characters try to come up with words that end in *y,* Vaccaro spells out "G-A-Y," eliciting a burst of say-it-ain't-so passion from her companion. As they roll around on the bed, the Scribbage pieces become embedded in his flesh.

The script called for the actress to disrobe completely. She refused. "You never are supposed to take your clothes off," she explains. "Because it's hard to do, and in those days nobody did that. This was one of the first [American films] to do nudity. John's lament was 'Oh, good God! Everybody thinks I'm doing a blue movie.' It was America—so puritanical. John didn't think nudity was such a big thing. He'd already done it in *Darling,* and he said, 'Julie Christie wore these fucking pasties, and then in the middle of the scene she hated them, so she pulled them off.' But he said to me, 'Well, do what you must.' I think Jon Voight had a codpiece or whatever they wear in England. I mean, pasted on, for Christ's sake. It was all over his pubes, the glue. It was horrible. I asked Ann Roth, who was a friend of mine, 'Annie, what the hell am I going to do? I'm so nervous. Oh my God, I'm not thin, I'm not skinny, I don't look gorgeous. Please, Annie! Do something for me.' So she went out and got a fox coat and brought it in to me, and I put it on nude, and we showed it to Schlesinger, who said, 'Oh, lovely. Fucked in fox.' When I was down on the floor in that sex scene, he had the handheld camera over me, and he was, like, bending down in my face. He said, 'Come now, dahling. Do it now. Come, dahling.'"

When shooting was all over, Schlesinger had no idea what he had in the can. He used to refer to it as "a pile of shit." And he was exhausted, and often depressed. At the end of production, he had found himself in Texas with Voight, shooting one of the "flash-present" scenes, one where the actor runs naked down a road. Schlesinger had an anxiety attack, so deep were his fears about the film. Recalls Voight, "I was putting my shirt on, walking around the side of this van, and there was John, and he was red, he was sweating, he was, like, shivering. I didn't know what was wrong. I thought he was having a stroke. And I said, 'John, what's the matter?' He said, 'What're we making here anyway? What will they think of us?' I grabbed him by the shoulders just to shake him out of it, and I said, 'John, we will live the rest of our artistic lives in the shadow of this great masterpiece.'"

Voight would be proved right, but doubts continued to plague Schlesinger even as the film came together in postproduction. Recalls Hellman, "John's last words to me, before we went in to show it to U.A. for the first time, were 'Honestly, tell me the truth, do you really think that anyone in their right mind is going to pay money to see this fucking rubbish?' We were scared shitless. The U.A. people were so pissed off at us that they wouldn't even speak to us on the way in." According to David Picker, when the film ended, with Ratso dead in the bus, Joe Buck's arm around him, and the mournful sound of John Barry's *Midnight Cowboy* theme filling the theater, "there was dead silence. [My uncle] Arnold, who was sitting behind me, leaned forward and said, 'It's a masterpiece.' The room exploded. Everybody was crying. It was one of the most extraordinary screenings I've ever been to."

Of course, *Midnight Cowboy* was not for everyone. The ratings board slapped it with an X rating—the first X-rated movie released by a studio. The ratings system was less than a year old, and an X didn't yet signify pornography, only that this was a film for strictly adult audiences. But the rating was going to cost the company money, because it virtually precluded a sale to network television and limited the picture's exposure in many markets. U.A. refused to cut a frame.

Says Hoffman, of one screening, "I remember people leaving the theater in droves, like a row. Bob Balaban blows Jon—eight people got up. The movie goes on a little bit more, something else happens, another row gets up." *Variety* called it "generally sordid," Rex Reed wrote that it was "a collage of screaming, crawling, vomiting humanity," and Roger Ebert declared that it was "an offensively trendy, gimmick-ridden, tarted-up, vulgar exercise in fashionable cinema."

But those were the days when filmmakers, especially the British and Europeans, and audiences too, were far ahead of the reviewers. *Midnight Cowboy* premiered on May 25, 1969, at the Coronet Theater, on Third Avenue in New York. "A fucking smash hit," recalls Hellman. As Childers remembers it, "Opening night, there was a 10-minute ovation, and the next day a friend of ours called and said, 'You've got to go down and check out the lines—they're all the way round to the 59th Street Bridge, like 14 blocks over.' John said, 'I can't let anybody see me.' So I said, 'Hide in the men's department of Bloomingdale's and look at the lines through the window.'"

The picture would gross $44.8 million before its run was over, the equivalent of $200 million today. When Oscar-time rolled around, it got seven nominations: picture, director, adapted screenplay, actor (for both Voight and Hoffman), supporting actress (Sylvia Miles), and editing. Hellman ran into George Roy Hill, who had directed *The World of Henry Orient,* and who that year had *Butch Cassidy and the Sundance Kid* in competition for best picture. (The other nominees were *Anne of the Thousand Days; Hello, Dolly!;* and *Z.*) "George confidently expected to win," Hellman continues. "He said words to this effect: '*Midnight Cowboy* is a terrific movie. You should be very proud. And don't be too disappointed, but the studio's told me that we've got a lock on it.' I went into the theater [on Oscar night] thinking that I was wasting my time. John Schlesinger didn't even come. He was in London, making *Sunday Bloody Sunday.* We got nothing until Waldo Salt took best writer of something adapted from other material. Then Schlesinger iced it. He took it away from George Roy Hill. Then I thought, Jesus, I guess it's possible. When I heard it, 'best picture,' I was stunned. I had nothing prepared. I was scared out of my wits. I remember going up on the stage and looking around and not wanting to break down. I made the shortest acceptance speech in the history of the Academy." How *Midnight Cowboy* swayed the generally conservative Academy is still something of a mystery, but perhaps Picker puts his finger on it when he says simply, "The picture did fabulous business, and it's a great fucking movie."

It was the spring of 1970, the height of the struggle against the Vietnam War. "There was a lot of political turmoil," recalls Voight, whose sympathies were with the demonstrators. "When I went to the Academy Awards, there was a split down the middle. Frank Sinatra and John Wayne and Bob Hope, I'd grown up with them, I admired them, but I was also of the new breed that wanted to see something changed. We were the sons of Brando. We didn't want to change our names—something simple like that—'No, I am who I am, I want to see the warts. When I work, I don't give a damn about having the perfect light and perfect makeup.' We wanted to see it as it was. Tell other stories. *Midnight Cowboy* was a perfect example of that."

Voight had been chosen to give out the Oscar for best screenplay. "At some point, they said, 'Jon, you gotta be on the other side of the stage.' So I took this long walk, just alone walking backstage, very aware of all the legacy of it—I didn't want to close down the Academy Awards, but I also wanted to represent whatever the values were I was carrying. And coming toward me in this little three-foot space was Fred Astaire. I thought, This is one of the greatest artists ever, coming toward me. We reached each other in the middle of this thing, me six foot two or three and Fred, slight of figure, shorter. And he looked up and said, 'Oh, Jon! Hi. Let me stand aside.' I said, 'No, no, please—let me stand aside for you.' 'Great work,' he said. 'Well, thank you, thank you.' Then I stepped aside. He went on, and I looked back, and it was Fred Astaire! That was the meeting of the two generations in the appropriate way, with tremendous regard for each other."

From *Vanity Fair*, March 2005

MYRA BRECKINRIDGE

Swinging into Disaster

by Steven Daly

So there he is: Mike Sarne, actor turned pop star turned photographer turned movie director, tooling down West London's Chiswick High Road in his silver mid-50s Thunderbird. It's some roadster, this Thunderbird: Sarne has had it up to 140 miles per hour out on the motorway, and he's even managed to flip the thing over, thanks to its simply rotten suspension.

The year is 1968. London is in its Late Swinging period, and few are oscillating more wildly than Mike Sarne, the street-smart son of Czechoslovak immigrants who fled the Nazis, and a known Face in all the Ace Places. Sarne (né Scheuer) has had a No. 1 smash in 1962 with "Come Outside," a jaunty novelty song in which he woos, in fake Cockney accent, a lower-class dolly bird. As a self-taught photographer, he has snapped Twiggy, Marianne Faithfull, Celia Hammond, "Patti Boyd and the whole gang." As a self-taught director, he has helmed *Joanna,* a quintessentially Swinging film about a middle-class dolly bird. Twentieth Century Fox, which is distributing the film, is pleased with its reception, and according to Sarne's agent at William Morris, everybody wants a piece of Swinging Mike.

So Mike Sarne is hot, and he knows it—dig?

On this particular day, Sarne is returning home from London's ultra-swank Claridge's hotel, where he's had a meeting with this character named Robert Fryer, a Fox-affiliated movie producer with a heavy pedigree in Broadway musicals. Fryer has been deputized to ask Swinging Mike if he is interested in directing a project that will surely send his profile stratospheric: the film adaptation of *Myra Breckinridge*, the outrageous best-selling novel by Fryer's friend Gore Vidal.

So Sarne gives ear to Fryer's *Breckinridge* pitch and takes a copy of Vidal's book. The young director pilots the old Thunderbird back to West London, and parks near his Chiswick house (where, not incidentally, Sarne has bedded no less a 60s sexpot than Brigitte Bardot).

"As I put the key in the lock," says Sarne today, "the book opened in the middle at this well-thumbed page, where this sodomy scene is going on. And I'm reading about this dildo going into the backside of some young guy. And I'm thinking: Are they serious, the William Morris Agency, Twentieth Century Fox, this funny, fey little producer?"

As far as directing this thing went—forget it. "I chucked it," says Sarne. "I don't know what happened to that copy of the book. And I forgot about it."

But only for a while. When he did ultimately succumb to *Myra Breckinridge*'s abundant charms, Mike Sarne would end up making a celluloid disasterpiece that is to this day pilloried as one of the worst films ever made. *Myra Breckinridge* managed to offend in equal measure the literary world, *ancien régime* Hollywood, and demimonde hipsters—and although its $4-million-plus budget was merely average for the time, the film also destabilized one of the great movie dynasties.

All these years later, most of the parties involved have filed this vilified project somewhere in the darker recesses of their minds—yet for Mike Sarne the memory will never fade. It was an experience that branded him, at 31, a Hollywood pariah with no chance of redemption.

"I'm the innocent party in this whole story," Sarne now protests. "I mean, you probably don't believe me, but I am the innocent party in this whole debacle."

——————

How do you solve a problem like *Myra*? This, in the winter of 1968, was the question facing Twentieth Century Fox, and in particular company executives David Brown and Richard Zanuck. Fox had triumphed in the bidding war for Gore Vidal's novel, paying a vertiginous $900,000 for movie rights to a book that had scandalized the nation and soared to the top of best-seller lists in February of that year. A book that was the subject of such pre-release notoriety that publisher Little, Brown opted to provide no review copies to the press.

The public ate *Myra Breckinridge* up, although the book was, in best-seller terms, a rare beast—not to mention a seemingly unlikely candidate to be tamed by movie adaptation. Vidal's phantasmagorical satire revolves around a central character bent on reforming the nation's uptight attitude toward sex through a one-woman jihad against the modern American male; a character who goes from Myron to Myra with the flick of a surgeon's knife, then lights out for Hollywood to claim a family inheritance from a retired cowboy actor; a character, it should be noted, whose secondary mission is to violate the lovingly described buttocks of an insolent young buck named Rusty. Throughout the book Myra, a film classicist who is obsessed with Hollywood's 1935–45 Golden Age, gushes forth a riotously entertaining internal monologue that lauds the obscure, real-life movie intellectual Parker Tyler while elegantly skewering the sloppy sensibilities of modern youth. Everything about the younger generation and its popular culture makes Myra sick: from its slack-jawed locutions to its slovenly dress to its maddening inability to appreciate the prolific oeuvre of producer Pandro S. Berman.

The book-buying American public had by 1968 been primed by Harold Robbins's lust-filled works, and lathered by Jacqueline Susann's pill-popping sex maniacs and their priapic partners—but *Myra Breckinridge* administered strokes of quite a different and altogether more literary sort. When the English critic John Weightman called *Myra Breckinridge* "a queer, queer book," he was not referring to the title character's rampant expression of what we might now call "the gay sensibility," a sensibility that today is associated with impressive spending power. *Myra Breckinridge*'s large constituency was certifiably mainstream: a mass audience looking for its kink quotient in any available form, even if it came packaged with lengthy ruminations on the parlous state of straight American manhood and the finer points of James Craig's performance in *Marriage Is a Private Affair*.

Best-sellers had always been prime movie fodder, and if this was an unusual novel, the late 60s was an era where few of the old certainties applied, a period in which the studios were desperate to figure out a youth market that was making hits of such iconoclastic statements as *Bonnie and Clyde* and *The Graduate*. In March 1968, when the rights to make *Myra Breckinridge* were won by Twentieth Century Fox, that company was being guided by the odd-couple power duo of Richard Zanuck, 33, and David Brown, 51. The former was the son of Fox's nominal president and major shareholder, Darryl F. Zanuck, one of the company's founders, who by the late 60s was domiciled chiefly in Europe. It was, Richard once remarked, like "working for Howard Hughes."

Zanuck *fils* was a stocky, streetwise former athlete who, as Fox's head of production, demanded that his cinematic offspring be above all else functional and populist. By contrast, David Brown, the vice president in charge of Fox's story department, was every inch the East Coast literary gent, dapper, bewhiskered, and refined of manner. Brown had risen to the position of managing editor at *Cosmopolitan* (he'd later wed the magazine's most famous editor, Helen Gurley Brown) before being tempted west in 1951 by Darryl Zanuck. But for a brief return to publishing, Brown remained with Fox for two decades thereafter, developing the network of literary contacts that earned him a reputation for being "the best nose in the business" when it came to raw material for the movies.

In August 1969, Richard Zanuck staged a dramatic coup at Fox, installing himself as president and reducing his father to chairman. Darryl Zanuck told his son that he had perpetrated "the con job of the century," yet the younger Zanuck felt that this hubristic move was a necessary step toward the financial rationalization that a management consultant's report had prescribed for the company. Ever since 1963, when *Cleopatra* and its record-busting budget had nearly bankrupted the company, Fox had been a troubled operation. The huge success of 1965's *The Sound of Music* had kept the studio afloat, but it had followed that picture with an expensive string of famous flops: *Star!; Doctor Dolittle; Hello, Dolly!*

The days of Hollywood's studio system may have been long gone by 1969, but the new regime of Zanuck and Brown inherited what the latter calls a "benevolent dictatorship" at Twentieth Century Fox. "We didn't bet the studio on every picture we made," says Brown. "In those days," he notes, "Hollywood was fun. It wasn't stressed out." Yet, if he and Richard Zanuck were not exactly betting the studio on *Myra Breckinridge,* the stakes were still substantial. (By way of comparison to the $900,000 Fox paid for Vidal's novel, the studio had bought *Valley of the Dolls,* Jackie Susann's eminently filmable 1966 blockbuster, for just $200,000.) Thus the challenge of translating *Myra Breckinridge* to the big screen looked likely to get Brown and Zanuck as close to "stressed out" as anything they'd handled in all their years together at Fox. The outcome would certainly affect the reputations of Brown and Zanuck, within the film industry in general and with Zanuck's disgruntled father in particular. It was imperative that Fox find a writer who could make cinematic sense of the Vidal book while keeping its more salacious passages within Hollywood's standards of moral decency. And, of course, deliver box-office dynamite in the process.

Gore Vidal's contract with Fox gave him first crack at writing the screenplay, and attached him to the project as a co-producer. Vidal was not new to the screenwriting dodge: as a long-term-contract writer for MGM, he had made an uncredited but significant contribution to *Ben-Hur,* the 1959 blockbuster that won a still-record 11 Oscars. *Myra Breckinridge* may have presented a more complex challenge, but Vidal (who responded to *Vanity Fair*'s questions in writing) maintains that in crafting the script he was able to "get around the most censorable parts," and as far as the ticklish task of finding a suitable director went, he claims, "Bud Yorkin [*Divorce American Style*] and I discussed the possibility of his directing the movie before it was bought by Fox." Vidal was subsequently disappointed that the studio executives "started to drag their feet" on the matter. According to Hugh Fordin, then an executive at Fox, the company offered the picture to several of its favorite "old-fashioned" directors, none of whom was able to understand the original material.

The studio also rejected successive drafts of Vidal's script. "What Gore turned out was a totally different screenplay—it had nothing to do with the book," says Hugh Fordin. "I'll never forget it: I walked into David Brown's office and said, 'What's that expression on your face?' He said, 'I just read a screenplay to a totally different movie! Gore didn't use a thing of it!' " Vidal denies outright this accusation.

"I thought it was good," says Zanuck in defense of Vidal's final script. "But it lacked that touch of craziness and zaniness that his very idea evoked. It wasn't quite on the page. You just can't make a film in the ordinary sense, using a beginning, middle, and end in narrative terms. It had to be told in as outrageous and bizarre a way as the book itself."

———

Enter once more Mike Sarne, 29-year-old former pop star, flaxen-haired charmer, and all-around main-chance artist. Just six years earlier, Sarne had been a blond and somewhat suave student of Russian at London University, supplementing his meager grant with bits of acting, modeling, and singing, when he scored his fluke hit single. He subsequently took up photography and, once established in that field, tried his hand at shooting movies. A short film he directed drew the attention of Fox, which, eager to tap into the energy of the British scene, agreed to finance his first feature, *Joanna*. According to Sarne, it was during a street-corner meeting in London that Richard Zanuck himself gave Sarne the green light to spend a chunk of the studio's impressive *Sound of Music* profits. *Joanna* was a modestly budgeted and manageably hip soufflé of a film that drew some decent notices and performed respectably enough when it was released in 1968. This may all sound larky and serendipitous, but the way Sarne tells it, the whole of Swinging London was just one big low-hanging fruit for a likely lad such as himself, with credentials, connections, and looks.

Toward the end of 1968, Sarne found himself in a New York hotel as the guest of a producer friend who wanted him to direct a less than appealing picture. Sarne, who says he was without local currency, had been reading in the trades about Fox's rejections of Vidal's costly scripts—perhaps, he thought, having warmed somewhat to the novel's humor, he could help the studio out. And so, even though several months earlier he had failed to follow up on Robert Fryer's initial approach about directing the film, the cashless Sarne set out to walk across town to see David Brown in Fox's West Side offices. The Englishman was in good odor with Fox, thanks to *Joanna*'s success. So just like that, Mike Sarne pitched up at Brown's doorstep and announced himself to the receptionist. "Oh, Mr. Sarney, yes," she said. "I'll see if he's available." Remarkably enough, the Anglo arriviste had to wait just a few minutes for an audience with Richard Zanuck's right-hand man. Sarne brought up *Myra Breckinridge,* and, he says, Brown responded, "It's driving me crazy. Dickie doesn't want to do it, he wishes he hadn't touched the fucking thing. What a piece of shit. I wish I hadn't talked him into it."

The feckless emissary of Swinging London sat down and offered Brown his simple and elegant solution to the problem called *Myra Breckinridge.* Here's how to frame the narrative, said Sarne: Myron wakes up at the end in a hospital bed having imagined the whole thing. In other words, the oldest wrinkle in the book: "It was all a dream." (Sarne today laughs at the simplicity of the idea. "Yup—just like *Dallas.*") David Brown cottoned to this new director in a big way. "Sarne was funky and seemed to fit the material," he offers. (Brown, like Richard Zanuck, insists that his recollections regarding *Myra Breckinridge* are somewhat hazy.)

Sarne now claims he wasn't looking for money from Brown, much less a directing job—he just wanted to help. "I'm an ideas person," says Sarne with a shrug. His dream conceit went over big. Brown loved it. Instant hit. The very "outrageous and bizarre" idea, perhaps, that Zanuck felt Vidal's screenplay lacked.

Right away David Brown got on the phone to Richard Zanuck in L.A. "Dick, I've got Mike Sarne in front of me." Brown explained

Sarne's pitch to Zanuck while eyeing his guest. "So," says Sarne, "he says to me, 'I want you to fly out to the coast. Let's go.'" Sarne may have been somewhat blithe about the prospect, but Fox, he soon realized, was deadly serious: Brown promptly bundled the director onto a jet for L.A. to meet with Zanuck.

"And now, a flashback," says Sarne. "I did a film once [acting] with Brigitte Bardot. It was called *Two Weeks in September*. We became quite close on it. And she said to me, 'Don't go to Hollywood, because they eat people like you and me for breakfast every day.'

"So Zanuck says to me, 'This sounds cool, Mike—are you going to direct this picture for us?' I'm hearing Brigitte saying in my head, 'They'll eat us for breakfast, Michael.' And I say, 'No, no, no, I'm just going to write the script. . . . I'll do it back in London.'"

Zanuck interjected: "We could get you a place in the Hills, Brentwood . . ." There was talk of an office, a secretary—$1,000 a week in expenses. "That's when a thousand dollars was a thousand dollars," says Sarne, who nonetheless insisted that London was where he wanted to get married and buy a home, where he wanted to be close to his aging father.

But Richard Zanuck hadn't gotten where he was by deferring to the talent, no matter how "swinging." So he dangled before Sarne the kind of numbers that looked to European eyes as big as the HOLLY-WOOD sign: $75,000 to write, with $25,000 for revisions. "Seventy-five grand," Sarne marvels. "Now they're weakening me; my knees are beginning to buckle, O.K.?"

In one last attempt to leave open an escape route, Sarne suggested that there should be a "mutual option" in his contract that would allow Fox to go with another director should it so choose, and, more important to Sarne, that he should have the option to pass on directing *Myra Breckinridge* should he so choose.

"So Dick Zanuck says the most fateful words I've ever heard in my life," says Sarne. "He leans forward over his desk. He says, 'Mike, a mutual option is no option.' And as he said that, I could see the 75 grand disappearing down the tubes."

So, almost as casually as Sarne had walked in to see David Brown, he signed on as *Myra*'s savior with the full blessing of both Zanuck and Brown. It is fair to say that by the time the movie was unveiled for America's cinema-going masses a year and a half later all three men—and, in fact, just about everyone associated with the film—wished that they had never attempted to coax Gore Vidal's lithe volume forth from the realm of print.

———

If Mike Sarne was in, Gore Vidal was out. The creator of *Myra Breckinridge* resigned his co-producer role as soon as Fox hired Sarne. Vidal remembers being shown *Joanna* by David Brown and Richard Zanuck after they acquired the rights to his novel. "It was very bad. British. A flop," Vidal says. He recalls being told later that "a pop singer called Michael Sarne would write and direct *Myra*, presumably on the strength of *Joanna*." Sarne himself was perfectly aware of Vidal's contempt for his work; he well remembers the author's comment that *Joanna* was "40 commercials looking for a product."

"My last act as co-producer," says Vidal (who would nevertheless stay in contact with the producer Robert Fryer as a backstage kibitzer throughout the coming months), "was to tell Dick 'n' Dave [Zanuck and Brown] that Sarne, no more a writer than a director, could never handle so complex a job. But a force higher than D&D was guiding them to the poorhouse."

At a meeting with Dick 'n' Dave and Fryer at New York's St. Regis hotel, Vidal offered a prediction: "This time next year Fox will be in the hands of the receivers," he said. In Brown's breezy and engaging autobiography, *Let Me Entertain You*, he recounts Vidal's exit after this summary judgment. "As he went out of the room," writes Brown (who puts the meeting at the Plaza), "he stumbled over Fryer, who was lying in the hallway, quietly sobbing. Or was he laughing?"

———

These days, Mike Sarne resembles a slightly downscale version of Beatles producer George Martin, minus the regimental diction and clad in brown brogues and a blue blazer that have definitely seen better days. The heavy lines around Sarne's blue eyes reveal that he has clearly flinched at the untold blows that have assailed him, yet his face has been etched by wisdom rather than bitterness about what befell

him in Hollywood. He is a maddeningly discursive and endlessly entertaining raconteur who delights in every absurd curveball life has
thrown at him, whether it be romps with Bardot, novelty-song stardom, or million-dollar meetings in London squares. But even Sarne's
well-honed sense of absurdity was stretched by *Myra Breckinridge,*
the project Zanuck gave him as a "reward" for *Joanna.*

Sarne arrived in Los Angeles to begin writing on January 15,
1969, bringing with him Tanya, his wife of just one day, a schoolteacher and former go-go dancer. "Funky" Mike was putatively in
Hollywood to help Fox embrace the youth revolution that had stood
the film business on its head. He, however, had entered the film
business not to destroy Western capitalism or nuke cinematic convention, but to simply rid himself of "the smell of poverty" he remembered from his childhood.

"I'm thinking I'll write the script and get the fuck out of here,"
says Sarne. Come the spring of 1969 he was beginning to understand
the odd nation he had been hired to satirize, and to figure out a way
to harness this troublesome mistress named Myra. His initial work
was done in Room 64 of the storied Chateau Marmont hotel on Sunset Boulevard, where parts of the film would, per Vidal's novel, be
filmed—and where the smell of poverty rarely rises above the sweet
scent of bougainvillea plants outside one's window.

But even if Sarne could find a way to translate *Myra Breckin-*
ridge for the big screen, what kinds of actors could possibly populate
such a gut-busting, rectum-rupturing farce? It wasn't until that question was addressed that the *Myra Breckinridge* project shrugged off
the mantle of industry time bomb and took on the aspect of a significant public event. Or, if you prefer, a train wreck.

Myra's chief antagonist in the book is Buck Loner, a seedy cowboy star—a perfect comic vehicle, Sarne thought, for spry movie veteran Mickey Rooney. But the next thing Sarne knew, John Huston
had moseyed up to Fox and expressed interest in the role. How could
any studio say no to the still-active part-time actor and director of
The Maltese Falcon and *The African Queen*? "I can't even describe
to you now how threatened I felt," says Sarne, the Hollywood green-
horn. "He's fuckin' John Huston, for Chrissake!"

Sarne's ideal choice for the salty casting agent Letitia Van Allen was another Hollywood legend, Mae West—no matter that the 76-year-old actress had not worked since 1943's *The Heat's On*. (She had, it is true, made a guest appearance on television's *Mister Ed* in 1964.) West may have at this point looked like as big an anachronism as Myra Breckinridge herself, but Sarne was onto something. The hourglass-contoured actress had, with her slyly sexed-up persona, blazed a trail for sexual comedy in the 30s. (One of the famous lines attributed to her: "Is that a pistol in your pocket, or are you just glad to see me?") And she remained an icon not just of gay culture but of the counterculture in general. Fox agreed to go along with this far-out notion—if Sarne could persuade the actress, whom he calls a "neglected national treasure," to come on board.

Mike Sarne took Bobby Fryer along to meet Miss West at the Ravenswood, the Hollywood apartment building she owned, occupying the penthouse apartment. In a scene Sarne compares to "something out of *Sunset Boulevard*," he and Fryer were ushered in by West's male companion, an "aging muscleman" with Tony Curtis coiffure. Noting the uniformly pale-pink décor (including chiffon draperies), and the nude statue of West on the piano, Sarne perched himself on the actress's pale-pink sofa and waited.

Mae West finally tottered into the room, clad from head to toe in pale pink, and respectfully listened to her suitors. Then she informed them that if she should deign to join their little enterprise she would be writing her own material. Fox subsequently offered West $300,000 for the role; with Sarne egging her on over Fryer's strenuous objections, she held out for, and got, a very healthy $350,000.

There could be few more perfect illustrations of David Brown's remark that Hollywood used to be "fun" than the way Sarne went about the key assignment of casting his leading lady. He and producer Fryer first trawled for their Myra on a giddy tour through the transvestite bars of Los Angeles and San Francisco.

This was a rare break in the tension between the two men at the center of *Myra Breckinridge*, whom Fox had forced to become the most unlikely of bedfellows. Their sensibilities were as different as their dress codes, Fryer favoring tweeds and Gucci moccasins, Sarne preferring a tank top, bell-bottoms, and bare feet. Sarne describes Fryer, who died in May 2000, as "a strange, ginger-haired guy, with eczema all over his face. He was very nervous and giggled a lot—you know, this funny little guy."

This "funny little guy" was actually something of a Face himself, albeit in circles slightly more exalted—that is, squarer—than those in which Mike Sarne spun. Robert Fryer was in 1969 a highly accomplished Broadway producer (*Mame, Sweet Charity*) who had lately managed to expand his purview into movie production, making *The Boston Strangler* and *The Prime of Miss Jean Brodie* for Fox, which then attached him to *Myra Breckinridge*. He might have enjoyed his tour of West Coast drag clubs (though he still preferred Angela Lansbury for the lead role), but he had never really taken to Mike Sarne, even at their initial London meeting. Now he fiercely resented having the young Englishman forced upon him.

The winners of Sarne and Fryer's transgendered talent search were dutifully screen-tested, but Sarne could not really see the ballbusting role of Myra resting on any of the drag queens' broad shoulders. "They weren't particularly great actors, but they were very good as women," he notes.

Warhol "superstar" Candy Darling (né James Slattery) did a twirl for Sarne's camera, but still no dice. Sarne had met Warhol through the artist Roy Lichtenstein, who'd done the ad campaign for *Joanna*, and he was close enough to the silver-haired sphinx to share with him his trepidation about *Myra Breckinridge*. In classically passive fashion, Warhol told Sarne, "Oh, just leave it alone. You can't get out of this."

In a desperate attempt to fill the biggest role in his problematic Hollywood debut, Sarne mentioned the name Raquel Welch to Richard Zanuck. (*Unknown transvestite? Premier box-office sex symbol of the day? Sure, what's the diff?!*) At which point Zanuck mentioned that Fox happened to have Miss Welch, then 28, under contractual obligation to make a picture for the company—and for a knockdown price of $125,000. The trades were soon spreading the word: Raquel Welch is . . . Myra Breckinridge!

"I'm quite happy with Raquel doing it," recalls Sarne, who nonetheless screen-tested her. "Because she has a marvelously artificial way of acting. And you could totally believe that she was a sex change in a mad sort of way. . . . To me she fitted kind of stylistically into my

Pop-art gallery. And Mae fit into that, too: the pose, the walk—'I'm Pop art, I'm a Marvel comic.'"

When Welch showed up at Sarne's recently rented Malibu beach house to discuss the project, he was surprised to see her wearing a very non-Marvel caftan, worn perhaps in deference to his supposed underground credentials. This former beauty queen and weather girl was, she now says, desperate to find a more edifying use for the mind-blowing sexual triumphalism she evinced in hits such as *One Million Years B.C.* and *Fantastic Voyage*. Sarne and Myra came along at just the right time.

"I thought if I played an erudite, articulate person who was multifaceted and who was struggling between the masculine and the feminine sides of his/her nature that this was a great opportunity to do lots of amazing things as an actress," says Welch. "I was really attuned to the fact that I really needed to do something that showed that I had more ability than I was given credit for at that time—that I wasn't just a body and a face."

The face of Myra's male alter ego, Myron—which looms as a presence in Vidal's book and is accorded visual manifestation in the movie—came to Mike Sarne in a cathode flash. One evening the director happened across Rex Reed, the photogenic movie critic, on a TV talk show. The saturnine scribe was, says Sarne, "camping about, criticizing movies." Reed had attained notoriety for his dryly trenchant movie-star profiles and bitchy movie reviews (*Joanna* was among his victims). Reed declined to be interviewed for this article, but in 1970, shortly before the film came out, he wrote a long, acerbic article for *Playboy* about the making of *Myra Breckinridge* to accompany a "wild pictorial" the magazine had derived from the film's somewhat harmless orgy scene. Reed, who had no previous film experience, described his reaction when Fox approached him to play the part of film theorist Myron: "Under no circumstances was I interested in playing a homosexual who has an operation to make him into a woman." Fox assured Reed that this aspect of Myron's character would be masked by the dream conceit, and that he would have approval over his sections of the script.

Although Sarne had handed in a draft of his screenplay and managed to agglomerate a phenomenal if unlikely cast for *Myra Breckinridge*, he was unperturbed in the summer of 1969 when he noticed that the term of his directorial contract with Fox was about to expire with no shooting date in sight. "I had this funny feeling they didn't want to start," Sarne says. "Gore was doing everything to stop this picture getting made, the gossip was starting. I felt my life drifting away. In Hollywood, there are hundreds of writers and people on option for doing things, waiting for the studio to call, and their expenses are being picked up . . . "

Among the published rumors about Sarne's project was an allegation that Vidal was offering to pay Fox $75,000 if it would fire the director. A source close to Vidal disputes any cash offer, but allows that the author was prepared to forgo part of his remuneration should Sarne be dismissed.

Sarne claims his bags were already packed for a flight back to London and freedom when the Fox messenger arrived at his beach house with news that a September 15, 1969, start date had been set for *Myra Breckinridge*. Now he would have to honor his side of the contract and direct the thing (which ended up rolling on September 22).

Still, for all Sarne's protestations, Fox's financial emoluments were more than handsome. And socially, he was well ensconced among a hip crowd of fellow Europeans headed by the director Roman Polanski. Among the locals, Sarne could count as friends perma-swingers Warren Beatty and Robert Evans, plus up-and-coming superagent Sue Mengers (who represented Vidal and was a model, it is said, for *Myra Breckinridge*'s Letitia Van Allen character).

On August 9, 1969, Sarne had received a call in Malibu telling him that on the previous night Sharon Tate, Roman Polanski's wife, had been brutally murdered along with four others at her home on Bel Air's Cielo Drive. (Polanski was in Europe on business the night of the murders.) In the wake of the horrendous crime, as the frantic hunt for Tate's unknown killers began, Polanski came to stay briefly at Sarne's place, bringing with him a phalanx of F.B.I. agents, who slept around the house on sofas and in armchairs.

In the months before Charles Manson and his associates were

apprehended and jailed for the Cielo Drive massacre (and another killing, in Silverlake), anyone who knew Polanski was both suspect and potential target. A pair of Mike Sarne's neighbors showed up on his doorstep, dressed in their swimsuits, asking him to boot his friend out. Roman stayed.

The temper of the times was markedly changing, and not just within the gilded precincts of the Malibu Colony. Before the Manson murders, recalls Sarne, Hollywood's European crowd "were the little darlings. When Sharon was murdered, we were no longer the darlings. Between the time that Sharon was murdered and the time they caught Manson, a big anti-foreigner thing kicked in, you know.

"There was a cool wind through California. So suddenly I wasn't so funny anymore. *Myra Breckinridge* wasn't so funny anymore. It wasn't the Love Generation anymore."

———

Embattled producer Bobby Fryer had meanwhile managed to convince Fox that if it insisted on keeping Sarne as director, it should at least commission a brand-new screenplay to override Sarne's. That Fox acceded to this demand showed how little confidence it had in Sarne as a writer, and how little control it had over the project as a whole.

Fryer's choice of writer was David Giler, an unproduced screenwriter who had first appeared in Fryer's office pitching an adaptation of Tom Wolfe's *The Electric Kool-Aid Acid Test*. Giler immediately heard that Gore Vidal regarded him, like Sarne, as a "bunny." Giler also happened to know Sarne socially, yet this connection did not inhibit the newcomer from quickly proposing that Fox replace Sarne with no less a talent than George Cukor, the director of such immutable Hollywood classics as *The Philadelphia Story*, *The Women*, and *Adam's Rib*. Giler says he wanted to play *Myra Breckinridge* straight, to "do this thing like it was *The Philadelphia Story* and let the outrageousness take care of itself."

According to Giler, Fox agreed with his and Fryer's request that should Giler's script prove to be acceptable Cukor (born in 1899) would replace Sarne on the project. (*Jumped-up likely lad from England? Ancient filmmaking deity? Sure, what's the diff?!*) "There was a parallel situation going on," marvels Giler, who would later, as a writer-producer, own a piece of the *Alien* franchise. "There were two movies happening at this point."

At a meeting with the film's cast members, Giler ventured to discuss one of his ideas with Mae West. "I said something about how maybe her character could have known the John Huston character 30 years ago, or something like that," says Giler. "An icy chill comes over the room. Mae leans over and pats me on the hand and says, 'Mae West never plays a character over 26.'"

West was adding to the proceedings surreal touches worthy of Luis Buñuel. "She also handed out a mimeographed sheet of things she wanted in the movie," Giler recalls. "Well, by Point 2 it was clear to me that she had not read the book—or the script. And Point 3 was 'two musical numbers.' I thought, How do I get through this meeting?"

Gore Vidal sent a telex from Rome endorsing David Giler's new script. Fox too seemed to approve. Yet Brown and Zanuck never did bring in George Cukor to replace Mike Sarne—which is why Giler now speaks of being on the "losing side" of the *Myra Breckinridge* struggle. By Mike Sarne's account, the idea of being on the "winning side" appealed to him not a whit. He had been quite aware of the Cukor plot—and had fully endorsed it. Anything to get out of his bind. "I said, 'That's fantastic! Go for it!'" says Sarne, who notes that another of Fryer's Myra candidates was Elizabeth Taylor.

———

A week before shooting was to begin on the Fox lot, the principal cast members gathered in John Huston's suite at the Hotel Bel-Air for one final read-through of the latest script, which had been cobbled together from both sides' versions. Raquel Welch was dismayed to find that the Giler/Sarne hybrid pages were no more coherent than any of the other versions she'd read.

"I went into the bathroom and had myself a cry," says Welch. "And when I came out John Huston was standing there. I had red eyes and everything, and he said, 'My darling, what's the matter?' I said, 'Mr. Huston, I'm just so scared, I don't know what to think. They keep rewriting this script, and I think it's getting worse—is it getting worse or is it getting better? Couldn't you help?' And he said,

'Darling, don't you worry about a thing. It's just a movie, it's only a movie.'"

For all her unassuaged despair, Welch says she never once considered quitting the film. When the shooting date rolled around she strapped it on like a trouper and strode onto the Fox lot. She had even, in the interests of goodwill, made a pre-production trip to Mae West's Ravenswood penthouse. "What's your name again?" asked the older actress. (Rex Reed later revealed that West said of Welch, "She's a sweet little thing, but no real woman would play this part.")

———

Even Myra Breckinridge could not have been anything but proud of Fox's choice of costumers for the picture being made in her name. In charge of Mae West's raiment would be none other than Edith Head, Hollywood's nonpareil wardrobe mistress, a 72-year-old veteran of pictures such as *All About Eve, Sunset Boulevard,* and *Rear Window,* and a winner of eight Academy Awards.

Accoutrements for Welch and the rest of the cast would be provided by newcomer Theadora Van Runkle, a 30-ish costumer whose stellar work in *The Thomas Crown Affair* and *Bonnie and Clyde* had not only dazzled Hollywood but also set alight the wider fashion world. Thanks to Van Runkle's beautifully conceived and executed retro designs, Welch would never look more breathtakingly fine than she did in *Myra*.

Despite the double generation gap between *Myra's* two leading ladies, there was palpable tension between them. Before filming, Sarne had sold Mae West on the idea of wearing only black and white throughout the picture, as a visual homage to old Hollywood. On the day that West and Welch were scheduled to share a scene together, Welch showed up in a Van Runkle–designed black dress with a white ruff collar that plunged around her décolletage. The dress was, says Welch, "confiscated" and later returned with the ruff sprayed light blue. She and West performed their scene, but not together—they never occupy the same frame in *Myra Breckinridge*.

That was just the beginning of *Myra's* problems. Co-producer James Cresson quit after a week. A publicist was fired for leaking stories about all the dramas besetting the production. And John Huston developed an implacable grudge against Sarne, who had called him a "hack" in a magazine interview. (Sarne insists that he was misquoted and had merely said that Huston "can't act.") So the older man would listen to Sarne's instructions, then ignore them. Between takes Huston groused about the no-smoking clause in Mae West's contract, which was cramping his style, cigar-wise.

Fox executives noticed that not all smokers were complying with this particular directive from Miss West. "The aroma or stench of pot seemed to be rising off the Fox lot while we were making the movie," says David Brown. "Pot is a felony in California. And the haze could not have emanated from one person." Sarne was not oblivious to the dope nimbus over the set, which he attributes mainly to the young extras who were working on *Myra,* and to the cast and crew of *Beyond the Valley of the Dolls,* the comparably scabrous picture being shot next door. Directing that project was sexploitation potentate Russ Meyer, whose ability to spin huge profits from tiny budgets (his 1968 *Vixen* had turned $72,000 into more than $6 million) persuaded Richard Zanuck to let him loose on a major studio picture.

Any tales of on-the-set felonies worried David Brown less than the "terrible reports" he was getting daily about the state of the *Myra Breckinridge* production. No one seemed able to guess what Sarne— whom several of the film's survivors describe as "arrogant"—might do from one day to the next day, or which parts of David Giler's script he might include and which parts of his own. Even at this late stage, with the meter running at a furious rate, a constant volley of memos flew among Sarne and Fox and Fryer, haggling over script details.

Even Raquel Welch succumbed to the memo madness, David Giler told a visiting journalist: "She types up these ten-page position papers and insists on reading them to me. Can you imagine anything more frightening than that?"

Rex Reed, in his *Playboy* article, depicted a movie set taken to the brink of chaos by an amateurish director who had also committed the sin, in Reed's eyes, of being unlettered. ("He hates scenes with any kind of dialog," Reed seethed.) By Reed's account, the film was pushed further over the edge by the wounded-animal skittishness of

Raquel Welch and the dickless dithering of the suits at Fox, "the gray little people who survive all the administrations because they never make a commitment to anything."

Whatever Mike Sarne's vision for *Myra Breckinridge* may have been, it proved highly elusive to his collaborators, a state of affairs which provoked both aggravation and bemusement. "I remember Edith turned to me once," says Theadora Van Runkle, "and she said, 'Thea, do you think we're working on a dirty movie?' And I said, 'Yeah, I think we are.'" Meanwhile, Sarne says his use of a red-white-and-blue color motif in the film led to accusations by Richard Zanuck that he was "pissing on the flag." Raquel Welch, who wore a Stars and Stripes bathing suit in one scene, describes how Bobby Fryer infuriated Sarne by having one of the sets repainted from red, white, and blue to drab olive overnight.

Despite the apparent hysteria that was consuming the production of *Myra Breckinridge,* Mike Sarne insists that more often than not the common response was laughter. "The thing you have to understand," says Sarne, "is that at a lot of these meetings everyone was holding their sides and falling to the floor with laughter. Richard Zanuck was running to the bathroom!"

Nor would Zanuck take Sarne seriously when the self-professed reluctant director requested that the studio solve its problems by firing Fryer and putting him "out of his misery." Zanuck "sort of laughed," says Sarne. "No, no, no," the executive said, "you two are going to have to stick together."

Even Raquel Welch bears out Sarne's talk of relative good humor in the face of rampant disorder. "Mike would show up and say, 'Right, where's Sexy Rexy in his ice-cream suit?'" says Welch, mimicking a cheerful English accent. "And Rex would show up in a tweed suit with elbow patches, carrying a pipe." Reed wore the white suit per Sarne's instruction, but never for a moment bothered to mask his contempt for the director.

According to David Brown, Reed reached the end of his tether when he was asked to deliver the line Myron utters when he wakes up in the hospital at the end of the film. (It's all a dream, remember?) The line is: "Where are my tits?!" Reed refused on grounds, presumably, of taste. Brown threatened to have another actor voice the line, and to make it painfully prominent. So, near the end of *Myra Breck-inridge*, one can enjoy the sight of the fastidious film critic reluctantly intoning, "Where are my tits?!"

======

Reed would have his revenge in spades, bad-mouthing the picture at every opportunity. The *Los Angeles Times*'s Joyce Haber frequently published anti-Sarne vitriol from, among others, Reed, Giler (who was quoted wondering why the Kennedys died and Sarne lived), and Fryer. "We thought we might be able to get rid of Sarne publicly," says Fryer's co-producer James Cresson. "It's amazing Zanuck didn't fire our asses." [Cresson died in 2004.]

In 1969 the media had not quite succumbed to the false-insider consciousness of our own era, where Hollywood politics are deconstructed for us and served up as actual entertainment. Only the most overblown works in progress were found newsworthy, films such as *Gone with the Wind* and *Cleopatra*. *Myra Breckinridge* could claim none of the latter film's internecine love affairs, continent-hopping locations, or stratospheric costs, but it nonetheless managed to become the subject of national fascination. There was something compelling about this *Myra* thing, with its heady brew of star power, generational dissonance, corporate folly, and good old-fashioned smut.

Gossip columnists quaffed freely of this concoction, and even opinion-making magazines such as *Life* and *Time* filed dispatches from the front lines, the latter wondering on its November 28, 1969, cover, which featured a mannequin version of Myra / Welch, CAN TODAY'S SEX SYMBOL FIND HAPPINESS AS MYRA BRECKINRIDGE?

After 12 weeks of shooting, Fox finally stepped in and pulled the plug on the whole farce on December 19, 1969, but had to allow Sarne to finish the film with more shooting in January. All the studio could do in defense of *Myra Breckinridge* was to place an ad in *The Hollywood Reporter*. THINK 20TH. TOGETHERNESS, it said. The accompanying photograph said otherwise. There was Welch, pneumatic and Stepford-serene; Reed, aloof as ever; Mae West, looking more like a Madame Tussaud's exhibit than a working actress; and game old John Huston in cowboy drag. Then there was Sarne, bearded and beatific, resembling a superannuated beach bum, and little Bobby Fryer, grinning and bearing it. "Motley" doesn't begin to describe the way this ensemble looked.

<hr>

However fractious the filming of *Myra Breckinridge* may have been, Mike Sarne's completed movie was, in its prerelease form, by no means regarded as a lost cause. For all the bad juju that had consumed the set, no one quite knew how the public would respond to Sarne's distinctive take on Vidal. Such were the uncertainties of the time that the filmmakers left test screenings with the distinct feeling that they could be onto something big.

During editing, Sarne had another one of his ideas, and a pretty good one: he would leaven Myra's lurid odyssey by cutting in clips of classic Hollywood films as appropriately absurd punctuation to the action. Sarne says he was inspired in this by the movie montages Stan Sheff used to create and project at the Whisky à Go Go; David Giler claims the whole thing was there in his script. Either way, Fox gave Sarne the run of its archives, so *Myra Breckinridge* now had a cute gimmick that might have been called postmodern had it come a decade later.

By both Sarne's and Zanuck's accounts, the director's final cut went over well at a test screening in Newport Beach in Orange County, and even better when it was previewed in San Francisco. By Sarne's estimate "about 3,000 gays" whooped and hollered appreciatively at the film's every innuendo and arch Hollywood reference. As Sarne recalls the screening, "They're getting all the gags, they're getting every little nuance—they're loving it! And some of them are dancing in the aisles. They were dressed up as movie stars, some of them—you know?"

One of Sarne's most treasured moments in the film is a scene in which Welch's Myra performs diligent fellatio on Rex Reed's Myron (don't worry about the metaphysics involved). In the original version, as Myron reaches crisis the director elected to cut to one of his old Hollywood clips: "a scene," says Sarne, "where Shirley Temple was milking a goat, and as she milks the goat, the goat squirts the milk in her face. And she goes 'Ohhhh!'" This particular cut went down well at the San Francisco screening, Sarne recalls.

"At that point the fucking theater exploded. It went, 'BOOM!,' like an atom bomb. The whole place went, 'Aaaaaah . . .' and then one big BOOM! Zanuck is holding his sides—he can hardly stay in his seat. . . . The gays were loving it—everybody was loving it."

Exultant scenes followed. "Zanuck was kissing me and cuddling me and groveling on the floor. We were hugging each other. We said, 'We got a hit, we got a hit!'" raves Sarne. "Kissing each other, drinking, punching each other, 'This is it, this is it . . . We've turned it around and made it a popular hit.'"

And not just a gay hit, either. Because in those days, before the demographic arts informed Hollywood's every move, "gay" was not considered a demographic at all. According to David Brown, the "gay market" had, for better or for worse, not been a factor in the making of *Myra Breckinridge*. "We weren't homophobic," says Brown. "We were just homo-ignorant."

After Sarne returned to L.A. from the San Francisco triumph, he felt as if he were "king of the hill." And then reality struck. Sarne noticed a change in Richard Zanuck, who had seemed to be in his corner during the filming of the picture. Back then, says Sarne, Zanuck was all mischief: "He talked about the rape scene: 'How you going to shoot the rape scene? How do you show the dildo?' It was like a boys' night out, you know, all the time."

It was a different Dick Zanuck who called Sarne into his office to talk about "that Shirley Temple scene." "I said, 'Which one?'" says Sarne. "Because I had about three or four of them. 'You know, the one where the goat squirts the milk in her face . . . that's got to go.' I said, 'Sorry, bubby, it's staying—it's the best scene in the film, the biggest laugh in the film. . . . In San Francisco, you were pissing yourself laughing. I remember, you had to go to the toilet.'"

Zanuck was quite insistent. Sarne reminded him that the scene had already been cleared by Fox's legal department. "He was getting really upset now, embarrassed," says Sarne. "He said, 'I've got a telegram here from my father, Darryl, who I haven't spoken to in 18 months, saying that the president of the United States [then Richard

Nixon] has called him, telling him that shot has to go, because Shirley Temple, who's a delegate to the United Nations, has heard about it and she's furious and that it's got to go.'"

Richard Zanuck says that at the time he was not estranged from his father, and that he does not remember excising Temple's goat-squirt scene from the film. Regardless, no such scene appears in the finished picture.

Sarne insists that Shirley Temple was just the beginning. Other veteran stars began to throw their weight around. "It seemed like every day somebody had an objection to something," says Sarne. "I ended up having to pull out all these clips from the film. You just can't do that and expect a film to hold up—you've totally destroyed its rhythm." The director estimates that 15 minutes were cut from his original version of *Myra Breckinridge*.

<hr>

According to *The New York Times,* a 2,000-strong crowd bellied up to the barricades outside New York's Criterion Theater on the night of *Myra Breckinridge*'s June 23 premiere. Fittingly, this was an un-quiet gathering: windows were smashed, civilians pitched into the street, policemen injured, arrests made.

Many of the spectators were there to gawk at Raquel Welch in all her sex-bomb splendor; quite another contingent was drawn by the prospect of glimpsing Mae West, who'd reportedly taken her first plane trip in 15 years just to attend. For the observant viewer, the premiere offered a re-enactment of the film's on-the-set dramas: according to Welch, when she arrived in front of the theater, "two men grabbed me by the arms and pushed me through a side door." Welch says she was held in a side room until it was time for her to take her seat. She was informed that Mae West—who had been sitting in line in the limo behind hers—had no intention of sharing the red carpet with her junior co-star.

Inside the theater, after the mink stoles had been parked, the cummerbunds loosened, and the lights dimmed, the audience was greeted by the startling image of Rex Reed lying awake in some *Barbarella*-esque operating theater. He was being attended by a cigarette-chomping and clearly nonsterilized surgeon, played by John Carradine. For no explicable reason there was a small audience in this operating theater—and it applauded enthusiastically when Carradine gelded Reed with a neat flourish. Cut to: the title sequence, in which the marvelously overripe Reed and Welch do a soft-shoe number along Hollywood Boulevard to Shirley Temple's "You Gotta S.M.I.L.E. to Be H.A. Double P. Y." Cut to: footage of a nuclear explosion. Cut to: Welch in *One Million Years B.C.* So far, so camp.

But, sitting among the swells in the audience, David Brown and Richard Zanuck realized something was wrong as the film unspooled. "Even our wives weren't laughing," says Brown, who allows that the "bizarre" sense of humor that he and Zanuck shared may have on this occasion diverged from the popular taste.

On the plus side, Mae West was in classic form in *Myra Breckinridge,* vindicating Sarne's decision to let her write her own lines. At one point she asks some young hunk how tall he is. "Six feet seven inches," he replies. West pauses until the audience can just about see it coming: "Forget about the six feet—let's talk about the seven inches."

And she got her two musical numbers, staged as a grand and inexplicable nightclub act, replete with a phalanx of vaguely Fosse-ish black male dancers. Like the rest of *Myra Breckinridge*'s principals, West was acting in her own movie. As *The New York Times* put it, there were "various degrees of stylization" on display throughout the picture. Raquel Welch, every inch the movie goddess that Myra aspired to be, delivered the character's wordy mission statements with spokesmodel sincerity, and even brought a certain vim and vigor to her violation of poor Rusty (played by the unknown Roger Herren). But it wasn't enough. Rex Reed was always skirting the scenes, heavy-lidded and dripping with disdain for the whole undertaking. (He, too, was permitted to write some of his own dialogue.) And as the gone-to-seed Buck Loner, John Huston played it broader than the Mesa Grande, as though to ensure that even the cheap seats got at least something out of the whole farrago.

Sarne's Hollywood setting is a carnal buffet where hypocrisy is denoted by faux-chamber-music trills and burlesque stings. (Sarne blames the movie's ham-fisted political satire on David Giler.) Sarne's prescient use of vintage-movie clips does here and there goose the narrative, and even manages to transform the buggery scene into a tour de force of sorts. Yet there is at the heart of the film a profound contradiction that its makers somehow never bothered to address: Gore Vidal's *Myra Breckinridge* was anti-Pop; Sarne's approach was unabashedly Pop.

Raquel Welch sums up the movie with admirable acuity: "There was this strange bouquet of personalities that were attached to this film, and each one of them was bigger than life in their own sphere. And you thought, Maybe this is the best idea that ever happened, and maybe it's the worst."

The critical vote on that particular issue was a landslide. *The Wall Street Journal* was at least blunt, calling *Myra* "distasteful, offensive, dishonest." Other reviewers made great sport of Sarne and Vidal's ungainly love child. "About as funny as a child molester."—*Time*. "A tired, smirking elephant with no place to go."—*The New York Times*. "A Hobson's choice of unprecedented unpleasantness."—*Newsweek*.

Even Myra's erstwhile idol, Parker Tyler, came out of the woodwork to give the film two thumbs down: in a letter to *The New York Times*, Tyler said he'd already been "travestied" by Vidal's book and was now being "wretchedly vulgarized" by Sarne's film.

Mike Sarne did not attend the premiere of *Myra Breckinridge*, and was not around to read his reviews. Sarne was at the time ensconced in an apartment on Rome's Piazza di Spagna, working on a movie idea possibly even more outlandish than the one he'd just completed. John Phillips, the leader of the Mamas and the Papas who served as a musical consultant on *Myra Breckinridge*, had enjoined Sarne to direct a "semi-documentary" that would cast the two pals as none other than Lord Byron and Percy Bysshe Shelley, with their respective ladies in appropriately parallel roles. This consumptive-poet buddy movie would come to nothing.

Back in America, *Gore Vidal's Myra Breckinridge* (as it was officially known) was being presented to cinemagoers as a titillating taste of taboo: "The Book That Couldn't Be Written . . . Is Now the

Movie That Couldn't Be Made!" The crass come-on worked momentarily: the film enjoyed a more than respectable box-office debut, breaking by an impressive margin the first-day records of major theaters in New York and Hollywood. Then, David Brown recalls, the reviews started to hit home, unopposed by positive word of mouth. Business slumped dramatically. And, according to Vidal, the film even caused a precipitous drop in the sales of the *Myra Breckinridge* paperback.

As the movie tanked, Fox's other kinky youth-market contender, *Beyond the Valley of the Dolls,* shimmied into profitability. Russ Meyer's film, written by Roger Ebert, may have been little more than a ragbag of pseudo-shocking generational clichés, post-Manson violence, and barely coherent plotlines, but it cost only $2 million to make and earned more than $10 million at the box office. From such proceeds the studio could afford to pay the $1.45 million in damages that was posthumously awarded in 1975 to *Valley of the Dolls* author Jacqueline Susann—a friend, incidentally, of the David Browns—over the misuse of her title.

Gore Vidal's prediction of receivership for Fox did not quite come true, but the combined moral taint of *Myra Breckinridge* and *Beyond the Valley of the Dolls* did help to bring down the curtain on the Brown-and-Zanuck regime. At a September 1970 meeting of the Twentieth Century Fox board, Darryl Zanuck stood up and, in admirably dramatic form, channeled the ill feeling that was building up toward his son and David Brown. He brought the board's attention to another sexy number they were hoping to pimp to America's moviegoers: Philip Roth's onanistic comedy *Portnoy's Complaint,* bought for half a million dollars. Zanuck *père* had prepared for the Fox board members—all of whom he himself had appointed—a detailed inventory of the Roth novel's off-color words, which by one account he proceeded to read in full: "Cock—16 . . . Shit—29 . . . Shove it in me, big boy—1." All eyes turned to the men responsible. "Tits—13 . . . "

"We expected right there and then a hand on our shoulder and a voice to say, 'You're fired,'" recalls Brown. Zanuck the younger plays down the impact of his father's recital, but the hand on the shoulder came soon enough. Two days before the end of 1970, the

Fox board met in New York and fired David Brown and Richard Zanuck. (On the credit side of their ledger, the two men had brought *M*°*A*°*S*°*H*, *Butch Cassidy and the Sundance Kid*, and *Patton* to Fox.) The pair would get their groove back in the realm of independent production, bringing the world mega-hits such as *The Sting* and *Jaws*; they have both thrived in Hollywood ever since. Darryl Zanuck resigned from Fox in May 1971. He died in 1979.

For his part, Gore Vidal says that all he has ever seen of the *Myra Breckinridge* movie is a clip that ran before one of his many TV interviews. The book is still regarded as a highlight of an unimpeachable literary career; Harold Bloom proposed it as part of the Western canon.

———

The cast of the movie may have been seen as guilty by association, but any embarrassment was transitory. Mae West was wheeled out one more time, for 1978's *Sextette*, another disastrous romp that did not significantly blemish her legend. [West died in 1980.] Rex Reed subsequently took on a handful of acting roles; he still writes about movies in *The New York Observer*. John Huston acted and directed many more times before his death in 1987; *Myra Breckinridge* constitutes barely a footnote in his several biographies.

Raquel Welch says the film took some of the sheen off her mainstream appeal, and certainly it didn't help her escape the sex-symbol cul-de-sac. The actress says it would take another four years before anyone recognized her talents as a "light comedienne," in 1974's *The Three Musketeers*.

Curiously enough, Mike Sarne chanced to showcase in *Myra Breckinridge* two TV sex symbols of the near future. Playing the part of Mary-Ann—a pretty girl whom Vidal's book describes as "mentally retarded" and whom Myra attempts to seduce on-screen—was future Charlie's Angel Farrah Fawcett. (Fawcett, through her publicist, declined to be interviewed for this article.) In the sublimely apt role of "Stud," *sans* trademark mustache: Mr. Tom Selleck!

Mike Sarne would spend the 70s attempting to recover from his ill-starred fling with Myra. In the wake of the film's release he realized that his calls to the William Morris people were not being returned—nor, it seemed, did anyone else in Hollywood care for his society. It didn't have to be that way, since, according to Tanya Sarne, the director had turned down several projects while making *Myra Breckinridge*. Over time, Sarne says, he has come to see himself as the "patsy" in the whole mess, and there are those who agree with that view, among them Sue Mengers, who reflects, "If anybody was going to be bullied, it was Michael."

"Zanuck and Brown threw Sarne to the wolves," says Hugh Fordin, now a record-label owner and producer of Broadway-cast albums. Fordin believes the studio knew that *Myra Breckinridge* was unfilmable when it passed the project to Sarne. "*Myra Breckinridge* was the fault of Fox not knowing what to do, and they shouldn't have done it in the first place. Big book, fabulous author—that's all it was to them." Adds the big book's fabulous author: "They only bought it for the dildo scene."

In the mid-70s, Sarne exiled himself to Brazil (somewhat in the manner of fugitive Great Train Robber Ronnie Biggs, whom, appropriately enough, he met) and in 1975 made a picture called *Intimidade* for the South American market. He returned to London in 1977, and shortly thereafter was divorced from his wife, with whom he had had two children. Tanya Sarne now enjoys international renown as the designer behind the label Ghost. Mike Sarne, meanwhile, is raising the three kids he's had with his French girlfriend; he makes a living by acting, painting, and directing the odd commercial. "You call this a living?" he asks with a vaudevillian shrug.

It all might have been so different had Twentieth Century Fox just paid him his writer's fee and let George Cukor take over. "They might have made a sad little picture that wouldn't have done anyone any harm," Sarne muses. Who knows, he says, "a lot of people might have found it a worthy project."

We will never know how George Cukor's *Myra Breckinridge* would have panned out, and for many years it was almost impossible to view even the Mike Sarne version, except on grainy videotape bootlegs or at rare midnight-movie screenings. [But thanks to the film's enduring reputation as a cult item, Fox finally granted *Myra*

Breckinridge a DVD release in 2004—and in doing so managed to add yet one more layer to this mille feuille of cinematic folly. The *Myra Breckinridge* DVD features two separate commentary tracks, which offer hilariously polarized interpretations of the same on-screen action. In his director's commentary, Mike Sarne indulges in a good deal of belated score-settling, casually sniping at anyone who sullied his grand vision and tossing in the odd homophobic crack for good measure. When Raquel Welch takes her place in the sound booth, she remarks, "I can't believe I took this part"; she continues in a similarly bemused vein throughout, creating one of the cattiest (and funniest) "extra features" ever to appear on a major-studio DVD and forever enshrining the legend of *Myra Breckinridge*.]

"That's the strange thing about this silly, superficial movie," said Mike Sarne, during *Myra*'s pre-DVD limbo. "And the silly, superficial project and all its shallow meretricious qualities It still has a sort of horrible grandeur. And especially for me."

From *Vanity Fair,* April 2001

TOMMY

Tommy *Dearest*

by James Wolcott

A shaming admission. Until the Year of Our Redeemer 2007, I had never seen the complete movie version of the Who's rock opera *Tommy*, a gaping pothole in my pop-culture upbringing that I find puzzling, faintly embarrassing, borderline perverse.

It was a movie I assumed I knew, and yet had avoided lashing myself to the mast to see from start to finish. I had seen clips from the film, was familiar with its most notorious crescendos, knew the soundtrack backward and sideways; I had pounced on the original *Tommy* double album when it was unleashed, in 1969 (for Who fans, it was our patriotic duty), the release of the single "Pinball Wizard" barely hinting at the visionary ambition and roiling disquietude of Pete Townshend's cathartic quest. As a pip-squeak reporter from *The Village Voice*, I had even been granted rare backstage access when the Who played Madison Square Garden in 1974, too reluctant to approach the jet-lagged, work-exhausted Townshend, who sat slumped in a chair like a beaten prisoner before rallying himself to go out on stage and whip himself into windmill-guitar action as lead singer Roger Daltrey, chipper backstage, pranced like a centaur beneath his Pre-Raphaelite curls, bassist John Entwistle held his position like an eternal sentry, and drummer Keith Moon created blitzkrieg thunder and a heavy precipitation of flying sweat. So I was primed for *Tommy* when it brazened its way into movie houses a year later, causing a fluster. Yet I held off, shied away from seeing it. If my reluctance had a name, its name was Ken Russell.

Russell, the director of *Tommy*, is the sort of cultural upheavalist for whom the phrase "aging *enfant terrible*" seems to have been custom-fitted. Like Otto Preminger, Alfred Hitchcock, Federico Fellini, and, in our own day, Mel Brooks and Quentin Tarantino, Russell is more than a traffic cop in a canvas chair conducting for the camera; he's an impresario, each movie part of a larger sales pitch for the director's signature brand.

Russell first rattled the commissary cart in the 60s as a director of documentaries at the BBC on the composers Prokofiev, Elgar, and Delius. What Russell did in his pioneer efforts seems tame now— reconstructing events in the composers' lives, bringing their sexual conflicts to the fore—but they were revelatory and scandalously controversial at the time, not only violating the prim protocols of BBC house style but injecting high art with pop hallucinogenic hyperbole.

———

There was a whole heap of moaning and groaning in Russell's movies: the nude-wrestling scene in his adaptation of D. H. Lawrence's *Women in Love*, between Oliver Reed and Alan Bates (which, in certain angles, resembled a pork-sword fight between two burly bears); the phantasmagoria attending Glenda Jackson as Tchaikovsky's lunatic wife, Nina, in *The Music Lovers* ("Whose fantasy are we in when Glenda Jackson writhes in torment in a blue-green madhouse and, in one sequence, is seen deliberately lying across a grating, spreadeagled, while the madmen locked below reach up under her skirt?," Pauline Kael wondered in *The New Yorker*); the nuns-gone-wild orgiastics of his screen version of Aldous Huxley's *The Devils of Loudun* (where, wrote critic Penelope Gilliatt in *The New Yorker*, "the epileptic rhythms of the editing are revved up with a score that might be program music for the onset of psychosis").

No, his was not a light touch, and when Russell got his paws on the charming musical *The Boy Friend*, I was reminded of Evelyn Waugh's fright at the prose of Stephen Spender: "To see him fumbling with our rich and delicate language is to experience all the horror of seeing a Sèvres vase in the hands of a chimpanzee."

Now, *Tommy* was no priceless vase that required gentle handling. It was closer to a Molotov cocktail of cleansing fire. "What *Tommy* proclaims with the first blast of its Beethovenish horn is the red dawn of revolution," wrote the critic Albert Goldman, whose musicological background as a Wagner enthusiast (and co-editor of the anthology *Wagner on Music and Drama*) enabled him to be the first to glimpse *Tommy*'s possibilities as a total theatrical sensory bombardment. The blissy, mud-honey, communal spirit of Woodstock had been savaged with pool cues at the Altamont racetrack (where Hell's Angels, functioning as security, had beaten and stabbed to death a young black man named Meredith Hunter during a free Rolling Stones concert), and the hippie multitudes were awaiting marching orders. "The love days are over, [*Tommy*] trumpets, now come the days of wrath. War is the opera's real theme, war of generation against generation, war between the younger generation and its own leaders."

Goldman once sat the great jazz drummer Elvin Jones down to grade the talent of his rock counterparts, and played him the "Underture" to *Tommy*. Jones, a hard man to impress, was impressed. "See there, where the tempo started to die, how he picked it up! The man is a drummer. Everything he plays, he *contains* it."

Moon's drumstick heroics were more than virtuosity. Percussion supplies the raging heartbeat of *Tommy*. "Beating a tachycardiac tattoo of alarm, battle, and triumph for a good half of its total length, *Tommy* reminds us that revolutions carry their colors in their drums," Goldman wrote. But by the time *Tommy* entered pre-production, the colors had been drained. In his autobiography, *Altered States*, Russell describes meeting "Manic Moon" during a recording session for *Quadrophenia*, where the concatenation from Moon's drum kit reminded Russell of the Blitz. "Six months later," Russell writes, "Moon was a wreck. His crazy lifestyle had reduced him to a pathetic shadow not strong enough to knock the skin off a rice pudding. And there were times when Pete had to replace him with an anonymous session man. I began to wonder if he'd be fit enough to play Uncle Ernie, the lecherous old man who debauches Tommy."

Moon was up to the sordid task once the cameras started rolling, playing Uncle Ernie with a pervy, scurvy brio matched in the film only by the bullfrog glower of Oliver Reed as Tommy's rotter of a stepfather. Off-camera, according to Joseph Lanza's aptly titled *Phallic Frenzy—Ken Russell and His Films* (Chicago Review Press), Reed kept himself entertained by airing out his dangler. "At the slightest provocation, he'd whip out what he called, 'My snake of desire, my wand of lust, my mighty mallet.'" His hellraising had repercussions. After Reed waved his willy at a resort where they planned to shoot the Holiday Camp sequence, the proprietor banned *Tommy*'s cast and crew from the property.

Its war drums muffled, the film version, unlike the original album, was no rallying cry for generational insurgency. It was instead all-out psychodrama, a case study *in excelsis*. Physically abused, sexually molested, chemically vandalized, this Tommy—"the first autistic hero in the history of opera" (Goldman), who shuts down after he's witness to the primal Freudian scene of seeing his mother's lover murder his father after the father catches them in flagrante delicto—is a Kasper Hauser–ish specimen whose victimization and exploitation supply the crucible of redemption and the catapult into stardom.

In our culture, stardom *is* redemption, fame the desired payoff for past suffering as a pissed-upon nobody. That's why *Tommy* endures while so many other rock efforts from that period have dated. Its battered-innocent protagonist, played with blue-eyed beatitude by Roger Daltrey, is the forerunner to *A Child Called "It,"* Augusten Burroughs's *Running with Scissors,* the fiction of J. T. Leroy, and the entire trauma ward of Oprah literature—the virgin prince of victim culture. Deaf, dumb, and blind, a pawn in everyone's grubby game, a pinball wizard whose supersensitive touch makes him unbeatable (his match against Elton John, whose humongous lumberjack boots are the movie's supreme coup of costume genius, is one of the standout set pieces), Tommy liberates his senses and sensibility when he smashes a mirror and, in the flood of sensation, achieves enlightenment. Enlightened, he becomes a messiah figure, a pop Christ (the *T* in Tommy serving as his logo cross) who attracts bikers and stoners alike to his gospel revivals, gliding above them like a paper airplane mailed from heaven. A figure of light, he nevertheless casts a shadow. Every pop savior with charisma to burn and the stage as his pulpit bears the magic beans of a potential fascist. They become what they displace.

It may seem quaint today, children of the corn, but you come-latelies have no idea of the spell cast in the late 60s by the specter of a rock messiah overturning the social order and assuming dictatorial powers over hordes of Hollywood extras. Incense, pot fumes, and gunpowder mingled in the insurrectionary air! Dionysian energy gone berserk was the basis of dystopian scare films such as *Wild in the Streets* (where an American pop star is elected president and everyone over the age of 30 is herded into retirement homes where they're force-fed LSD) and *Privilege* (where a British pop star presides over a Nuremberg-like rally as an obedient mob chants, "We will conform!"), and of the Doors' anthem "Five to One," from the album *Waiting for the Sun,* which puts the deadwood of society on notice that they're about to be swept downstream by demographic forces ("They got the guns / But we got the numbers"),

It was the dissolute insolence of the Doors' lead singer and leather-trousered shaman, Jim Morrison, that helped disillusion Townshend to the whole rock-star deity trip. As Lanza writes in *Phallic Frenzy,* "Townshend based his 'Sally Simpson' vignette—when an avid girl fan gets mutilated while rushing to reach the messianic Tommy on the stage—on witnessing Jim Morrison throw a fan a sucker punch just as a woman in the audience fell on her face while trying to touch the Lizard King." In *Tommy,* it's the jackbooted Oliver Reed who does the maiming, but the lesson is the same: the dynamic between idols and idolizers is a sick co-dependency, perceives Townshend; when delirium reigns, the slightest provocation may incite a feeding frenzy. Tommy's angelic form is a communion host his fans would eat alive if they could. Ken Russell's gusty temperament, meteorologically ill-suited for so many subjects, was perfect for *Tommy.* Hysteria was always right up his alley, with pandemonium just around the bend.

Which is why the true star of *Tommy,* its true hero and animating force, isn't Tommy, or Roger Daltrey, or the director calling the shots, or even the great Tina Turner as the orgasmatronic Acid Queen, but Ann-Margret as Tommy's mother, Nora. In her silver catsuit, Ann-Margret's Nora is pandemonium personified, the mother of all mothers. The all-American go-go-girl curvaceousness that vitalized *Viva Las Vegas* whenever Ann-Margret gyrated with Elvis (making it his least crappy musical) ripened into mad dervish disco divahood in *Tommy.* Bravery is what drives her bravura. Surviving a steep, dangerous fall off a stage in Lake Tahoe a couple of years earlier that could have put her permanently out of commission, she nevertheless held nothing back here. Hers is a performance beyond vanity, beyond good and bad, beyond good and evil, beyond camp—a pure projectile of kamikaze dedication. "In this process of morphing from a glitzy and safe Hollywood vixen into another of his maniacal harridans, Ken Russell should have canonized her Saint Ann-Margret," writes Lanza.

Let us canonize her in his stead, for in the course of the film she frolics in a frigid stream, has her false fingernails torn off, and lets her mascara run wild. Her tour de force is the solo orgy in a bedroom done up in Peggy Lee satiny white where, in a drunken, deranged fury at seeing Tommy's face popping up on every channel, she flings an empty champagne bottle and smashes the TV screen, only to be inundated with a dam burst of soap suds (which turned pink from a cut Ann-Margret incurred from a shard of broken glass), baked beans (a nod to the cover of *The Who Sell Out,* where Daltrey soaked in a bathtub full of Heinz beans), and, the *pièce de résistance,* a septic explosion of dark chocolate. Lanza: "Soon Russell has her groveling among the foam and fudge, whipping up an orgasmic rage as she straddles a sausage shaped (and now chocolate lubed) pillow. Ann-Margret's husband, the producer Roger Smith [also a former actor on TV's *77 Sunset Strip*], happened to walk onto the set while all of this transpired. He looked aghast and speculated then and there that his wife's career as a glamour queen had come to an end."

Perhaps it had, but what a way to end it! Using her body as a paint roller, Ann-Margret threw herself into a fearless fit of performance art, predating Karen Finley's chocolate-smeared onstage agonizings by a full decade. After her showstopper, Tommy's tribulations seem like post-nasal drip.

=======

In the initial enthusiasm over the phenomenon of *Tommy*, there was the innocent hope that a new rock art form had been forged, "a poperatic tradition," in Goldman's phrase. It was not to be. Pete Townshend later followed *Tommy* with the equally effortful but less linear and concentrated *Quadrophenia*, where the multiple personalities of the Who contended inside the teenage psyche of a 60s mod named Jimmy. *Quadrophenia* was later made into a movie and adapted for the stage, but despite the punch of individual songs, it lacked an overarching iconographic design and remained, in the words of one rock critic, more of a "cultural monument" than a pleasure.

Ken Russell followed *Tommy* with *Lisztomania*, which cast Roger Daltrey as the composer Franz Liszt wigging them out in 19th-century Europe and whose ad campaign promised that the film "out-Tommys 'Tommy.'" It wished. There was so much obtrusive, overblown phallic symbolism that it's a wonder someone's eyes weren't poked out.

Even with successful follow-through, it's doubtful that the rock opera would have flourished as a going genre into the present. Rock is no longer its own religion, the elevated altar of mystics and martyrs. Our sensibilities don't aspire to be absorbed into the mother ship of Wagner's dream of *Gesamtkunstwerk*, the total integration of the arts into an oceanic whole. The bombastic scope of tabernacle-scaled works of Tormented Genius seems anachronistic to us now. In the era of the iPod and laptop, our music—the soundtracks of our lives and the playlist in our heads—is downloadable, portable, swappable, remixable. (Farewell, rock opera; hello, jukebox musical.)

We don't want to be subsumed into something bigger. We want something smaller to become part of us, incorporated into the repertoire. When Tommy's autistic condition was cracked open, his mind awakened to what it was like Out There and his arms embraced the sky. We prefer it In Here, with the hood down.

From *Vanity Fair's Movies Rock*, Fall 2007

SATURDAY NIGHT FEVER

Fever Pitch

by Sam Kashner

Robert Stigwood, the 42-year-old Australian impresario known as "the Darryl Zanuck of pop," was out of his mind. That was the talk in Hollywood, Bill Oakes remembers, on September 25, 1976, when his boss held a lavish press conference at the Beverly Hills Hotel to announce that the Robert Stigwood Organisation—RSO—had just signed John Travolta to a million-dollar contract to star in three films. Oakes, then in his mid-20s, had worked for the Beatles and had once been Paul McCartney's assistant. By this time he was running RSO Records, which boasted Eric Clapton and the Bee Gees among its roster of pop stars. "Everyone thought it was madness," says Oakes, "because nobody had ever made the transition from television to movie stardom. So, a lot of us thought to pay a million dollars for Vinnie Barbarino [Travolta's character on the TV sitcom *Welcome Back, Kotter*] is going to make us a laughingstock."

Stigwood wanted Travolta to star in the movie version of *Grease,* the long-running Broadway musical (in which Travolta had already appeared as Doody, one of the T-Bird gang members, in a road company). Five years earlier, Stigwood had auditioned the actor—then just 17—for *Jesus Christ Superstar,* and though Ted Neeley got the job, Stigwood had penciled himself a note on a yellow pad: "This kid will be a very big star."

But Stigwood's option for *Grease* stipulated that production could not begin before the spring of 1978, because the musical was still going strong. While they waited, Stigwood and his lieutenants began to look around for a new property.

A few months before, an English rock critic by the name of Nik Cohn had published a magazine article entitled "Tribal Rites of the New Saturday Night." Appearing in the June 7, 1976, issue of *New York,* the article followed the Saturday-night rituals of a group of working-class Italian-Americans in Bay Ridge, Brooklyn, who held dead-end jobs but lived for their nights of dancing at a local disco called 2001 Odyssey. Cohn's hero, named Vincent, was a tough, violent guy but a great dancer who yearned for a chance to shine, and to escape the mean streets of Brooklyn.

On an icy winter night in 1975, Cohn had made his first trip to Bay Ridge with a disco dancer called Tu Sweet, who would serve as his Virgil. "According to Tu Sweet," Cohn later wrote, "the [disco] craze had started in black gay clubs, then progressed to straight blacks and gay whites and from there to mass consumption—Latinos in the Bronx, West Indians on Staten Island, and, yes, Italians in Brooklyn." In 1975, black dancers like Tu Sweet were not welcome in those Italian clubs; nonetheless, he liked the dancers there—their passion and their moves. "Some of those guys, they have no lives," he told Cohn. "Dancing's all they got."

A brawl was in progress when they arrived at 2001 Odyssey. One of the brawlers lurched over to Cohn's cab and threw up on his trouser leg. With that welcome, the two men hightailed it back to Manhattan, but not before Cohn caught a glimpse of a figure, dressed in "flared, crimson pants and a black body shirt," coolly watching the action from the club doorway. "There was a certain style about him—an inner force, a hunger, and a sense of his own specialness. He looked, in short, like a star," recalled Cohn. He'd found his Vincent, the protagonist of his New Journalism–style piece.

Later, Cohn went back to the disco with the artist James McMullan, whose illustrations for the article helped persuade Cohn's underwhelmed editor in chief, Clay Felker, to run it. The title was changed from "Another Saturday Night" to "Tribal Rites of the New Saturday Night," and a note was added insisting that "everything described in this article is factual."

In the 1970s it was almost unheard of to buy a magazine article for a movie, but "Tribal Rites" attracted enough attention that producer Ray Stark (*Funny Girl*) and a few others bid on it. Cohn had known Stigwood back in London and liked him. Stigwood came from humble stock: farm people in Adelaide, Australia. He'd made his way to London in the early 1960s and ended up managing the Beatles organization for Brian Epstein. Ousted in the power struggle that followed Epstein's death, Stigwood went on to create RSO Records, and in 1968 he branched out into theater, putting together the West End productions of *Jesus Christ Superstar*, *Hair*, and *Grease*. His movie-producing career began five years later, with the film version of *Jesus Christ Superstar*, followed by *Tommy*, the rock musical written by the Who and directed by the flamboyant Ken Russell, which became one of the biggest movies of 1975.

So the deal was made, and Cohn was paid $90,000 for the rights.

Now they had to find a director.

In Los Angeles, Stigwood's assistant, Kevin McCormick, a brilliant, lean 23-year-old from New Jersey, went from office to office looking for one. "Kid, my directors do movies," one agent promptly told him. "They don't do magazine articles." But while McCormick was packing to return to New York, the phone rang, and it was the agent saying, "Kid, you're in luck. My client came in and looked at this, and he's interested. But you should see his movie first."

"So we saw *Rocky* on Monday, and we made a deal," recalls McCormick, now president of production at Warner Bros. The client was director John Avildsen, and he brought in screenwriter Norman

Wexler, who had earned his first Academy Award nomination for the screenplay for *Joe*, the popular 1970 film about a bigoted hard hat, played by Peter Boyle. (Incidentally, the film gave Susan Sarandon her first screen role.) Wexler had also co-adapted Peter Maas's *Serpico* for the screen (which brought him a second Oscar nomination). That seemed fitting, as Al Pacino was something of the patron saint of Cohn's article, as well as of the film—in the story, Vincent is flattered when someone mistakes him for Pacino, and in the movie, the poster from *Serpico* dominates Tony Manero's Bay Ridge bedroom, going face-to-face with Farrah Fawcett's famous cheesecake poster.

Wexler, a tall man, often wrapped in a trench coat, puffed on Tarrytons so continuously he was usually wreathed in cigarette smoke. McCormick thought of him as "a sort of tragic figure, but enormously sympathetic." A manic-depressive, Wexler was on and off his meds; when he stopped, all hell broke loose. Karen Lynn Gorney, who played Stephanie Mangano, Tony's love interest in the movie, remembers, "He would come into his agent's office, or try to pitch a script to somebody, and start giving nylons and chocolates to the secretaries." He could turn violent, and was known to sometimes carry a .32-caliber pistol. In the grip of a manic episode, he once bit a stewardess on the arm; on another flight he announced that he had a plan to assassinate President Nixon. "You've heard of street theater?" he yelled, holding up a magazine picture of the president. "Well, this is airplane theater!" He was arrested and escorted off the plane.

But McCormick was pleased when the script came in. At 149 pages, "it was way, way, way, way too long, but quite wonderful. I think what Norman did so well was to create a family situation that had real truth, an accurate look at how men related to women in that moment, in ways that you would never get away with now." Wexler transformed Vincent into Tony Manero and gave him a young sister and a favored older brother who breaks his mother's heart by leaving the priesthood. During one row at the dinner table, Tony explodes at his mother when she refuses to accept that her eldest has turned in his collar: "You got nuthin' but three shit children!" he yells. Tony's mother—played by acclaimed stage actress and Off Broadway playwright Julie Bovasso—bursts into tears, and Tony is overcome with remorse.

Before John Travolta became a teen idol, he was a dancer. "I think my first turn-on to dance was James Cagney in *Yankee Doodle Dandy,* when I was five or six," recalls Travolta on a break from filming the musical version of John Waters's *Hairspray* in Toronto. "I used to try to imitate him in front of the television set. I liked black dancing better than white dancing. I used to watch *Soul Train,* and what I wanted to create was a *Soul Train* feel in *Saturday Night Fever.*" That famous strut to the Bee Gees' "Stayin' Alive" in the opening scene? "It was the walk of coolness. I went to a school that was 50 percent black, and that's how the black kids walked through the hall."

"Nobody pushed me into show business," Travolta says. "I was aching for it." Born in 1954 in Englewood, New Jersey, he was one of six kids, five of whom pursued careers in show business. His mother, Helen, was an actress who taught in a high-school theater-arts program and who set a record for swimming the Hudson River. His father, Salvatore (known as "Sam"), once played semi-pro football and was a co-owner of Travolta Tyre Exchange. John's parents agreed to let him drop out of Dwight Morrow High School, in Englewood, at 16, for one year, to pursue a theatrical career. He never went back. Soon after, in 1970, Travolta caught the attention of agent Bob LeMond when he appeared as Hugo Peabody in a production of *Bye Bye Birdie* at Club Benet in Morgan, New York. LeMond quickly got him work in dozens of TV commercials, including one for Mutual of New York, in which Travolta played a teenager crying over the death of his father.

Travolta moved to Los Angeles in 1974 and auditioned for *The Last Detail,* but lost the role to Randy Quaid. He landed a small role as Nancy Allen's creepy, sadistic boyfriend in Brian De Palma's *Carrie,* just before auditioning for *Welcome Back, Kotter,* the ABC sitcom about a group of unteachable Brooklyn high-school students called the "Sweathogs" and their local-boy teacher, played by the show's creator, Gabe Kaplan.

After signing to play the dumb but sexy Italian kid, Vinnie Barbarino (who thrilled the girls with his goofy grin, curly forelock, and swiveling snake hips), Travolta landed the lead role in Terrence Malick's *Days of Heaven.* But ABC wouldn't let him out of the *Welcome Back, Kotter* production schedule, and Richard Gere took his place. "I thought, What's happening here? Will I ever get my big break?" Travolta recalls.

What Travolta didn't know was that he had already gotten his big break. The network was receiving 10,000 fan letters a week—just for him. Soon there were beefcake Vinnie Barbarino posters everywhere—that cleft chin, those cerulean eyes. His public appearances were mobbed. When his 1976 debut album was released, thousands of female fans packed E. J. Korvette's record department in Hicksville, Long Island, and an estimated 30,000 fans showed up at what was then the world's largest indoor mall, in Schaumburg, Illinois. When *Carrie* was released, Travolta's name appeared above the title on some movie marquees.

ABC asked him to star in his own show, based on the Barbarino character, but Travolta turned it down, worried about ever getting a major film role. Then Robert Stigwood called.

While still appearing on *Welcome Back, Kotter,* Travolta had played the lead in an ABC TV movie called *The Boy in the Plastic Bubble,* the true story of a teenage boy who had been born without an immune system. It aired November 12, 1976, and his co-star was Diana Hyland, who played his mother. Hyland—often described as "a Grace Kelly type"—had appeared on Broadway with Paul Newman in *Sweet Bird of Youth,* but was best known as Susan, an alcoholic wife on the TV series *Peyton Place.* A romance flowered between 22-year-old Travolta and 40-year-old Hyland, which baffled many who knew the young actor, and was toned down so as not to raise too many eyebrows in the press or alienate his teen fan base.

It was Diana who persuaded Travolta to take the role of Tony Manero. "I got the script, I read it that night," Travolta recalls. "I wondered if I could give it enough dimension. Diana took it into the other room, and in about an hour she burst back in. 'Baby, you are going to be great in this—great! This Tony, he's got all the colors! First he's angry about something. He hates the trap that Brooklyn and his dumb job are. There's a whole glamorous world out there waiting for him, which he feels only when he dances. And he grows, he gets out of Brooklyn.'" Travolta remembers answering, "'He's also king of the disco. I'm not that good a dancer.' 'Baby,' she said, 'you're going to learn!'"

Stigwood "just had blithe confidence that the movie's going to be up and ready to go," according to McCormick. "And he had no financier. He was financing it himself with his new partners, for two and a half million dollars. I knew that the budget was at least $2.8 [million] already. I had a stomachache every day. We were making this low-budget movie out of 135 Central Park West—we literally put together the soundtrack in Stigwood's living room."

And they had to hurry: Travolta and Stigwood were slated to film *Grease* soon after. This was just a little movie to get out of the way.

After six months of prepping, a huge problem reared its head: the director turned out to be all wrong. McCormick noticed that Avildsen was becoming increasingly difficult. "First he couldn't figure out who the choreographer should be. We met endlessly with [New York City Ballet principal dancer] Jacques D'Amboise. [Alvin Ailey star] Judith Jamison we talked to for a while. So, it just got to a point where Avildsen wanted to be put out of his misery. He was acting provocatively: 'Travolta's too fat. He can't dance, he can't do this, he can't do that.'"

Avildsen brought in a trainer, ex-boxer Jimmy Gambina, who had worked with Sylvester Stallone on *Rocky*, to get Travolta into shape, "which was really good," McCormick says, "because Travolta is prone to be soft and not that energetic, and Gambina ran him like he was a fighter." But Avildsen still wasn't satisfied, and wondered if maybe Travolta's character "shouldn't be a dancer—maybe he should be a painter. It was just weird. It became Clifford Odets," recalls McCormick. Travolta, ultimately, wasn't happy with Avildsen, either; he felt the director wanted to smooth Tony's rough edges, make him the kind of nice guy who carries groceries for old ladies in the neighborhood—another Rocky Balboa.

Just weeks before filming was set to begin, Stigwood summoned Avildsen to an emergency meeting. That morning, Stigwood had learned, Avildsen had been nominated for an Oscar for *Rocky*. McCormick says, "Robert walked in and said, 'John, there's good news and bad news. The good news is you've just been nominated for an

Academy Award. Congratulations. The bad news is you're fired.'"
(Avildsen won the Oscar.)

"Now what do we do?" McCormick asked Stigwood.

"We get another director."

So, John Badham came on the scene, three weeks before principal photography was to begin. Badham was born in England, raised in Alabama, and educated at the Yale School of Drama. Like Travolta, he came from a theatrical family. His mother was an actress and his sister, Mary, had played Scout, Atticus Finch's daughter, in *To Kill a Mockingbird*. It was her connection to Gregory Peck that had gotten her brother's foot in the door in the industry: in the mailroom at Warner Bros. At 34, Badham still had few credits to his name—some television and a baseball movie starring Billy Dee Williams, Richard Pryor, and James Earl Jones (*The Bingo Long Traveling All-Stars & Motor Kings*). He had just jumped from—or been pushed out of—directing *The Wiz*, because he objected to 33-year-old Diana Ross being cast as Dorothy. McCormick sent him the *Saturday Night Fever* script and promptly flew him to New York.

When Travolta met Badham, he was surprised that his new director knew so little about New York. The actor took it upon himself to show Badham Manhattan and Brooklyn. "I said, 'Let me be your guide. Let me take you by the hand and show you New York and its environs—the real New York. I know this town.'" He was a quick study, says McCormick. "Badham, the most unmusical guy in the world, brought in the choreographer, who was fantastic"—Lester Wilson. Travolta had already been working with Deney Terio, a disco dancer who would later host a TV disco competition called *Dance Fever*, but it was Wilson, many in the crew believe, who breathed life into the movie.

Wilson was a black choreographer who had worked with Sammy Davis Jr. as a featured dancer in *Golden Boy* on Broadway and in London. A legend in gay dance clubs, he'd won an Emmy for choreographing Lola Falana's television specials. Paul Pape, who played Double J, the most aggressive member of Tony Manero's entourage, says, "Deney Terio did show John the moves, and I give him credit for that. But I don't think Lester Wilson got nearly the credit that he deserved. The movie was Lester."

Travolta describes Wilson as "such an interesting guy. He taught me what he called his 'hang time.' He would smoke a cigarette to greet the day, and he infused my dancing with African-American rhythm. I'm the kind of dancer who needs thought and construction—an idea—before I dance. I need an internal story. Lester would put on some music and he would say, 'Move with me, motherfucker—move with me!'"

Before they could start filming, they had to get the setting just right. Lloyd Kaufman, co-founder of Troma Entertainment and the film's executive in charge of locations, says, "We looked at every disco in Manhattan, Brooklyn, and Queens, and even considered converting a loft to our own specifications, before deciding to go with 2001 Odyssey, in Bay Ridge. That was always our first choice, since that's where the story really happens." The movie, except for two days' filming on the West Side of Manhattan and the Verrazano-Narrows Bridge scenes, was shot entirely in Bay Ridge.

Filming in Brooklyn brought a whole new set of challenges. It was a rough place, and the production started to have some neighborhood problems. A firebomb was thrown at the discotheque, but it didn't cause any serious damage. McCormick asked John Nicolella, the production manager on the shoot and a tough Italian character, "'What the fuck is this about?' And he said, 'Well, you know, it's a neighborhood thing. They want us to hire some of the kids.' Then these two guys appeared on the set, pulled me off to the side. 'You know, you're being disruptive to the neighborhood. You might need some security. And if you want to put lights on the bowling alley across the street, Black Stan really wants seven grand.'" They paid him.

Tom Priestley, then a camera operator on his first feature film, says, "We all grew up on locations in New York because Hollywood had all the studios. We had one or two stages that were decent. But most of the time, all our work was in the streets. We didn't have all the bells and whistles that Hollywood had. And that's what made us, I think, tough and adaptable. You figure if you can work in New York you can work anywhere."

To research his character, Travolta began sneaking into 2001 Odyssey with Wexler. So great was his popularity as Vinnie Barbarino he had to disguise himself in dark glasses and a hat. Before he was spotted, he watched the Faces—the cool, aggressive dancers Cohn had based his article on—concentrating on every detail of their behavior. When he was recognized—"Hey, man! Hey, it's fuckin' Travolta!"—the actor noticed how the disco's alpha males kept their girls in line. "Their girlfriends would come up, and they'd say, 'Hey, stay away from him, don't bug Travolta,' and they'd actually push the girls away. Tony Manero's whole male-chauvinist thing I got from watching those guys in the discos," says Travolta.

Priestley remembers, "I would've thought the real guys [in Brooklyn] would have resented a film like this, like we've come to make fun of them or something, but they loved it. There was one brother-and-sister team that was very good. Remember, all those people in the show are extras. You see them dancing next to Travolta and Donna Pescow [who played Annette]. They were really good dancers."

———

There were no special effects in *Saturday Night Fever,* except for the smoke rising from the dance floor. Bill Ward, the film's sole gaffer, explains that it wasn't from dry ice or a smoke machine—it was "a toxic mix of burning tar and automobile tires, pinched from a Bay Ridge alley." It created such heat and smoke that at one point they had to wheel in oxygen for Travolta. The filmmakers also went to great trouble and expense—$15,000—to put lights in the dance floor, designed to pulsate to the music. The walls were covered with aluminum foil and Christmas lights. When the club's owner saw the dailies for the first time, he said, "Holy shit, you guys made my place look great!"

Filming began on March 14, 1977. "The first day's location was outside the dance studio," recalls McCormick. "I got a phone call from the production manager, and he said, 'This is chaos!' I came out and there were 10,000 kids on the streets, and we only have four security guys. So we had to shut down for a couple of hours while we just regrouped and tried to figure out a way to make it work. It was the first time that we actually had a sense of who John was." By the end of the first day, they had to shut down and go home because "there was no place you could point the camera without seeing 15,000 people. We'd have to put out fake call sheets and get out there at 5:30 in the morning" to avoid the crush of fans.

Brooklyn-born actress Donna Pescow, who breaks your heart as Annette, the foolish local girl whose adoration of Tony nearly destroys her, was in the makeup trailer with Travolta when fans surrounded them and started rocking the trailer back and forth. "That was terrifying," she remembers. "So, they got the right people in the neighborhood, who said, 'Don't do that anymore.' They were practically paying protection—I mean, it was really tough." Karen Lynn Gorney, however, felt that the sheer energy released by thousands of Travolta's female fans yelling "Barbarino!" added to the set. "It helped the film," she says. "A lot of female hormones raging around— that might have been a good thing. Women aren't supposed to express their sexuality, but that's what you get, all that screaming and crying, because they're sitting on their gonads."

A personal tragedy was unfolding for Travolta, however: Diana Hyland's struggle with breast cancer. By the time he began preparing to play Tony Manero, she was dying. Travolta made many trips from New York to Los Angeles to be with her through her illness, so he was in a state of constant jet lag and distress. Two weeks after shooting began, he flew to the West Coast to be with Diana one last time. "He did not know Diana was sick when he fell in love," Travolta's mother, Helen, later told *McCall's* magazine, "but he stuck with her when he did know." On March 27, 1977, Hyland died in his arms.

Andy Warhol was on Travolta's return flight to New York. He later wrote in his diary, "John Travolta kept going to the bathroom, coming out with his eyes bright red, drinking orange juice and liquor in a paper cup, and he put his head in a pillow and started crying. I saw him reading a script, too, so I thought he was acting, really cute and sensitive-looking, very tall. . . . You can see the magic in him. I asked the stewardess why he was crying and she said, 'death in the family,' so I thought it was a mother or father, until I picked up the paper at home and found out that it was Diana Hyland, who'd died of cancer at forty-one, soap-opera queen, his steady date."

Karen Lynn Gorney later said that she could feel Diana's spirit on the set, "protecting him, because he was going through deep grief and he had to get through it. If he fell into the grief, he wouldn't be able to pull himself out of it. But he was very professional and he was right there on the money. I remember the scene at the Verrazano Bridge when I lean over and kiss him. The poor thing was suffering so, and that kiss was totally spontaneous. That wasn't Tony and Stephanie—that was because I really saw he was hurting."

There's another lovely scene between Travolta and Gorney, when Stephanie agrees to accompany Tony to a Brooklyn restaurant. "We wanted to see how much of it we could do in one shot," Badham says about that scene, which was filmed through the restaurant's window, so you see them through a glorious, dreamlike reflection of a city skyline—"magic and distant." They try to impress each other with their savvy and their cool, but they are hilariously unpolished. (Stephanie informs Tony that worldly New Yorkers drink tea with lemon.) "These kids are trying to pretend like they're a lot more sophisticated than they are," Badham says, "though obviously anybody that says 'Bonwit Taylor' hasn't quite got it all together." As the scene unfolds, the light subtly changes, late afternoon moving into dusk.

———

Badham and Travolta clashed on a number of occasions. When Travolta first saw the rushes of the opening scene, in which a stand-in— shot from the knees down—takes that famous walk along Brooklyn's 86th Street to the beat of "Stayin' Alive," he insisted that his character wouldn't walk like that. He made Badham reshoot the scene, this time with Travolta strutting down the avenue. Later, when Travolta got his first look at how his big dance solo had been edited, he had a meltdown. "I was crying and very angry because of the way the dance highlight was shot. I knew how it should appear on-screen, and it wasn't shot that way. You couldn't even see my feet!" The sequence had been edited for close-ups, so that all his hard work—the knee drops, the splits, the solo he had labored over for nine months—had been cut off at the knees. He knew that for the scene to work, he had to be seen head to toe, so no one would think someone else had done the dancing for him. One of the most famous dance numbers in the history of film almost didn't make it to the screen.

"I called Stigwood," Travolta says, "crying and furious, and said, 'Robert, I'm off the movie. I don't want to be a part of it anymore.'"

Stigwood gave Travolta license to re-edit the scene, over Badham's objections. At 23, Travolta knew what he wanted and what he could do, and he was protecting his character and his dazzling moves.

"The Bee Gees weren't even involved in the movie in the beginning," says Travolta. "I was dancing to Stevie Wonder and Boz Scaggs." Once they came in, however, everything changed.

Afterward, Stigwood thought of the Bee Gees as co-creators of the movie. "Those first five songs," says Bill Oakes, "which I put on the first side of the soundtrack double album—'Stayin' Alive,' 'How Deep Is Your Love,' 'Night Fever,' 'More than a Woman,' and 'If I Can't Have You' [written by the brothers Gibb but sung by Oakes's wife at the time, Yvonne Elliman]—that's the side you couldn't stop playing." But in 1976, before Stigwood bought the rights to Cohn's article, "the Bee Gees were broken," remembers McCormick. "They were touring Malaysia and Venezuela, the two places where they were still popular. They were a mess. Everybody [in the group] had their own little soap opera." But Stigwood "still had this innate ability to spot where a trend was going, like he had this pop gyroscope implanted in him," he adds.

The Bee Gees are three brothers—Barry, Robin, and Maurice Gibb—who were born on the Isle of Man and grew up in Australia, and whose first big hit, "New York Mining Disaster 1941," had some people believing that it was secretly recorded by the Beatles under a pseudonym. It was followed by two more hits: "To Love Somebody" and "How Can You Mend a Broken Heart." Quick fame and riches put tremendous strains on the group—they broke up, tried solo acts, regrouped, and by the time of *Saturday Night Fever* were considered a dated 60s band, awash in drugs and alcohol and legal problems. Nonetheless, Stigwood signed them to his record label and released "Jive Talkin'" to radio stations anonymously, because no one wanted to hear from the Bee Gees. Oakes recalls that in the early 1970s "it was hard just getting the Bee Gees back on the radio, because they were virtually blacklisted." But when "Jive Talkin'" hit, people were surprised to learn that "these falsetto-singing disco chaps were in fact your old Bee Gees—that again was Stigwood's genius." The song and the album it came from, *Main Course,* were huge hits. Even though they weren't a disco band—they didn't go to clubs, they didn't even dance!—Stigwood felt they had "the beat of the dance floor in their blood," Oakes says.

When Stigwood told the band about Cohn's article and asked them to write songs for the movie, they were back living on the Isle of Man, for tax reasons. Barry Gibb suggested a few titles, including "Stayin' Alive" and "Night Fever," but it wasn't until they convened at the Chateau D'Heurouville studio, in France, to mix a live album called *Here at Last Live,* did they flesh out those songs—and they wrote them virtually in a single weekend.

Stigwood and Oakes turned up in Heurouville, and the Bee Gees played their demos: "How Deep Is Your Love," "Stayin' Alive," "Night Fever," "More than a Woman." "They flipped out and said these will be great. We still had no concept of the movie, except some kind of rough script that they'd brought with them," according to Barry Gibb. "You've got to remember, we were fairly dead in the water at that point, 1975, somewhere in that zone—the Bee Gees' sound was basically tired. We needed something new. We hadn't had a hit record in about three years. So we felt, Oh jeez, that's it. That's our life span, like most groups in the late 60s. So, we had to find something. We didn't know what was going to happen."

Oakes mixed the soundtrack on the Paramount lot. Senior executives would call across the commissary to ask, " 'How's your little disco movie, Billy?' They thought it was rather silly; disco had run its course. These days, *Fever* is credited with kicking off the whole disco thing—it really didn't. Truth is, it breathed new life into a genre that was actually dying."

The music had a profound effect on cast and crew. Priestley remembers, "We all thought we'd fallen into a bucket of shit, and then we heard that music. It changed everything. We didn't hear the soundtrack until we were about three weeks into the movie. But once you heard it, you said, 'Whoa!' An aura came over it. I mean, I'm not a disco fan, but that music transcends disco." For the first time, everyone dared to think this movie could be big. Gorney, whose father was Jay Gorney, the songwriter who wrote such hits as "Brother, Can You Spare a Dime" and "You're My Thrill," had the same reaction: "The first time I heard the music I said, 'Those are monster hits.'"

"How long was the *Fever* shoot?" asks Karen Lynn Gorney rhetorically. "Three months and 30 years, and it's not over yet. I seemed to be always working on the film, because of the dancing. Physically, I was weak when I started. I was terrified, because the first time I danced with John he'd been working for half a year on this stuff. I felt like I was trying to dance with a wild stallion—he was that strong."

An actress and dancer who was well known at the time as Tara Martin Tyler Brent Jefferson on ABC's endlessly running soap opera *All My Children,* Gorney landed the part after sharing a cab with Stigwood's nephew. When he described the movie to her, she asked, "Am I in it?" She then auditioned for Stigwood in his apartment in the San Remo, on Central Park West. "I remember this giant silk Chinese screen along the wall—the whole history of China. I did the best acting of my life in front of him." She landed the part of Stephanie, a Brooklyn climber who has already made the big move to "the city" and is hell-bent on self-improvement—taking college courses and drinking tea with lemon. Tony reminds her of the neighborhood she's trying to escape. It's a touching and comic role—at one point, while showing off her erudition in her Brooklyn accent, she insists that *Romeo and Juliet* was written by Zefferelli. "I was trying to convince myself to stay away from Tony," she says about her role, "because he wasn't going to get me anywhere. I wanted you to see the voices in her head saying, 'Oh, he's too young. He doesn't have any class.'"

There was some early grumbling about Gorney when filming began. Certain crew members felt she was too old for the part, and that her dancing wasn't up to par. (She had sustained serious injuries in a motorcycle accident a few years earlier.) But Pauline Kael, in her review of the film, found the performance affecting: "Gorney wins you over by her small, harried, tight face and her line readings, which are sometimes miraculously edgy and ardent. The determined, troubled Stephanie . . . is an updated version of those working girls that Ginger Rogers used to play." Her toughness, her ambition—even her comic cluelessness—contribute to the authenticity of the film. As does an accent so thick it needs subtitles.

The other important female character is Annette, played by Donna Pescow. She auditioned for the role six times—three for Avildsen, three for Badham. When she got the part, at 22, she said it was the first Christmas in years she wouldn't have to work at Bloomingdale's selling ornaments. She had spent two years at the American Academy of Dramatic Arts, in New York, trying to get rid of her Brooklyn accent, but when she finally landed the role, she had to reclaim it. Legendary casting director Shirley Rich told her, "Donna. Move back home, hang out with your parents. You sound like you don't come from anywhere."

"I grew up never calling it 'Manhattan.' It was always 'the city'—'We're going to the city,'" Pescow recalls. "I was living with my folks because it was close to the set, and I didn't drive. And so the Teamsters used to pick me up. My first night of shooting, my grandfather Jack Goldress drove me to the set in Bay Ridge. He was a former lighting man in vaudeville and then a movie projectionist at the RKO Albee, so movies were not a big thing for him. He was more interested in finding parking."

Badham rehearsed Pescow and the Faces for a couple of weeks, "just to get us to be kind of a gang. We went to the clubs together. Travolta couldn't go because he was too recognizable, but the other guys went. I'd never been in a discotheque, ever."

———

One of the first scenes shot with Donna was the gang-rape scene, still a harrowing thing to watch. An acting coach at the American Academy once told her, "If you play a victim, you're lost," and she seems to have followed that advice. Though we cringe at the way her character is abused, we see her strength and her resilience. In her effort to become the kind of woman who can attract Tony, she allows herself to be abused by the boys she probably grew up with, went to school with, danced with. Yet her character has the most insight into how women's roles were changing: Tony contemptuously asks her, "What are you anyway, a nice girl or you a cunt?" To which she replies, "I don't know—both?"

"John Badham and I had a running disagreement" about that scene, Pescow remembers. "I said, 'She's a virgin.' He said, 'No, she's not.' That's why I never played it as if she were really raped—she wasn't—she was off in her own little world," offering up her virginity, by proxy, to Tony Manero.

Pape admits how difficult it was to film that scene. "What Donna did was an incredible piece of acting. We were really worried it was going to affect our friendship. We talked about it a lot before we did it. We had to go into this choreographed situation where you're violating your friend with no concern for her feelings whatsoever. We had to go to a place where we weren't protecting her at all. She was willing to give it up to the wrong guy. And what did she really want? She just wanted to be loved."

Everyone on the set seemed to respond to Pescow's vulnerability. Says Priestley, "The crew just loved her. She was so great. But we all felt sorry for her. There's that great scene where she walks up to Tony and says, 'You're gonna ask me to sit down?' And he says, 'No,' but she said, 'You'd ask me to lie down.' She was perfect—it was so Brooklyn. I mean, the little outfit with the white fur jacket? It makes you feel bad for every girl you screwed over."

Tony Manero's Faces—his entourage of homeboys who watch his back, admire his dancing, keep the girls from bothering him, and rumble with the Puerto Ricans were played with pathos and humor by Pape (Double J), Barry Miller (Bobby C.), and Joseph Cali (Joey). When he first moved to New York from Rochester, Pape says, "Pacino was the actor to be—he was the hottest thing. He was the presiding spirit of the movie. When Tony comes out of his room in his underwear and his Italian grandmother crosses herself, he says, 'Attica! Attica!'—that's from *Dog Day Afternoon*." Pape managed to land this, his first film role, on his first audition—almost unheard of—and his character was a kind of "lieutenant figure who could easily have been the leader. But he had one flaw: he had a bad temper. That's why he was in second position."

Like his cohorts, Cali, a stage-trained actor, would end up being typecast by the role of Joey. "People thought I was that street guy. I had to be Joey," he later said. Miller, as the hapless Bobby C., has the most shocking moment in the film when he falls—or jumps—to his death from the Verrazano Bridge. He's depressed because his girl-friend is pregnant and he knows he has to marry her, ending his carefree days as one of Tony's entourage.

The actors rehearsed for a few weeks in Manhattan, around Eighth Street and Broadway. "We just played basketball together and did that scene where we're making fun of the gay guys," Pape says. "We were all brand new—it's what we'd been dreaming about, having a chance to prove ourselves. We all improvised well together." (Travolta, in fact, was an inspired improviser. Manero's overbearing father slaps him on the head during an argument at the dinner table. Travolta improvised, "Would you just watch the hair? You know, I work on my hair a long time, and you hit it! He hits my hair!")

In prepping for their roles, the Faces went to Times Square with the costume designer, Patrizia von Brandenstein (who would later win an Oscar for her art direction on *Amadeus*). The wardrobe was bought off the rack, adding to the film's authenticity. "We were buying all these polyester things, picking out all this costume jewelry. She had a great feel for it," Pape says. Von Brandenstein found Travolta's famous white suit at a boutique in Bay Ridge just under the El. "It was 1977," says Priestley. "You had to have bling—all the gold around your neck, the pointy shoes. You had to have the suit. It was called 'the Hollywood Rise.'"

Pape took inspiration from the crush of local Barbarino fans hanging around the shoot. "It wasn't just that they were there to see Travolta," he says. "If they could get within five feet of you, they wanted to be sure you were doing them right. They didn't want Hollywood bullshit. These were the guys who went to the clubs on the weekends, who worked in the paint stores, who had the dead-end jobs. This was important to them. It wasn't just about hanging around movie people. It was like, Yeah, you're welcome to be here. But regardless of what you think, respect it. This is our life, this is our world. One of the guys said, 'You can touch it, but don't spit on it.'"

━━━━━━

The Verrazano-Narrows Bridge looms over *Saturday Night Fever* as a nearly mythical structure. Named after the 16th-century Italian explorer Giovanni da Verrazano, the bridge is a source of ethnic pride for Italian-Americans. When it opened, on November 21, 1964, it was the longest suspension bridge in the world, connecting Brooklyn and Staten Island. An American achievement with an Italian name, it symbolizes the realization of unreachable dreams. Tony knows that bridge, and in one scene he lovingly describes its history, its dimensions, its grandeur. It's where Tony's entourage—full of alcohol and sheer animal energy—hang from the girders and dare one another to climb higher. The crew spent three harrowing nights filming on the Verrazano, and it was a nightmare, as the March weather veered from freezing on one occasion to nearly 90 degrees on another. The high winds posed additional threats to the camera crew and stuntmen. Doubling as Travolta's stand-in and wearing Tony Manero's shoes and pants, Priestley, the camera operator for the scene, took a handheld camera out on the bridge's main beam and filmed himself with just a key grip holding his waist. "I was young. You couldn't sense danger then. But you're 600 feet off the water. I had my camera in my hand and we just did it. We wanted to show Hollywood we could make great films."

"They were talking about putting a guy wire on us," Pape reminisces, "and I said, 'No.' I just jumped up on the cable to show them I could swing around. There was no safety net. I was [hundreds] of feet above the water. All that was improvised—it wasn't planned. I just jumped up there and said, 'Let's do it, let's get it done.'"

The cast and crew thought that Paramount didn't care about *Saturday Night Fever.* "They gave us an office on the lot the size of a broom closet," Oakes says. "They didn't believe in it. Only Stigwood knew it was going to be something big. It was just the studio's 'little disco movie'—that was the phrase that haunted me."

———

In fact, word was getting back to Michael Eisner, newly ensconced as Paramount's head of production, that the movie was too vulgar. At previews in Cincinnati and Columbus, half the audience walked out because of the language and sex scenes. McCormick remembers being paged in Kennedy Airport: "I pick up the phone and it's Eisner, who starts screaming at me because we'd only taken two 'fuck's out. It became one of those ridiculous arguing sessions, where they said,

'Take out two "fuck"s and I'll let you have one "spic."' Stigwood finally agreed to take two 'fuck's out of the movie, and that was it—he wouldn't change." They did leave in the term "blow job," however, which, some believe, is the first time the phrase was uttered in a feature film. (Attempts to reach Eisner were unsuccessful as this article first went to press.)

It wasn't just the language. Some of the suits at Paramount were made uncomfortable by the way Travolta was so lovingly photographed in one scene—preening in front of the mirror in his bikini briefs, his gold chain nestled in his chest hair—by the cinematographer Ralf D. Bode. "We got all kinds of hassle," remembers Badham. "We were letting some man walk around in his underwear, showing his body off." The image of lean, sexually vibrant Travolta was so homoerotic that the production designer, Charles Bailey, put up that Farrah Fawcett poster just to cool things off.

There was another little problem that Paramount had to deal with before the film could ever be released. *Hairspray* would not be the first time John Travolta dressed in drag. Letting off steam at the end of the shoot, Travolta and members of the crew filmed a mock wedding at the disco—for laughs—with John dressed as the bride and one of the grips appearing as the groom. "They wanted to blow Paramount's mind," Bill Ward explains. But when the studio executives arrived, according to Tom Priestley, "they didn't see the humor in it. They sent someone to take control of the film, and I'm sure they burned it."

Stigwood released the music before the film—his strategy not only worked, it changed the game. "He basically pioneered an entirely new way of doing business in the distribution of films, records, stage, and television," Oakes believes. "I think his being from Australia had a lot to do with it—that sort of buccaneering adventurism, that entrepreneurship. I don't think he would have been as successful if he'd been English."

Eisner was skiing in Vail two weeks before the movie opened, on December 7, 1977. "I heard 'Stayin' Alive' at the lift, at the bottom, and then we went up to the top, to the restaurant, and they were playing 'Stayin' Alive' there, too, so I called up Barry Diller, head of Paramount, and I said, 'Do we have a hit here?' And then it opened,"

Eisner has recounted, and Travolta "was the biggest thing that ever happened." When the film debuted, at Grauman's Chinese Theatre, it was a phenomenon. In its first 11 days, it grossed more than $11 million—it would go on to gross $285 million, and the soundtrack became the best-selling movie soundtrack album of all time (until Whitney Houston's *The Bodyguard,* in 1992).

———

Travolta, who thought they were just "doing a little art film in Brooklyn," was stunned. Not only did it breathe new life into disco, it changed the way American youth looked: "Thousands of shaggy-haired, blue-jean-clad youngsters are suddenly putting on suits and vests, combing their hair and learning to dance with partners," wrote *Newsweek.* The Abraham & Straus department store in Brooklyn even opened a "Night Fever" men's-wear boutique. John Travolta look-alike contests were drawing lines two blocks long. Fans no less prominent than Jane Fonda and *Chicago Tribune* movie critic Gene Siskel—who saw *Saturday Night Fever* 20 times—bid on Travolta's suit when it was auctioned at a charity benefit in 1979. Siskel outbid her at $2,000. (It's now valued at $100,000 and has ended up in the Smithsonian Institution.)

Pape and Pescow went to see the film in a theater in Brooklyn. "It was my first time seeing it with the people that we made it about," recalls Pape. "It was amazing. They were talking back to the screen, they were screaming and yelling, and as we came out of the theater, we were caught. But the crush was not mean—the crush was, 'You nailed it! What part of Brooklyn are you from?' It was a crush of affirmation."

The film was, finally, so authentic, Karen Lynn Gorney believes, that it was more of a documentary. "We improvised for two weeks, so that by the time it came to filming, Badham just shot what was happening. It wasn't acting."

For the Bee Gees, once the music hit, life became insane. "*Fever* was No. 1 every week," remembers Barry Gibb. "It wasn't just like a hit album. It was No. 1 every single week for 25 weeks. It was just an amazing, crazy, extraordinary time. I remember not being able to answer the phone, and I remember people climbing over my walls. I was quite grateful when it stopped. It was too unreal. In the long run, your life is better if it's not like that on a constant basis. Nice though it was."

When the reviews came out, Travolta noticed his manager, Bob LeMond, quietly weeping in the Palm Court of the Plaza Hotel. He was reading Pauline Kael's review in the December 26, 1977, *New Yorker*. To this day, Travolta treasures Kael's words: "[He] *acts* like someone who loves to dance. And, more than that, he acts like someone who loves to act. . . . He expresses shades of emotion that aren't set down in scripts, and he knows how to show us the decency and intelligence under Tony's uncouthness . . . he isn't just a good actor, he's a generous-hearted actor."

———

The Academy of Motion Picture Arts and Sciences nominated Travolta for a best-actor Oscar, along with Richard Dreyfuss, Woody Allen, Richard Burton, and Marcello Mastroianni (Dreyfuss won, for *The Goodbye Girl*). But the Bee Gees were snubbed. Stigwood threatened legal action, and McCormick threw an "anti–Academy Awards party" at his house, in Los Angeles, in protest. The guest list included Marisa Berenson, Tony and Berry Perkins, Lily Tomlin, and the writer Christopher Isherwood—even Ava Gardner showed up. "It was the last blush of *Saturday Night Fever*" for McCormick. "It was over after that, for me."

The movie changed John Travolta's life. What Brando and James Dean had been to the 1950s, Travolta was to the 1970s. *Saturday Night Fever*, believes Travolta, gave the decade its cultural identity. Pape felt that it was just Travolta's fate: "Sometimes it's time for you to have the brass ring. It's like, in John's life, it was meant to happen, and everybody just has to get out of the way." When movie stardom hit for Travolta, there was no one else in his stratosphere. "I had the field to myself," he recalls. "A few years later, Cruise would come along, and Tom Hanks, and Mel Gibson, but for a long time there was no one else out there. It was like Valentino-style popularity, an unimaginable pinnacle of fame. It's not that I wanted competition. I just wanted company."

For Pape, the movie "was like getting strapped onto a rocket ship. I became almost a victim of my own success. All the stage training I'd had, all the stuff that I'd done, it was starting to work against me, because the only work I was being offered were similar kinds of things. The very thing that made us trapped us." Pescow, who won the New York Film Critics Circle Award for best supporting actress for the film, later got rave reviews playing a waitress on television in the short-lived *Angie.* After that, she "spent years waiting for a film part to come through. And when it didn't I realized I was turning my entire life into a waiting room. I wasn't going to do that anymore." Today, Pape is in demand doing voiceovers for television and film, and he's C.E.O. of his own production company, Red Wall Productions. And Pescow's return to acting was not an insignificant one. As if to forge a link between Tony Manero and Tony Soprano (could there possibly be a white suit hanging among the other skeletons in Soprano's closet?), Pescow appeared in the controversial final episode of *The Sopranos.*

By the end of the 90s, Joseph Cali had occasionally turned up on television, in shows such as *Baywatch* and *Melrose Place,* but he now primarily sells high-end home-theater equipment for Cello Music & Film Systems, a company he founded six years ago. Gorney has appeared in dozens of independent films since *Saturday Night Fever.* She might well have ushered in the era of the tough heroine with the thick Brooklyn accent, embodied by actresses such as Marisa Tomei, Debbie Mazar, and Lorraine Bracco.

McCormick now says that working on *Fever* "was the most exciting time of my life. I couldn't get up early enough, and I couldn't wait to see the dailies every night. It went from a dark winter of John losing Diana to a glorious summer. And we didn't know at the end how it was going to work out. All I prayed for was that it would be enough of a success that I'd get to work on another movie." His prayers were answered. At Warner Bros., McCormick has overseen such films as *Syriana, Charlie and the Chocolate Factory, The Perfect Storm, Divine Secrets of the Ya-Ya Sisterhood, Fight Club,* and *Blood Diamond.*

Stigwood's comet also continued to burn—for a while. *Fever* was followed by *Grease,* which did even better at the box office. But inevitably, perhaps, Stigwood and the Bee Gees fell out. The band filed a $120 million lawsuit against him, which would later be settled out of court. RSO folded in 1981. "I know I'd worked for a magician—an alchemist," McCormick says, but after *Saturday Night Fever* "you could never get him interested in anything again. He really had no serious desire. He wanted to be safe. And all that money went offshore to Bermuda," where Stigwood maintained a baronial estate for a number of years. Oakes says, "He removed himself from everyday life, almost like Howard Hughes. He was literally on his yacht, or in a suite somewhere. To get him to go out was a major achievement."

—————

Travolta believes that "the big difference between me and Stigwood was, when something is that big, people feel in a way that they'd rather get out if they can't replicate that incredible success. He pulled up his ladder, moved to Bermuda, decided to get out of the game." For Travolta it was different. "It was never just about money. I'd wanted to be a film actor my entire life. For Stigwood, if it wasn't the pinnacle every time, he wasn't going to stay."

Travolta found himself in the wilderness, too, after the success of *Grease*. His third film for RSO, *Moment by Moment*, with Lily Tomlin, was a disappointment for everyone. (Critics nicknamed it *Hour by Hour*.) In 1983, Stigwood co-produced a sequel to *Saturday Night Fever* called *Staying Alive*, with its writer-director Sylvester Stallone. Although Norman Wexler co-wrote the screenplay, the movie was a disaster. "I called it *Staying Awake*—it was ego gone mad," recalls Oakes. "It was shorter, five times more expensive, and not any good." Oakes withdrew from Hollywood soon after. "That's when I said, 'I'm putting down my tools.'" After writing a film for Arnold Schwarzenegger (*Raw Deal*, in 1986), Wexler started turning down work. "I was fired by my agent," he told friends gleefully, before returning to playwriting. His last play, in 1996, was a comedy, *Forgive Me, Forgive Me Not*. He died three years later.

Travolta's career had a brief boost with two comedies, *Look Who's Talking* and *Look Who's Talking Too*, in 1989 and 1990, but by

1994, when he came to the attention of an intense young filmmaker new in Hollywood, his asking price had plummeted to $150,000. Quentin Tarantino was a huge fan of Travolta's, and he cast him in the role of Vincent Vega, a hit man who can dance, in *Pulp Fiction.* After *Welcome Back, Kotter* and *Saturday Night Fever,* it was the third time a character named Vincent would transform Travolta's career.

As for Nik Cohn, he admits that "in America I have always, and will always be, the guy that did *Saturday Night Fever.*" Twenty years after its release, he published an article in *New York* magazine explaining how he had come to create the character of Vincent, cobbling him together from all the Faces he'd seen while trawling through pop-culture venues in the U.K. and America. There was in fact no Tony Manero, except for the one made flesh by Wexler's screenplay and Travolta's performance. For Cohn, "the whole phenomenon was just Travolta, because his particular gift is sympathy. There's something about those puppy-dog eyes and the wetness around the mouth. And the other ingredients—my character, the Bee Gees' music, Wexler's script—they all had their function. But it would not have been a touchstone, it wouldn't have worked with anybody else—nobody else could have done it."

⸻

In the early 80s the disco craze ended with a thud, followed by a backlash, from which the Bee Gees have never quite recovered. Those embarrassing white suits and platform shoes went to the back of the closet, or have been sold on eBay, and the disco sound evolved into the four-on-four beat of club divas such as Madonna and hip-hop artists such as Wyclef Jean (who remade "Stayin' Alive" as "We Trying to Stay Alive"). In 2005, a memorabilia company called Profiles in History put the 2001 Odyssey dance floor up for auction, but the attempt just ended up in a lawsuit. The nightclub continued to exist, for a while anyway, at 802 64th Street in Brooklyn, with a new name—Spectrum—ending its life as a gay, black dance club, where the disco craze first began.

But the characters of *Saturday Night Fever* live on in the collective imagination. I remember a moment nearly 10 years after the film when the poet Allen Ginsberg asked the Clash's Joe Strummer if he believed in reincarnation, and Strummer jumped the gun and said he'd like to come back as "Tony Manero, the guy from *Saturday Night Fever*—he had great fucking hair." Bay Ridge calling! Bay Ridge calling!

From *Vanity Fair's Movies Rock,* Fall 2007

REDS

Thunder on the Left

by Peter Biskind

When one of Arnold Schwarzenegger's aides called Warren Beatty a "crackpot"—among other choice epithets—after Beatty had taken a few shots at the California governor not long ago, one thing the aide refrained from calling Beatty was a "dilettante." Because, as anybody who has even a glancing familiarity with his career knows, Beatty has been a very serious political amateur for decades, at least since he backed Bobby Kennedy for president in 1968, and then became a visible supporter of gun control after Kennedy's assassination. Four years later he was doggedly pounding the pavement for George McGovern, helping to organize a then groundbreaking series of rock-concert fund-raisers. It was during this period—the night after McGovern won the Democratic nomination at a deeply divided convention in Miami, which Beatty attended—that he took a break from campaigning to hole up in a hotel room and spend four days working on a treatment that would eventually become *Reds*, one of the most audacious and politically literate movies ever to come out of Hollywood.

Released on December 4, 1981, *Reds* is a sprawling, three-hour-and-twenty-minute homage, of sorts, to the Russian Revolution as well as to the high passions that animated the largely forgotten American left in the years before, during, and after World War I. The film is an achievement nearly unparalleled in the history of American cinema—ambitious, complex, and entertaining in equal measures. It is partly a biopic, centered on the short but eventful life of the writer and activist John Reed, one of the few Americans buried in the Kremlin, whose account of the bloody birth of the Soviet Union, *Ten Days That Shook the World*, is a classic of political journalism. It is partly a love story, re-creating Reed's tumultuous relationship with fellow journalist Louise Bryant. It is partly a historical drama that chronicles, among other things, the rise of Bolshevism and the birth of the Communist Party of America. And it is partly a documentary, one that rescues from oblivion 32 actual survivors of that period who serve as a kind of Greek chorus.

Not only did *Reds* pioneer the blend of fact and fiction that later came to be known as "docudrama," it was also an unapologetic, if critical, major-studio treatment of Communism, lavishing on this mostly taboo subject the vast resources at Hollywood's disposal: a big budget, A-list stars, and, in this case, the brains, skills, and talents of the best and the brightest of Hollywood's most recent—and probably final—golden age. All of this at a moment that could not have been less hospitable to the subject. Beatty began shooting the picture in 1979, the year the Russians invaded Afghanistan; production continued throughout 1980, the year America elected a new president, Ronald Reagan, who campaigned with open hostility to the Soviet Union and, once in office, would famously dub it the "evil empire." *Reds* was so unlikely a film for Hollywood, and its timing so unpropitious, that many in Beatty's orbit, including the screenwriter Robert Towne and the film critic Pauline Kael, begged him not to make it, convinced that *Reds* was a folly.

Looking back from the present, a time characterized by the corporate consolidation of the movie industry, filmmaking by committee, and creative timidity, the fact that *Reds* was made at all is almost incomprehensible—testimony to the vision and persistence of one man. As one of Beatty's longtime collaborators, the late production designer Dick Sylbert, once told me, "Talk about obsessed! His ability to will something to happen was mind-boggling."

Reds was a labor of love, but labors of love—Kevin Spacey's *Beyond the Sea* and John Travolta's *Battlefield Earth* come to mind—are generally dubious propositions in the film business; studio executives are right to run for the hills when a powerful star, director, or producer knocks on the door with a personal project to which he or she has long given tender care, and this was never truer than in the late 70s, a time when the once astringent talents of the New Hollywood were giving way to bloat and self-indulgence. While Beatty was pitching *Reds* (which he might have described as the movie David Lean would have made had Gillo Pontecorvo, director of *The Battle of Algiers*, put a knife to his throat), United Artists was still looking down the barrel of Francis Ford Coppola's troubled, much-delayed, and phenomenally expensive *Apocalypse Now*. Worse, UA was about to wade knee-deep into the quicksand of Michael Cimino's studio-busting *Heaven's Gate*. Universal, meanwhile, was still reeling from *Sorcerer*, Billy Friedkin's expensive 1977 flop, and was about to lose a bundle more on Steven Spielberg's overproduced, unfunny comedy, *1941*. *Reds* and Martin Scorsese's *Raging Bull* would be exceptions that proved the rule, although the former, with its lengthy dialogue scenes devoted to parsing the factional infighting on the American left, was still a big mouthful to swallow. Beatty, who at the time was coming off the huge comedy hit *Heaven Can Wait*, which minted money for Paramount, was probably the only star with the clout (or desire) to launch a major motion picture that would dramatize the Russian Revolution from a not entirely unsympathetic perspective—and get a studio to pay for it. As former Paramount production head Bob Evans puts it in his inimitable fashion, "Warren could dictate what he wanted to make. [*Reds*] was his come shot after *Heaven Can Wait*."

Born to comfortable circumstances in Portland, Oregon, John Reed had gone to Harvard. Once he cast off the remnants of his bourgeois background—says Beatty, "It took me quite a while to get over the fact that he was a cheerleader at Harvard"—Reed came into his own as a journalist, poet, and radical, torn between his aspirations to art and to political activism, a conflict Beatty could relate to. And, like Beatty at the start of his career, when the actor's dating games made him a fixture of the gossip columns and sometimes upstaged his considerable gifts as a performer, Reed had something to prove. He was too much fortune's child—too good-looking, too well-off, too talented—to be taken seriously. Upton Sinclair once called Reed "the Playboy of the Revolution," something else Beatty could relate to.

Reed was also an adventurer, inexorably drawn to the action. And in the teens of the last century, the action was on the left, among American unions such as the Industrial Workers of the World (also known as the Wobblies) and, abroad, in places such as Mexico, where the peasants were making a revolution with machetes—and, better yet, the volcano that was czarist Russia. Reed went to Russia three times: in 1915 to cover World War I, in 1917 as a participant-observer in the Russian Revolution—he was in St. Petersburg when the czar's Winter Palace fell—and in 1920 to plead for Soviet accreditation of his newly formed Communist Labor Party. When he wanted to return to America, the Soviets refused to let him go. He tried to cross the border into Finland and landed in a Finnish jail for his trouble. He was finally released to the Soviets, and spent what little was left of his life working in their propaganda ministry, writing and making speeches. He died of typhus in 1920, three days before his 33rd birthday.

The love of Reed's life was Louise Bryant, a dentist's wife he lured from Portland to New York to join the ranks of artists and revolutionaries who peopled Greenwich Village. She too was a journalist with large appetites: she had an affair with Eugene O'Neill, went to cover World War I from the front in France, and followed Reed to Russia twice, all the time struggling to carve out her own career. After Reed's death she tumbled downhill into alcoholism, drug addiction, and poverty. She died in 1936 at the age of 50.

Beatty recalls coming across Reed's story in the mid-1960s. He says, "When you're very, very young, you hear, 'John Reed: Harvard guy gets over [to Russia] and ends up being buried in the Kremlin wall,' and then you find out later that he traveled with Pancho Villa, so after you read *Ten Days That Shook the World*, you read *Insur-*

gent Mexico," which was Reed's first book. The film editor Dede Allen recalls Beatty's mentioning the idea of putting Reed's life on film as far back as 1966. "We were sitting in a Chinese restaurant having lunch when he said, 'Have you ever heard of Jack Reed?'

" 'Yes.'

" 'I'm going to do his story one day.' "

In 1966, "one day" was still more than a decade off—Beatty was then in the midst of producing and starring in *Bonnie and Clyde*—but he was serious about Reed, whose story clearly had vivid cinematic potential. The actor had taught himself some Russian and in 1969 visited the Soviet Union with his then girlfriend Julie Christie. The Soviet director Sergei Bondarchuk, who had just filmed *War and Peace,* wanted to make a movie about Reed himself and asked the actor to star in it. But Beatty didn't like the script and turned Bondarchuk down. Instead, Beatty told me, "I asked [the Soviet authorities], 'Can I talk to some people who might have known Reed?' They said there was this woman who claims to have had an affair with him. I said, 'Can I meet her?' They took me out to her apartment on the seventh floor of one of those temporary-looking postwar buildings. She was about 80. Her mother was close to Lenin's wife, and there is a picture of her, at the age of 15, an incredibly beautiful little girl, standing next to Lenin. I said, 'Did you have a romance with John Reed?' She said to me in Russian, 'A romance? I fucked him!' I said, 'Were you ever in a labor camp?' And she said, 'Oh, yes.' I said, 'How long were you there?' She said, 'Oh, 16 years.' I said, 'How do you feel about Stalin?' She said, 'Only hate. But of course the revolution is in its early stages.' It was at that moment I thought, I have to make a movie about that kind of passion. I'm going to make it without the Russians. And just the way I want to make it." In Beatty's eyes, Reed had for too long been the exclusive property of the Soviet Union. "I felt some sort of need to protect this poor American who was buried in the Kremlin wall. His ideals were not owned by Soviet Communism."

━━━━━━

For all the similarities between Beatty and Reed, the differences are striking as well. Where Reed was impulsive and given to extreme solutions, politically, Beatty is deliberate, slow to act, and liberal, not radical. He worked on Reed's story, fitfully, throughout the early 1970s, writing about 25 pages. At the time, he was hitting his stride professionally, a cinematic polymath who was able to do everything well and often did. Not only was he one of the most sought-after leading men throughout the late 1960s and the 1970s, but his love life was still manna to the gossip sheets. With *Bonnie and Clyde,* which had kicked off the New Hollywood revolution, in 1967, he had become one of the first actors to succeed at hands-on producing, so much so that on subsequent projects he was known as the equal of canny studio negotiators such as Frank Wells and Barry Diller. He produced, co-wrote, and starred in two successful comedies, 1975's *Shampoo* and 1978's *Heaven Can Wait,* the latter of which he co-directed as well, with Buck Henry. Nevertheless, according to Henry, while on the set of that film Beatty had to listen to Christie, his co-star, mock him for being lightweight. The John Reed film would be far from a comedy, and Beatty knew that if he was ever going to make it this was the time, when he had both clout and command of his craft.

In 1976 he had finally found a writer for the project: Trevor Griffiths, a successful playwright whose London hit, *Comedians,* Mike Nichols was taking to Broadway. A Marxist intellectual, Griffiths wasn't about to get his head turned by a movie star. According to Jeremy Pikser, a protégé of Griffiths's, whom Beatty hired as a research consultant and who later went on to co-write *Bulworth* with Beatty, "Trevor felt, 'I'm a historian, a playwright. You're a Hollywood movie star. What can you tell me about how to tell the story of John Reed?' I couldn't imagine two less likely people to have an effective collaboration."

To Griffiths it was clear how much Beatty identified with Reed. "Warren spoke as if he was the reincarnation of Jack Reed," Griffiths says. "Reed was a golden boy. I would get that sense as we talked that Warren had been born to play him. Or Jack Reed had been born so that at a later moment Warren could play him!"

Griffiths's wife was killed in an airplane crash while he was working on the script, which delayed a first draft considerably. He finally finished around the end of 1977. "Warren rang me up and said, 'This is wonderful. This is just terrific. I've got to read it again,'" he recalls. "When he rang me again about it, a week later, there was a completely different tone to his voice. He basically wanted to start again, keep the outline, keep the shape, keep some of the characterizations, and begin again. And, indeed, that's what we did."

According to Pikser, "The first script was much more tendentious. Humorless. It was much more historical, in that the relationship between John Reed and Louise Bryant was not nearly as modern. And Reed was more of a character than a vehicle for Warren Beatty. In one scene, Reed embraced Louise and said, 'Your hair smells like damsons.' Damsons are a kind of plum, and they do exist in America, and they are likely something that Reed might have known about and, as a poet, might have made a reference to. But Warren's attitude was 'What the fuck is a damson? And I sure would never say that about a woman! What kind of an idiot is this guy Trevor Griffiths? It must be some sort of English thing.' But I don't think Warren hated the script any more than he hates other first drafts. He never has a draft he likes. It's never 'O.K., now the script is done,' in my experience. It's like 'Let's work on it.' You go into a film re-writing while it's being shot."

Says Beatty, "That draft had serious problems. There was no tension between Bryant and Reed. What I needed to do was pit her feminism against his chauvinism, turn a woman who was in love with a man against that man."

Griffiths returned to New York in the middle of 1978 to hash out the script with Beatty. "We sat down in a hotel bedroom at the Carlyle and we worked for about four and a half months," Griffiths recalls. "It was a pretty unpleasant four and a half months . . . really painful. I was sitting in a room for six or eight hours a day with a guy that I was increasingly growing to detest, and who was increasingly growing to detest me. That's the Sartrean version of hell."

In his everyday exchanges, Beatty is invariably polite and soft-spoken, with a dry wit. When he's relaxed and unguarded, as unguarded as he ever gets, he's ribald and funny. He rarely loses his temper, rarely allows himself to get annoyed or irritable. But script meetings are, for Beatty, something else: free-for-alls, extreme combat. "When you're collaborating, you have to be able to take the gloves off," Beatty says. He is a firm believer in the adage that two (or more) minds are better than one. He calls them "hostile intelligences." But, observes Pikser, "it's often more hostile than intelligent." He goes on, "Warren functions creatively in a pugilistic manner. He likes to fight. It's not fun to fight with a stupid person, so he likes to have smart people to fight with. You stop working on the script, he's sweet as honey. You start working on a script, you can expect to be abused. Anybody who's ever worked with him who doesn't admit that is lying. That's how he is with Robert Towne, that's how he is with Elaine May, but they love it. They throw things, they scream. They swear at each other. I think they feel that this is what it means to be creative. The first time I met Towne"—the screenwriter kibitzed on *Reds,* as did writer-director May, more extensively—"he walked up to me and he said, 'I just want you to know something.' Right up in my face. 'I don't give a fuck about history.' I was like, 'What do you want from me, man? I'm just a kid here.'"

———

After the four-and-a-half-month stint at the Carlyle, Griffiths told Beatty in late August or September 1978—nearly two years after their work on *Reds* had begun—that he had to go back to London. Beatty said, "I'm coming with you!" So they ended up together again, this time working at the Dorchester hotel, in London. "The atmosphere around us was poisonous, terrible," says Griffiths. "It was messy, it was vile, it was foulmouthed on both sides."

There is a key sequence aboard a train near the end of the script during which Reed berates Zinoviev, a Soviet functionary, for rewriting his speeches. Suddenly, in the middle of the dispute, the White Army, the counter-revolutionaries, attack the train. Griffiths complained about the scene.

"Do we really need this scene?" he asked. "What is important is the argument, not the attack on the train."

"Listen," Griffiths recalls Beatty's saying. "One thing you have to learn: in a movie, one bullet is worth a thousand words."

"That's terrible, because I'm a writer, and all I've got are words," exploded Griffiths. And then, he recalls, "Beatty exploded, and I exploded again and walked out of the room, packed my bag, and left. And never saw him again."

Of course, Beatty was right. *Reds* was not a novel or a play, it was a movie, a popular entertainment, or at least that was the hope. Would people go for it? "That's the great thing about Warren," says Pikser. "It's a gamble. That's what makes it fun. If he thinks there's no chance that people will hate it, he's not interested in doing it."

━━━━━

It was Leslie Caron, a former flame of Beatty's, who once observed that he "has always fallen in love with girls who have won or been nominated for an Academy Award." Caron qualified, Christie too, and so did Diane Keaton, who had won Best Actress for *Annie Hall*, in 1977. Slender, pale as porcelain, and radiating a nervous intelligence, Keaton was an original. She was adorable as Woody Allen's neurotic match in *Annie Hall*, and single-handedly started a fashion trend with her gender-bending mix-and-match wardrobe of ties, trousers, and skirts.

"I remember the first time I ever saw Warren. I must have been about 26," Keaton recalls, placing the incident in the early 70s when her career was just beginning to flower. "It was at the Beverly Wilshire Hotel. They used to have a bookstore there, and I was inside, and I looked out and saw him in the lobby. I thought, My god, he's so beautiful. It was like there was a light. He looked at me for a second, and then [his eyes] passed me by. I thought, I'll never know him. He'll never be somebody in my life."

But she was wrong. A few years later they hooked up during the frenzy that followed upon the success of *Heaven Can Wait*, and Beatty became equally intoxicated, though the relationship proved to be a difficult one. According to Pikser, who spent a lot of time with the couple, "Warren was always trying to please Diane. Which was not easy. Which is why he wanted to do it so much. It's no fun for him if it's easy. He really likes women who kick his ass. He always moaned about it, but I think it's what drew him to her. She was very difficult." Pikser adds, "It was a very contentious, complicated relationship. It was very volatile. He bought her a pair of handcuffs, as either a Christmas or a birthday gift. I took that as an ironic comment on her feeling that he wanted to constrain her. Or maybe they were just into that!" (Says Beatty, "God help me, no, I've never been into that. The idea of handcuffs as sexual paraphernalia has always made me laugh. And there would be about as much chance of Diane Keaton being into that kind of stuff as there would be of her becoming interested in skydiving.")

Beatty—who has a long history of working with current and former lovers—wanted Keaton to play Bryant. He regarded her as something of a muse, or at least that's what he told the press at the time: "If Diane Keaton had not made *Reds*, I don't know what I would have done." He says now, "She's always surprising. And that's fun. It would have been kind of heavy going to have these two idealists go through this idealistic period without some surprises. And some laughs."

When Beatty had first asked Keaton to play Bryant, the actress was skeptical. "I didn't really believe it was going to happen," she recalls. "He would say, 'We're going to shoot now,' and then we would not shoot now, and then he would say, 'O.K., the next few months, probably,' and it kept getting put off and put off for what seemed like an endless amount of time. So it really wasn't a reality until we were actually in England, and we started to shoot. And then I believed we were doing it."

———

The other key role was Eugene O'Neill, Reed's friend and Bryant's lover. The historical O'Neill was tall and lanky, with a boozer's pallor. Beatty first thought of casting James Taylor, who had the look of an addict, someone who knew pain. Or Sam Shepard, of which the same was true. In the end he chose his pal Jack Nicholson, with whom he had appeared in *The Fortune* (1975) for Mike Nichols. As the story goes, Beatty tricked Nicholson into accepting the smallish but important part by ostensibly asking for advice. "I told him I needed someone to play Eugene O'Neill, but it had to be someone who could convincingly take this woman away from me," Beatty once told an interviewer. Without missing a beat, Nicholson responded, "There is only one actor who could do that—me!"

Nevertheless, says executive producer Simon Relph, "Warren

worried and worried about casting Jack, because, frankly, both of them were too old to play the parts. When we met with Jack, he was doing *The Shining*. It was towards the end of the film, and Kubrick had got him into the most shambolic state. A kind of grotesque figure appeared. We only had three or four months before shooting. Warren said to me, 'Do you think Jack can get in shape?' I said, 'If he wants to do it, I'm sure he can.' He did really want to do it. When it was time, he appeared, having shed a huge amount of weight, and all the years. He was fantastic."

The rest of the cast included Maureen Stapleton, who would prove to be splendid as Emma Goldman, the anarchist; Paul Sorvino, who played Italian-American firebrand Louis Fraina, a leader of the infant Communist Party of America; and Gene Hackman, who had the small part of a magazine editor. Beatty was largely using British locations to stand in for American ones such as Provincetown and Greenwich Village, and because he was worried the locales wouldn't be convincing to U.S. audiences, he took care to populate the picture with veteran Hollywood character actors such as Ian Wolfe, R. G. Armstrong, Jack Kehoe, and M. Emmet Walsh, who were familiar to audiences from dozens of movies. Beatty also cast some non-actors in important roles. George Plimpton, the editor of *The Paris Review*, played a fashionable publisher who tries to seduce Bryant. Plimpton was offered the part when he nearly tripped over Beatty while the actor was asleep on the floor of the Playboy Mansion; Plimpton later clinched the deal by putting the moves on Keaton with such conviction during an audition that Beatty yelled, "Stop it!" Another non-actor, the novelist Jerzy Kosinski, was brilliant as Zinoviev, the Soviet apparatchik. An outspoken anti-Communist who had been born in Poland, Kosinski initially turned Beatty down because he feared he would be kidnapped by the K.G.B. while on location in Finland.

─────────

Beatty hadn't originally intended to act in or direct the film. He knew how difficult it was simply to produce. He considered casting John Lithgow, who physically resembled Reed, but eventually decided to do it himself, just as he became convinced there was no one else to hold the reins behind the camera. He told Dick Sylbert, "I can't

trust anybody to direct this movie but me. If Kubrick called me tomorrow I'd turn him down. But I hate the idea. To be a director, you
have to be sick." He surrounded himself with collaborators who
could help him, and was able, as he had in the past, to attract the best
in the business. Sylbert, who had just put in three years as head of
production at Paramount, was arguably the most skilled production
designer in Hollywood and had worked with Beatty on *Shampoo.*
Dede Allen, whose innovative cutting created the jackrabbit velocity
that helped drive *Bonnie and Clyde* to critical and commercial
success, was the best editor in New York. Vittorio Storaro, who was
responsible for Bernardo Bertolucci's stunningly photographed pictures and had most recently survived *Apocalypse Now,* was a master
of lush color and the moving camera—though what worked for Bertolucci didn't always work for Beatty, who was raised at the knee of
George Stevens, the Hollywood classicist who had directed him in
The Only Game in Town and who never moved his camera.

Beatty came up with the idea of filming talking-head interviews
with survivors of the period who knew or knew of Reed; they were
called the Witnesses. Pikser remembers, "The way it was explained
to me was 'Look, the thing that kills historical dramas is exposition.
We have an audience which doesn't know the first fucking thing
about any of this stuff, and if we're going to educate them with the
dialogue, it's going to be deadly—it will ruin the film. So why not just
take the bull by the horns, and let's say, "We're going to make a little
documentary, and we'll get the information we need, but it won't be
purely didactic. It will be funny. It will have entertainment value."'
It was brilliant."

Mischievously, Beatty begins the film with the Witnesses talking
about the unreliability of memory, its lapses and the tricks it plays.
The interviewees included Roger Baldwin, who founded the American Civil Liberties Union, and the writers Rebecca West and Henry
Miller, whose *Tropic of Cancer,* published by Grove Press in 1961,
struck an early blow for the "sexual revolution" when the Supreme
Court ruled it literature, not pornography. Dede Allen remembers
how Beatty had read an interview with Miller where he described
himself as "the Warren Beatty of his day." Says Allen, "Miller had
nothing to do with Jack Reed, but Warren just wanted to interview

him." (Beatty says Miller knew Emma Goldman, and Beatty wanted his take on the period.) Pikser wrote Miller a polite letter. Miller wrote back saying, "You seem to be after the same kind of academic crap I've always hated my whole life. I think I would be terrible for you. There's no way you could make use of me. I don't think I would like to meet you. I don't think you would like to meet me." Pikser was crushed, wrote an abject apology: "You misunderstood me. We think you'd be great, blah-blah." He showed it to Beatty, who said, "Throw that out. Send him a telegram: PERFECT! WHEN CAN WE ARRIVE?" Pikser did so, and the next thing he knew he had an invitation to dinner at Miller's house, along with the young actress Brenda Venus, Miller's final, though platonic, girlfriend. (He was a spry 88.) His only request was that Beatty help Venus find a movie part. (There was no role for her in *Reds*.)

After Griffiths walked out, Beatty continued to work on the script by himself, and then brought in Elaine May, with whom he had written *Heaven Can Wait*. May presented herself as kooky and fragile, a delicate flower, someone unequipped to deal with the real world, an impression she nurtured and seemed to enjoy, because she would make jokes about it. But once she swung into writing mode, she was like another person: confident, self-assured, and opinionated. Some of the work was done at the Plaza Athénée in Paris—one of several hotels around the world where Beatty liked to hang out. May would fly in on the Concorde. At the hotel she'd use the floor of her suite for a desk, laying out on the rug six or seven different scenes, each one in three versions written in longhand on yellow lined paper. Housekeeping was barred from the room, so that after a few days (she never went out) room-service trays covered with dirty dishes and leftover food were stacked in piles. She chain-smoked tiny cigars and let the ashes fall where they might.

May, whose contribution to the script—and later the editing process—was incalculable, focused on the scenes between Reed and Bryant, and Bryant and O'Neill. Unlike Griffiths, May understood that Beatty was the star, that Reed was in large part a vehicle for him, and that the Reed-Bryant relationship had to have contemporary resonance; the tension between the two protagonists, although rooted in the historical reality of the period, had to crackle with the passions that roiled the 1970s, particularly the women's movement. According to Pikser, she said, "I don't know anything about this history." But somebody needed to, so she insisted that he be integrated into the process. Holding up some pages, she would say, "Jack and Emma Goldman need to fight here. I don't know what the fuck they would fight about," and throw him a pad.

———

Beatty had been financing script development and the pre-production of *Reds* out of his own pocket. "That's the way I usually do things, because I'm what is called a control freak," he explains with a laugh. But he was not about to launch into a film as expensive as this one might be without studio backing. By this time the studios had recovered from the New Hollywood fever of the early 1970s, were sitting up in bed and beginning to eat solid food, especially Paramount, now run by a group of Young Turks recruited from television—Barry Diller, Michael Eisner, and Don Simpson—and presided over by the choleric but brilliant financier Charles Bluhdorn, chairman of Paramount's parent corporation, Gulf & Western. *Heaven Can Wait* had made a lot of money for Paramount, and when the Oscar nominations were announced in February 1979, the film received nine. While making it, Beatty had charmed Bluhdorn, and he already knew Diller, who headed the studio, through Democratic Party politics, but Beatty knew that *Reds* was still going to be a tough sell.

He did what he always did: he played the field, making the studios compete for his favors. He had interested Warner Bros. in the picture. Still, Paramount was his first choice, and the executives there were both wary and intrigued. "I'd been hearing about *Reds* for years," says Diller. "It's like remembering when you first heard about Santa Claus. It was pervasive. I was fascinated by it. I thought it was an impossible idea for a movie, but Warren created success with *Heaven Can Wait*, and if you create success you are entitled to extra room." Diller, Eisner, and Beatty had a dinner with Bluhdorn in New York to discuss *Reds;* the Gulf & Western chairman's blessing would be prudent for a film as potentially expensive and controversial as this one. Diller remembers that Bluhdorn was enthusiastic about the project, but in Beatty's recollection Bluhdorn was cooler toward the idea, and Beatty's pitch hardly made *Reds* sound like a nobrainer: "Look, this is an iffy project about a Communist hero who dies in the end. It may be a very dodgy commercial subject. If you say no, there's no hard feelings, and I'll take it somewhere else."

"How much is it gonna cost?" asked the Austrian-born Bluhdorn, who spoke in a thick accent his executives enjoyed mimicking.

"I've got to be honest with you," Beatty answered. "I don't know. But it's a long, long movie." Beatty subsequently gave Bluhdorn a copy of what then passed for the script and sat outside his office door while he read it. Bluhdorn finally said yes. But, Beatty recalls, "he made the movie because he didn't want to lose the movie."

And a few days later, Bluhdorn came down with a bad case of buyer's remorse. Bluhdorn told Beatty, "Do me a favor. Take $25 million. Go to Mexico. Keep $24 million for yourself. Spend the one million on a picture. Just don't make this one." Beatty replied, "Charlie, I have to make this movie." Beatty then got a call from one of Bluhdorn's pals. (The Gulf & Western head was suspected of nurturing Mob connections, among them the attorney and Hollywood fixer Sidney Korshak, though Beatty says the caller was not Korshak.) The man said, "If you know what's good for you, you shouldn't make this picture!" Beatty replied, "I'm going to do this movie and I'm going to forget that I got this call." Finally, Bluhdorn acceded to the inevitable and agreed to finance the film, whose budget was then hovering in the $20 million range.

Once the studio agreed to do the picture, the executives reversed field, forcing Beatty to start production before he wanted to. "I didn't consider the script to be ready, but then, I never consider any script to be ready," he says. "But I did say I can be much more economical if I have another month. To prepare and rehearse, etc." According to Beatty, who believed that waiting could help him shave millions off the budget, the studio replied, "*No.* The contract says you start on this date, and if you don't start on this date, you're in default, and we have no arrangement." Continues Beatty, "It was odd."

He wondered if Paramount was looking for an excuse to pull the plug on the picture. Finally, he acquiesced. "So I started—kind of slowly. There are some movies that you make that just can't be clarified on paper, and they make themselves as you go along. You adhere to Napoleon's battle plan. When they asked him how he planned a battle, he said, 'Here's how I do it—first I go there, and then I see what happens.'"

———

Principal photography began in early August of 1979 in London. Recalls Simon Relph, "The budget was actually quite low, given how ambitious a film it was, but it started to swell once we began shooting, and it became clear that we were never going to do it in the time we were supposed to. We more than doubled the production time. I think the original intention was probably 15 or 16 weeks. We actually shot the film over a whole year, some 30-odd weeks, plus these 'hiatuses' where Warren went back to the drawing board."

The picture was plagued by the same problems that befall most productions, but with a movie this big, shot in five countries, the snafus were magnified tenfold. The crew had to wait for snow to fall in Helsinki and for rain to stop in Spain, where at one juncture there was an insurrection by the extras, about 1,000 of them, gathered for a crowd scene. The day was very hot, and the extras had been up since four in the morning. The caterers had failed to give them breakfast rolls, and by lunchtime they were starving, with little more to eat than fruit, while they watched the crew chow down on a three-course meal. "They came storming into where we were eating, banging trays, and looking to turn over tables," recalls production manager Nigel Wooll. Beatty, who was furious with him and Relph, handled the situation like the enlightened capitalist he is, in a manner that might have made Reed turn over in his grave. As Wooll recalls, "He said, 'O.K., bring the two ringleaders here, and let me talk to them.' He told them, 'You're right. We apologize, and we'll put you in charge of extras, and we'll pay you more money.' They both said yes, and there was absolutely no problem at all. He took the sting out of the tail."

The problems caused by the extras were nothing compared with those caused by the actors. Says Wooll, "Maureen Stapleton wouldn't fly to London. We wanted her in November, but in November there are no oceangoing liners across the Atlantic because it's too rough. So we offered to put her on the Concorde, which would have been three and a half hours, with a doctor who would put her to sleep, but she wouldn't do it. She was absolutely happy to come on a tramp steamer. It was supposed to take about two weeks. But of course it broke down halfway across and had to be towed into Amsterdam. So that was another delay. Then of course she has to get a train, and the boat from Amsterdam back to London. A horrendous trip."

Meanwhile, on the set, "Do it again" had become the operative phrase. Beatty shot an impressive number of takes. He generally liked to give himself lots of choices in the editing room, and always thought that the best take was just around the corner. Explains Beatty, "I don't ask for a lot of takes except when I'm directing and acting in a scene. It's no fun for the person who's acting with you to be watched. It kills the performance. You can't say, 'Well, no, I want you to change this and open your eyes there,' and so forth, all that bullshit—you don't. What you do is you do it again. And you hire good actors."

Customarily, a director will say "Cut" at the end of a take, and the cast and crew will break while the director of photography prepares for the next one. According to Wooll, Beatty "wouldn't stop the camera. Instead of going to Take 1, Take 2, Take 3, he'd do it all in one run until the roll of film ran out, after 10 minutes. He would just say, 'Do it again,' 'Do it again,' 'Do it again.'" But this created its own peculiar problems. Wooll recalls, "We burned out three camera motors because they overheated. I've never, ever burned out a camera motor before or since. It was extraordinary." One day they discovered that the focus was soft on some of the dailies of the scenes between Keaton and Nicholson. "We were going crazy," remembers Dede Allen. The default response would have been to fire the focus puller, but Vittorio Storaro demurred. After some investigation, he discovered, in Allen's words, "that the magazine would get hot and slightly move the film from the gate by the most minute amount," thereby distorting the focus.

Some of the actors welcomed the challenge of working for Beatty. Says Paul Sorvino, who did as many as 70 takes for one of his scenes, "It was a point of pride with me to do as many as Warren wanted. It was like 'Yeah? You want another one? How 'bout 10 more? How about 20 more?' It was that young macho thing in me that said I could stand up to anything Warren [dished out]. I thought he felt he had to strip the actors down. A lot of directors do that in a cruel way, skinning them, flaying them. But Warren just wanted the best that I had, so I gave it to him."

Others weren't so amenable, especially since Beatty, ever opaque on set, rarely told the actors precisely what he wanted. According to one source, Maureen Stapleton did more than 80 takes of a scene, her head further slumping onto her shoulders with each re-do. Another day, after another set of multiple takes, she reportedly inquired, "Are you out of your fucking mind?" Beatty just smiled and said, "I may be, darling, but do it again anyway." Says another source, "I saw several actors actually break down and start crying. Jack was almost in tears. In one scene with Diane, I remember him screaming, 'Just tell me what the fuck you want and I'll do it!' Literally, his eyes filled with water from the frustration of not knowing why he was asked to do it again." Says Beatty, "Put it this way: It was a scene of great frustration, and a scene of great emotion. Maybe [Nicholson's reaction] just means I'm a good director! What was it that Katharine Hepburn once said—'Show me a happy set and I'll show you a dull movie.'"

Keaton had mixed feelings about Beatty's methods. "I enjoy that kind of process of discovery by doing things over and over," she says. "But at the same time I didn't exactly feel like I knew what I was doing. It was really Warren's performance, not my performance. Because he worked so hard. He was so thorough, and he was never satisfied, and he pushed me and pushed me, and frankly I felt kind of lost. And maybe that was his intention in some way, for [the character]."

Whatever it was he was looking for, Beatty got some of the best work of their careers from Nicholson and Keaton, helped enormously by Beatty and May's dialogue, alternately passionate, biting, and just plain funny, as when O'Neill, who is in love with Bryant, can't resist telling her—she's acting in an amateur production of one of his plays—"I wish you wouldn't smoke during rehearsals. You don't act as if you're looking for your soul, but for an ashtray."

Gene Hackman's part was small, just two scenes. He had taken the role as a favor to Beatty, whom he was fond of. Hackman was also sensible to the fact that Beatty had kick-started his career by casting him as Buck Barrow in *Bonnie and Clyde,* for which he was nominated for best supporting actor. "It was such a pleasure to work for Warren, even though he did a lot of takes," the actor says. "It was close to 50. He didn't say a lot to me. There's something about somebody who is that tough and perseveres that way that is attractive to an actor that wants to do good work. So I hung in there. And finally it gets you out of the text. You just have these words that are flowing out of you. But all those takes—I was going blind. After Take 5, I'm kind of finished. I had no idea how they would change. I don't think that I ever verbalized anything to him in terms of my annoyance—I just sucked it up—but he must have known. When he called me to do *Dick Tracy*"—the film Beatty made for Disney, in 1990—"I said, 'I love you, Warren, but I just can't do it.'"

Assistant editor Billy Scharf, who would later work on *Ishtar* (the 1987 flop starring Beatty and Dustin Hoffman and directed by May), explains Beatty's working method best: "A lot of people say Warren overshoots. I know that not to be true. Directors who come back with insufficient material are doing a disservice to the opportunity. They get intimidated by stars. Warren is not. In the movie, when Reed wants to leave Russia and go back to America, Zinoviev tells him, 'You can never come back to this moment in history.' Warren felt that way when he shot. He believed that that was the time and that was the place, and he had to take advantage of the opportunity to the hilt. He had the resources, and he wanted to use them, because he knew he would never get another chance."

There was a literal price for the slow pace, as the executives at Paramount were well aware. Recalls Diller, "It was really not possible to budget the movie. We did a kind of estimate [in pre-production], and we were, of course, terribly wrong. I don't know what we would have done if we knew what the real cost was. I doubt we would have done it, but who knows?"

Says Beatty dryly, "I think there was probably a point when Paramount would have preferred not to be involved."

As the bills piled up, the relationship between Beatty and Diller deteriorated. At the end of long shooting days, Beatty got on the phone with the Paramount head, and the two men screamed at each other. "Within a week we were a week behind [schedule]," says Diller. "And it just went on from there. They just had all sorts of problems. They had production problems. They had weather problems. They had fatigue problems. They had Warren-and-Diane problems. It was all on the fly, which is a dopey way to make a movie. It was just a mess, and it went on and on. It was one of those rough, rough shoots that made everybody unhappy."

But Diller was in a bind. "Here's the dumbassness of that," he continues. "I should have forced him not to be Warren. But that would have been stupid. That's his process. That's how he functions."

Wholly exasperated, Diller ceased returning Beatty's phone calls. "I was so angry with him, I thought it was just pointless to talk to him. I wanted to make him feel guilty. I thought that would have some effect. That was naïve."

———

As months passed, and the wrap date was forever just over the horizon, mordant jokes about the production were heard on the set, some of which found their way into the "Grabber News," an occasional broadsheet put out by several crew members. The sheet reported that *The John Reed–Louise Bryant Story*, the film's working title, was a popular term for Seconal sleeping pills, and suggested alternative titles such as *The Longest Day* and *The 39 Takes*.

Rumors swirled: about the budget, about Beatty's extravagance, about the script rewrites, about the status of his relationship with Keaton. The set was closed to journalists, which only fed the flames. Beatty's health suffered. He lost weight and developed a cough. Recalls Pikser, "Warren felt isolated. He used to say to me, 'You and I are the only two people who give a fuck about what this movie is say-

ing.' Which is true. You had hundreds of people working on this picture, and for them it was a gig. 'We did *Agatha* last month and we're
doing this this month.' And Warren felt like he's bogged down in the
Philippines fighting the Japanese. And nobody else cared if he's going to win or not."

Beatty's relationship with Keaton barely survived the shoot. It
is always a dicey proposition when an actress works with a star or
director—both, in this case—with whom she has an offscreen relationship. "It's like running down a street with a plate of consommé and
trying not to spill any," Beatty says. Moreover, the director admits,
his perfectionism only added to the stress: "Making a movie together
if you've got someone who is even moderately obsessive-compulsive
is hell on a relationship." Keaton appeared in more scenes than any
other actor, save Beatty, and many of them were difficult ones, where
she had to assay a wide range of feelings, from romantic passion to
anger, and deliver several lengthy, complex, emotional speeches.
George Plimpton once observed, "Diane almost got broken. I thought
[Beatty] was trying to break her into what Louise Bryant had been
like with John Reed." Adds Relph, "It must have been a strain on
their relationship, because he was completely obsessive, relentless."

Says Keaton, "I don't think we were much of a couple by the
end of the movie. But we were never, ever to be taken seriously as
one of the great romances. I adored him. I was mad for him. But this
movie meant so much to him, it was really the passion of his professional life—it was the most important thing to Warren. Completely,
absolutely. I understood that then, and I understand now, and I'm
proud to have been part of it."

———

Some people who worked on the picture felt that the relationship
between Reed and Bryant reflected Beatty and Keaton's offscreen
dynamic. In the film, Reed and his circle don't take Bryant entirely
seriously; in one scene, he criticizes her for writing an article about
the Armory Show—three years after the fact—at a time when the
world was going up in flames. In real life, while Beatty was in pre-
production on *Reds,* Keaton was putting together a book of photographs of hotel lobbies. "Diane wanted to be serious in certain ways

that Warren was ambivalent about," Pikser says. "To really have been a partner in Diane's quirkiness, the singularity of her pursuit of the obscure and the avant-garde, which to me was a product of a restive and intelligent mind, and also to some degree a compensation for insecurity about her intellectual powers, for him would have been heavy lifting. There was a way in which he wanted to pay obeisance to her intellectual pursuits, but at the same time there was a sense on her part that he didn't really respect or appreciate them. So when Warren says in *Reds*, 'You're doing a piece on an art exhibition that took place three years ago . . . maybe if you took yourself a little more seriously, other people would, too.' Can you imagine what Warren really thought about her taking photographs of hotel lobbies?"

Keaton says she had an intuitive understanding of Bryant: "I saw her as the everyman of that piece, as somebody who really wanted to be extraordinary, but was probably more ordinary, except for the fact that she was driven. I knew what it was like not to really be an artist. I knew what it felt like to be extremely insecure. I knew what it was like to be envious." But both she and Beatty emphatically reject the notion that the Reed-Bryant relationship was in some sense analogous to their own. Says Keaton, "It was completely different. I didn't find myself dead in a stairway, drunk. Also I don't think that we're that important, historically, Warren and I. Sorry to say." For his part, Beatty credits Keaton with much more self-awareness than Bryant possessed. Nor, he says emphatically, was the actress in any way in his shadow. "She had just made one of the great, great movies—*Annie Hall*. She had won the Academy Award. She was very much in demand."

The simmering tensions in the couple's relationship seem to have boiled over while they were shooting the last scene in the movie: Reed's death, from typhus, in a squalid Moscow hospital with Bryant at his side. Says art director Simon Holland, "It was at the time when he and Diane were about to split. And it was Warren's death scene, and he couldn't sort of concentrate on what was happening—he couldn't even see how Diane was acting." Beatty did take after take and eventually, according to Holland, he sat up and asked Zelda Barron, the script supervisor, "How was that, Zelda? Was she all right?" Beatty was likely concerned with continuity issues, but some on the set interpreted his question to Barron as an invitation to evaluate Keaton's performance—a breach of thespian protocol. According to Holland, "Diane just went, 'Warren Beatty, you'll never do that to me again.' And she walked out. And that was it." Adds location manager Simon Bosanquet, who was also there, "She went to the airport and left. It was a real exit and a half, a wonderful way to end."

Of this anecdote, Keaton says, "It does ring a bell," and "No, I'm not going to talk about that at all." According to Beatty, it's "completely not true" that he asked Barron to critique Keaton. "I have never asked that question of anyone. It's just not something you do. When we were shooting that scene, there were other matters between me and Diane that really didn't have anything to do with the movie. Nobody knew what was transpiring between me and Diane. Nobody knows what's going on between me and any of the actors. And often I don't know either."

———

By the time *Reds* wrapped in the late spring of 1980, editing was already under way in New York. The editorial staff was so big—65 people—it seemed like every editor in New York who could walk and talk had been hired. "We were working six and seven days a week," says editor Craig McKay. "I was screening dailies 16 hours at a clip. Marathons."

The most immediate problem facing the editors was the enormous amount of footage that Beatty had shot. "I was overwhelmed with film," recalls Dede Allen. The party line, she says, was that *Reds* had not exceeded the recent total racked up by *Apocalypse Now*: 700,000 feet of exposed film, about 100 hours' worth. As Allen recalls, "It got to the point where I never discussed [footage] with anybody. That was verboten. [But] I know it was more than 700,000 feet. Are you kidding?" According to Wooll, "We went through over two and a half million feet of film." One source in a position to know claims Beatty shot three million feet—roughly two and a half weeks' worth of screen time—with one million feet actually printed. (The total footage, shipped from London to the U.S. in one big load, is said to have weighed four and a half tons.) Beatty himself can't remember an exact figure, but says, "It's axiomatic that the cheapest thing we have is film. It's the hours that people spend on the day that cost you money. But that's a hell of a lot less time than coming back and adding another shot."

And still Beatty returned for more shooting, scenes that he was not satisfied with as well as new material—which meant that the brutal script work continued on, too, even into late November, for dubbing, with an early-December release date breathing down everyone's neck. Elaine May continued to be an indispensable part of Beatty's team. He felt that she was one of the few people in the inner circle who didn't have her own agenda. At one point, having hurt her ankle, she couldn't walk without a cane. It was late, he wanted her help with a script question, but she wanted to leave. According to an eyewitness, he grabbed her cane while she screamed, "Give me back that cane—I want to get out of here." Beatty had so much confidence in May's judgment that he scrapped an entire sound mix that had taken weeks of work to put together because she didn't think it was as effective as the down-and-dirty temp mix that the sound department had put together months before.

McKay was cutting one of Beatty's scenes, sorting through the takes, when he came across a close-up in which it was clear to him that Beatty was giving his best line reading. But it was a side angle, and there were crow's-feet faintly evident at the corner of his eye. McKay remembered that the actor had once told him, "You've never seen a narcissist until you've met me—I'm the biggest narcissist in Hollywood." McKay said to his assistant, "He's gonna react to that, but that's his best take."

"Yeah, he's gonna want you to take it out, because he doesn't look too good."

"Well, I'm gonna leave it in, because it's his best work as an actor, and we don't know if he's going to spot it or not."

When McKay was ready to show him the sequence, Beatty sat down at the editing bay and folded his arms across his chest as McKay ran the scene for him. According to the editor, he said, "It's good, it works." Then he paused for a moment and added, "You know that shot of me where I say this, this, and this?"

"Yeah," McKay replied.

"Don't you think it's got a little too much character?"

"Warren, it's your best performance."

"Well, it's good, but it's not quite the tone I want. Find something else." And he walked out of the room.

———

Beatty had long since patched up his relationship with Diller and Paramount. Around Christmas of 1979, five months into filming, Diller and Eisner had flown to London to see five hours of footage prepared specifically for them. They loved it, and from that point on, the studio was fully behind *Reds,* though some observers wondered if Bluhdorn was hedging his bets when he picked up *Ragtime,* another long historical epic set in vaguely the same time period, from producer Dino De Laurentiis. Oddly, Paramount would release it a mere two weeks before *Reds.*

As Beatty's picture moved toward completion, he screened a near-final cut for the executives, first for Diller and then for Bluhdorn. There was a protocol for these screenings: the guest of honor was never on time. How late he was depended on where he stood in the pecking order. If a screening was scheduled for Beatty himself at eight in the evening, he might show up at any time after that, but never at eight. When he screened the film for Diller, Beatty arrived punctually at eight, but Diller was late. (Nicholson was at that screening, and he'd yell, in his Nicholson voice, "Hey, Dil, hy'a doin', Dil?") At the screening for Bluhdorn in New York, Beatty and Diller were on time, but Bluhdorn was late. (He was accompanied by bodyguards, who locked the doors of the room.) During the intermission, picking food off silver trays, the Austrian mogul said something like, "Varren, yoo haf made a vonderful movie. It is fantastic. I luf you in it, espccially, but I haf vun question." "What is that, Mr. Bluhdorn?" "Vill it zell in Indiana?"

———

Postproduction concluded at the end of November 1981, more than two years after shooting had begun, three years after pre-production commenced. As Sylbert put it, "The shooting time was about 50 weeks. We shot in studios all over Europe. We shot in every fucking country in the world. We came back and filled the studios here in

L.A. We were in New York. We were in Washington. You couldn't pay for that picture today."

Beatty declined to do publicity for the movie—he said it should speak for itself—making a difficult marketing job more difficult. The press had already begun sniping about the picture's cost, which may never be known. The official figure Paramount was giving out was $33.5 million. Beatty says he's not sure, maybe $31 million, which would be the rough equivalent of $80 million today. The numbers cited in the press, which weren't really based on anything but one another, gradually crept up into the $40 millions. The journalist Aaron Latham, in *Rolling Stone,* quoted unnamed Paramount sources who put the final tally near $50 million but, again, this is a figure best taken with a grain of salt. (For comparison's sake, the budget of *Heaven's Gate,* then the record holder in nonconstant dollars, was estimated at $44 million.)

It didn't help the movie's profile that the British producer David Puttnam (*Midnight Express*) took it upon himself to launch a crusade against out-of-control filmmaking and began giving interviews chastising Beatty for overspending. Puttnam called *Reds* "lunacy," telling the columnist Marilyn Beck that "Beatty should be spanked in public," that it was "a desperately damaging thing for him to have indulged himself as he has." Worse, it was "despicable" for Paramount to have enabled him. It probably escaped no one's notice, at least in Hollywood, that Puttnam had produced *Chariots of Fire* (reported budget: $5.5 million), which could be expected to go up against *Reds* at Oscar time.

In the end, Paramount was forgiving about the money spent on *Reds:* the studio had tax-sheltered the picture with Barclay's Bank, and had also put together a currency deal, hedging pounds against dollars, which went Paramount's way. "That was just a piece of bird-brained luck that took any sting from *Reds,*" Diller says. "By the time the picture was finished, we were in profit!"

The exhibitors' screenings were predictably discouraging. Theater owners complained about the length and the subject, said things such as "Oh my God, Communism—I know it's a part of our history, but do we have to have a movie about it?" According to Patrick Caddell, the Democratic pollster and consultant, a friend of Beatty's

from the McGovern days who was advising on the marketing campaign for *Reds,* Paramount feared a right-wing backlash against the
film. But despite a few hostile editorials, nothing much materialized,
perhaps because Beatty had headed off conservatives by screening
the film—in a remarkable coup—for Ronald Reagan in the White
House. Reagan told Beatty he liked it, though the president "wished
it had a happy ending."

The reviews, for the most part, were glowing. Vincent Canby
called *Reds* "an extraordinary film" in *The New York Times,* "the best
romantic adventure since David Lean's *Lawrence of Arabia*"—high
praise indeed. In *Time,* Richard Corliss wrote, "*Reds* is a big, smart
movie, vastly ambitious and entertaining, full of belief in Reed and in
the ability of a popular audience to respond to him. It combines the
majestic sweep of *Lawrence of Arabia* and *Doctor Zhivago*—David
Lean and Robert Bolt's mature and exhilarating epics—with the rue-
ful comedy and historical fatalism of *Citizen Kane.*"

Seen today *Reds* still seems as fresh as the moment it was
released—this despite the fact that the lure of the idealism it drama-
tizes runs counter to the cynicism that has dominated political dis-
course for the past generation. Like the Soviet Union itself, John
Reed and Louise Bryant may have been doomed, may even have
been foolish, but they enlivened their politics with passion and idealism, and in Reed's case, he sacrificed his life for his beliefs. The inten-
sity between Beatty and Keaton is tangible on-screen and gives the
film its heart. Ultimately, Reed and Bryant are "comrades," the title
of Griffiths's first draft, and the word Reed whispers to Bryant on his
deathbed. More than just lovers, more than just revolutionaries, they
have made political lives, lived their politics, and *Reds* is above all a
tribute to that. Beatty's gamble in making a movie with his partner
paid off; he didn't spill the consommé. Instead, he did what true *au-
teurs* must do: make an intensely personal film, in this case out of big
themes and big ideas, out of a chunk of history that in other hands
could easily have remained indigestible.

"*Reds* marked the end of something, in the subject matter and
the willingness to gamble," Beatty says, reflecting on his film today.
"What moved the late 60s and 70s was politics. *Reds* is a political
movie. It begins with politics and it ends with politics. It was in some

sense a reverie about that way of thinking in American life, one that went back to 1915." But it was also, he says, a reverie about the two decades just past, about Beatty's own generation. "*We* were those old lefties that were narrating this movie," he continues. "We, me. *Reds* was a death rattle."

⸻

R*eds* was released on December 4, 1981, in nearly 400 theaters, a medium-size opening. The length precluded it from playing more than once a night, limiting the box office, which was good but not great. On February 11, 1982, the Academy of Motion Picture Arts and Sciences announced that the film had gotten 12 Oscar nominations, the most since *A Man for All Seasons,* in 1966, and two more than *Reds'* nearest competitor in 1982, *On Golden Pond.* The nominations included those for best picture, best director, best actor, best actress, and best adapted screenplay (which was credited to Griffiths and Beatty). Beatty's four personal nominations, matching a feat he had accomplished with *Heaven Can Wait,* set a record. (Only Orson Welles had also been nominated four times for the same film, but just once, for *Citizen Kane.*)

In the end, *Reds* won only three Oscars: best director, best cinematography, and best supporting actress, for Stapleton. The biggest disappointment was inexplicably losing best picture to Puttnam's *Chariots of Fire.* It was a nasty twist of fate. As Sylbert put it, Beatty and Puttnam "hated each other. [The loss] broke Warren's heart, because that was really the first time he'd had a chance to do everything he ever dreamed of." But Beatty, at this point exhausted by *Reds,* had his Oscar and other consolations. He had screened the picture for Elia Kazan, who directed Beatty in his first picture, *Splendor in the Grass,* in 1961. Kazan had apparently not liked *Shampoo,* and had told Beatty at the time, "You know, Warren, you should have talked to me about that picture before you made it." But after seeing *Reds* the man who had made *A Streetcar Named Desire* and *On the Waterfront* called Beatty and said, "You really are a good director."

From *Vanity Fair,* March 2006

ABOUT THE
AUTHORS

PETER BISKIND has been a contributing editor at *Vanity Fair* since 1999. Formerly the editor in chief of *American Film,* he was also executive editor of *Premiere.* Biskind's books include *Seeing Is Believing: How Hollywood Taught Us to Stop Worrying and Love the Fifties* (Pantheon, 1983); *Easy Riders, Raging Bulls: How the Sex-Drugs-and-Rock 'n' Roll Generation Saved Hollywood* (Simon & Schuster, 1998); *Down and Dirty Pictures: Miramax, Sundance, and the Rise of Independent Film* (Simon & Schuster, 2004); and *Gods and Monsters: Movers, Shakers, and Other Casualties of the Hollywood Machine* (Nation Books, 2004). He is currently at work on a biography of Warren Beatty.

STEVEN DALY became a contributing editor at *Vanity Fair* in 1999. Prior to that, he was a contributor to *Rolling Stone, Interview, The Face, GQ, Details,* and *Spin,* where he served as music editor. He was a U.S. cultural correspondent for BBC Radio 1 from 1994 to 1997. Daly contributes to *The Sunday Telegraph* magazine, in Britain, and is a co-author of *alt.culture* (HarperCollins, 1995) and *The Rock Snob's Dictionary* (Broadway, 2005).

LAURA JACOBS has been a *Vanity Fair* contributing editor since 1995, writing profiles on fashion designers, actors, and figures in the performing arts. Jacobs was editor in chief of *Stagebill* for eight years, is the dance critic for *The New Criterion*, and is the author of *Barbie in Fashion* (Abbeville, 1994), *The Art of Haute Couture* (Abbeville, 1995), *Beauty and the Beene* (Abrams, 1999), *Women About Town* (Viking, 2002), and *Landscape with Moving Figures* (Dance & Movement Press, 2006).

DAVID KAMP joined *Vanity Fair* as a contributing editor in 1996. Previously, he was an editor and writer at *GQ*. He started his career as a writer and editor for *Spy*, working under future *V.F.* editor Graydon Carter. Kamp is the author of the food-world history *The United States of Arugula* (Broadway, 2006) as well as the co-author of the humor books *The Rock Snob's Dictionary, The Film Snob's Dictionary, The Food Snob's Dictionary*, and *The Wine Snob's Dictionary.*

SAM KASHNER became a contributing editor at *Vanity Fair* in 2007. Prior to that, he was a frequent contributor to *GQ*. Kashner is the author of *Sinatraland: A Novel* (Overlook, 1999) and *When I Was Cool* (HarperCollins, 2004). He is also the co-author, with Nancy Schoenberger, of *Hollywood Kryptonite* (St. Martin's, 1996), which was the basis for the 2006 film *Hollywoodland*, and *A Talent for Genius: The Life and Times of Oscar Levant* (Villard, 1994), which is slated to be made into a film, with Ben Stiller as the great hypochondriac pianist.

SAM STAGGS has written for a variety of publications, including *Vanity Fair* and *Architectural Digest*. He is the author of *All About "All About Eve": The Complete Behind-the-Scenes Story of the Bitchiest Film Ever Made!* (St. Martin's Griffin, 2001); *Close-up on Sunset Boulevard: Billy Wilder, Norma Desmond, and the Dark Hollywood Dream* (St. Martin's, 2002); *When Blanche Met Brando: The Scandalous Story of "A Streetcar Named Desire"* (St. Martin's,

2005); and *Born to Be Hurt: The Untold Story of "Imitation of Life"* (St. Martin's, 2009).

JAMES WOLCOTT joined *Vanity Fair* as a contributing editor in 1983, left in 1992 to be a staff writer at *The New Yorker,* and returned in 1997. He has a monthly *V.F.* column covering the media, politics, and pop culture, and writes the popular James Wolcott's Blog, at vanityfair.com. In 2003, he received a National Magazine Award for Reviews and Criticism. Wolcott began his career in the circulation department of *The Village Voice* in 1972 and became a regular contributor two years later, writing some of the earliest articles about the punk scene. Wolcott has written numerous reviews for such publications as *The New Republic, The New Criterion,* and *The Nation.* He is also the author of *The Catsitters* (HarperCollins, 2001), a novel, as well as *Attack Poodles and Other Media Mutants* (Miramax, 2004). He is working on a memoir about New York City in the 70s.

ACKNOWLEDGMENTS

EDITOR Graydon Carter

V.F. BOOKS EDITOR David Friend
MANAGING EDITOR Chris Garrett
DESIGN DIRECTOR David Harris
PRODUCTION DIRECTOR Martha Hurley
ILLUSTRATOR Tim Sheaffer
EDITORIAL ASSOCIATES
Jessica Flint, Jonathan Kelly,
Tim Mislock, Feifei Sun
COVER DESIGN Paul Buckley

Special thanks go to Penguin's incomparable team, led by Kathryn Court and Stephen M. Morrison and including Sabrina Bowers, Kate Griggs, Rebecca Hunt, and Heidi Stokes.

We extend our gratitude as well to *Vanity Fair*'s Dori Amarito, Dina Amarito-DeShan, John Banta, Aimée Bell, Dana Brown, Peter Devine, David Foxley, Anne Fulenwider, SunHee C. Grinnell, Heather Halberstadt, Bruce Handy, Michael Hogan, Claire Howorth,

Paloma Huerre, Punch Hutton, Ellen Kiell, Beth Kseniak, Wayne Lawson, Sara Marks, Amanda Meigher, Edward J. Menicheschi, Chris Mueller, Cullen Murphy, Peter Newcomb, Elise O'Shaughnessy, Henry Porter, Jeannie Rhodes, Michael Roberts, Jane Sarkin, Jocelyn Selig, Krista Smith, Doug Stumpf, Piper Vitale, Robert Walsh, Julie Weiss, and Susan White, along with everyone on the magazine's art, copy, online, photography, production, public-relations, research, and special-projects staffs.

We are also grateful to our friends and colleagues at Sabin, Bermant & Gould; the Wylie Agency; and the Rights and Permissions Department of Condé Nast Publications.